Stalin and the
Cold War in Europe

THE HARVARD COLD WAR STUDIES BOOK SERIES
Series Editor
Mark Kramer, *Harvard University*

The Struggle for the Soul of the Nation:
Czech Culture and the Rise of Communism
Bradley F. Abrams

Resistance with the People:
Repression and Resistance in Eastern Germany 1945–1955
Gary Bruce

Triggering Communism's Collapse:
Perceptions and Power in Poland's Transition
Marjorie Castle

At the Dawn of the Cold War:
The Soviet-American Crisis over Iranian Azerbaijan, 1941–1946
Jamil Hasanli

Mao and the Economic Stalinization of China, 1948–1953
Hua-yu Li

Redrawing Nations:
Ethnic Cleansing in East-Central Europe, 1944–1948
Edited by Philipp Ther and Ana Siljak

Stalin and the Cold War in Europe:
The Emergence and Development of East-West Conflict, 1939–1953
Gerhard Wettig

Stalin and the Cold War in Europe

The Emergence and Development of East-West Conflict, 1939–1953

Gerhard Wettig

ROWMAN & LITTLEFIELD PUBLISHERS, INC.
Lanham • Boulder • New York • Toronto • Plymouth, UK

ROWMAN & LITTLEFIELD PUBLISHERS, INC.

Published in the United States of America
by Rowman & Littlefield Publishers, Inc.
A wholly owned subsidiary of The Rowman & Littlefield Publishing Group, Inc.
4501 Forbes Boulevard, Suite 200, Lanham, Maryland 20706
www.rowmanlittlefield.com

Estover Road, Plymouth PL6 7PY, United Kingdom

British Library Cataloguing in Publication Information Available

Library of Congress Cataloging-in-Publication Data
Wettig, Gerhard.
  Stalin and the Cold War in Europe : the emergence and development of
East-West conflict, 1939–1953 / Gerhard Wettig.
      p. cm. — (Harvard Cold War studies book series)
  Includes bibliographical references and index.
  ISBN-13: 978-0-7425-5542-6 (cloth : alk. paper)
  ISBN-10: 0-7425-5542-9 (cloth : alk. paper)
   1. Cold War. 2. Europe—Politics and government—1945– 3. Soviet Union—
Politics and government—1945–1991. 4. Soviet Union—Foreign relations—
Europe. 5. Europe—Foreign relations—Soviet Union. I. Title.
  D843.W448 2007
  940.55'4—dc22
                                                                    2007012388
Printed in the United States of America

⊗™ The paper used in this publication meets the minimum requirements of
American National Standard for Information Sciences—Permanence of Paper for
Printed Library Materials, ANSI/NISO Z39.48-1992.

Contents

Acknowledgments

From 1966 onward, it was my primary task in the Federal Institute of East European and International Studies in Cologne (Germany) to analyze current Soviet policies in the Cold War. After the breakdown of the USSR in the early 1990s, I was interested in looking at these policies in retrospect. The first opportunity for this was provided by working with a commission set up by the Nobel Institute in Oslo to support academic access to the archive of the Russian Ministry of Foreign Affairs with means provided by the MacArthur Foundation. I have greatly benefitted from the profound knowledge of my colleagues there—Jonathan Haslam, Sven Holtsmark, William Taubman, and Odd Arne Westad. My research on the contemporary history of Soviet policy toward the West that developed during the 1990s received valuable stimuli and information from the conferences and the other activities of the Cold War International History Project at the Woodrow Wilson International Center for Scholars in Washington, D.C.

The continuation of my research after I had retired in 1999 and the Federal Institute in Cologne had closed down was made possible largely by the Common Commission for Research on Recent History of German-Russian Relations of which I was a member until 2003 and under the aegis of which I have been working to this day. I am much indebted to unfailing support from its two chairmen, Horst Möller and Aleksandr Chubar'ian, and its German secretary, Eberhard Kuhrt. During my repeated stays in Berlin when I used both the archives of the former GDR and the various academic libraries in the city, I enjoyed hospitality and the manifold help of the Berlin Department of the Institute for Contemporary History, notably from its head Hermann Wentker and its secretary Hannelore Georgi. As student assistants, Ruth Wunnicke, Sebastian Nagel, Larisa Strese-Gassiev, and Theresa

Kilian have supported me in finding the materials underlying this study. Encouragement was provided by Christian Ostermann and, of crucial importantance, by Mark Kramer to whom I am greatly indebted. He has welcomed the idea to write this book from the very start, kept my spirits up all the time, and has been most helpful in getting the manuscript into The Harvard Cold War Studies Book Series. Last, but not least, I thank the publisher Rowman & Littlefield and all those who have taken care of the book there: Jessica Gribble who did the correspondence and advised me to cope with technical difficulties, Anna Schmöhe who was responsible for production, and Jane McGarry who took the pains of copyediting.

1

Introduction

Most works on the Cold War, which was waged mainly in the European theater, are essentially based on Western sources and hence largely reflect Western perspectives and perceptions.[1] This book has been written to fill the gap. It is a study not on the Cold War in general but on East-West conflict as seen and handled by the USSR, that is, by Stalin who controlled Soviet foreign policy. Documents that have become available from archives in Moscow and, less importantly, in other capitals of former socialist countries, provide substantial insight into internal Soviet decision making and Stalin's reasoning on major problems. To be sure, access to Russian files was never unlimited and, after a short period of more liberal practice, has become more restricted again. Nonetheless, significant evidence is available on the basis of archival materials declassified at one time or another, published documents, and findings in studies by other, notably Russian historians. This book is essentially based on this triple source of information, which is complemented by reference to East German and occasionally East European files. On this fundament, new light is shed on Stalin's role both during the years of more or less outspoken East-West tension from 1939 through 1947 and after the open outbreak of the Cold War in mid-1947.

The 1945–1947 period, when confrontation developed under the constraints of postulated cooperation, has usually been included in historical portrayals of the Cold War. Occasionally, Lenin's seizure of power in Petrograd in 1917 is felt to have been its starting point. While this view can be justified by the fact that the Russian communists have always challenged the rest of the world on grounds of political principle, their power was insufficient for attempts to promote revolutionary ambitions after all "bourgeois" countries had stabilized by late 1923. At the same time, the USSR was

1

exhausted by devastating wars. It faced a "revolutionary ebb" that did not allow for offensive action against foreign states but required a defensive attitude. Stalin proclaimed limitation to "socialism in one country" as his political postulate for the time being. Only when, in pursuit of his expansionist aims, Hitler faced confrontation with Western Europe, notably Britain, in 1939 and needed Soviet backing, was the Kremlin leader put into a position to exploit conflict in the outside world for breaking the chains of "bourgeois" containment and renewing the "revolutionary" challenge to neighboring countries. This is why, in this study, the pact with Hitler has been chosen as a point of departure to investigate Stalin's policy of expansion, which set the stage for the Cold War.

Focusing attention on the Cold War and its prehistory implies that political developments in the relevant theaters of East-West conflict at that time, and not all European countries, are the topics of investigation. Until early 1945, this relevant area was essentially Eastern Europe as the region that came within the reach of Soviet power but also was of some—major or minor—interest to Britain and the United States. When, at the end of World War II, the victorious armies of East and West conquered Germany, the focus increasingly shifted to this country. The USSR and the Anglo-Saxon powers had agreed to occupy it jointly but by separate zones and sectors. Accordingly, they were both in direct geographical contact and in a situation of political competition, which resulted in confrontation when envisaged cooperation failed. As a result, the defeated main enemy country became the primary battlefield of the Cold War in the postwar period.

To be sure, there were other points of East-West disagreement. Soviet ambition to extend power beyond occupied territory and to spread the communist system was resisted by the Anglo-Saxon governments in other geographical areas as well. As the allegiance of regions such as, particularly, Iranian Azerbaijan, Finland, Czechoslovakia, and Yugoslavia was not finally determined, it was a source of dispute. The enforcement of incomplete socialist transformation in unwilling but Soviet-controlled East European countries invited British and U.S. opposition which, however, was less strong than it could have been and ultimately proved unsuccessful. But even if the United States and Britain had made a maximum effort to stop the introduction of communist rule in Soviet-occupied territories, their resources to make the USSR comply were limited. Given that the control of Germany was crucial, the conflict on Eastern Europe was only of second-rate importance. At the end of 1946, the discordant wartime allies had managed to settle some of their minor disputes but this did not fulfill their hopes that such resolution would promote agreement on major differences, notably in Germany. On the contrary, shortly afterward open conflict resulted. The political struggle for Germany became the central element of the emergent Cold War tension and hostility.

While this study is the first one to put German postwar development into the context of Soviet Cold War policy, development in the occupied East European countries (as a result of which the "outer empire" of the USSR emerged) has already been the subject of Donal O'Sullivan's book, *Stalins "Cordon Sanitaire."*[2] The topical focus, however, is different. The current volume pays primary attention to the systemic aspect as the crucial factor underlying East-West conflict. The focus is on how Stalin imposed systemic transformation along Soviet lines on the countries under his control. Comparison between his internal statements and recurrent patterns of action provides a basis for inferences on his strategy to enforce both adoption of Soviet-type socialism and permanent submission to Soviet power. The results of this analysis indicate that, from the very beginning, the political approach in the Soviet zone of Germany was basically the same. What differs is simply the time frame. Given that Stalin controlled but part of the country as a whole and wanted to avoid open rupture with the Westen co-occupiers, he felt that he must be more cautious and hence slow down his pace until the United States gave him freedom of action by its withdrawal from Europe.

Conflict over systemic transformation was invariably linked to competition for political control. As long as the Cold War was being waged, systemic issues were also issues of power politics. While, in the early years under perceptions of wartime cooperation, this appears to have ocasionally been ignored by major Western leaders, Stalin and his entourage always expressed belief in ideological tenets of principled opposition to the outside world. Among analysts, it has been open to controversy whether, or to what extent, the profession of adherence to Marxist-Leninist doctrine reflected political attitude or had to be seen as lip service that legitimized political decisions based on other, more pragmatic considerations. This study shows that detailed evidence on internal statements indicated that doctrinal elements largely shaped action. Ideological terms therefore are an important key to understand the meaning ot Soviet statements. A number of them—particularly *democracy, antifascism,* ascription of *peaceful* intent, *imperialism, militarism, fascism,* and *reactionary* attitude—imply crucial messages. In the Kremlin's vocabulary, the first three characterizations indicate political association with the USSR, mostly on the basis of full-scale political and ideological consensus, while the latter four terms serve as labels to verify rejection of Western democracy and its adherents. That meanings ascribed to these terms fundamentally differ from those ascribed in the West serves the purpose of projecting opposite messages to communist cadres and Western listeners when using one and the same statement. It should also be noted that, in Moscow's verbiage (which is taken over in this study), *socialism* refers to the Soviet system, while *communism* is a political characteristic of persons, parties, and regimes committed to it.

This study does not seek to clarify the general problem that has been the subject of controversy between the traditionalist and revisionist schools of thought. Western behavior is taken into account merely to the extent required for providing context to Soviet action. For this reason, judgment on the two sides' respective responsibility for the outbreak and ensuing intensification of the Cold War is a priori excluded. To be sure, the findings on the Kremlin's policy are relevant for this problem, but comparison of the two opposing sides' policies would be required for a final judgment. It may be noted, however, that increased information on Soviet decision making resulting from some measure of access to internal documents has given a major impulse to reinforcing the postrevisionist trend that has taken exception to revisionist philosophy.[3]

NOTES

1. See, for example, Daniel Yergin, *Shattered Peace. The Origins of the Cold War and the National Security State* (Boston: Houghton Mifflin 1978); Michael Dockrill, *The Cold War, 1945–1963* (Basingstoke: Macmillan 1988); John Wilson Young, *Coldwar Europe 1945–1991* (London: Arnold 1996); Marc Trachtenberg, *A Constructed Peace: The Making of the European Settlement 1945–1963* (Princeton, NJ: Princeton University Press 1999); Yvan Vanden Berghe, *Der Kalte Krieg 1917–1991* (Leipzig: Leipziger Universitätsverlag 2002); Rolf Steininger, *Der Kalte Krieg* (Frankfurt/Main: Fischer Kompakt 2003); Bernd Stöver, *Der Kalte Krieg* (Munich: C. H. Beck 2003); Jost Dülffer, *Europa im Ost-West-Konflikt 1945–1991* (Munich: Oldenbourg 2004). As a rare effort to summarize research on Soviet aspects of Cold War history, see John Lewis Gaddis, *We Now Know: Rethinking Cold War History* (Oxford: Clarendon Press 1998).

2. Donal O'Sullivan, *Stalins "Cordon Sanitaire": Die sowjetische Osteuropapolitik und die Reaktionen des Westens 1939–1949* (Paderborn: Schöningh 2003).

3. See, inter alia, John Lewis Gaddis, "The Emerging Post-Revisionist Synthesis on the Origins of the Cold War," *Diplomatic History* 7, no. 3 (Summer 1983), pp. 171–200; Dockrill, *The Cold War*, pp. 12–50; Gaddis, *We Now Know*, pp. 8–25; Geir Lundestad, "How (Not) to Study the Origins of the Cold War," Odd Arne Westad (ed.), *Reviewing the Cold War. Approaches, Interpretations, Theory* (London: Frank Cass 2000), pp. 64–80; Antonio Varsori, "Reflections on the Origins of the Cold War," Odd Arne Westad (ed.), *Reviewing the Cold War. Approaches, Interpretations, Theory* (London: Frank Cass 2000), pp. 281–302.

2

Prelude to
Postwar East-West Conflict

IDEOLOGICAL FUNDAMENTS OF SOVIET POLICY

When the communists seized power in Russia, they acted on the assumption that the Soviet Union was a revolutionary challenge to the rest of the world. The Russian "working class" had thrown off the yoke of exploitation and oppression. The "class comrades" in the other countries were expected to follow their example. In the end, worldwide elimination of the capitalist system was to result. In Lenin's view, it was not by coincidence that anti-"bourgeois" revolution had started in Russia where the "bourgeoisie" was weak: The chain of capitalism had been broken at its weakest link. Once it was no longer intact at one point, it would break everywhere. The European countries would continue the revolutionary process and make it succeed on a global scale. The next country expected to rid itself of capitalism was Germany. Lenin regarded winning over Germany as decisive. It was the biggest and strongest nation on the Continent and would open the door to the West.

The revolutionary goal was to install socialism by means of "proletarian dictatorship," which would destroy the old order. At the beginning of his political career, Lenin had admitted that he was an enemy of democracy. When he realized, however, that rejection of democracy was most unpopular not only among his liberal antagonists but among workers and socialists, he advocated "true" democracy, explaining that people's power had to be created "materially" rather than "formally." As he saw it, the "working class," under the leadership of the Bolshevik party as its political "vanguard," was the "real" people. According to this argument, democracy was synonymous with proletarian dictatorship, while democracy in its usual meaning had to be seen as a mere set of formal rules designed to conceal exploitation and repression by the "bourgeoisie." From then on, Lenin's followers had this interpretation in mind whenever they advocated democracy. As a result, "democracy" was practically the same thing as communist party dictatorship, which was justified as the only way of putting the people into control. Western democracy was referred to as a "bourgeois" or "formal" one as opposed to "true democracy."

Lenin's idea that socialism (his version of "democracy") was to prevail all over the world implied an approach to foreign policy that differed from traditional practice. The first step when his regime had taken power was to appeal to the "tormented and harrassed peoples" to reach an understanding on terminating war. Underlying these proclamations was no expectation that foreign governments might be induced to withdraw from armed conflict: The leaders of other countries were seen as notorious "imperialists" who, on the basis of their role as class representatives of the "bourgeoisie," were inherently unwilling to abandon the goals they sought to achieve by military action. It was the people who had to rise against war and their governments who waged it. Accordingly, interstate war had to be transformed into revolutionary war. Creating of peace required the elimination of both "imperialistic" governments and the system of "imperialism" (defined as the latest variant of capitalism). The worldwide establishment of socialism under communist rule was required to create peace. History had assigned this struggle to the "working class" and its domestic allies (such as the land-seeking peasants in Russia) under the guidance of the communist party. It was only on this basis that international understanding and peace among nations would become possible. "Class solidarity" among the workers of all countries was predestined to put an end to "bourgeois" statehood and the resultant separation and conflict among states. In this perception, diplomatic intercourse between states did not serve any positive purpose. When, in his assumed function as people's commissar of foreign affairs, Trotsky took charge of Russia's diplomatic apparat, he saw his task in issuing revolutionary appeals and expected them to elicit positive response in the outside world. There would be no need for another kind of action.

Failure of Revolution Outside the USSR

Reality proved to be different. Lenin's peace appeal made Imperial Germany seek a separate peace treaty with Russia, which would free its military forces for war against the West. This was not what the communists had had in mind. Rather than help the *kaiser's* regime prevail in war, they wanted to strain it increasingly as a precondition for its being toppled by revolutionary upheaval. At the same time, the communists protested against the harsh peace conditions with which they were confronted. Feeling that the German workers would rise against the "imperialistic war" in support of their "class brethren" in Russia, they announced a situation of "neither war nor peace." But there was no rebellion against the *kaiser* and the "bourgeois" regime in Berlin. The imperial high command exerted pressure and threatened to take advantage of the Russian military collapse that had resulted from Bolshevik revolutionary subversion. The prospect that the German army would invade the defenseless country and put an end to communist rule was imminent. Lenin did not want to lose power. So he decided that he had no choice but to accept the German conditions. When he defended his decision against criticism by his peers, he argued that the "revolutionary" upheaval outside Russia took more time than had been expected but would inescapably follow some time later. The concessions would then be revoked.

This prediction was correct. Half a year later, imperial Germany collapsed as a result of domestic riots, and the Russian communists got rid of the conditions imposed on them. But their expectation proved illusory that Germany would turn away from capitalism, adopt the Soviet system, and join the USSR. While traditional interstate relations remained in force, the Kremlin's hope for revolutionary change outside Russia and concomitant willingness to foster it continued. While Lenin understood that he had to adapt to the current traditional character of the international system as long as he had to deal with "imperialistic states" and their governments, he stuck to his belief that fundamental, "revolutionary" transformation of the international system was preordained by history and had to be promoted by maximum effort. Accordingly, diplomacy could not be dispensed with under prevailing conditions but had to be complemented by revolutionary effort. A dual foreign policy emerged. Diplomatic tasks were assigned to the People's Commissariat of Foreign Affairs, while the Communist International (Comintern) had to instruct the "brother parties" in other countries on their domestic policies. To the extent possible, they were to foster systemic change or, at minimum, cooperation with the USSR. Both institutions were equally controlled by the party leadership. Given that the two institutions were not infrequently directed at contradictory purposes, there were occasional frictions among them.[1]

In the early years after Bolshevik takeover in Russia, there were repeated attempts to export "revolution" into Central Europe. In 1920, the Red Army expelled Polish troops from Ukraine and then started a counteroffensive. Lenin's hope to conquer Warsaw, which would allow the USSR to occupy all of Poland and to invade Germany where a strong communist party would provide support, was frustrated by Soviet defeat in a decisive battle at the Vistula River. Nonetheless, the Kremlin continued to seek systemic change in the outside world. When, in 1923, Germany was in crisis, action appeared promising. Stalin pressed the communist party leaders (who initially hesitated but then submitted to instructions from Moscow) to prepare for insurrection.However, as the scheduled date in October approached, political and military conditions had basically changed. There was no chance for success any longer. German party leader Heinrich Brandler reacted by calling off planned action. As there was no time to ask for Soviet approval, he took the decision by himself. For Stalin, this was an impardonable disobedience, which he punished at the earliest possible moment. While Brandler had spared disaster to his party as a whole, the Hamburg section had not received his message in time; it took up arms, and suffered defeat after short combat.[2]

Containment of International Aspirations

From fall 1923 onward, the situation in Central Europe increasingly stabilized and made Soviet hope for mass upheaval against the capitalist system illusory. Stalin, who had succeeded Lenin, spoke of a "revolutionary ebb." This implied a fundamental change in the correlation of forces between socialism and capitalism. The USSR was a large country but a weak power. It was therefore felt in the Kremlin that, for the time being, there was no more possibility to spread the "revolution" to other countries. Instead, all effort had to focus on preserving it in one country. Rather than being able to challenge the world, Stalin feared that the capitalist powers might unite to destroy the Soviet Union as the hotbed of socialism. To prevent this, diplomatic skills were required more than ever. The cultivation of interstate relations was more important than ever. While this enhanced the domestic position of the People's Commissariat of Foreign Affairs, Moscow continued to cherish the idea of adamant antagonism toward the rest of the world and the historical mission of eliminating the old order. To be sure, there was no chance of progress for the time being but the "revolutionary" mission had to be preserved. Although the Comintern could not but reduce its effort to destabilize foreign countries from within, it had to remain committed to the principle of "revolution." In order to be able to resume its task when opportunities would offer themselves again, its organizational pattern was upheld and completed.

Stalin's concept of "socialism in [but] one country" begged the question of how the USSR might maintain itself against much stronger "imperialistic" enemy states. As Richard Crockett has pointed out, one of Lenin's fundamental innovations of Marxism had been to link socialist revolution to war among capitalist countries.[3] According to his doctrine of "imperialism as the highest stage of capitalism," economic dynamics were pushing their leaders to internecine conflict by necessity. An inherent systemic need for expansion had turned capitalism into "imperialism." The resultant conflicts—"interimperialistic contradictions"—had resulted in World War I, which had crucially weakened the capitalist system by mutual destruction, revolution in Russia, and emergence of the first socialist state. Stalin concluded that, given "imperialism's" continuing existence, the process was bound to repeat itself. Another world war would break out and make the "imperialist" states again destroy each other. The USSR had to preserve neutrality in its deadly struggle until the "working class" would once more rise up against war and exploitation. Then the Red Army would have to intervene and to replace the old system by socialism.[4]

This concept must be seen against an ideological background of a teleological perspective. According to Marxist-Leninist doctrine, there was a predetermined series of successive "historical formations" from capitalism to socialism and communism (defined as the ultimate stage of socialism when all the dreams of mankind would come true). Therefore capitalism had to be seen as the inferior sociopolitical order that had to be fought on moral grounds and would be eliminated in the end by historical necessity. This implied that both domestic and international relations had to be handled on the basis of "class" criteria. For this reason, the imperative of "class struggle" against the capitalist, respectively "imperialistic" enemy and his allies had to take precedence over any other consideration. At the same time, it was necessary to implant the idea in the minds of the "masses" that the USSR and its communist followers were the only political forces to promote "historical progress" and to achieve salvation of mankind. To be sure, these prescripts often did not provide direct guidance and were open to differing practical conclusions (which then allowed for some degree of pragmatic decision making) but they created patterns of reasoning that were bound to shape policy in a highly self-assertive, unscrupulous, and hostile direction.[5]

Status Quo Orientation in the 1920s and 1930s

After World War I, defeated Germany and socialist Russia were treated as pariahs. As the victors' principal enemy, Germany was subjected to deliberate humiliation, a big loss of territory, a heavy load of reparations, and occupation of its western provinces. Russia was treated as an outlaw for both having left the wartime alliance and challenging the outside world. As a result, both countries were interested in supporting each other. Their governments decided to ignore systemic antagonism and to start large-scale economic, limited political, and secret military cooperation. When, in the mid-1920s, Germany improved relations with France and Britain, its need for Soviet backing decreased. Nonetheless, until 1933 all German governments continued cooperation with the Kremlin, whose relations with the West European powers remained tense. In 1919, Britain had sent troops to Russia in support of Lenin's enemies in the civil war, and France created an East Central European *cordon sanitaire* of alliances against both Germany and the USSR.

Hitler's advent to power changed international relations fundamentally. The Nazi leader subjected the communists to severe repression and announced an anti-Soviet course but also challenged the West European defenders of the status quo. Nonetheless, the Kremlin felt that the new situation offered a chance. "Interimperialistic contradictions" might mature and result in war among the powers of the outside world. As had been internally stated as early as in 1929, any intensification of antagonism between revisionist countries such as, notably, Germany and the Western camp was bound to improve Soviet security.[6] For some while, Stalin was hopeful that the new regime in Berlin would precipitate a crisis of capitalism and internecine war among the "imperialists." In an apparent attempt to foster such a development, he wanted to maintain cooperation with Germany despite prosecution of the communists. It took more than a year until he concluded that, for the time being, he had no option but to unite with the Nazi power's opponents. The USSR entered the League of Nations (which Hitler had left), instructed the communists abroad to direct their efforts against "fascist" Germany, and made them enter government coalitions with democratic parties in West European countries.[7] Underlying this policy of "antifascist" unity was the intent to prevent a German attack against the Soviet Union. The Kremlin's propaganda line was preservation of peace. In novels and films, war was depicted as an imminent threat.[8]

Alignment with the West European status quo powers did not imply a merely defensive attitude. Referring to Lenin, Stalin made clear

> that, after having taken power in one country and organized socialist production, the proletariat will be forced by the power of circumstances to undertake a [military] campaign against the other retarded reactionary capitalistic countries in order to help the proletariat of these countries to free itself from the bourgeoisie.

The Soviet leader explained that it was wrong to think that the Bolsheviks would fight only to defend themselves against attack.

> There are situations when the Bolsheviks themselves will attack; if war is righteous, if circumstance is suitable, if conditions are favorable, they will attack themselves. They are by no means against offensive military actions, not against any war. That we are currently propagating defense—this is a disguise, a disguise. All states put on masks: "if you are living with wolves, you will have to cry like a wolf." It would be silly to expose all your inside and to put it on the table. People would say that you are a fool.[9]

Such willingness to exploit opportunities for forceful territorial expansion resulted not only from socialist but imperial motives. Stalin saw himself as a Russian leader who had inherited the tsars' empire and would follow in their footsteps.[10] In spite of Hitler's extreme hostility, which frustrated any Soviet attempt at normalizing mutual relations, Stalin maintained his preference for siding with Berlin rather than London and Paris and continued to hope for the restoration of previous cooperation.[11]

Increasing Frustration Over West European Appeasement Policy

In the late nineteen thirties, Soviet alignment with Western Europe was increasingly under strain. Stalin strongly disapproved of British and French indulgence regarding Hitler's extension of power. After the German *führer* annexed Austria in March 1938, the Kremlin leader tried to set up an international front of joint resistance against further expansion but met with refusal in London and Paris.[12] The two governments did not want to align themselves with a regime they saw as discredited by both revolutionary designs toward the outside world and mass terror within its own country. The British also believed that Hitler simply wanted to include all ethnic Germans in their national homeland—a motive they felt to be morally justified. They therefore did not want to oppose his policy of bringing his countrymen "back home into the *Reich.*"

In the Kremlin's view, the crucial test whether the West European powers would oppose German expansion jointly with the USSR was the September 1938 crisis. France and Britain were committed to defending Czechoslovakia against Berlin's claim to the Sudeten territory inhabited by ethnic Germans. Stalin felt that containment of Hitler was crucial and indicated willingness for support. The two West European governments felt that their troops would have to attack Germany's western borders and expected the Soviet Union to employ its forces for direct defense of the threatened country. This plan required Red Army transit through Poland and Romania. But the leaders in Warsaw and Bucharest refused permission. They suspected that once Soviet troops were on their soil, they would stay and initiate communist revolution. This prospect seemed all the more plausible as Stalin did nothing to allay this fear. He was obviously uninterested in agreement at the price of Soviet guarantees not to intervene in internal affairs. In retrospect, he argued that, from the very start, he had not expected the Czechs to fight. The British and the French lost hope that it was possible to counter German attack effectively and concluded that peace had to be bought by handing over the Sudeten territories to Germany.

In view of this result, Stalin strongly complained that the West European leaders had chosen to appease Hitler rather than to resist him. At the 1938 October Revolution anniversary, he declared that a "second imperialistic war" had already been started by the German, Italian, and Japanese aggressors, and he blamed Britain and France for being unwilling to resist the threat jointly with the USSR. He suspected that they saw "fascist" power as

a suitable antidote to socialism.[13] Stalin also blamed them for having excluded him from decision making. The USSR had been denied recognition
as a great power and put into a position of dangerous isolation. Would the
two West European countries continue their policy by directing German expansion against the Soviet Union?[14] Were they willing to exploit Hitler as a
tool to fight and destroy the USSR as their "class enemy"? Stalin felt that
"fascist" attack with West European backing was a definite possibility.[15] In
his perception, a deadly danger emerged: Rather than indulging in internecine war, the "imperialists" might unite against the Soviet Union before they would, of course, fight each other as predicted. If the USSR was
chosen to be the object of Hitler's aggression, the German army would have
to cross Poland, which was allied to Berlin since 1934 and had been given
a bit of Czechoslovak territory in 1938.

Stalin felt that the threat of an *entente* between Germany and other countries against the USSR had to be prevented. There was little hope that it
might be countered by seeking rapprochment with the Poles who traditionally had an anti-Soviet attitude, but he did not see this as promising and
preferred to take the German bull at his horns by making his ambitions
turn against the West. As early as in 1937–1938, Stalin had expressed distrust in the British and French and indicated interest in coming to terms
with Berlin.[16] In October 1938, the Soviet press speculated that the German
policy on Poland would result in loss of its national independence. Germany would put partitioning this country on the international agenda.[17]
The implict message was that the USSR (which was the only country to take
the other part of the territorial prey) was willing to take part. In early 1939,
there was an increasing number of signals from Moscow that relations with
Germany might be improved. On 1 February, the government daily *Izvestiia*
carried an article by the official news agency TASS which, allegedly re-
sponding to British speculations on Soviet-German rapprochement, concluded that their author was concerned that current differences between
Moscow and Berlin might not be an unchangeable factor of international
politics. Did Stalin want to deliver the message that the British, not the Germans, had an interest in such tension? Two weeks later, the party journal
Bol'shevik expressly raised the specter of Soviet-German collaboration but
cautioned that the potential partner could not be trusted. This may have
been a hint to the Nazi government that mutual cooperation was useful but
required assurances to the USSR.[18]

BREAKING CONTAINMENT OF SOCIALISM

On 10 March 1939, Stalin blamed Britain and France for failure to comply
with agreed policies of collective security. They were spreading lies on al-

leged Soviet military weakness in order to turn the Germans to the East and provoke conflict between them and the USSR. He pleaded for "business-like contacts" with all countries and added he would not allow warmongers to involve his country in war and to make it by getting chestnuts out of the fire for others. He also predicted the decline of world capitalism to result from a comprehensive economic crisis which already entailed imperialistic war. Capitalistic derangement would continue and lead to another wave of revolutionary upheaval.[19]

The governments of Britain and France had concluded the Munich Agreement feeling that Hitler wanted to complete the nation state by including ethnic Germans. They grew suspicious when he tried to rally the Poles behind him by offering "generous" conditions if they would join him in fighting the status quo. His underlying imperialistic attitude clearly surfaced when, in mid-March 1939, he annexed the Czech-inhabited regions of Bohemia and Moravia, set up a satellite regime in Slovakia, and made continuing cooperation with Poland conditional on its willingness for an arrangement on the "*Corridor*" which, on the basis of the 1919 Versailles Treaty, had been ceded to it and separated Eastern Prussia from the main part of Germany. On 26 March, the government in Warsaw finally refused any consideration of the demand. After, on 23 March, Hitler had forced Lithuania to return the Memel territory that it had annexed in 1923, Stalin claimed the two Northern Baltic countries, Latvia and Estonia, for his sphere of interest by unilaterally extending a "guarantee" to them. By implication, he accepted that Lithuania was part of the German power sphere.[20]

Against this background, the British government repudiated appeasement of Hitler and extended an unconditional guarantee to Poland. This was a fateful step. Warsaw was allowed to determine whether Britain—and also allied France—would have to go to war. Even more importantly, the USSR was put into the privileged position of a courted power that would be able to sell its willingness for support. Each side, the West European countries and Germany, was bound to be vitally interested in Soviet support. If the Kremlin would commit the Red Army to the defense of Poland, Hitler was confronted with both a superior military coalition and the haunted prospect of a permanent two-front war. But if he managed to exact a pledge of neutrality from Moscow, he was likely to feel that the West European countries would be unable to prevent conquest of Poland and might even be deterred from entering war. Thus Stalin would decide whether German aggression against Poland was promising. He could play off Hitler and his adversaries against one another for the highest bid.[21] In the words of a leading Soviet functionary, the USSR was like a rich bride who knew her price and would marry only for adequate payment.[22]

Negotiations with Britain and France

Stalin's suspicion of Britain and France was not reduced by their turn-around. What had made the British provide a guarantee with no regard for the Soviet attitude? Which motive was underlying their continuing attempts to come to terms with Hitler? When, in spring, London and Paris began to seek Soviet commitment to the defense of Polish integrity, Stalin felt that this might be a ruse designed to expose the USSR to the thrust of a German attack against Polish territory, while they would sit and wait for the *Wehrmacht* and the Red Army to exhaust each other. In addition to this, he was generally averse to employing his forces for foreign purpose, as he had already made clear in his speech on 10 March. Why should he commit resources to fulfilment of another side's promise of assistance to a country that he felt was profoundly anti-Soviet? Nonetheless, Stalin accepted negotiations. In spite of his effort to elicit interest in Berlin,[23] he had thus far no German option. The prospect of siding with the West would prevent isolation if Hitler changed his policy again and turned against the USSR. It was also useful as a signal to Hitler that it was in his interest to counter the threat of Soviet alignment with his opponents by making an offer to the Kremlin.[24] To make him feel that Soviet–West European agreement was indeed imminent, Stalin instructed the communist parties to propagate cooperation with Britain and France.[25]

The tripartite negotiations were impaired by mutual distrust from the very start. The governments in London and Paris—and even more so their Polish protegés and the other East Central European leaders, all of whom abhorred the Soviet military presence—suspected that the Red Army would spread communist revolution wherever it would enter. The Kremlin added to this fear by demanding that its troops must be granted access also to regions not required for fulfilment of their military task. In contrast to this, Britain and France wanted to limit the risk of socialist transformation by a clear-cut accord that provided for armed assistance but stipulated political restraint. Commitment to the League of Nations principle of collective security was to be the guideline. The USSR wanted to avoid unequivocal obligations not only on political good behavior but Poland's defense as well. It demanded a broad mandate to "protect" many other states, notably the Baltic countries. At a later stage, the Soviet delegates expressly claimed that also Finland, Romania, Turkey, Greece, and Belgium had to be protected from threat by preventive military measures—if necessary against their will. Any reference to the League of Nations was rejected. Any proposals for compromise were declared unacceptable; only unconditional fulfilment of Soviet demands would counter the threat. When the Western side refused to comply, it was blamed for seeking to engage the USSR in endless talks and for avoiding any serious agreement. Such "humiliation" was intolerable.[26]

Stalin explained to his aides that he wanted not to protect Poland but to enhance Soviet security against prospective German attack across Polish territory. Negotiations had to be oriented at preparing joint action to meet this challenge. He accused the West of dragging its feet. Instead of seeking agreement, it wanted to direct Nazi aggression against the USSR.[27] At the end of June, Zhdanov publicly accused the Western governments of procrastination. Hence their sincerity was doubtful. They were using the issue of guarantee to the Baltic states as a pretext to make the negotiations fail. Britain and France responded by suggesting that the Soviet military presence there might secretly be accepted in the event of direct German aggression. The Kremlin declined, saying that there was a danger of indirect aggression that must be taken into account, and it rejected the proposal that the USSR might be permitted intervention if a foreign government were forced to abandon neutrality under threat.[28]

The Decision to Conclude the Pact with Hitler

During spring 1939, Moscow exchanged views with Berlin and finally succeeded in making clear that the price for alignment would be higher than merely a share of the Polish prey. During the following weeks in July and early August, Soviet demands concerning the Northern Baltic countries and parts of Romania were spelled out in more detail.[29] In mid-July, the Comintern instructed the communist parties to initiate a political campaign that would both denounce the "fascist aggressors" and "unmask double-faced Western behavior." Alleged trends in West European countries to "capitulate" to Hitler's policy also required chastisement. Accordingly, the "German fascists" were no longer portrayed to threaten peace exclusively. At the same time, the absence of an accord with Berlin made Stalin maintain the option to put the blame mainly on the Germans.[30] In early August, the Soviet side insisted in negotiations with Britain and France that agreement on two problems was required: the kind of operations to be assigned to the Red Army in the event of war with Germany, and the availability of Polish and Romanian territory for Soviet advance to the front line. The talks were deadlocked when the British and French negotiators refused to authorize the Red Army's presence in both countries by saying that they were independent states that had to decide themselves on their affairs.[31]

When, in early August, outlines of a prospective agreement crystallized in Soviet-German talks,[32] the Kremlin gave clear expression to its demands in a draft of a military accord with Britain and France that had been approved by Stalin and Molotov. A number of possible scenarios were envisaged: German attack on France and/or Britain, on Poland (on the premise that London and Paris would render military assistance), on Romania (also by

Hungarian and Bulgarian forces, if the British and French would intervene militarily on behalf of the attacked country), and on the USSR (through Finnish, Estonian, and Latvian territory). In all these cases, the Soviet side planned to insist on a binding commitment of the two West European countries to instantly engage all their forces in an all-out offensive against Germany and in maximum armed support to the Soviet Union. A similar obligation would have to be taken by Poland if it would take part in the struggle. The USSR, however, would not employ all troops but spare most of them as "reserves." Internally, the Polish and Romanian attitude was given as a major reason for withholding a major part of Soviet forces. It was also posited that the Red Army must be permitted any adjacent countries such as Poland, Estonia, and Latvia and to create maritime bases in Helsinki, Hanko, Tallinn, and on Finland's and Estonia's islands in the Baltic Sea. If Romania or the USSR would become targets of aggression, Turkey was to put its fleet under Soviet command in order to defend the Dardanelles and to blockade enemy ports—provisions that would undermine a crucial component of Turkish sovereignty. When, at the start of the negotiations on a military accord, the Soviet side tabled these demands, the British and French delegations declined discussion, saying that they were not authorized to talk about this.[33]

When, on 8 August, Stalin received a message from Hitler indicating interest in an accord to allow German attack on Poland in exchange for a Soviet free hand with regard to a number of East Central European countries and territories, he instantly agreed.[34] To be sure, he continued to feel that the Nazi leader was the main enemy but noted with satisfaction that his calculus had been correct: The German dictator joined him in toppling the status quo and was willing to pay a high price for Soviet neutrality, which would allow him to go to war.[35] For the talks on what was then called a non-aggression pact, Hitler sent Ribbentrop to Moscow. Even before the German foreign minister arrived, Stalin was confident that agreement would be achieved: He instructed the West European communists to assert that, contrary to allegations in the "bourgeois press," the prospective treaty was no obstacle to an accord with Britain and France on joint resistance against aggression. It was justified as an instrument to protect peace and to frustrate the plans by "bourgeois reactionary circles" and "social democratic capitulationists" who wanted to direct [Nazi] aggression against the USSR. It would also serve to make Britain and France seek agreement with the Soviet Union seriously. Communist struggle against the aggressors, notably German "fascism," was bound to continue.[36]

In his negotiations with Stalin and Molotov on 23 August, Ribbentrop offered what the West had failed to concede: Secret protocols would give the Kremlin a free hand concerning Northern Latvia, Estonia, Finland, and Romania. The USSR might also take its share of Polish territory after German attack. This was more than Stalin had hoped to get. Exploiting the situation, he demanded also Southern Latvia. This was accepted. The pact as such implied that Germany renounced any support of its "Anticomintern Pact" ally Japan in the current war against the Soviet Union.[37] Stalin boasted to his aides that he had outwitted Hitler.[38] He had taken a considerably bigger territorial share than his counterpart. In his view, this was a crucial advantage in the military conflict with Germany to which he was looking forward in some future. The Nazi leader, however, equally felt that he had deceived the other side. For him, winning time was decisive. Britain and France were prevented from getting Soviet support to save Poland, which would thus be unable to defend itself. Germany was spared the prospect of a protracted two-front war and, after a number of other victories, the necessity to be strong enough to defeat "Bol'shevizm." The USSR's territorial gains were seen as temporary and unimportant. When war would break out later, Germany would no longer be in a difficult situation as at present and, with no engagement elsewhere, its superior forces would easily conquer additional Soviet territory.[39] To allay British and French concerns, the Kremlin officially declared that a mutual non-aggression pledge had been made, which implied Soviet neutrality. However, this was "neutrality of a special kind," as was internally stated.[40]

The Problem of Stalin's Underlying Intent

Characteristically, the USSR had invariably confronted Britain and France with maximalist demands. Did Stalin really feel that they might fulfill all of them under the pressure resulting from their difficult situation? Or did he see the talks simply as a device to evoke an alternative offer by Hitler? If he had indeed been initially serious in seeking agreement, when did he cease to hope for an accord with Britain and France? A major argument to justify that, contrary to preceding propaganda, the USSR preferred alignment with Nazi Germany to joining defense against "fascist" aggression, was the accusation that the two West European countries had wanted their partner to play the role of a "servant" who had to shoulder their burden with no permission to pursue his own interest. The implication is clear: Britain and France had rejected Soviet expansionist demands that Hitler had not hesitated to satisfy.

Most historians feel that Stalin preferred an accord with Germany already when, for lack of another at this time, he accepted negotiations with the West European powers.[41] On the basis of Soviet archival sources that have recently become available, Sergei Slutsch has argued that, as early as immediately after the Munich Agreement, Stalin clearly sought cooperation and alignment exclusively with Hitler and eschewed any understanding with the West.[42] In contrast to this, a few other authors—notably

Ingeborg Fleischhauer and Gabriel Gorodetsky—are convinced that he made his deal with Hitler as a result of frustration over unsatisfactory British and French offers.[43] Donal O'Sullivan takes the view that, for a long time, he pursued different lines of policy simultaneously in order to keep his options open as long as possible. Only when the choice was clear to the full extent, he decided to side with Hitler.[44] Stalin clearly had no German option prior to the message from Berlin on 8 August 1939, and hence he was bound to negotiate but with the West. Simultaneously, there is no doubt that he made a sustained effort to provoke an offer from Berlin and ordered his delegates to take maximalist positions in their talks with their British and French counterparts with whom he can hardly have expected to comply. At a minimum, he felt that Germany was bound to make an offer sooner or later and that this would allow him to press for maximum gain. If Paris and London were unwilling to give what he wanted, Berlin was likely to be more accommodating.

Another controversy has developed over the kind of achievement Stalin sought when he rejected agreement with the West and decided to support Hitler. While official Soviet historiography until the late 1980s both denied the existence of secret protocols and claimed that the treaty with Hitler was but an instrument to win time for preparing a defense against German aggression, Mikhail Semiriaga has argued that Stalin saw a need for territorial expansion on the basis of his perception that the USSR was a beleaguered fortress that, for this reason, had to be reinforced by any means possible.[45] Internal statements indicate that extension of both Soviet power and the socialist system was sought. In the Kremlin's view, the world war unleashed by the pact with Hitler was a starting point for developments that would ultimately result in taking over all of Europe.[46] Donal O'Sullivan apparently feels that both traditional Russian imperialism and willingness to spread the Soviet system were crucial.[47] Bianka Pietrow-Ennker has pointed out that alignment with Germany, rather than Britain and France, held the promise of lifting Japanese pressure on the USSR. Accordingly, it offered a better chance to maintain Soviet security and to allow for active policy in the European theater.[48]

Laure Castin-Chaparro, Aleksandr Chubar'ian, A. S. Sakharov, and O'Sullivan quote internal statements according to which the doctrine of "interimperialistic contradictions" shaped Stalin's decision.[49] It may be seen as a confirmation that the Soviet leader expected a long indecisive battle to result between Germany and its enemies that would mutually wear them down, and he was unpleasantly surprised when this hope was frustrated by Hitler's *blitzkrieg* victories in 1940 that made Germany the dominating power on the European continent.[50] An address on 7 September 1939 to leading Comintern cadres provides insight into Stalin's considerations when he concluded the pact with Hitler.

War is taking place between two groups of capitalist countries (poor and rich ones with regard to colonies, raw materials etc.) for partition of the world, for domination of the world! We are not averse to their struggling hard and to weakening each other. It is not bad if, by the hands of Germany, the situation of the richest capitalist countries (in particular England) is shattered. Without knowing and wanting it, Hitler disorganizes and undermines the capitalist system. The position of communists in power is different from [that of] the communists in opposition. We are masters at home. The communists in capitalist countries are in opposition, the bourgeoisie is in power there. We can maneuver and incite one side against the other so that they will quarrel better. The non-aggression pact helps Germany to some extent. The next moment [will be] to incite the other side. The communists of the capitalist countries must decisively stand up against their governments, against war.

Before the war, it was completely correct to support the democratic regime against fascism. During the [current] war between the imperialistic powers, this is not correct any longer. The previous division of capitalist governments in fascist and democratic ones has lost its previous meaning. The war has resulted in a radical change. Yesterday's united people's front [of the communists and the democrats] was there to alleviate the slaves' situation under the capitalist regime. Under conditions of imperialistic war, the issue of eliminating slavery is put on the agenda! To take the position of yesterday (united people's front, national unity) would mean slipping off to the bourgeoisie's position. This slogan is removed.

The Polish state was previously (in history) a state of the nation since the revolutionaries defended it against partition and enslavement. At present, the fascist state [of Poland] suppresses the Ukrainians, Belorussians etc. Annihilating this state under present conditions would mean one bourgeois-fascist state less! It would not be bad if, as a result of smashing Poland, we would extend the socialist system to new territories and populations.

We would have preferred agreement with the so-called democratic countries and have conducted negotiations to this end. But the English and the French wanted us as their servants and, in addition to this, did not want to pay for it. We, of course, did not go as servants. . . . The working class must be told: The war is being waged for world domination; it is being waged by the masters of the capitalist countries for their imperialistic interests. This war will not give anything to the workers, to the working people, except suffering and privation. [One has] to stand up resolutely against war and its culprits. Unmask the neutrality of the bourgeois neutral countries which advocate neutrality for themselves but support war in other countries for the sake of profit.[51]

These explanations served as guidance for subsequent instructions by Comintern head Georgii Dimitrov to the communist parties abroad.[52]

The Hitler-Stalin Pact was a shock to foreign communists who, until then, had enthusiastically abided by Soviet instructions to fight the "fascists" who prosecuted their comrades in Germany and elsewhere. Now they were ordered to oppose "imperialistic war" of both Hitler and the West

European governments. Given that the communists were able to hamper only the West's military effort, such "struggle against the two imperialisms" amounted to supporting the German aggressor who continued to prosecute any followers and sympathizers of Soviet "bolshevism." Disbelief of, and opposition to, Stalin's new policy spread among foreign communists who, until then, had been unconditionally obedient. Only after a number of weeks did the Kremlin manage to overcome resistance.[53] On 17 September 1939, the Soviet Union invaded Poland pretending to save its eastern parts from "fascist occupation." Eleven days later, the arrangement under the secret protocols was modified. Germany was allotted a larger part of Poland, while most of Lithuania was added to Moscow's "sphere of influence." Leaving all of central Poland to the Germans, Stalin gave credence to his claim that he simply wanted to recuperate previous territory up to the "Curzon line," which was alleged to be Russia's "ethnic frontier." The Baltic countries, Finland, and the Romanian province of Bessarabia were portrayed as historically associated with the USSR. Accordingly, an unnatural state of affairs was terminated when the Kremlin acquired "influence" there.[54]

Sovietization of the Countries Annexed Under the Pact with Nazi Germany

Stalin hastened to exploit the situation created by the pact with Hitler. On 25 September 1939, he informed Berlin that he was going to "solve the Baltic problem" on the basis of the accord reached on 23 August. Two days later, Estonian foreign minister Karl Selter was summoned to Moscow where he was made to sign a "treaty of mutual assistance" that allowed for Soviet military bases in Estonia. On 5 October, Latvia had to conclude a similar treaty; on 10 October, Lithuania was imposed the same kind of arrangement. In mid-June 1940, when international attention was focused on the breathtaking German advance into France, the second phase of annexation was initiated. Soviet NKVD troops raided border posts of Estonia, Latvia, and Lithuania. The Kremlin claimed that the three countries had violated their obligations under the treaties of assistance, adding six-hour ultimatums that new governments must be formed. Seeking to avoid Soviet massacres of civilians, the leaders in Tallinn, Riga, and Vilnius accepted the demand. Upon this, envoys from Moscow issued lists of persons to become cabinet members. At the same time, there were Soviet pledges to respect national independence.

The next step by the Kremlin was to organize demonstrations that demanded that the national president had to resign and that election for a new parliament was required. The postulated elections were held in mid-July under the Soviet military's strict control. Voting was based on but one single list of candidates selected by the occupation power; attempts to provide for a policy alternative were crushed. The elections were held in an atmosphere of all-pervasive terror. On the basis of previous planning, as early as in mid-June tens of thousands of civilians including children had been deported from each country to far-away inhospitable parts of the USSR and put into forced labor camps under unbelievably cruel conditions. State administration was smashed and substituted by Soviet institutions with Soviet cadres. The NKVD secret police plus new juridical courts and public prosecutors were employed to assure full-scale repression. A few days before the elections, single candidates lists were introduced which, according to official statements, were approved by 92.8 percent of the voters in Estonia, by 97.6 percent in Latvia, and by 99.2 percent in Lithuania. While national independence had not been put into question during the elections, the resultant parliaments immediately asked for admission to the USSR, which was naturally "granted" by the Supreme Soviet in Moscow. As everywhere under the Kremlin's power, the peasantry and the "bourgeoisie"—industrialists, bankers, businessmen, and even small traders and craftsmen—were expropriated. All "means of production" were taken over by "the people," that is, the imposed Soviet party nomenklatura.[55]

In the first half of July, when the Baltic countries were still nominally independent, the Kremlin issued secret orders that declared them to be a military district of the USSR. Their armies were first termed "people's armies" and then "territorial corps of the Red Army." Also before the mid-July elections, command was assumed by Soviet military commissars, while the native officers were transported to the USSR under the pretense of being given "additional training." Most of them were shot, the others sent to forced labor camps for physical liquidation.[56] Deportation of national elites was intended to decapitate society in the interests of eliminating sociopolitical and national identity. In the other parts of the "sphere of influence" acquired by the pact with Hitler—Eastern Poland, Bessarabia, and Northern Bukovina—similar sovietization processes were initiated. The Katyn mass murder of Polish officers is a well-known incident in the context of decapitating national societies. In many respects, treatment of the territories annexed in 1939–1940 created a pattern of how to employ military and police power for imposing the Soviet system and Soviet domination on foreign populations. While force was brutally used, the Kremlin was careful to create an appearance to the outside world that transformation resulted from the people's own will. The methods largely presaged Soviet action in conquered Eastern Europe a few years later.

Limits to Soviet Expansion and Cooling Down of Relations with Germany

When the Baltic countries were made to sign "treaties of mutual assistance," Stalin tried to play the same game with Finland. On 5 October 1939, he summoned a representative from Helsinki to the Soviet capital for "political consultations." But his demands for surrender of territories, stationing of troops at the Hangö peninsula, and demilitarization of the areas bordering the USSR were rejected. Stalin then decided to attack the recalcitrant Finns. On 26 November, the Kremlin protested that Finland had allegedly bombarded a village in the USSR (an infringement of Soviet territory that was physically impossible for the pretended culprit). Three days later, Moscow declared war and formed a Finnish satellite government that was alleged to be the representation of the Finnish working people. Stalin expected that the country would be subjugated within a short period of time. But the Finnish Communist Party chairman in Moscow exile, Arvo Tuominen, failed to play the role assigned to him. As the crisis mounted, he managed to leave for Sweden. There he declined the post of prime minister in a Soviet-installed government and even appealed to the "Finnish workers and comrades" to join the national defense effort against the USSR. To be sure, the Kremlin replaced him by Otto Kuusinen but any basis for the satellite regime to gain influence and for communist sabotage groups to take action was destroyed. The Finnish troops resisted the invader most stubbornly. The Red Army prevailed only after long and fierce battle without, however, being able to break the military resistance altogether. At this point, the British appeared ready for military intervention. The Kremlin saw the risk of both wasting too many resources on a minor achievement and prematurely getting involved in war. As Stalin did not want this, he renounced annexation and sovietization and was content with the Finnish surrender of border strips and military bases.[57]

Stalin's initial effort to incorporate Finland was one of the factors that created distrust in Berlin. Annexation of Northern Bukovina, in excess of the secret protocol provisions, was another point of irritation. Hitler suspected that the Soviet leader would seek domination of the Balkans, which he saw as his exclusive sphere of influence. When the USSR incorporated nearly all Lithuania (of which but a minor share was taken by Germany), further ill-feeling resulted in Berlin. On his part, Stalin's expectation that war would wear down both the Germans and their adversaries was frustrated when the Wehrmacht speedily occupied Denmark, Norway, the Benelux countries, and France in spring 1940. Feeling that maintaining agreement with the Germans was more important than ever, he took recourse to appeasement tactics. For example, he tried to make them accept an arrangement that would allow the communists in France and other countries to continue their legal existence on a limited scale. In exchange for this, he would oblige his followers there to support occupation policies unconditionally. This deal, however, was rejected by the Germans. Upon this, he ordered the "brother parties" in Western Europe to discontinue compromising contact with the Wehrmacht authorities and to take a national position without, however, antagonizing the occupiers.[58]

Stalin was seeking to appease the Germans also by satisfying their appetite for deliveries from the USSR. He even offered them a "strategic" relationship. At the same time, however, his interest in territorial expansion increased. After he had completed annexation of the Baltic countries, he made clear in Berlin that he wanted a "free hand" in Northern Europe and the Balkans. He also sought German support in the Black Sea region, in the Middle East, and in other parts of Asia.[59] Tension among the partners of the 1939 treaty resulted. But Stalin did not budge, feeling that war with Germany could not possibly break out as long as the Wehrmacht was confronted with Britain, which was supported by the military contributions of its empire and by an increasing amount of deliveries from the United States. The Soviet leader could not imagine that Hitler might enter another military conflict before war with the West had been terminated. Against this background, he was also sure that Germany could not dispense with the oil and the raw materials from the USSR. To be sure, Moscow and Berlin were bound to be antagonists in the long run but war among them appeared to be still far off.[60]

REVERSAL OF ALIGNMENT AND MODIFICATION OF POLICY

As a result of the German attack on 22 June 1941, the USSR found itself in an unexpected alliance with Britain. When, in December, Foreign Minister Eden went to Moscow, which had just escaped conquest by a narrow margin, Stalin tried to make him confirm his annexations in 1939–1940 and agree to even more territorial gains, the establishment of military bases abroad, the control of the Danish and Turkish Straits, and an alliance obligation for Romania. In return, he suggested that the British do likewise and extend their power to Western Europe. Underlying this was the very idea of "spheres of responsibility" that had shaped his pact with Hitler. Eden declined.[61] After Prime Minister Churchill had equally rejected these plans[62] and the United States (which had entered the war against Germany) also did not want to support Soviet expansion, Stalin concluded that it was useless to seek Western approval. In his view, the Anglo-Saxon leaders' negative attitudes were motivated by "bourgeois class interest" that did not allow for extension of the Soviet system. He was not prepared, however, to renounce socialist transformation. In his view, expansion of power required a systemic fundament. The two sides' objectives in war proved to be incompatible. This was a major problem for Stalin, who was aware that he badly needed cooperative relations with his allies to maintain military defense, to reconstruct his country after the war, and to further his policy goals generally.[63] So he could not afford to alienate them openly.

Western attitudes helped Stalin to cope with his dilemma. The leading circles in London and Washington were impressed by Soviet suffering. Previous rejection of the USSR as a revolutionary threat to international security gave way to an image of a heroic ally who, on the basis of his sacrifice, deserved unconditional support against the Nazi invaders. Harry Hopkins, a close friend of U.S. President Roosevelt, went to Moscow with an offer to support the USSR's war effort by massive land lease deliveries. The financial modalities were most generous and were not made conditional on any Soviet restraint concerning political action in territories that would be occupied by the Red Army. The American envoy did not make the slightest attempt to exploit awareness in the Kremlin that victory crucially depended on shipment of armaments and other materials from the West, notably the United States. As a result, no strings were put on Stalin's prospective policy of socialist transformation.[64] At the same time, the Soviet leader succeeded in exacting approval of his claim to control over Eastern Europe: His Western allies accepted the argument that this was necessary to prevent another German aggression. Accordingly, deployment of Soviet troops, creation of "friendly governments," and establishment of a "democratic order" suitable to eradicate fascist and aggressive tendencies were recognized to be indispensable. The anti-Soviet *cordon sanitaire* of the prewar period would have to be replaced by a "security belt" to protect the USSR.[65]

In Western interpretation, this concept provided for "friendly governments" in neighboring countries that would comply with Soviet foreign policy but freely take their decisions on domestic affairs. In particular, sociopolitical self-determination of the respective states would not be infringed. In reality, however, lacking obligation with regard to enforcement of socialist transformation and recognition of a claim to "friendly" government policy provided Stalin with a rationale to both veil and justify compulsory measures not only to install regimes but to impose sociopolitical transformation as he would like. His determination to exploit the situation thus created to the maximum extent surfaced when surrender of defeated German allies was on the agenda. The Soviet side invariably insisted that an armistice must not terminate the state of war (but implicitly allow for continuing control by the victor), that the military commander of the occupying power had to be accorded exclusive responsibility not limited by any interallied body, and that undesirable exile governments must not be permitted to return to their countries.[66] At the same time, Stalin was willing to sign declarations on national independence, non-intervention, and democratic freedom. Verbal approval of Western principle would soothe concerns in the West and do no harm. After all, practical interpretation depended on the correlation of forces in the respective region.[67]

The Kremlin concealed its envisaged systemic goals by declaring that, in Poland as in other countries, it simply wanted the domestic power structure to be "democratic" and an "antifascist" national front government to be formed. Party pluralism and creation of a "democratic, not a Soviet order" were sought and would be extended to society by expropriation of big landowners and nationalization of banks, big industry, mining, and transport. Central economic planning was required to protect "normal supply" and prevent "disorder and speculation."[68] The sociopolitical order thus portrayed was termed a "new type of democracy" that pretendedly did not differ much from Western democracy but would simply be complemented by a socialist element (which, in Western perception, did not imply Soviet patterns). The explanation that a "parliamentary," respectively "national," "road to socialism" would be taken[69] was intended to create the impression that the principles of parliamentary democracy and national independence would be respected. When, in fall 1943, Churchill indicated that the small countries of Eastern Europe were afraid of communist revolution, Stalin replied that such fears were unfounded.[70] But the Kremlin's statement that a "road to socialism" would be taken implied to the initiated that the ultimate goal was the introduction of the Soviet system.

Pretended Abandonment of Revolutionary Intent

Both the Sudeten crisis of 1938 and the negotiations with Britain and France in the following year had made clear to Stalin that foreign leaders suspected the USSR to seek revolutionary transformation. He realized that this was a crucial handicap in his alliance with the Anglo-Saxon powers. So he tried to create the impression that he no longer wanted extension of his sociopolitical system. He therefore put dissolution of the Comintern on the Moscow agenda. On 8 May 1943, he internally explained: "Under present conditions, the Comintern as the leading center of the communist parties has become an impediment for their [these parties'] independent development and to fulfilment of their specific tasks." The envisaged dissolution would also serve to facilitate the recruitment of political cadres among prisoners of war from enemy countries, notably Germany, Italy, Hungary, and Romania. These people were "bourgeois"-minded and would reject communist indoctrination but accept training if they felt that the ideological barrier had been removed. The communist parties abroad would have better chances of domestic success when they were no longer seen to receive instructions from Moscow and could present themselves as champions of national interest.[71]

As early as in December 1941, a massive training program had been initiated for foreigners to serve as political and administrative cadres in their home countries when these had been conquered by the Red Army. Given that only a few communist emigrés were available whose number was insufficient to provide the necessary key personnel, selected prisoners of war were also prepared for the prospective task of rebuilding and transforming the domestic system of their respective countries.[72] The trainees, who have aptly been termed "Moscow cadres" by Peter Erler,[73] were envisaged to enforce Soviet policies at home under control by communist top functionaries unconditionally devoted to Stalin who would return with them from the USSR. The first "Antifa (that is, antifascist) school" for Germans opened in May 1942. The CPSU selected the trainees, prescribed the teaching program, and provided the lecturers, while the German Communist Party (KPD) in Moscow exile had no say whatsoever. As was explicitly stated, training cadres for employment at home was a task of the Soviet party, not the German one. Candidates from communist families, defectors from the Wehrmacht, and people with appropriate "class" backgrounds were preferably admitted. At first, there was no specific communist indoctrination as it was felt that this was not required in the beginning and would only make useful people unwilling to enlist.[74]

To direct these and other "revolutionary" activities, the Comintern's organizational structure was preserved to the full extent. Dimitrov and his staff kept working in what was now called the Soviet Central Committee Department of International Information. As before, the CPSU leadership and ultimately Stalin provided the national bureaus with instructions. Some parts of the previous Comintern were termed "institutes": its Press and Propaganda Department operated as "Institute 205," and the First Department with its international network of agents and radio transmitters became "Institute 100." An additional "Institute 99" was set up to manage the "National Committee Free Germany" (Nationalkomitee Freies Deutschland, NKFD), which was formed after more than one hundred thousand men had been taken prisoner of war as a result of the German Stalingrad army's surrender early in 1943.

The principal task of the NKFD was to persuade the German soldiers in the trenches to lay down their weapons and withdraw from Soviet territory. As was alleged, it was in their national interest to cooperate with the USSR for putting an end to war and thus save their home country from impending disaster. To add credibility, prisoners of war were made to join the appeal. To this end, promises were given in what appeared to be a process of negotiation.[75] But the People's Commissariat of Domestic Affairs in charge had no authority to make any pledges, and Soviet policy retained its punitive anti-German orientation. The purpose underlying the NKFD's activity was both to make the enemy forces surrender and to veil communist intent by national slogans.[76] To make Soviet policy appear aimed at attainment of normal goals that would allow for national independence of other countries and did not imply "revolutionary" change, Stalin took the decision that conquered countries would not be incorporated into the USSR (as had been the practice before). They would remain separate states but informally be subjected to comprehensive Soviet control.

Three Different Soviet Approaches to Policy on Europe

Soviet performance in Eastern Europe demonstrates that Stalin was determined to extend his power and system to conquered countries. Control by the Red Army was crucial but he also saw acceptance, or at minimum acquiescence, by his Western allies as essential. He therefore skilfully exploited their willingness to come to meet demands for security. In defeated enemy countries, measures that were actually designed to establish communist power were veiled as being necessary for other purposes. While international law did not allow for intervention in internal affairs of an occupied country, Western leaders agreed that the USSR must replace "fascist" regimes for the sake of "democratization." In Soviet terminology, however, these words had quite another meaning than in the West. The Kremlin exploited the appearance of political consensus to initiate what in fact was socialist transformation directed against Western democracy and Western influence.

In Italy and France, which would be occupied by Anglo-Saxon troops, Stalin faced the problem of what instructions he should give to the communists there. In either country, they had joined anti-German resistance in 1941, organized underground forces, and won sympathy as the most outspoken enemies of "fascism." As a result, they appeared capable of seizing power by some kind of putsch. But in his view, another factor, the troops of Britain and the United States, was crucial. Their presence determined the "correlation of forces" more than anything else and hence did not allow for communist takeover and elimination of the "bourgeois" parties. As a result, the Italian and French "brother parties" had to cooperate with the "domestic clients" of the Anglo-Saxon powers and to join government coalitions under their leadership.[77] It appeared natural to Stalin that both the USSR and the West would impose their respective system where their armies would take control.[78]

For a long time, Stalin was not sure whether he would be able to exercise decisive influence on German matters. This apparently continued even after agreement with the Anglo-Saxon powers on joint occupation of Germany in fall 1943 which provided for control of but one part of the country. In the event that the Anglo-Saxons would not deceive the USSR but allow it to get its share, Stalin looked forward to initiate in his zone of occupation basically the same kind of policy as existed in the other territories controlled by the Red Army. Seeking not to alienate the Western co-occupiers, he simply planned the approach to be more cautious and gradual. Given that the United States and Britain would be able to monitor Soviet performance in more detail, the ultimate goal had to be concealed more carefully. Therefore measures that were clearly indicative of the intended direction had to be delayed until the USSR was in a dominating position after American disengagement from Europe. Stalin was hopeful that the United States would withdraw again as after World War I.

Stalin's Concept for Eastern Europe

Lenin had seized power in Russia by establishing "dictatorship of the proletariat." Stalin felt that, for the sake of continuing agreement with the West, this proclamation must not be repeated in the occupied countries. He saw no need for this either since the situation would be fundamentally different. In Russia, the task had been to defeat a powerful enemy. As early as in December 1941, the Kremlin leader had been sure that the USSR was on the winning side and would control East European countries at the end of war. As in the territories annexed in 1939–1940, class struggle would already have been decided. Conquest and occupation by the Red Army would have broken the power of the ruling classes. But while Hitler had not cared for Soviet use of brutal force in Eastern Poland, the Baltic countries, and elsewhere, the Anglo-Saxon allies were sensitive to despotism and violence. Therefore, consideration for their scruples rather than rash action to create accomplished facts was required. On the basis of military conquest, communist takeover without mass terror and heavy loss of human life was feasible. At the same time, such performance appeared necessary to allay Western concerns. Therefore, systemic transformation was envisaged as a long-term process that would be enforced as smoothly as possible and take place in a context of pretended national independence.

In summer 1946, Stalin explained his East European policy to Polish leaders as follows:

> After the First World War, dictatorship of the proletariat emerged with us in Russia. By what was it caused? We had strong enemies, we had to crush three principal [enemies]—the tsar, the landlords, and the rather strong class of Russian capitalists that had its ties with foreigners. To defeat these forces, power was needed based on force, that is, dictatorship. For you, the situation is completely different. Your capitalists and landlords have compromised themselves by their ties with the Germans to such an extent that they could be smashed easily. They have displayed no patriotism. With such a 'sin', no one wanted to associate himself with them. Undoubtedly, also the Red Army helped to eliminate the capitalists and landlords in Poland. This is why you have no basis for dictatorship of the proletariat.[79]

Stalin argued that Soviet military victory in Eastern Europe had defeated also the class enemy there. This allowed for "an easier, less bloodletting road of development" than proletarian dictatorship. As a result, socialism had to be attained not by forceful change including brutal measures of radical expropriation but by taking the "road of socio-economic reforms," that is, initiation of sociopolitical transformation by nationalization of big industry and business and the banking system. Small enterpreneurs, craftsmen, and traders must not be antagonized. Big lands had to be expropriated; an agrarian reform would give it to small peasants.[80] The Kremlin leader failed to tell his Polish interlocutors (who were aligned with the communists but did not agree with them fully) that respect for small property was planned to be but temporary. In the long run, any private enterprise of trade and land was unacceptable.

In a conversation with his long-time aide Dimitrov who became leader of Bulgaria after the war, Stalin made clear that the communists must merge in due course with the other "parties of the working people" to create a united party that would be essentially communist but not appear so to the public. They would thus be provided with a broad mass basis notably among the peasants (who, in Bulgaria as in most other East European countries, were the large majority of the population). A program of but minimum political requirements would be required. Tasks must be defined for "any concrete period." The communists would use the anouncement of intermediate objectives as a "very convenient mask" to conceal their ultimate goal. This was important not only in the domestic context but also internationally. The time for the maximum program would come later. Stalin emphasized that the Soviet experience must not be repeated since the situation was completely different.[81]

Once the Red Army had basically decided the class struggle by occupying the country, it was necessary to translate military control into domestic transformation. "Exploitation of such institutions of the bourgeois order as parliament and other institutions" would serve this purpose. Stalin made clear that the "reforms" thus enforced did not directly result in the creation of socialism. For an extended period of time, "petty and medium capitalists" in the cities and the countryside were bound to be a major element of society. But once "big private banks," "private big industry," and the "classes of big capitalists and landlords" had disappeared, a regime of industry control and satisfaction of people's consumption needs would allow societies to "approach socialism without struggle full of bloodshed."[82] The Soviet leader argued that his new approach did not imply deviation from Leninist principles. To be sure, introduction of the Soviet system would not result immediately but ultimately ensue. Allowing for systemic "concessions" (which were understood to be temporary) to soothe both the West and native "bourgeois" groups was a merely tactical approach. During a critical

initial period, opposition to the early steps of socialist transformation had
to be minimized. The pretense that the effort was simply directed at an "antifascist-democratic" multiparty system with additional sociopolitical elements served the purpose of neutralizing opposition. Before communist
control would be consolidated, it was essential to spread illusions that the
USSR wanted some kind of democracy not basically different from the
Western variant.[83]

In the Kremlin's view, it was crucial for systemic decisions on occupied
countries to avoid arousing concern among the Anglo-Saxon allies. As a
People's Commissariat on Internal Affairs (NKVD) commission emphasized when, in January 1944, it submitted guidelines for sociopolitical
transformation of Eastern Europe, the USSR was "interested in that the state
structure of these countries is based on the principles of broad democracy
in the spirit of the people's front idea." Enforcement of this concept required caution. Particular attention had to be paid to the fact that the main
threat to peace and security might result "from premature revolutions since
these can provoke escalation of tension in relations with the West."[84]

Stalin's Concept of Communist Policy in Western Europe

In July 1943, Marshal Badoglio overthrew Mussolini in Rome, formed a
new government, and sought an alliance with the Anglo-Saxon powers that
had already taken Sicily and were starting military operations on the Italian
mainland. Stalin faced indecision among the Italian communists whether
to cooperate with the regime or oppose it. To be sure, the new leaders had
served the dictator and continued to advocate preservation of the monarchy
but now they were allies against the Germans. The Kremlin leader felt in
Moscow that seeking to oust Badoglio would challenge the Americans and
the British and initiate civil war. Before the Italian Communist Party head
in Soviet exile, Palmiro Togliatti, left for his home country, Stalin provided
him with political guidance on 3 March 1944. The two men agreed that
conflict between the fascist defectors from Mussolini and "anti-fascist"
forces must be avoided. National unity was called for; social revolution and
domestic struggle were inappropriate for the time being. Communist restraint and left-wing participation in government was the best way to serve
the needs of both Italy and the USSR. Stalin wanted to avoid provocation
of Britain and the United States by a communization effort which, given
their military presence, he declared would be futile from the very beginning.
Togliatti agreed and issued an appeal to cooperate with Badoglio, referring
to the common national interest.[85]

When, after their landing in Normandy, American and British troops had
broken German defenses and were pouring into France in summer 1944,

the communists in the country's resistance movement took armed action to seize control wherever possible and succeeded in some regions. On the whole, however, General de Gaulle prevailed, whose troops had joined the Anglo-Saxon forces when they entered the country. In October, he formed a government that was recognized by all allies including the USSR. The new French leader went to Moscow to conclude a friendship treaty and to recognize the Kremlin's Lublin government for Poland. As a result, there was no Soviet backing for taking an intransigent position against the "bourgeois" regime in Paris: Stalin told de Gaulle on 26 November that the French communists had to join the government coalition and to take a cooperative attitude. They were expected to play a substantial role in domestic French politics on this basis. The general agreed to accept them as political partners provided that they would submit to his leadership.[86]

In a preceding conversation with their leader Maurice Thorez on 19 November 1944, Stalin had argued that a popular front strategy along the lines of the mid-1930s was required (which, for psychological reasons, must not be termed so):

> It is quite possible that de Gaulle will take steps to isolate the communist party. Comrade Stalin thinks that, in this event, it would be good if party would have [domestic] allies. The party must look around and look for allies among the [left liberal] radicals [. . .] One must look for allies also among the socialists. It is necessary to create a bloc against reaction. It is necessary to employ also socialists in this bloc. Perhaps some more elements can be found who can be used in this bloc. One must organize certain forces that will be grouped around the communist party for defense and, when the situation will change, also for attack. The communists should not look for those people among the socialists who, at some time, have said something against the Soviet Union. We know the socialists well. The socialists are the left wing of the bourgeoisie. For us, the main thing is to create a leftist bloc. How strong the communist party may be, must not be the only force that opposes the reaction. The communist party must not be isolated. The party's current task is establishing close ties with the trade-unions and the young people. The youth [organization] must not be called communist youth. It has to be taken into account that some people are apprehensive of the flag. One has to consider this.

Repeating that the French party should seek to strengthen its weak domestic position by bloc-building, Stalin indicated

> that de Gaulle will be urged to think about steps against the communists, and even if he himself does not want these steps, he will be pressed by the British and the Americans who want to install a reactionary government in France as at any place where this can be done. Therefore, the party must have allies, even if initially they are weak.

Stalin also told Thorez that communist-controlled armed forces must be disbanded. He argued

> that it must be taken into account that, in France, there is a government now which is recognized by the allied powers. Under these conditions, it is difficult for the communists to have parallel armed forces since there is a regular army. The communists might be put the question for what purpose they need parallel armed units. As long as there was no provisional government, as long as there was no rear zone which could be used, the existence of such units made some sense. But for what purpose shall these units exist now when there is a government which has an army? Such may be the arguments of the communists' enemies. These arguments may be convincing for the average Frenchman. Therefore, the position of the communist party is weak and will be weak when it maintains armed forces. It is difficult to defend this position. Therefore, the armed units must be transformed into another organization, into a political organization, and the weapons must be hidden. Comrade Stalin explains that he has touched this question since he has got the impression that the communists have not realized yet that the situation in France has changed. The communists are bragging and continue to pursue their old line [directed against the pro-German Vichy regime], while the situation has become another one.[87]

Stalin justified his instruction saying that the French communists must guard themselves against threat and prepare for gaining influence in the long run. An even more important motive was his view that any challenge to Britain and the United States within their sphere of power had to be avoided. Also, communist participation in West European governments would be a barrier to prevent use of these countries by the "imperialists" in Washington and London.[88]

Considerations on Germany

Ever since Lenin, the Kremlin saw Germany as the key country that would guarantee domination of the whole Continent. In the early years of the Soviet state, there had been repeated efforts to gain control of it. In contrast to Trotskii and other rivals for power in the USSR, Stalin had learned the lesson that the "revolutionary ebb" had made achievement of this objective impossible. As late as in 1943 and 1944 when the Red Army had already put the Wehrmacht on the defensive, he was not confident yet whether he would be able to exercise decisive influence on Germany. He therefore wanted to make sure that it at least would be prevented from becoming a threat again. As the USSR argued when pressing for an interallied decision, the best method for this was dismemberment.[89] At first, the Anglo-Saxon powers were inclined to comply but then grew increasingly hesitant.[90] In Moscow, the Peoples Commissariat of Foreign Affairs was made to devise plans on possible implementation but Stalin also had another option in mind. As the premise of central authority underlying a 1944 concept on postwar policy in Germany indicates,[91] he equally considered the possibility to maintain unity of the enemy country if socialist transformation would prove feasible.

At the Moscow conference in October 1943, the United States and Britain both committed themselves not to seek a separate deal with Germany and expressed their willingness to allow for Soviet participation in future decisions on Germany by accepting joint occupation.[92] Upon this, Stalin decided to have a political strategy worked out that would provide for gradual socialist transformation of the defeated country. To be sure, he was not certain yet whether he would be in a position to implement this plan. Would the Anglo-Saxon powers really forego an opportunity to exclude him from decision making on Germany by making a separate deal with the enemy? Would they abide by projected zonal division if their troops would advance further? If, on the basis of such or other contingencies, the USSR would be prevented from dominating the whole country, Stalin continued to feel that he had to make sure that its potential for future attack was neutralized by creating a number of German states. Only when, at the end of March 1945, he was sufficiently confident that he would be able to exercise decisive influence on German postwar development, he dropped his demand for dismemberment. From then on, he saw long-time occupation as crucial for Soviet security.[93]

Laure Castin-Chaparro has concluded that continuing insistence on the demand of German dismemberment in diplomatic exchange with the West resulted from caution: Stalin wanted to make sure that in any case the USSR would be protected against aggression. This was his minimum objective but he always preferred having a united Germany provided that he would control it and be allowed to initiate socialist transformation.[94] This inference is plausible. Stalin demonstrated his preference for unity by never paying any attention to the plans of dismemberment duly worked out in the Foreign People's Commissariat while he continually provided the members of the KPD commission on postwar policy with guidance. There was no statement underlying their effort, which would have been tabled without preceding consultation with, and approval by, Dimitrov who, on his part, had received instructions from the Kremlin leader.[95] The mere fact that dismemberment planning was assigned to diplomats, while postwar strategy in a centrally organized Germany was worked out by party cadres, indicates preference for the latter option: in matters of primary importance, Stalin generally turned to the party apparatus.[96]

The action program worked out on this basis was essentially similar to the Soviet concept for Eastern Europe. However, the situation to cope with was more complicated as a result of Western participation in occupation. Modifications were therefore required. Nonetheless, the fundamental opening statement presented by Wilhelm Florin emphasized that confrontation of "reaction" and "progress" in Germany required "imperialist reaction" to be smashed. This implied that the goal was a domestic order along Soviet lines. To be sure, Florin denied any such intention by the USSR but this did not mean anything: such an assertion was used also to conceal the true character of Soviet policy in Eastern Europe. Florin expressed hope that Hitler might be overthrown by insurrection initiated by the communists. In this event, outright defeat of Germany would be prevented. To be sure, occupation by the three allied powers and destruction of the war machinery had been firmly decided but other aspects of postwar development continued to be open. On the basis of interallied agreement, the "reactionary circles in the United States and England" were likely to particpate in occupation. As these political forces were most suspicious of communist policy and hostile to both German "national and social interest" and a "genuinely democratic community of [European] peoples," particular attention was required to cope with them. As a result, the KPD was confronted with a number of mutually interrelated tasks:

(1) To continue supporting the alliance of the three great powers and to do nothing that might allow the reactionary circles in the United States and England to make this alliance break apart;
(2) but simultaneously to thwart the plans of the reactionary forces concerning Germany;
(3) to attain with regard to Germany's domestic transformation the maximum of what the international situation and the correlation of power within Germany itself permit.

In view of the complicated situation, an announcement of a socialist program of action would be harmful. It would not only foster domestic opposition but facilitate Roosevelt's overthrow by reactionary forces.

Therefore, all our central program slogans can and may only be directed at overthrowing fascism, at overpowering the aggressive [political] forces of imperialism, and at achieving bourgeois democracy as people's government. This line is correct also from an intra-German viewpoint since it must be our objective as before to divide the German bourgeoisie and to include one part of it in the national front. Can it be expected that one part of the German bourgeoisie will take another direction than most of the reactionary forces? Yes! Why? The reactionary forces in England and the United States want to subject Germany to their imperialistic control. They are supported by certain liberals who say: "Let us create a Western plan which must be more attractive than the Soviet Union's Eastern plan." But intelligent bourgeois circles in Germany also

realize that German industry and trade can flourish once more only in an independent Germany.

Its "progressive circles" had to be mobilized by the argument that British-
American policy was incompatible with national independence. The "bourgeoisie" would thus have to make a choice between an Eastern and a Western orientation, with a resulting split that must be skilfully deepened and
exploited. This would allow the communists to seek a compromise with the
progressive party. Pursuing this policy, they had to be most careful not to
jeopardize the Soviet alliance with the United States and Britain. To increase
the split within the German bourgeoisie still further, the communists had
to argue that Russia was a profitable market and that, for this reason, an
Eastern orientation served the national interest. The "party of the working
class," that is, the KPD, must form an alliance with other political forces to
assume responsibility. In spite of all "maneuvers and tactics," it had to keep
in mind that socialism was the ultimate goal. Clarity in matters of principle
was required. For the time being, only "militant democracy" was on the
agenda but the perspective of "class struggle" had be maintained.[97]
   Particular attention was paid to the possibility that the Western occupation powers might support "national traitors," that is, anti-Soviet political
forces in Germany. To prevent this, it was crucial to veil the systemic character of the conflict. If the "class struggle" were perceived as such, domestic
German and foreign Western "imperialists" were likely to join their efforts.
"Premature" action that would disclose the underlying socialist intent had
to be avoided. A "direct course toward socialist revolution" carried the risk
of confrontation with the United States and Britain and might result in defeat of both socialism and the "international working class." Restraint in
pursuit of political and social objectives was therefore required. For the
time being, only the roots of the "imperialistic," that is, capitalist, system
had to be eradicated by socioeconomic transformation.[98]

GUIDELINES FOR SOVIET INTERVENTION
IN INTERNAL AFFAIRS OF CONQUERED COUNTRIES

The crucial problem in countries taken by the Red Army was how to translate occupation power into control of domestic development. To this end,
Western willingness to support "antifascist" action and to allow for "democratization" with a socialist element had to be exploited. To make this
policy succeed, the communists in the respective country were called upon
to initiate a process of slow, gradual sovietization designed to be impercep-
tible so as not to impair the Soviet interest in continuing cooperation
with the Anglo-Saxon countries and to minimize the risks inherent in the

"correlation of domestic forces." As a result, the political conditions in Soviet-occupied Eastern Europe fundamentally differed from those in Western Europe (with an Anglo-Saxon military presence) and Germany (under an interallied occupation regime). Despite this difference, the communists in all these three regions were instructed to form coalitions with the other parties. This, however, implied divergent strategic orientations and concepts.

In Eastern Europe, the Kremlin used several methods to impose its will. Personnel of its choosing, notably Moscow cadres trained for their jobs in the USSR, were put into crucial power positions to make them fulfill orders to initiate sociopolitical transformation. Soviet power to grant or refuse admission of parties allowed for deciding rules of political interaction. Supreme state authority was a basis of control of all matters of domestic policy. In Western Europe, all this was lacking. Neither were there cadres whom the Soviet party had trained and selected, nor did the communists enjoy support by an occupation power. Like all the other parties, they were subjected to the rules of democratic competition. As a result, they could not claim a "leading role" in domestic politics as they were enabled to do within the Kremlin's power sphere. Given their being backed by only a minor part of the population, they had to accept junior positions.

In Germany, Stalin initially hoped for a workers' uprising to oust Hitler. This would put the communists into a strong position. Nonetheless, he always saw a need to maintain cooperation with the Western powers that would take part in occupying the country. While this requirement was even more relevant when, by remaining passive, the "working class" failed to promote communist domestic power, the Soviet military authorities were in a position to render any support to them within their zone. Extension of the resulting sociopolitical "achievements" to the other parts of Germany depended on whether the communists would gain both people's support and acceptance, or at least acquiescence by the Western occupation powers. As a result, Stalin was even more interested than in Eastern Europe to deceive both domestic opinion and Western governments about his long-term goal. In Germany, the allied "imperialistic powers" had direct power to prevent the transfer of measures aimed at sovietization in the long run and to back, even mobilize, "bourgeois" opposition against them.

Initiation of Sociopolitical Transformation

Stalin felt that socioeconomic transformation was indispensable to establish Soviet control. Underlying this belief was the Marxist-Leninist doctrine that, as a "material basis," distribution of the means of production shaped social and political relations. Expropriation would deprive the "bourgeoisie" of its power in both the cities and villages and rally the working masses behind their "class party" which, as their representation, would take control of the economic process. Once social relations based on property changed, similar change of political relations was bound to follow. This conviction explains why, for example, Stalin ordered expropriation of landowners in his zone of Germany in mid-1945, when even the KPD leaders did not want it. He understood that, at this point of time, chaos in society and lack of food would thus be greatly increased further.[99] Stalin, of course, was aware of this, too, but felt that, given a situation of general turmoil and want, change could be imposed more easily than under more stable conditions. In his view, priority had to be given to laying the fundament of the new political order before existing social structures had been allowed to reconsolidate. Other measures might be delayed if necessary but elimination of the "bourgeoisie's" social and financial power by expropriation of landed and industrial property was accorded absolute priority.

The need to initiate systemic change through socioeconomic transformation was reflected in internal statements only. In public, respective measures were depicted as "reforms" that complemented political democracy and its institutions. While, in Stalin's explanations to East European communist leaders, there was a fundamental difference between "new democracy" and Western democracy, statements to the outside were designed to create the impression that they were essentially identical. As long as Moscow wanted to maintain cooperative relations with its Western allies (that is, prior to the outbreak of open confrontation in mid-1947), it always tried to persuade people that the East European version of democracy was a mere modification of the Western model. In the case of East Germany, the fiction that the Soviet-imposed order was a mere variant of "bourgeois democracy" was maintained even until 1952.

In spite of the crucial importance ascribed to it, land reform was but an interim arrangement that would have to be revised in due course. While it was recognized to be necessary for breaking the social power of the big landowners, emergence of a "petty bourgeoisie on the countryside" was not ultimately the sought objective. As in the USSR when Lenin had taken power, it appeared useful to mobilize the peasantry in support of the socialist cause by giving them land. Private ownership thus created, however, was not in accordance with the socialist imperative that the means of production must be common property, that is, put under national control to be exercised by the Moscow cadres. Collectivization of agriculture would be necessary once appropriate political conditions were created at a later date. "Reform" along Soviet lines also implied setting up unified "societal organizations." From the very start, trade unions and associations to represent all kinds of social, professional, and other groups had to be set up in such a way that there was only one organization for each category and competition for membership and popularity among them was excluded. This program, which was mandatory in all of Soviet-controlled Eastern Europe except for

Czechoslovakia (where, on the basis of his pact with Beneš,[100] Stalin did not set up an occupation regime and refrained from direct intervention), alleged that these were "above party" organizations. They were, however, managed by communist cadres who owed their positions to the occupation power and gradually developed into affiliates of the communist party. While, during the initial period, they allowed for some diversity, they prepared for a pattern of social and political uniformity which, after this, was increasingly enforced.

Bloc Politics in Occupied Countries

While Stalin saw his task in making sure that Soviet military power in occupied countries was duly translated into control of domestic politics and creation of sovietizing structures, both Western governments and non-communist activists in Eastern Europe initially hoped that he was willing to allow for genuine democracy. This was largely based on the fact that a number of different political groups including social democratic and "bourgeois" parties were admitted. But the multiparty system authorized by Soviet authorities had an inherent bias. Except for Czechoslovakia, activities by political parties were made conditional on abiding by the rule of bloc politics. In Romania where the government had initiated surrender and, on this basis, was willing for friendly relations but not all-encompassing subordination, the Soviet occupation power took pains to replace it by a cabinet that was not only dominated by the communists but subjected to the bloc rule of non-disagreement. Bulgaria, which had not been at war with the USSR, was attacked by the Red Army to allow for occupation and subsequent creation of a multiparty bloc under communist leadership. That Poland was an allied country did not prevent Stalin from subjecting it to what, for all practical purposes, was a harsh occupation regime. On this basis, he imposed a tightly Soviet-controlled government bloc. When Berlin came under exclusive Soviet control, he also initiated a party bloc there, hoping that it would extend its reach to all of Germany.

All the parties that were permitted activity had to accept membership in an "antifascist" bloc obliging them to act only in mutual consensus. By this, expression of individual political positions was prohibited as a matter of principle. Any statements and decisions on policy required unanimity among all participants. The Moscow cadres at the top of the communist party would refuse to change their stand and insist that the others must comply, if necessary by indicating that the occupation wanted the decision. Opposition then maintained was insubordination to Soviet authorities, hence likely to entail harsh punishment. Occasionally when this threat failed to produce the desired effect, occupation officers would even intervene directly. Profession of views divergent from bloc consensus thus achieved was illegal. Elections (which the Kremlin had pledged to the Western allies) thus did not offer policy choices. People were simply allowed to indicate preference for one of the parties that had to follow equally the line prescribed by the Kremlin. Nonetheless, election results were not irrelevant. Not only did they reflect the population's attitude to official policy and thereby express judgment on the regime's claim to legitimation by the people's will but determined the filling of visible political positions, to some extent.

The bloc system thus allowed the USSR to exercise domestic control indirectly. While the public in the respective country increasingly sensed that political decisions were basically pro-Soviet oriented, these nonetheless seemed to result from debate among native politicians. In the Kremlin's view, concealment of its political role was crucial. During a critical initial period, this appeared necessary to neutralize resistance against occupation policy and to prevent the domestic opponents and their "class brethren" in the West from joining forces. Notably measures likely to arouse rejection must not be allowed to be seen as having been caused by Soviet influence.[101] No one informed on the true origin of official policy was permitted to hint at this in talking to anyone else or to note previous intercourse with occupation authorities in the files. As a rule, it is therefore not from sources of the country concerned but from reports by Soviet officials to their superiors in Moscow that direct evidence is available.[102]

Stalin wanted to make the satellite regimes look not only autochthonous but "bourgeois democratic" as well. He was therefore in recruiting "bourgeois" politicians willing to follow communist bloc leadership and to support socioeconomic "reform." Oskar Lange in Poland, Gheorghe Tătărescu in Romania, Zoltán Tildy in Hungary, and Jurho Paasikivi in Finland were chosen to fill major, publicly visible positions during an interim period. He hoped that this would positively impress both the West and domestic audiences in the respective countries and make them believe that there was genuine "bourgeois" participation in policy making.[103] Similarly, Stalin liked to put noncommunist officials of mostly "bourgeois" origin into many top administrative positions on which public attention was focused. The second man to work behind the scenes was then a reliable communist cadre who took control of the apparatus and the decision-making process. Also, crucial departments with responsibility for personnel, general police, secret police, youth, and so on were taken over by communists whenever possible.

KPD leader Walter Ulbricht mentioned another aspect of bloc politics. The "working class" had to emerge as the decisive political force. But its vanguard, the communist party, was not sufficiently prepared yet to take the leading role in Germany. It was for this reason as well that a multiparty alliance and a coalition government were needed for an interim period. Not all political groups were acceptable as bloc partners. Parties with incompatible orientations—advocates of "imperialist democracy" and "monopolistic capitalism"—could not be tolerated. To be accepted, parties were required to adopt "antifascist" positions and take an "anti-imperialistic" attitude. Two kinds of alliances were envisaged: permanent, "natural" ones with related social forces (such as the peasants and all working people) willing to submit to the communist vanguard party, and temporary accords with "bourgeois" parties that could not be politically assimilated but were necessary for attainment of interim objectives. The Social Democrats were seen to belong to the first category: They would have to accept organizational unity with the communists under their control in due course. This, however, was a long-term perspective: Like the "old communists" who had not undergone training in the USSR, they were seen to be immature. New cadres had to be recruited both to create a Soviet-controlled majority within the party and to fill crucial administrative positions required to smash the old state machinery. A huge training program was envisaged directed at preparing them for their tasks and making them accept strict "internationalist" discipline. At the beginning, Marxist-Leninist indoctrination was secondary; it would have to take place only at a later date.[104]

Dynamic Aspects of Bloc Politics

In all East European countries except Czechoslovakia, the communists were but a minor group. They were particularly weak in Romania where there were less than a thousand adherents, and in Poland where the party (which Stalin had dissolved in the late 1930s) was set up again only by emissaries from the USSR and met with resistance in practically all parts of society. Not only there, neither the Moscow cadres nor "trustworthy" comrades at home were available in sufficient numbers. There was an acute shortage of administrative, police, and other professionals deemed acceptable. While laws and decrees on subjects of even minor importance were largely devised by Soviet authorities,[105] implementation depended on indigenous cadres. Noncommunists had to be employed on a large scale. There was no alternative but to fill, with the exception of crucial "commanding heights," most positions in state and society with "politically unreliable" personnel. If these people would prove unconditionally obedient, they might possibly be allowed to stay. Otherwise, they were liable to be ousted for failure to meet expectations or on subsequent occasions of cleansing. On the basis of Soviet instructions and with funding exacted by the occupation authorities, the Moscow cadres started large-scale party programs to train personnel who would both meet political requirements and, in the second place, be competent. To the extent that the new cadres would be available, replacement of all unreliable administrators, policemen, and other "specialists" was envisaged.[106]

From the very beginning, the multiparty system established by the Soviet occupation authorities was planned to be but temporary. Once the communists had acquired a predominant position and created a mighty Stalinist party organization, they would be able to absorb the social democrats. Foundation of a "united working class party" was intended both to eliminate the competitor for support by the working population and to strengthen the communist personnel basis. After this, elimination of the "bourgeois" political forces had to be put on the agenda to the extent domestic and international conditions would allow. This was envisaged to be a successive process. The basis was provided by the mechanism of bloc politics: "Bourgeois" politicians and parties would have to face issues that forced them to choose between unconditional surrender and outright rejection. If they chose the former, they would survive but alienate their followers and thus marginalize themselves. In the latter case, defamation as deviators from the "antifascist-democratic" consensus, "traitors" to the people, and as similar political criminals was bound to result, with ensuing isolation, prosecution, and liquidation.

The Moscow cadres, ultimately the Kremlin, would be in charge of the process: They were the ones to determine the kind of issue that was put on the political agenda at a given moment, and to decide which part of the "bourgeoisie" was the target of attack. It was up to them which divisive issues were successively employed as instruments to separate "progressive forces" from "reactionary elements" and to render both of them powerless by self-emasculation or futile self-sacrifice. Such procedures of political elimination could be repeated endlessly until the communists had gained unlimited power. Only politicians who had actually adopted communism and were unconditionally supportive of Soviet policy would remain.

The Special Case of Germany

The KPD commission in Moscow failed to discuss in concrete terms how the "road to socialism" might be taken in Western-occupied Germany. Even if systemic mimicry worked as planned, the Anglo-Saxon powers were unlikely to allow for full-fledged socioeconomic transformation and a "leading role" by communist cadres on the basis of bloc politics. There was little chance that interallied agreement as sought by the Kremlin would extend to these matters. The Soviet side was interested in avoiding discussion on divisive systemic issues and, in addition to this, insisted on the military commanders being accorded supreme authority individually. When the People's Commissariat on Foreign Affairs prepared a proposal on zonal division, it did not provide for joint decision making by the occupation powers. The

Kremlin accepted the idea of some common exercise of authority only when the British offered a very favorable territorial agreement that was tied to a proposal to this effect. This plan was also beneficial in that Berlin, as the seat of an interallied control body, was envisaged to be an exclave far within the USSR's power sphere and would hence be subjected to predominant Soviet influence. Stalin naturally agreed.[107] The agreement on control that ensued defined the spheres of individual and joint responsibilities in vague terms[108] and thus allowed the Soviet side to claim or deny the need for interallied decision making at will.

As it turned out after occupation, the Kremlin exploited the agreement to reject any say by the Western powers in the Soviet zone but veto any undesirable measure in their part of Germany. The geographical position that the USSR was accorded at the place of the allied control machinery greatly enhanced chances to impact the defeated country's postwar development. As subsequent action was to demonstrate, Stalin was well aware of the accruing political advantage.

INTERALLIED CONFLICT ON SOVIET INTERVENTION IN OCCUPIED COUNTRIES

The Anglo-Saxon powers supported the USSR by massive deliveries of war materials but disagreed with its policy on Eastern Europe. This was reciprocated by Stalin's suspicion that the capitalist countries would seek to create an anti-Soviet political front. He also stuck to his previous conviction that conflict with "imperialism" was inevitable sooner or later.[109] Underlying the Soviet distrust of the allies was, inter alia, their failure to open a "second front" in Western Europe with no delay whatsoever to relieve the Red Army of military pressure. The Kremlin leader argued that his troops offered resistance to the Wehrmacht under most adverse conditions, while the allies abstained from fighting the enemy, and did not accept the argument that the British and Americans were already involved in vehement struggle against the Germans in North Africa and did what they could to support the USSR by sending masses of war material. Stalin wanted more deliveries and insisted on another war theater to be opened in the West.[110] In internal exchange, he suspected that Western refusal to fulfill his demand indicated the capitalists' intent to make him get their chestnuts out of the fire. After all, Soviet survival was at stake, while the Anglo-Saxon powers were safe. He felt that notably Churchill wanted to eliminate socialism by making the USSR bleed to death. When the prime minister had achieved this, he would initiate agreement with Germany.[111]

In return, Western, notably British distrust was fueled by the fact that the USSR failed to respect the borders and the political system of crucial, even allied, East European states. This was not without reason. As early as in December 1941, the Kremlin had internally stated that adjacent countries would have to accept both "democratic" structures and regard for Soviet security.[112] The Moscow leaders saw the requirements of security and system as closely interrelated. They claimed a "special role" in the "struggle for liberation from fascism." Any decision on Eastern Europe's postwar order would have to take this into due account.[113] In London, suspicion of Soviet policy on Poland had never ceased. After all, the United Kingdom had gone to war for Polish integrity that had been violated as much by Stalin's USSR as by Hitler's Germany. Anti-Soviet feeling intensified both when it became known that the Polish officer corps that had surrendered to the Red Army had been murdered at Katyn and when, in response to Polish protest, the Kremlin broke off relations with the government in London exile.[114] Conflict was increased further when cadres from the USSR set up the Polish communist party again and organized a leftist front organization to support it. However, all attempts by the Moscow cadres failed to win adherents or allies in the country. The underground forces of the *Armia Kraiowa* fighting against the German occupiers recognized the anticommunist government as a legitimate authority, and they were vehemently opposed even to mere contact with Soviet envoys and followers.[115]

When, in summer 1943, the Red Army was on the verge of entering foreign territory, the leaders of Britain and the United States felt that, for the sake of not allowing the Soviet system to be imposed on unwilling countries, its responsibilities had to be limited to temporary military control. But the Kremlin was already preparing for setting up a communist regime in Poland,[116] and it failed to pledge non-intervention. It simply promised "broad" government participation of individuals who "were sympathetically disposed toward the cause of the allies' victory and capable of fostering re-establishment of local government institutions organized on democratic fundaments."[117] As was internally explained, international supervision of Soviet occupation policy had to be prevented. It would "needlessly bind hands" and foster insubordination by the Poles, the Turks, and others.[118] All enemy countries—Finland, Romania, Hungary, and Germany— were envisaged to accept unconditional surrender and to take material obligations that would both benefit the USSR and provide it with levers of economic control.[119]

Controversy Over Eastern Europe in 1942–1943

Stalin exploited Italy's surrender to the United States and Britain at the exclusion of the USSR in July 1943 by demanding that control by the victorious power on the spot would have to apply also to the USSR in Eastern Europe. In his portrayal, Anglo-Saxon negotiations with Badoglio had set a precedent for full freedom of action wherever the Red Army would defeat the enemy.[120] As a result, the allied foreign ministers agreed at the Moscow conference in October 1943 that the recipient country of an enemy state's surrender was entitled to define the conditions alone. To be sure, allied control commissions were envisaged but they would be chaired by the occupying power and have no real authority. This arrangement provided the basis for the respective Soviet diplomatic missions to become centers of "advisor" networks that "regulated" political, economic, military, and other aspects of life in all countries "liberated" by the Red Army.[121] As the Anglo-Saxons expressly conceded, the USSR alone would define the terms of surrender to be imposed on Finland, Hungary, and Bulgaria (which was not even at war with the Soviet Union). The Soviet side also succeeded in killing the proposal that mutual consultation was required when allied forces entered foreign territory. Commonly agreed rules of occupation were thus excluded.[122] In early 1945, Stalin failed to back the communist insurgents in Greece. As recompensation, the Anglo-Saxon allies were expected to acquiesce in a Soviet-dominated government imposed on Romania.[123]

At the Moscow conference, the Americans and the British failed to veto the Soviet annexation of Eastern Poland and to exact Soviet permission for arms deliveries to the Polish underground resistance movement. As Molotov explained, it was crucial for such weapons to fall into "reliable hands" and to be used for the "purpose intended." The USSR wanted an independent Poland but had to make sure that the Poles entertained "friendly feelings."[124] At the Teheran Summit shortly afterward, Churchill explained to Stalin that Britain was vitally interested in restoring Poland as a strong and independent country. While he did not insist on any specific frontiers, he pressed for a binding commitment that would allow for reasonable compromise. Stalin avoided an answer saying that he had not seen a need yet to formulate his position.[125] The problem was then discussed by the foreign ministers. Eden emphasized that his government merely desired to prevent the Polish problem from becoming a source of interallied friction. "Some sort of an agreement of opinion" was required. Molotov agreed but no accord on practical details resulted.[126]

In subsequent talks, the British could not shatter Soviet determination to retain the 1939 annexations. The Soviet side argued that the Poles might be indemnified by large German provinces. Churchill did not agree but, when Roosevelt denied him support, he felt that some agreement had to be reached; otherwise the Kremlin would unilaterally set up a communist regime after having taken possession of the country. He therefore put pressure on the Polish exile leaders to come to meet major territorial demands.[127] Their concessions, however, did not pay. Stalin declared himself dissatisfied when they failed to fulfill all his demands. He blamed them for unwillingness to cooperate under any conditions, unless another war might teach them a lesson. Given that this attitude prevented him from finding "any Poles one could talk to," he decided to act on his own. He used the "Union of Polish Patriots," an organization created by the communist party along with a number of satellite groups that had equally been set up by envoys from the USSR and failed to have backing in the country, to become the nucleus of a government designed to enforce Polish compliance and eliminate Western influence.[128]

Czechoslovakia was easier to cope with. When its "bourgeois" leader-in-exile, Edvard Beneš, went to Moscow in late fall 1943, he was willing to meet Stalin's conditions requiring ethnic cleansing—the expulsion of several millions of Sudeten Germans from Bohemia and Moravia and also the Hungarian population from Southern Slovakia. During a long train ride, Beneš was informed by a high-ranking diplomat on what he was expected to accept. As a result, Beneš not only unconditionally agreed to Soviet foreign policy but pledged that he would act only in accordance with the Kremlin and invariably submit to its guidance. "Prague must have the same policy as Moscow"; its "delegates at international conferences will always follow you." He promised close "postwar collaboration" in military and economic affairs, coordination of military planning, adoption of the Kremlin's military theory, standardization of arms and ammunitions along Soviet lines, and cooperation on air defense and distribution of airfields. Czechoslovak economic management would have to be based on collaboration. Declaring that the ethnic Germans of his country were "rich people" outside the democratic consensus, Beneš identified his interest in expulsion with the communist interest to expropriate major landowners and all industrialists. He therefore pledged confiscation and nationalization also of Czechoslovak-owned big lands and all factories, mines, steelworks, and banks.[129]

Beneš subsequently indicated in public that he would take a "national road to socialism."[130] Stalin was most satisfied. In his view, the arrangement was a model to be implementation elsewhere.[131] This may be surprising given that a number of domestic "reforms" imposed on other countries were not included in the program. But what the Kremlin leader wanted was not compliance with any detail. There were two things that made the Beneš approach appear as a promising road to socialism. On the one hand, the Czechoslovak leader's pledge to break up major landed property and to nationalize industry and banking was crucial to destroying the capitalist system. On the other, the prospect of a strong communist party to initiate political change with no resistance by the "bourgeois" president made Stalin feel that the country could dispense with bloc politics. Against this background, he deemed it useful not to insist on this domestic decision-making mechanism. This would have required some kind of occupation regime the justification of which would have been difficult given that Czechoslovakia

had been recognized as an ally.[132] The fact that large territories to be evacuated by their populations would provide the communists with a material
basis of their political power increased Stalin's confidence that systemic
change was achievable also without bloc politics. The Czechoslovak variant
of "new democracy" therefore seemed to create a safe road to socialism with
no danger whatsoever of systemic conflict with the Anglo-Saxon powers.

Soviet Policy in Occupied East European Countries in 1944–1945

Against all odds, Stalin was determined to subjugate Poland totally,
which he saw as a crucial country for both setting up his empire in Eastern
Europe and opening the road to Germany. To be sure, he expected major
tension to result with Britain and the United States but felt that control of
Poland was both absolutely necessary and unlikely to create serious long-
term implications. In July 1944, when the Red Army had entered the country, a "Polish Committee of National Liberation" consisting of communists
and satellite parties was set up under direct control by the Soviet plenipo-
tentiary Colonel General Bulganin. Pretending that it was an indigenous
body that represented Polish society, this Lublin Committee (as it was
called after its place of foundation) took the role of a government authority on occupied territory and challenged the government in London. The
Kremlin thus tried to avoid the impression that it exercised occupation authority. It also sought to placate the allies by the use of moderate, seemingly
democratic language, and by expressing interest in an agreement with the
exile leaders in London, it was keen to eliminate any sympathizers with the
West in Poland. Both the underground fighters against German occupation
and the members of noncommunist parties were systematically perse-
cuted.[133] Against this background, the "Polish problem" was a point of continuing disagreement between the USSR and its Anglo-Saxon allies.[134]

When on 1 August, the *Armia Kraiowa* started an uprising in Warsaw to
assert its power in the capital, the Red Army (which had reached the other
bank of the River Vistula) stopped its advance at the edges of the Polish capital to allow the Wehrmacht to crush the insurrection. Moscow also denied
British and U.S. aircraft overflight and landing on occupied territory. This
prevented return missions. As a result, the two Western countries were unable to support the insurgents by dropping weapons, munitions, and other
supplies. To counter the impression that the USSR deliberately sacrificed
the insurgents, minor relief operations were permitted after they had become useless. Stalin then also accepted talks with the government-in-exile
but continued to have its followers seized and killed.[135] Trying to exploit the
offer, Churchill and Eden invited the Polish exile prime minister to join
their Moscow negotiations in October 1944. Hopeful that a basis for agreement might be created, they put him under pressure to accept Soviet an-

nexations. When he reluctantly expressed willingness to comply but insisted that the region of Lemberg (L'vov) must remain with Poland, Stalin declined. He declared, however, that he would allow the London Poles full participation in the Lublin Committee government if they would abandon their demand for L'vov. But when this condition had also been fulfilled, he increasingly watered down his pledge. At the same time, the Red Army continued to persecute and liquidate any persons and groups loyal to the exile government.[136] Stalin felt that he could afford to strain relations with London given that the British were prevented from military intervention by facts of geography and would avoid confrontation for the sake of maintaining the anti-German alliance.[137]

At the Yalta conference in February 1945, the three allied powers agreed that Poland would have to cede territories to the USSR and to get German provinces in return. Conflict over the kind of regime continued. Roosevelt tried to make Stalin accept democratic self-determination by saying that Warsaw would be obliged to maintain most friendly and cooperative relations with Moscow. Churchill suspected that the USSR would use this as a lever to impose comprehensive control. He emphasized that, for reasons of honor, his government would oppose any solution that did not leave Poland a free and independent state. While it must not be hostile to the USSR, it must be mistress in her own house. Churchill insisted that the Polish exile leaders were "good and honest men" whose inclusion into the Polish government should be possible, and he offered recognition of the Lublin government as an interim authority until free elections were held. Stalin replied that, for the USSR, Poland was a matter of not only honor but security. Throughout history, this country had been a corridor of attack against Russia. Its "independent, strong, and democratic" character was a "question of life and death." It was not for the great powers to create a government without consultation of the Poles themselves. The problem had to be settled with their consent. He justified refusal to accept the head of the government-in-exile as national leader by alleging that the London Poles had called their countrymen bandits and criminals. Churchill did not buy the story and pressed for an accord, saying that otherwise the Polish underground army was likely to clash with the Lublin government. Resulting bloodshed, arrests, and deportations would negatively affect the Polish question.[138]

Roosevelt tried to find a solution by proposing that the Poles from either side be heard. Stalin was evasive but made Molotov present a paper that seemed to come close to what the president wanted: The current provisional government would be complemented by "some democratic emigré heads" and then be recognized by the Anglo-Saxon powers. Its primary task was to prepare elections. This was accepted. During the discussion of details, it became clear that the Soviet leader saw the Lublin people as the nucleus of the Polish government. He justified this by saying that the emigré politicians had lost direct contact with the country. Churchill objected that, according to his information, the cabinet in Warsaw did not commend itself to the overwhelming masses of the people and was certainly not accepted abroad as its representation. He would be severely castigated at home if he agreed to the proposal. Most painful consequences would result for allied unity.

The prime minister outlined how genuinely free elections and a situation of equal opportunity to all parties might be provided. Stalin declined and argued that the government that had been set up in Poland was supported by the people. He also claimed that it was psychologically very important that its members had not left the country but remained there underground. When Churchill objected, Roosevelt failed to side with him: He accorded priority to avoiding interallied conflict and expected the Kremlin to allow for at least a center-left government based on tolerably free elections. The Soviet proposal that simply some emigrés should be added was not approved, but Stalin basically got his point when his interlocutors agreed to envisage "reorganization," not replacement, of the present government, if "on a broad democratic basis" that would include party heads from outside the country.[139]

Despite having largely given in to Soviet demands, the Western side, particularly the U.S. administration, hoped that a new start had been made that would limit the Kremlin's control of domestic affairs. This hope was already dampened when the Lublin Poles claimed they were entitled to choose whom they saw fit to take part in their government. Roosevelt saw his expectation clearly disappointed when, at the end of March 1945, the Soviet secret police NKVD seized sixteen Polish underground leaders who had wanted to participate in negotiations on government reorganization and put them to trial for alleged "crimes" and "diversions." Even upon this, the president of the United States refrained from open protest and expressed but "concern." Stalin saw no need to make his Polish satellites relinquish major positions of domestic power.[140] He did not change his attitude when Truman took office in Washington.[141] The Kremlin remained adamant.[142]

On 21 July 1945, basic agreement was reached on Soviet terms after the Polish exile prime minister, Stanisław Mikołajczyk, had vainly argued that, according to the Yalta compromise, his people were entitled to half of the cabinet seats. Instead, they were only accorded one-third. Contrary to the Kremlin's pledge that decision making on issues of organization and propaganda would be independent, the principle of bloc consensus was imposed. Assurances that political prisoners would be released and that foreign (that is, Soviet) forces and party, security, and other institutions would leave the country failed to be supported by concrete safeguards or plans of implementation. While the USSR sentenced underground leaders to long-term imprisonment and thus indicated unwillingness to ease repression, Britain and the United States gave their approval and recognized the enlarged Warsaw government as representation of the Polish nation. They therefore no longer permitted the exile leaders in London to speak on Poland's behalf. When the members of the exile government returned to Poland, the population greeted them enthusiastically.[143]

As early as in 1943, the Kremlin had attempted to make Romania change alliances. After the Antonescu government refused to accept the annexations of 1940 and opposition leader Iuliu Maniu failed to align himself with the USSR against the dictator, Soviet agent Emil Bodnăraş managed to organize an underground coalition in August 1944 to stage a *coup d'état* that would put the communists—two tiny groups by then—into power. This was preempted by King Mihai who, together with some generals, overthrew Antonescu to save the country. The monarch accepted the USSR's armistice terms (which, inter alia, envisaged the 1940 borders and military occupation) and ordered his troops to relinquish their arms. The Red Army invaded the whole country but, since the communists were unable to control the country and there were no "reliable" leaders, it had to accept an independent government. Internal quarrel in Bucharest, however, allowed the Kremlin to exert major influence as a political arbitrator. To expand their role in domestic politics, a number of small parties joined a "National-Democratic Front" that was increasingly dominated by the communists who enjoyed Soviet support. Given that the United States was uninterested and Churchill acknowledged the USSR's preeminent influence, the Red Army's concern to have its rear secured by Romania was the main obstacle to more active intervention in domestic politics.

In late November 1944, Stalin sent his close aide Andrei Vyshinskii to Bucharest; he then exploited both Romanian inability to fulfill all harsh armistice conditions and Bucharest's desire to have Northern Transylvania back from Hungary as levers to change the composition of government. To be sure, the military continued to keep the "power ministries" in their hands but the National-Democratic Front took crucial positions in administration and society. In February 1945, the Soviet proponents provoked a crisis to exploit support by the occupation power for enforcement of unlimited control. Vyshinskii again went to Bucharest and, in early March, installed a government that included only members subservient to the Front. The army's potential of resistance was neutralized by removal of major troop leaders and inclusion of two divisions staffed with ideologically trained prisoners of war in the regular forces. Reorganization of the police was initiated under Red Army guidance. The traditional parties, among which the Peasant Party and the liberals were most rooted in society, were excluded from government and subjected to intensifying persecution.[144]

Vyshinskii justified intervention by arguing that, in the Red Army's rear, order must be maintained and compliance with armistice conditions was required. The Anglo-Saxon allies protested, refused to recognize the new cabinet, and withheld diplomatic personnel from Bucharest. They argued that, contrary to tripartite agreement at Yalta, a number of parties had been excluded from government. Their statements, however, did not overly impress the Kremlin. Stalin felt that Soviet encroachment of domestic affairs was not criticized as such and that, as a result, Romania had been acknowledged to be within his sphere of influence. Vyshinskii's intervention put the communists into a dominant position. They controlled the party bloc and were free to initiate socioeconomic transformation. Bodnăraş was appointed general secretary of the government. On the basis of his experience in the USSR, he reorganized the Romanian secret police along Soviet lines to make it an efficient tool of repression. In spring and summer, the opposition was exposed to systematic intimidation. Given that "bourgeois" influence in society did not allow for open all-out repression, national leaders known to the general public were largely spared for the time being. Instead, local politicians, whose imprisonment would attract little attention, were the main targets. Both political persecution and strict control of radio and press were designed to prepare for unlimited communist dictatorship and physical liquidation of any opposition.[145]

Neighboring Bulgaria was a traditionally Russophile country that had entered war against Yugoslavia, Greece, and Britain but not the USSR. Leniency in Sofia had allowed the Kremlin to exercise major influence on domestic politics and to initiating sabotage operations in the early 1940s. In 1943–1944, it had sought to set up an all-party "Patriotic Front" that would make Bulgaria opt out of the war, install a new government, and prepare for elections. Despite increased Soviet pressure when the Red Army had entered Romania, this attempt failed to result in agreement until the end of August 1944. But on 2 September, a new government was formed that immediately announced neutrality and termination of the alliance with Berlin. It also tried to make the German troops leave the country, respectively to disarm them, and to enter negotiations with its previous enemies on ending the state of war. This prompted Soviet action. On 5 September, the USSR declared war, pretending that Bulgaria had to be prevented from assisting Germany and allowing the Wehrmacht to use its territory. On 9 September, the Red Army crossed the border and created the conditions for a communist coup d´état on the following night. Both the creation of a communist-controlled "Patriotic Front" and the conclusion of an armistice followed. Bulgaria was put in the position of a defeated country, the Soviet military commander in Sofia assumed supreme authority, and the communists whom he instructed took full control of domestic politics.[146]

Occupation of Romania opened the road to Hungary. Its leader Miklos Horthy had offered surrender and entered negotiations even before the coup d'état in Bucharest. The Soviet side indicated that it wanted the communists to play a crucial role in domestic politics by insisting that they must participate in the armistice talks. Horthy's attempt to put an end to war with the USSR failed as, assisted by Romanian forces shortly before their surrender to the Red Army, the Wehrmacht occupied his country and thus prevented it from opting out. To be sure, Moscow's Hungarian followers were made to create a government in Soviet-occupied Debreczen in November 1944, but an armistice resulted only on 20 January 1945. The USSR imposed harsh conditions that allowed it to seize vitally important material assets, take full control of internal affairs, and to hand administrative power to the communists. On 13 February, Budapest was taken after long and heavy battle. Within two more months, Western Hungary was conquered.[147]

Failure to Occupy Yugoslavia, Greece, and Finland

After Yugoslavia had been occupied by Hitler's and Mussolini's troops in spring 1941, Tito's communist partisans directed by Moscow fought against both the foreign invaders and their domestic opponents. They operated primarily in the mountains, which were difficult to reach. Feeling that these guerillas were the most efficient anti-German force in the country, the British not only sent them massive supplies by aircraft but also supported their struggle against the "bourgeois" elements in the resistance movement.[148] Against Stalin's advice, Tito declared his communist-controlled "anti-fascist" front to be the country's government in November 1943. To the Kremlin's surprise, Churchill immediately accorded recognition. After the Red Army had occupied Romania, it advanced into the northeastern lowlands of Yugoslavia. The German troops came under military pressure; their position was no longer tenable. As a result, it was easy for the communists to take over. They set up a most radical Stalinist regime all over the country with no regard for the Soviet feeling of need for caution. The idea of a parliamentary "national road to socialism" was rejected.[149] As a result of the Yugoslavs' enthusiasic profession of willingness to see Stalin as their leader, however, the man in the Kremlin was assured of their unflinching loyalty[150] and did not pay attention to indications of divergent attitude such as, notably, Tito's failure to integrate his secret service into the Soviet network and his statement that agreement on foreign policy must be sought by either side.[151] Organized largely by the Yugoslav communists, a partisan movement had also emerged in Albania that established "proletarian dictatorship" of a similar kind. Feeling that this was simply an annex, Stalin paid no attention.[152]

On the basis of a deal with Churchill and Britain's strong position in the Mediterranean, Stalin did not aspire to control of Greece and disagreed with the native communists on the need to take power. But Tito, whose partisans had taken care of the Greek party since 1941, supported its armed struggle against rival nationalist resistance movements as early as in 1943. In August 1944, when Soviet military envoys managed to establish contact with the rebels in Northern Greece, they persuaded them to lay down their weapons and to join the Athens government as a junior partner. Underlying this was the assessment that the Anglo-Saxons were bound to prevail and that armed struggle against regimes supported by their military was undesirable. Stalin resented independent action and wanted the Yugoslav leaders to focus on domestic affairs rather than enter into conflict in neighboring countries. Tito was angry about such interference and appealed to the Greek communists to continue their struggle. Encouraged by his prediction that the British would not intervene, they decided in December to disobey orders to disarm. But London chose to involve its troops, and the insurgents suffered defeat.[153]

Stalin seems to have been confident that his policy would prevail. He wanted Greece to be both weak and penetrable and to underlie a strong, popular communist party's influence. This required that its wartime military structure undergo change to become an effective political organization. Preferably, the party would be unable to assume power immediately but be capable to prevent any other domestic actors from taking action without its consent. When British influence would weaken in due course and the United States not step in, it would gradually penetrate and eventually overthrow the "bourgeois" state apparatus. Underlying the plan was the idea that the British must not be antagonized. Instead, their influence had to be gradually removed. As a result, all the Balkans would be dominated by the USSR in the end. In 1945, the situation seemed promising: While the Americans wanted not to get involved, British difficulties in controlling the situation in Greece were increasing. The Kremlin concluded that the British would not be in control much longer. To be sure, failure of the communist attempt to seize power by force indicated that they were in control for the time being. Given that this defeat warned against attempting another insurrection, Stalin hoped that the new party chairman, Nikos Zakhariadis, who was not discredited by the past, would elicit sufficient trust among the country's noncommunists to allow for mutual cooperation.[154]

When Stalin had taken the road of expansion in 1939–1940, Finland had been the only country to offer stiff military resistance. Its communists had failed to play the role assigned to them by the Kremlin, and Britain had threatened military intervention. Against this background, Stalin felt that it was particularly difficult to break Finnish resistance. It would take a major military effort and entail major international complications to impose control on this marginal country. Scarce resources would have to be committed for small gain. In September 1944, the Finns, who were under heavy military pressure but had reconsolidated their defenses, offered to change alliances. By this, Stalin was confronted with a choice between protracted struggle for occupying the enemy country and freeing his troops for other employment, and he concluded that the latter option was preferable, which allowed him to concentrate troops on attack against Berlin. To be sure, Finland had to accept harsh conditions but its democratic system and regime were preserved.[155]

Policy on Western Europe

Following Stalin's instructions, the communists duly entered coalition governments in Italy, France, and Belgium. By this, they contributed to political stabilization of early postwar Western Europe and gained the positive image of supporters rather than opponents of democracy. Widespread benevolence thus acquired was a major benefit for Soviet policy which, despite conflict over Eastern Europe, had earned a big capital of trust at the end of World War II. The Kremlin saw Greece as part of the Western sphere and instructed the communists there to join the government. They were instructed to seek extension of domestic influence, political conciliation, and infiltration rather than armed conflict. Moscow did not even object when the party signed an agreement that obliged it not only to submission but to unconditional acceptance of British orders.[156]

While Stalin exercised restraint in the Anglo-Saxon sphere of influence, he continued to seek further extension of his power, at least in the longer run. To be sure, the USSR was exhausted and unable to challenge its allies but would nonetheless have an impact on systemic development outside. In Moscow's view, there were several factors to provide for this. The Soviet Union would recover and regain strength. Even without U.S. aid, putative superiority of the socialist system over capitalism was bound to make it prevail over the Western countries in due course. The correlation of forces would take the same direction. On the basis of its position in Eastern Europe, the Kremlin would emerge as the only strong military land power on the Continent, while Britain and other countries would be in progressive decline. If Germany and other enemy states were permanently kept down and friendly countries such as Czechoslovakia were supported, power would shift fundamentally. Provided that peace was preserved, hegemony all over Europe would result within thirty to fifty years.[157]

The caveat that peace was required resulted from both the need for an extended period of recovery after devastating war and the Kremlin's desire not to get involved in another deadly struggle. Since Stalin was used to thinking in terms of historical regularity and repetition, he expected the United

States to withdraw to North America as it had after World War I. If his assumption was correct, there was an even more immediate prospect to achieve a dominant position in Europe. To make sure that his assessment of postwar performance was correct, he asked Roosevelt at Yalta when his troops would return home and based subsequent policy making on the president's answer that they would stay no longer than two or three years.[158] It is plausible that resultant overconfidence may have contributed to Stalin's overplaying his hand in the early postwar years. After all, assessment that isolationism would shape U.S. foreign policy, as after World War I, invited the conclusion that little regard for American political attitude was required. Simply, U.S. interest in "financial-economic expansion" would have to be taken into account. This did not interfere with Moscow's ambitions in Europe and might even be exploited for Soviet reconstruction. Britain, as an insular country and a maritime power with no major commitment to the Continent, carried little weight.[159]

Initial Steps of Policy on Germany in Early 1945

Stalin's attention largely focused on Germany. At Yalta, he demanded massive reparations to compensate for the enormous war losses suffered by the USSR, to punish the enemy and to keep him down. Churchill, however, remembered the baleful experience after World War I when excessive burdens on the defeated country had disrupted the international situation. On the basis of this experience, he adamantly opposed repetition and argued that Britain must not "be chained to a dead body of Germany." Roosevelt, too, expressed concern about economic consequences. Torn between such awareness and habitual inclination to satisfy the Kremlin, he wavered when his advisor Harry Hopkins shoved him a note saying that the Russians had given in so much and therefore deserved not to be let down. So he agreed to set a sum of twenty billion dollars, with half of it to go to the USSR, as a basis for further discussion. This would have to be paid by goods, production, and equipment—not in cash (as had been the case after World War I).[160] While, for the Anglo-Saxon statesmen, this implied merely a point of departure for future negotiations, the Soviet side subsequently insisted that it was a binding commitment that had to be honored to the full extent.

Stalin also vehemently demanded a binding and detailed decision on dismemberment of Germany. While Churchill and Roosevelt had begun to have doubts about it, they wanted to avoid open rebuff. At their suggestion, the tripartite European Advisory Commission (EAC) in London was to examine the problem. They did not pay attention to Stalin's remark that "transformation" (*pereustroistvo*) of Germany was necessary.[161] During the following weeks, the EAC discussed dismemberment. The Soviet representatives vainly insisted on its being enforced.[162] On 24 March, Molotov ordered the effort to be discontinued.[163] On 9 May, Stalin explained in public that "the Soviet Union celebrates its victory but does not intend to dismember or annihilate Germany."[164] While the Kremlin leader's confidence to gain decisive influence had considerably increased during the early months of 1945, evidence is lacking about why his position changed precisely at the end of March. After all, the stage had been set at Yalta already. It is plausible that, given Anglo-Saxon willingness there to meet his demands,[165] Stalin felt that his occupation partners would accept disguised socioeconomic transformation and communist bloc politics in Germany.[166] He is also likely to have expected that the USSR would prevail in all of the country after U.S. withdrawal, and he clearly saw imminent conquest of Berlin by the Red Army as crucial for the prospect of being able to exercise influence beyond his own zone of occupation.

NOTES

1. Cf. Bert Hoppe, "Stalin und die KPD in der Weimarer Republik," Jürgen Zarusky (ed.), *Stalin und die Deutschen. Neue Beiträge zur Forschung* (Munich: Oldenbourg 2006), pp. 25–31.

2. Bernhard H. Bayerlein, Leonid G. Babichenko, Friedrich I. Firsov, and Aleksandr Ju. Vatlin (eds.), *Deutscher Oktober 1923. Ein Revolutionsplan und sein Scheitern* (Berlin: Aufbau-Verlag 2003); Otto Wenzel, *Die gescheiterte deutsche Oktoberrevolution* (Münster: LIT-Verlag 2003).

3. Richard Crockett, *The Fifty Years War. The United States and the Soviet Union, 1941–1991* (London and New York: Routledge 1995), pp. 30–31.

4. As the most explicit statement see Stalin's report to the XVIIth Party Congress, 26 January 1934, in I. V. Stalin, *Sochineniia, Vol. 13* (Moscow: Politizdat 1951), pp. 291–306. Use of the word *contradiction* to mean "conflict" is rooted in Hegel's philosophy, which starts from the general assumption that reasoning is the basis of reality. Therefore, terminology of logic is seen as adequate for stating facts.

5. Relevance of this ideological pattern has been emphasized by L. N. Nezhinskii and I. A. Chelyshev, "O doktrinal'nykh osnovakh sovetskoi vneshnei politiki v gody 'kholodnoi voiny'," *Otechestvennaia istoriia*, 1/1995, pp. 3–27.

6. G. V. Chicherin to I. V. Stalin, 22 March 1929, V. V. Sokolov, "Neizvestnyi Chicherin," *Novaia i noveishaia istoriia*, 2/1994, p. 12.

7. "Introduction," Bernhard H. Bayerlein, Mikhail Narinski, Brigitte Studer, and Serge Wolikow (eds.), *Moscou, Paris, Berlin (1939–1941). Télégrammes chiffrés du Komintern* (Paris: Tallandier 2003), pp. 14–17; Bianka Pietrow-Ennker, *Stalinismus, Sicherheit, Offensive. Das "Dritte Reich" in der Konzeption der sowjetischen Aussenpolitik 1933–1941* (Melsungen: Schwartz 1983), pp. 30–59.

8. Donal O'Sullivan, *Stalins "Cordon Sanitaire." Die sowjetische Osteuropapolitik und die Reaktionen des Westens 1939–1949* (Paderborn: Schöningh 2003), p. 57.

9. Address by Stalin to the propagandists of Moscow and Leningrad, 1 October 1938, "I. V. Stalin o 'Kratkom kurse istorii VKP(b)," *Istoricheskii arkhiv*, 5/1994, p. 13.

10. See Stalin's toast at a meal with his aides on the twentieth anniversary of the October Revolution, 7 November 1937: Georgi Dimitroff, *Tagebücher 1933–1943*, ed. Bernhard H. Bayerlein (Berlin: Aufbau-Verlag 2000), p. 162.

11. Sergej Slutsch, "Stalin und Hitler 1933–1941: Kalküle und Fehlkalkulationen des Kreml," Zarusky (ed.), *Stalin und die Deutschen*, pp. 59–78.

12. Vojtech Mastny, *Russia's Road to the Cold War. Diplomacy, Warfare, and the Politics of Communism, 1941–1945* (New York: Columbia University Press 1979), p. 21.

13. Bianka Pietrow-Ennker, "Stalinistische Aussen- und Deutschlandpolitik 1919–1941," Bianka Pietrow-Ennker (ed.), *Präventivkrieg? Der deutsche Angriff auf die Sowjetunion* (Frankfurt/Main: Fischer Taschenbuch Verlag 2000), p. 79.

14. Pietrow-Ennker, "Stalinistische Aussen- und Deutschlandpolitik 1919–1941," *Präventivkrieg?* pp. 20–21.

15. Jonathan Haslam, *The Soviet Union and the Struggle for Collective Security in Europe 1933–1939* (London and Basingstoke: Macmillan 1984), pp. 195–201.

16. M. I. Semiriaga, "Sovetskii Soiuz i predvoennyi politicheskii krizis," *Voprosy istorii*, 9/1990, p. 51.

17. Jan Lipinsky, *Das Geheime Zusatzprotokoll zum deutsch-sowjetischen Nichtangriffsvertrag vom 23. August 1939 und seine Entstehungs- und Rezeptionsgeschichte von 1939 bis 1999* (Frankfurt/Main: Peter Lang 2005), pp. 24–25; Ingeborg Fleischhauer, *Der Pakt. Hitler, Stalin und die Initiative der deutschen Diplomatie 1938–1939* (Frankfurt/Main: Ullstein 1990), pp. 51–52. See also Pietrow-Ennker, "Stalinistische Aussen- und Deutschlandpolitik 1919–1941," *Präventivkrieg?* pp. 59–61.

18. Semiriaga, "Sovetskii Soiuz i predvoennyi politicheskii krizis," pp. 202–5.

19. Semiriaga, "Sovetskii Soiuz i predvoennyi politicheskii krizis," p. 205; Pietrow-Ennker, "Stalinistische Aussen- und Deutschlandpolitik," *Präventivkrieg?* pp. 81–82.

20. Lipinsky, *Das Geheime Zusatzprotokoll*, pp. 25–26.

21. Cf. Klaus Hildebrand, "Der Weg in den Zweiten Weltkrieg," *Mitteilungen der Gemeinsamen Kommission fuer die Erforschung der juengeren Geschichte der deutsch-russischen Beziehungen* (bilingual German-Russian publication), prepared by Eberhard Kuhrt, Vol. 1 (Berlin: Federal Ministry of the Interior 2003), p. 67 (translated version on p. 75 of the Russian section); Mastny, *Russia's Road*, p. 23.

22. Internal remark by Dmitrii Manul'skii in July 1939, quoted by O'Sullivan, *Stalin's "Cordon Sanitaire,"* p. 75.

23. Lipinsky, *Das Geheime Zusatzprotokoll*, pp. 26–27.

24. Cf. Haslam, *The Soviet Union and the Struggle for Collective Security*, pp. 205–209.

25. F. I. Firsov, ed., "Arkhivy Komintern i vneshniaia politika SSSR v 1939–1941 gg.," *Novaia i noveishaia istoriia*, 6/1992, p. 13.

26. Haslam, *The Soviet Union and the Struggle for Collective Security*, pp. 210–17; Anthony Read and David Fisher, *The Deadly Embrace. Hitler, Stalin, and the Nazi-Soviet Pact 1939–1941* (London: Michael Joseph 1988), pp. 90–133; Geoffrey Roberts, *The Soviet Union and the Origins of the Second World War. Russo-German Relations and the Road to War, 1933–1941* (London and Basingstoke: Macmillan 1995), pp. 70–82.

27. N. S. Khrushchëv, *Vospominaniia. Vremia, liudi, vlast', Vol. I* (Moscow: "Moskovskie novosti" 1999), pp. 224–26.

28. Semiriaga, "Sovetskii Soiuz i predvoennyi politicheskii krizis," p. 53; Fleischhauer, *Der Pakt*, pp. 249–54.

29. Lipinsky, *Das Geheime Zusatzprotokoll*, pp. 27–34, 39–40.

30. Firsov, "Arkhivy Komintern," pp. 13–14.

31. Fleischhauer, *Der Pakt*, pp. 303–13.

32. Lipinsky, *Das Geheime Zusatzprotokoll*, pp. 40–47.

33. Lev Bezymenski, *Stalin und Hitler. Das Pokerspiel der Diktatoren* (Berlin: Aufbau Verlag 2002), pp. 166–77.

34. Semiriaga, "Sovetskii Soiuz i predvoennyi politicheskii krizis," p. 53.

35. For detailed discussion of pro- and anti-status quo tendencies opposing each other in international politics at the end of the 1930s see Hildebrand, "Der Weg in den Zweiten Weltkrieg," pp. 62–67 (Russian translation on pp. 67–73 of the Russian book section).

36. Firsov, "Arkhivy Komintern," p. 14. For similar explanations to Western negotiators see Semiriaga, "Sovetskii Soiuz i predvoennyi politicheskii krizis," p. 53.

37. Fleischhauer, *Der Pakt*, pp. 314–403; Stefan Kley, *Hitler, Ribbentrop und die Entfesselung des Zweiten Weltkrieges* (Paderborn: Schöningh 1996), pp. 295–302; Gerhard L. Weinberg, "Offene Probleme und kontroverse Fragen," *Mitteilungen*, pp. 78–79 (translated version on p. 87 of the Russian section); A. O. Chubar'ian, "SSSR posle podpisaniia sovetsko-germanskogo pakta," *Mitteilungen*, p. 91 (translated version on p. 82 of the German section); O'Sullivan, *Stalins "Cordon Sanitaire,"* p. 77; Lipinsky, *Das Geheime Zusatzprotokoll*, pp. 47–75.

38. Khrushchëv, *Vospominaniia*, pp. 227–28.

39. Weinberg, "Offene Probleme und kontroverse Fragen," *Mitteilungen*, p. 79 (translated version on p. 87 of the Russian section); Lipinsky, *Das Geheime Zusatzprotokoll*, pp. 77–79.

40. A. S. Sakharov, *Rossiia: Narod, Praviteli, Tsivilizatsii* (Moscow: Institut Rossiskoi istorii RAN 2004), p. 367.

41. See, for example, Haslam, *The Soviet Union and the Struggle for Collective Security*, pp. 217–29; Roberts, *The Soviet Union and the Origins of the Second World War*, pp. 149–52; Aleksandr M. Nekrich, "The Two Nazi-Soviet Pacts and their Consequences"; David Wingate Pike (ed.), *The Opening of the Second World War* (New York: Peter Lang 1991), pp. 44–98; Semiriaga, "Sovetskii Soiuz i predvoennyi politicheskii krizis," p. 54.

42. Slutsch, "Stalin und Hitler 1933–1941," Zarusky (ed.), *Stalin und die Deutschen*, pp. 78–81.

43. Fleischhauer, *Der Pakt*, pp. 418–36; Gabriel Gorodetsky, *The Grand Delusion* (New Haven, CT: Yale University Press 1999), pp. 4–6.

44. O'Sullivan, *Stalin's "Cordon Sanitaire,"* p. 64.

45. Semiriaga, "Sovetskii Soiuz i predvoennyi politicheskii krizis," p. 51.

46. Sakharov, *Rossiia*, pp. 366–67.

47. O'Sullivan, *Stalin's "Cordon Sanitaire,"* pp. 76–85.

48. Pietrow-Ennker, "Stalinistische Aussen- und Deutschlandpolitik," *Präventivkrieg?* p. 80.

49. Laure Castin-Chaparro, *Puissance de l'URSS, misères de l'Allemagne. Staline et la question allemande, 1941–1955* (Paris: Publications de la Sorbonne 2002), pp. 39–41; Chubar'ian, "SSSR," *Mitteilungen*, pp. 105–6 (translated version on p. 96 of the German section); Sakharov, *Rossiia*, p. 367; O'Sullivan, *Stalin's "Cordon Sanitaire,"* p. 50.

50. Cf. "Introduction," Bayerlein, Narinski, Studer, and Wolikow, *Moscou, Paris, Berlin*, pp. 21–22; "Présentation," *Moscou, Paris, Berlin*, pp. 306–17.

51. Quoted from Dimitrov's diary by Firsov, "Arkhivy Komintern," pp. 18–19.

52. G. Dimitrov to the French communist party leadership, 9 September 1939, Bayerlein, Narinski, Studer, and Wolikow, *Moscou, Paris, Berlin*, pp. 74–75.

53. "Introduction," Bayerlein, Narinski, Studer, and Wolikow, *Moscou, Paris, Berlin*, pp. 18–21. For the relevant documents see pp. 74–239.

54. Cf. O'Sullivan, *Stalin's "Cordon Sanitaire,"* pp. 89–94; Sergei Slutsch, "17 sentiabria 1939 g.: vstuplenie SSSR vo Vtoroi mirovuiu voinu," *Mitteilungen der Gemeinsamen Kommission fuer die Erforschung der juengeren Geschichte der deutsch-russischen Beziehungen* (bilingual German-Russian publication), prepared by Eberhard Kuhrt (Berlin: Federal Ministry of the Interior 2003), pp. 144–45 (translated version on pp. 130–31 of the German section); Mastny, *Russia's Road*, pp. 26–27.

55. O'Sullivan, *Stalin's "Cordon Sanitaire,"* pp. 89–94; Uldis Pauls Strelis, "Deportation als Vernichtungsmethode," *Terroropfer unter zwei Diktaturen in den baltischen Ländern. Divu diktaturu terora upuri Baltijas valstis* (Riga: Tapals 2005), pp. 52–66; Lipinsky, *Das Geheime Zusatzprotokoll*, pp. 194–219; information by the Okkupacijas muzejs in Riga, 23 August 2005.

56. Information by the Okkupacijas muzejs in Riga, 23 August 2005.

57. Ruth Büttner, "Volksdemokratie und Sowjetisierung. Der Sonderfall Finnland (1944–1948)," Stefan Creuzberger and Manfred Görtemaker (eds.), *Gleichschaltung unter Stalin? Die Entwicklung der Parteien im östlichen Europa 1944–1949* (Paderborn: Schöningh 2002), pp. 376–78; H. M. Tillotson, *Finland at Peace and War 1918–1993* (Norwich: Michael Russell 1993), pp. 81–120; Arvo Tuominen, *Stalins Schatten über Finnland. Erinnerungen des ehemaligen Führers der finnischen Kommunisten* (Freiburg/Breisgau: Herderbücherei 1986), pp. 198–213.

58. "Introduction," Bayerlein, Narinski, Studer, and Wolikow, *Moscou, Paris, Berlin*, pp. 21–22; "Présentation," *Moscou, Paris, Berlin*, pp. 306–17. For relevant documents see *Moscou, Paris, Berlin*, pp. 319–422.

59. See notably Chubar'ian, "SSSR," *Mitteilungen*, pp. 91–106 (translated version on pp. 83–96 of the German section); O'Sullivan, *Stalin's "Cordon Sanitaire,"* pp. 119–27.

60. Lev Bezymenski, "Chto zhe skazal Stalin 5 maia 1941 goda?" *Novoe vremia*, 19/1991, pp. 36–40; Slutsch, "Stalin und Hitler 1933–1941," Zarusky (ed.), *Stalin und die Deutschen*, pp. 82–87.

61. See, in particular, record of conversation I. V. Stalin and V. M. Molotov–A. Eden, 16 December 1941, *SSSR i germanskii vopros 1941–1949. Dokumenty iz Arkhiva vneshnei politiki Rossiiskogo Federatsii*, ed. Historico-Archival Department of the Russian Ministry of Foreign Affairs and the Potsdam Center for Contemporary Historical Research, Vol. I: *1941–1945* (Moscow: "Mezhdunarodnye ostnosheniia" 1996), pp. 124–35; Soviet-British draft treaty, 18 December 1941, *SSSR i germanskii vopros 1941–1949*, I, pp. 135–36.

62. M. M. Litvinov to V. M. Molotov, 12 March 1942, *SSSR i germanskii vopros 1941–1949*, I, pp. 149–51; V. M. Molotov to I. M. Maiskii, 26 April 1942, *SSSR i germanskii vopros 1941–1949*, I, pp. 151–57; V. M. Molotov–W. Churchill, 21 May 1942, *SSSR i germanskii vopros 1941–1949*, I, pp. 159–61.

63. *Sto sorok besed s Molotovym. Iz dnevnika F. Chueva* (Moscow: Terra 1991), p. 76; V. V. Mar'ina, "VKP(b) i KPCh. 1945–1949 gg.," A. O. Chubar'ian (ed.), *Stalin i kholodnaia voina* (Moscow: Institut vseobshchei istorii RAN 1997), p. 127.

64. O'Sullivan, *Stalins "Cordon Sanitaire*," pp. 141–42.

65. T. V. Volokitina (ed.), *Sovetskii faktor v Vostochnoi Evrope 1944–1953, Vol. I: 1944–1948. Dokumenty* (Moscow: ROSSPÈN 1999), p. 9.

66. See, e.g., *SSSR i germanskii vopros*, I, pp. 219–22, 251–52; *Foreign Relations of the United States. Diplomatic Papers* [henceforth: *FRUS*] *1943, Vol. I: General*, Department of State Publication 7585 (Washington D.C.: Government Printing Office 1963), pp. 637–38.

67. Volokitina, *Sovetskii faktor*, p. 76.

68. G. M. Dimitrov to P. Finder, 2 April 1943, *Novaia i noveishaia istoriia*, 5/1964, p. 122.

69. T. V. Volokitina, G. P. Murashko, and A. F. Noskova, *Narodnaia demokratiia: Mif ili real'nost'?* (Moscow: "Nauka" 1993), pp. 236–39, 305–12; conversation I. V. Stalin, B. Bierut, and E. Osóbka-Morawski, 24 May 1946, *Vostochnaia Evropa v dokumentakh rossiiskikh arkhivov 1944–1953 gg.*, ed. Rossiiskaia Akademiia Nauk/Institut slvavianovedeniia i balkanistiki/Rossiiski Tsentr khraneniia i izucheniia dokumentov po noveishei istorii/Gosudarstvennyi arkhiv Rossiiskoi Federatsii, Vol. I (Moscow and Novosibirsk: "Sibirskii khronograf" 1997), pp. 457–58.

70. Vladimir Volkov, "The Soviet Leadership and Southeastern Europe," Leonid Gibianskii and Norman Naimark (eds.), *The Establishment of Communist Regimes in Eastern Europe, 1944–1949* (Boulder, CO: Westview Press 1997), p. 62.

71. K. M. Anderson and A. O. Chubar'ian (eds.), *Komintern i vtoraia mirovaia voina [collection of documents]* vol. 2 (Moscow: Institut vseobshchei istorii RAN 1998), pp. 353–79; N. Lebedeva and M. Narinskii, "Rospusk Kominterna v 1943 godu," *Mezhdunarodnaia zhizn'*, 5/1994, pp. 82–87; Grant M. Adibekov, "Ot ispolkoma Kominterna do otdela mezhdunarodnoi informatsii," *Bulgarian Historical Review*, 25 (2–3/1997), pp. 156–79; G. M. Adibekov, *Kominform i poslevoennaia Evropa, 1947–1956 gg.* (Moscow: Rossiia molodaia 1994), pp. 7–18; Georgi Dimitroff, *Tagebücher 1933–1943*, Bernhard H. Bayerlein (ed.) (Berlin: Aufbau Verlag 2000), pp. 694–708; Jörg Morré, *Hinter den Kulissen des Nationalkomitees. Das Institut 99 in Moskau und die Deutschlandpolitik der UdSSR 1943–1946* (Munich: Oldenbourg 2001), pp. 43–45.

72. See, inter alia, I. S. Iazhborovskaia, "Vovlechenie Pol'shi v blokovuiu politiku v 1940-e gody," A. O. Chubar'ian (ed.), *Stalin i kholodnaia voina* (Moscow: Institut vseobshchei istorii RAN 1998), pp. 88–90; Büttner, "Volksdemokratie und Sowjetisierung," Creuzberger and Görtemaker (eds.), *Gleichschaltung unter Stalin?* pp. 378–79; Peter Erler, "'Moskau-Kader' der KPD in der SBZ"; Manfred Wilke (ed.), *Die Anatomie der Parteizentrale. Die KPD/SED auf dem Weg zur Macht* (Berlin: Akademie Verlag 1998), pp. 229–91; "Einleitung," Peter Erler, Horst Laude, and Manfred Wilke (eds.), *"Nach Hitler kommen wir." Dokumente zur Programmatik der Moskauer KPD-Führung 1944/45 für Nachkriegsdeutschland* (Berlin: Akademie Verlag

1994), pp. 109–10, 112–15; Monika Tantzscher, "Vorläufer des Staatssicherheitsdienstes," *Jahrbuch für Historische Kommunismusforschung*, 1998, pp. 126–31. Cf. Hans Ehlert and Armin Wagner (eds.), *Genosse General! Die Militärelite der DDR in biographischen Skizzen* (Berlin: Ch. Links 2003).

73. Erler, "'Moskau-Kader' der KPD in der SBZ"; Wilke, *Die Anatomie der Parteizentrale*, pp. 229–91.

74. Jan Foitzik, *Sowjetische Militäradministration in Deutschland (SMAD): 1945–1949. Struktur und Funktion* (Berlin: Akademie Verlag 1999), pp. 35–39; Monika Tantzscher, "Vorläufer des Staatssicherheitsdienstes," *Jahrbuch für Historische Kommunismusforschung*, 1998, pp. 117–49.

75. See notably Morré, *Hinter den Kulissen des Nationalkomitees*, pp. 43–59.

76. Morré, *Hinter den Kulissen des Nationalkomitees*, pp. 61–91. For simultaneous Soviet policy on Germany see the documents in *SSSR i germanskii vopros*, I, pp. 201–312.

77. Stéphane Courteois, "Thorez, Stalin und Frankreichs Befreiung im Lichte von Moskauer Archiven," *Jahrbuch für Historische Kommunismusforschung*, 1998, pp. 77–78; Philippe Robrieux, *Histoire intérieure du parti communiste, Vol. II: 1945–1972* (Paris: Fayard 1981), pp. 78–81.

78. Milovan Djilas, *Conversations with Stalin* (New York: Harcourt 1962), p. 114.

79. Conversation I. V. Stalin–B. Bierut and E. Osóbka-Morawski, 24 May 1946, *Vostochnaia Evropa v dokumentakh*, p. 457.

80. Conversation I. V. Stalin–E. Osóbka-Morawski, St. Szwalbe, and J. Cyrankiewicz, 19 August 1946, *Vostochnaia Evropa v dokumentakh*, I, p. 511. As Leonid Gibianskij, "Osteuropa: Sicherheitszone der UdSSR, sowjetisiertes Protektorat oder Sozialismus 'ohne Diktatur des Proletariats'?" *Forum für osteuropäische Ideen- und Zeitgeschichte* 8, no. 2 (2004), pp. 134–35, has aptly observed, interpretation of Stalin's statement must take his respective addressees into due account. While Bierut chaired the communist party, Osóbka-Morawski, Szwalbe, and Cyrankiewicz were socialist leaders who had been included in the bloc but in summer 1946 disputed communist-imposed policy. Stalin was unlikely to be quite frank with the latter three but his explanation that the Polish road to socialism (which, in their perception, did not imply that the Soviet system was the ultimate goal) would not entail civil war and mass terror as had been the case in the USSR, was authentic. He rightly felt that this aspect of the process was apt to appeal to noncommunist "allies" and failed to mention the other aspect that communist dictatorship would result also in Poland.

81. I. V. Stalin to G. Dimitrov, 2 September 1946, cited by Gibianskij, "Osteuropa," pp. 136–37.

82. Conversation I. V. Stalin–B. Bierut and E. Osóbka-Morawski, 24 May 1946, *Vostochnaia Evropa*, p. 457–58. For more extensive explanations of the perception that nationalization of industry and banking and additionally distribution of land to small peasants was crucial to break the power of the old regime and establish communist rule, see Volokitina, Murashko, and Noskova, *Narodnaia demokratiia*, particularly pp. 236–39, 305–12; T. V. Volokitina, "Stalin i smena strategicheskogo kursa Kremlia v kontse 40-kh godov: Ot kompromissov do konfrontatsii," A. O. Chubar'ian (ed.), *Stalinskoe desiatiletie kholodnoi voiny. Fakty i gipotezy* (Moscow: Institut vseobshchei istorii 1999), pp. 13–18.

83. See, in particular, V. K. Volkov, *Uzlovye problemy noveishei istorii Tsentral'noi i Iugo-Vostochnoi Evropy* (Moscow: Izd. "INDRIK" 2000), pp. 59–81; Volokitina, "Stalin i smena," Chubar'ian (ed.), *Stalinskoe desiatiletie kholodnoi voiny*, pp. 13–14.

84. Quoted by V. O. Mar'ina, "V. V.: Sovetskii Soiuz i Chekhoslovakiia. 1945 god," *Novaia i noveishaia istoriia*, 3/2005, p. 10.

85. Silvio Pons, "Stalin, Togliatti, and the Origins of the Cold War in Europe," *Journal of Cold War Studies 3*, no. 2 (Spring 2001), pp. 3–11.

86. Stéphane Courteois, "Thorez, Stalin und Frankreichs Befreiung im Lichte von Moskauer Archiven," *Jahrbuch für Historische Kommunismusforschung*, 1998, pp. 77–78; Philippe Robrieux, *Histoire intérieure du parti communiste*, Vol. *II: 1945–1972* (Paris: Fayard 1981), pp. 78–81.

87. Report on conversation I. V. Stalin–M. Thorez, 19 November 1944, *Vestnik Arkhiva Prezidenta Rossiiskoi Federatsii* (supplement to *Istochnik*), 4/1995, pp. 152–58.

88. M. M. Litvinov to V. M. Molotov and A. Ia. Vyshinskii, 11 January 1945, *Vestnik Arkhiva Prezidenta Rossiiskoi Federatsii* (supplement to *Istochnik*), pp. 595–97; Vladimir O. Pechatnov, *The Big Three after World War II. New Documents on Soviet Thinking about Post War Relations with the United States and Great Britain*, Working Paper No. 13, Cold War International History Project (Washington D.C.: Woodrow Wilson International Center for Scholars 1995), p. 14.

89. *SSSR i germanskii vopros*, I, pp. 126, 138, 240–41, 252–67, 296–301, 305–12, 336–38, 441–54, 597–600; *Sovetskii Soiuz na mezhdunarodnykh konferentsiiakh perioda Velikoi otechestvennoi voiny 1941–1945 gg.*, Vol. *II: Tegeranskaia konferentsiia trëkh soiuznykh derzhav—SSSR, SShA i Velikobritanii (28 noiabria–1 dekabria 1943 g.). Sbornik dokumentov* (Moscow: Izdatel'stvo politicheskoi literatury 1978), pp. 166–67, Vol. *IV: Krymskaia konferentsiia rukovoditelei trekh sojuznykh derzhav—SSSR, SShA i Velikobritanii (4–11 fevralja 1945 g.). Sbornik dokumentov* (Moscow: Izdatel'stvo politicheskoi literatury 1984), pp. 59–64, 77–80, 225, 232; *FRUS. The Conferences of Cairo and Tehran 1943*. Department of State Publication 7187 (Washington D.C.: Government Printing Office 1961), pp. 602, 845–47, 879; *Berliner Jahrbuch für osteuropäische Geschichte*, 1/1995, pp. 282–88; *FRUS. The Conferences at Malta and Yalta 1945*, Department of State Publication 6199 (Washington D.C.: Government Printing Office 1955), pp. 611–16, 624–28, 656, 700, 709, 936, 947–48. Cf. G. P. Kynin, "Germanskii vopros vo vzaimootnosheniiakh SSSR, SShA i Velikobritanii," *Novaia i noveishaia istoriia*, 4/1995, pp. 115, 119–23; G. P. Kynin, "Die Antihitlerkoalition und die Nachkriegsordnung in Deutschland. Die Haltung der UdSSR nach Dokumenten des Archivs fuer Aussenpolitik Russlands," *Berliner Jahrbuch für osteuropäische Geschichte*, 2/1995, pp. 187–92; A. M. Filitov, "Problems of Post-War Confrontation in Soviet Foreign Policy during World War II," Francesca Gori and Silvio Pons (eds.), *The Soviet Union and Europe in the Cold War, 1943–1953* (Basingstoke and London: Macmillan; New York: St. Martin's Press 1996), pp. 16–18.

90. See their attitude as early as at the Moscow conference of foreign ministers in October 1943 as opposed to the Soviet stand: *FRUS 1943*, I, pp. 631–33.

91. Cf. R. C. Raack, "Stalin Plans His Post-War Germany," *Journal of Contemporary History*, 28 (1993), pp. 53–73; Erler, Laude, and Wilke, "Nach Hitler kommen wir," pp. 125–397.

92. *FRUS 1943*, I, pp. 721–23, 752, 757.

93. As early as in January 1944, a leading Soviet diplomat had internally stated that an at least ten-year period of occupation and another twenty to forty years of imposed interallied control were required in order to allow for enough time to acquire superior military power against any aggressor: I. Maiskii to V. M. Molotov, 11 January 1944, *SSSR i germanskii vopros*, I, pp. 334–38; *Vestnik Arkhiva Prezidenta Rossiiskoi Federatsii* (supplement to *Istochnik*), 4/1995, pp. 152–58.

94. Castin-Chaparro, *Puissance de l'URSS*, pp. 66–67, 87–90.

95. Raack, "Stalin Plans His Post-War Germany," pp. 55, 64–65, 69–70; "Zur programmatischen Arbeit der Moskauer KPD Führung 1941–1944," Erler, Laude, and Wilke, *"Nach Hitler kommen wir,"* pp. 72, 77–79, 89–96; "Einführung," Gerhard Keiderling (ed.), *"Gruppe Ulbricht" in Berlin April bis Juni 1945. Von den Vorbereitungen im Sommer 1944 bis zur Wiedergründung der KPD im Juni 1945. Eine Dokumentation* (Berlin: Berlin Verlag 1993), pp. 26–27; Morré, *Hinter den Kulissen des Nationalkomitees*, p. 76.

96. Gibianskij, "Osteuropa," p. 126.

97. Wilhelm Florin on 6 March 1944; Erler, Laude, and Wilke, *"Nach Hitler kommen wir,"* pp. 136–58 (quotations on pp. 142–44).

98. Statements by Anton Ackermann, Wilhelm Florin, Hermann Matern, Sepp Schwab, and Johannes Becher; successive drafts of an action program for public announcement by the envisaged "Bloc of Militant Democracy"; lectures by Wilhelm Pieck at the party training college near Moscow, 1 and 10 March 1945; and "Guidelines for the German Antifascists' Work in German Regions Occupied by the Red Army," 5 April 1945, Erler, Laude, and Wilke, *"Nach Hitler kommen wir,"* pp. 172–386; notes on conversations Dimitrov–Pieck, 9 August 1944 and 6 February 1945; Keiderling, *"Gruppe Ulbricht,"* pp. 118–23, 180–84; lectures by Pieck at the party training college near Moscow, 9 and 28 January 1945, Keiderling, *"Gruppe Ulbricht"* pp. 139–61.

99. Expropriation of land before harvesting created turmoil which, in many cases, entailed diversion of attention from the crops.

100. Jiří Kocian,"Vom Kaschauer Programm zum Prager Putsch. Die Entwicklung der politischen Parteien in der Tschechoslowakei in den Jahren 1944–1948," Creuzberger and Görtemaker (eds.), *Gleichschaltung unter Stalin?* pp. 301–17; Volokitina, "Stalin i smena," Chubar'ian (ed.), *Stalinskoe desiatiletie kholodnoi voiny*, p. 15.

101. Cf. Alexandr Haritonow, *Ideologie als Instiution und soziale Praxis. Die Adaption des höheren sowjetischen Parteischulungssystems in der SBZ/DDR (1945–1956)* (Berlin: Akademie Verlag 2004), p. 24.

102. See, for example, Trëkhletnyi opyt raboty Upravleniia informatsii SVAG (oktiabr' 1945–oktiabr' 1948), GARF, 7319, 19, 1, pp. 1–273.

103. Volokitina, *Sovetskii faktor*, pp. 9–11; Eduard Mark, *Revolution by Degrees: Stalin's National-Front Strategy for Europe, 1941–1947*, Working Paper No. 31, Cold War International History Project (Washington D.C.: Woodrow Wilson International Center for Scholars 2001).

104. Notes on Ulbricht's 17 April 1944 report taken by Wilhelm Pieck, Wilhelm Florin, and Sepp Schwab, in Erler, Laude, and Wilke, *"Nach Hitler kommen wir,"* pp. 161–72.

105. For an exemplary case see report by Major Nazarov included in the protocol of the 19 September 1946 session of the CPSU Central Committee commission set up to investigate SMAG Administration for Propaganda (excerpt), Bernd Bonvech, Gennadii Bordiugov, and Norman Neimark (eds.), *SVAG. Upravlenie propagandy (informatsii) i S.I. Tiul'panov. 1945–1949* (Moscow: "Rossiia molodaia" 1994), p. 182.

106. Cf. Haritonow, *Ideologie*, pp. 2–9, 24–25.

107. Jochen Laufer, "Die UdSSR und die Zoneneinteilung Deutschlands (1943/44)," *Zeitschrift für Geschichtswissenschaft*, 4/1995, pp. 325–30; *SSSR i germanskii vopros, 1*, pp. 334–38, 406–7, 414–17, 483–88, 549; Protocols on Zones of Occupation in Germany and Administration of the "Greater Berlin" Area (Engl. and Russ. original texts), 12 September and 14 November 1944, Alois Riklin, *Das Berlinproblem. Historisch-politische und völkerrechtliche Darstellung des Viermächtestatus* (Cologne: Verlag Wissenschaft und Politik 1964), pp. 293–304.

108. Agreement on Control Machinery in Germany (Engl. and Russ. original texts), 14 November 1944, Riklin, *Berlinproblem*, pp. 312–19. For preceding negotiations see *SSSR i germanskii vopros, I*, pp. 469–73, 478–83, 486–87, 489–90, 493–502, 517–20, 529–31, 545–47, 549.

109. S. A. Losovskii to I. V. Stalin and V. M. Molotov, 26 December 1941, *SSSR i germanskii vopros, I*, pp. 141–42.

110. M. M. Litvinov to V. M. Molotov, 20 January 1942, *SSSR i germanskii vopros, I*, pp. 145–46; record of conversation M. M. Litvinov–F. D. Roosevelt, 12 May 1942, *SSSR i germanskii vopros, I*, pp. 150–51; I. V. Stalin to V. M. Molotov, 2 June 1942, *SSSR i germanskii vopros, I*, pp. 163–64; record of conversation I. V. Stalin–W. Churchill, 16 August 1942, *SSSR i germanskii vopros, I*, pp. 165–66; Vladimir Pechatnov, "Kak Stalin pisal F. Ruzvel'tu (po novym dokumentam)," *Istochnik*, 6/1999, pp. 83–84.

111. I. V. Stalin to I. M. Maiskii, 19 October 1942, *SSSR i germanskii vopros, I*, p. 167. The United States was blamed for having sought to gain victory and power at the USSR's sacrifice as late as in the postwar period: situation assessment by Soviet ambassador N. V. Novikov, 27 September 1946, *Sovetsko-amerikanskie otnosheniia 1945–1948. Rossiia XX vek. Dokumenty pod obshchei redaktsiei Akademika A. N. Iakovleva* (Moscow: Izdatel'stvo "Materik" 2004), pp. 312–13.

112. Draft of secret protocol (first version), December 1941, *SSSR i germanskii vopros, I*, pp. 136–39.

113. Draft of secret protocol (second version), December 1941, *SSSR i germanskii vopros, I*, pp. 139–41.

114. Conversation V. M. Molotov–W. Standley, 26 April 1943, *Sovetsko-amerikanskie otnosheniia 1939–1945. Rossiia XX vek. Dokumenty pod obshchei redaktsiei Akademika A.N. Iakovleva* (Moscow: Izdatel'stvo "Materik" 2004), pp. 343–45.

115. "Introduction," Antony Polonsky and Bolesław Drukier (eds.), *The Beginnings of Communist Rule in Poland* (London and Boston: Routledge and Kegan Paul 1980), pp. 5–13; John Coutouvidis and Jaime Reynolds, *Poland 1939–1947* (Leicester: Leicester University Press 1986), pp. 86–102.

116. Gibianskij, "Osteuropa," p. 125.

117. V. M. Molotov to W. Standley, 14 September 1943, *SSSR i germanskii vopros, I*, pp. 251–52.

118. M. M. Litvinov to V. M. Molotov, 9 October 1943, *SSSR i germanskii vopros*, I, pp. 277–86.

119. E. S. Varga to M. M. Litvinov, 27 September 1943, *SSSR i germanskii vopros*, I, pp. 252–69; K. E. Voroshilov to V. M. Molotov, 6 October 1943, *SSSR i germanskii vopros*, I, pp. 269–75.

120. The argument was invariably employed whenever Britain and the United States would criticize Soviet intervention in internal affairs of conquered countries, see for example conversation I. V. Stalin–W. A. Harriman, 25 October 1945, *Sovetsko-amerikanskie otnosheniia 1945–1948. Rossiia XX vek. Dokumenty pod obshchei redaktsiei Akademika A. N. Iakovleva* (Moscow: Izdatel'stvo "Materik" 2004), pp. 82–83; conversation V. M. Molotov–W. A. Harriman, 20 January 1946, *Sovetsko-amerikanskie otnosheniia 1945–1948*, p. 151.

121. Volokitina, *Sovetskii faktor*, pp. 8, 10–11.

122. For more detailed explanation see Caroline Kennedy-Pipe, *Soviet Strategies in Europe, 1943 to 1956* (Manchester and New York: Manchester University Press 1995), pp. 36–38.

123. Peter J. Stavrakis, *Moscow and Greek Communism, 1944–1949* (Ithaca, NY, and London: Cornell University Press 1989), pp. 40–42.

124. Stavrakis, *Moscow and Greek Communism*, pp. 39–40; Coutouvidis and Reynolds, *Poland 1939–1947*, pp. 102–7; *FRUS 1943*, I: *General*, pp. 662–70; *Sovetskii Soiuz na mezhdunarodnykh konferentsiiakh perioda Velikoi Otzechestvennoi Voiny 1941–1945 gg. Vol. I: Moskovskaia konferentsiia ministrov inostrannykh del SSSR, SShA i Velikobritanii, 19–30 otiabria 1943 g. Sbornik dokumentov* (Moscow: Izdatel'stvo politicheskoi literatury 1978), pp. 252–53.

125. First Plenary Meeting, 28 November 1943, *FRUS. The Conferences at Cairo and Tehran 1943*, Department of State Publication 7187 (Washington D.C.: Government Printing Office 1961), p. 512.

126. Hopkins-Eden-Molotov Luncheon Meeting, 30 November 1943, *FRUS 1943. Conferences at Cairo and Tehran*, p. 575.

127. Fourth Session of 1 December 1943, *Sovetskii Soiuz na mezhdunarodnykh konferentsiiakh perioda Velikoi Otechestvennoi Voiny 1941–1945 gg. Vol. II: Tegeranskaia konferentsiia rukovoditelei trëkh soiuznykh derzhav—SSSR, SShA i velikobritanii (28 oktibria–1 dekabria 1943 g.). Sbornik dokumentov* (Moscow: Izdatel'stvo politicheskoi literatury 1984), pp. 147–48; Kennedy-Pipe, *Soviet Strategies in Europe*, p. 43.

128. Vojtech Mastny (ed.), "The Beneš-Stalin-Molotov-Conversations in December 1943" [minutes taken by J. Smutný], *Jahrbücher für Geschichte Osteuropas*, NF 20 (1972), pp. 376–80.

129. Mastny, "The Beneš-Stalin-Molotov-Conversations," pp. 376–96.

130. Haritonow, *Ideologie*, pp. 10–11.

131. Mastny, *Russia's Road*, p. 69; O'Sullivan, *Stalin's "Cordon Sanitaire,"* p. 242.

132. To be sure, Stalin did not hesitate to subject allied Poland to what was—not in form but in fact—an occupation regime. He decided to do this against great odds since he felt that otherwise Poland would have become both a political and geostrategic barrier to his ambitions. While he accepted the price for this in terms of conflict with the Anglo-Saxon powers, it would have strained interallied relations intolerably, if another case of such conflict had been created.

133. Harald Moldenhauer, "'Ihr werdet euch dem Sozialismus ohne blutigen Kampf annähern.' Kommunistische Blockpolitik und 'Gleichschaltung' der Parteien in Polen, 1944–1948," Creuzberger and Görtemaker (eds.), *Gleichschaltung unter Stalin?* pp. 89–95; Coutouvidis and Reynolds, *Poland 1939–1947*, pp. 113–36; "Introduction," Polonsky and Drukier (eds.), *The Beginnings of Communist Rule*, pp. 13–33, for relevant documents see pp. 191–260.

134. Conversation I. V. Stalin–W. Standley and A. D. K. Kerr, 11 August 1943, *Sovetsko-amerikanskie otnosheniia 1939–1945*, pp. 364–66; conversation V. M. Molotov–W. A. Harriman and A. D. K. Kerr, 11 January 1944, *Sovetsko-amerikanskie otnosheniia 1939–1945*, pp. 424–25; conversation V. M. Molotov–W. A. Harriman and A. D. K. Kerr, 16 January 1944, *Sovetsko-amerikanskie otnosheniia 1939–1945*, pp. 425–26; conversation V. M. Molotov–W. A. Harriman and A. D. K. Kerr, 16 July 1944, *Sovetsko-amerikanskie otnosheniia 1939–1945*, pp. 530–33.

135. Krystyna Kersten, *The Establishment of Communist Rule in Poland, 1943–1948* (Berkeley: University of California Press 1991), pp. 39–76. For details see conversation V. M. Molotov–W. A. Harriman and A. D. K. Kerr, 17 August 1944, *Sovetsko-amerikanskie otnosheniia 1939–1945*, pp. 572–81; Norman Davies, *Aufstand der Verlorenen. Der Kampf um Warschau 1944* (Munich: Droemer 2004) (the original English version was not available).

136. Conversation I. V. Stalin–W. Churchill, 14 October 1944, *Vestnik Arkhiva Prezidenta Rossiiskoi Federatsii* (supplement to *Istochnik*), 4/1995, pp. 144–47; conversation I. V. Stalin–W. Churchill and A. Eden, 17 October 1944, *Vestnik Arkhiva Prezidenta Rossiiskoi Federatsii*, pp. 148–52; Polonsky and Drukier, *The Beginnings of Communist Rule*, pp. 43–49 (relevant documents on pp. 261–401); Coutouvidis and Reynolds, *Poland 1939–1947*, pp. 137–61; Kersten, *The Establishment of Communist Rule in Poland*, pp. 77–117. For Stalin's preceding conversations with Polish leaders in early August 1944 see the documents in Volokitina, *Sovetskii faktor*, pp. 67–89. The Soviet protocol of his conversation with Churchill and other British representatives on 9 October 1944 is printed in *Istochnik*, 2/2003, pp. 48–53.

137. Report on conversation Stalin–Polish Committee of National Liberation, 9 October 1944, Polonsky and Drukier, *The Beginnings of Communist Rule*, p. 298.

138. Bohlen Minutes on Third Plenary Meeting, 6 February 1945, *FRUS. The Conferences at Malta and Yalta 1945*, pp. 667–71. See also Matthew Minutes on pp. 677–81.

139. See the documents and minutes relating to the plenary discussions on 7 and 8 February 1945 in *FRUS. The Conferences at Malta and Yalta 1945*, pp. 727–43, the Stettinius proposal of 9 February 1945, p. 804, the foreign ministers' discussion on 10 February 1945, pp. 872–73, and the agreed draft of 10 February 1945, p. 883 (final version on p. 938). Cf. Daniel Yergin, *Shattered Peace. The Origins of the Cold War and the National Security State* (Boston: Houghton Mifflin 1978), pp. 63–64; Kersten, *The Establishment of Communist Rule in Poland*, pp. 118–62.

140. Harald Moldenhauer, "'Ihr werdet Euch dem Sozialismus ohne blutigen Kampf annähern.' Kommunistische Blockpolitik und 'Gleichschaltung' der Parteien in Polen," Creuzberger and Görtemaker (eds.), *Gleichschaltung unter Stalin?* pp. 97–100.

141. Conversation between the foreign ministers of the United States, the USSR, and Britain, 22 April 1945, *Sovetsko-amerikanskie otnosheniia 1939–1945*, pp. 647–50; conversation H. S. Truman–V. M. Molotov, 23 April 1945, *Sovetsko-amerikanskie otnosheniia 1939–1945*, pp. 650–51; conversation V. M. Molotov–S. B. Davies, 23 April 1945,

Sovetsko-amerikanskie otnosheniia 1939–1945, p. 652; conversations between the foreign ministers of the United States, the USSR, and Britain, 23 April and 4 May 1945, *Sovetsko-amerikanskie otnosheniia 1939–1945*, pp. 682–83.

142. V. M. Molotov to Soviet ambassador in Washington, 6 June 1945, *Sovetsko-amerikanskie otnosheniia 1939–1945*, pp. 695–96.

143. Moldenhauer, "'Ihr werdet Euch dem Sozialismus ohne blutigen Kampf annähern,'" Creuzberger and Görtemaker (eds.), *Gleichschaltung unter Stalin?* pp. 100–102.

144. "K chitateliu," T. V. Volokitina, G. P. Murashko, and A. P. Noskova (eds.), *Tri vizita A.Ia. Vyshinskogo v Bukharest 1944–1946. Dokumenty russkikh arkhivov* (Moscow: ROSSPĖN 1998), pp. 6–12; "Documents," Volokitina, Murashko, and Noskova (eds.), *Tri vizita A.Ia. Vyshinskogo*, pp. 17–116; Kennedy-Pipe, *Soviet Strategies in Europe*, pp. 45–47; Ulrich Burger, "Von der Zusammenarbeit über die Konfrontation zur Auflösung. Die Strategie der Kommunisten in Rumänien zur Gleichschaltung des Parteiensystems zwischen 1944 und 1948," Creuzberger and Görtemaker (eds.), *Gleichschaltung unter Stalin?* pp. 128–42.

145. Ulrich Burger, "Von der Zusammenarbeit über die Konfrontation zur Auflösung. Die Strategie der Kommunisten in Rumänien zur Gleichschaltung des Parteiensystems zwischen 1944 und 1948," Creuzberger and Görtemaker (eds.), *Gleichschaltung unter Stalin?* pp. 142–45.

146. Marietta Stankova, "Das parteipolitische System in Bulgarien 1944–1949. Äussere Einflüsse und innere Faktoren," Creuzberger and Görtemaker (eds.), *Gleichschaltung unter Stalin?* pp. 170–89; Kennedy-Pipe, *Soviet Strategies in Europe*, p. 45; Gibianskij, "Osteuropa," pp. 126–27.

147. Bela Zhelitski, "Postwar Hungary, 1944–1946"; Gibianski and Naimark, *The Establishment of Communist Regimes in Eastern Europe*, pp. 73–76; Janos M. Rainer, "Der Weg der ungarischen Volkdsdemokratie. Das Mehrparteiensystem und seine Beseitigung 1944–1949," Creuzberger and Görtemaker (eds.), *Gleichschaltung unter Stalin?* pp. 320–25.

148. O'Sullivan, *Stalin's "Cordon Sanitaire,"* pp. 174–78.

149. Jerca Voduček Starič, "Stalinismus und Selbst-Sowjetisierung in Jugoslawien. Von der kommunistischen Partisanenbewegung zu Titos Einparteiensystem," Creuzberger and Görtemaker (eds.), *Gleichschaltung unter Stalin?* pp. 226–33; Geoffrey Swain, "Stalin's Vision of the Postwar World," *Diplomacy and Statecraft* 7, no. 1 (March 1996), pp. 86–87.

150. Jerca Voduček Starič, "Stalinismus und Selbst-Sowjetisierung in Jugoslawien," Creuzberger and Görtemaker (eds.), *Gleichschaltung unter Stalin?* pp. 220–29.

151. For Tito's willingness to be an equal partner, not a subordinate, see O'Sullivan, *Stalin's "Cordon Sanitaire,"* pp. 275, 280–81; Swain, "Stalin's Vision of the Postwar World," pp. 87–88; N. D. Smirnova, "'Grecheskii vopros' na parizhskoi mirnoi konferentsii," Chubar'ian (ed.), *Stalin i kholodnaia voina*, pp. 8–10; Stavrakis, *Moscow and Greek Communism*, pp. 26–40.

152. Peter Danylow, "Sieg und Niederlage der Internationale. Die Sowjetisierung der Kommunistischen Partei in Albanien," Creuzberger and Görtemaker (eds.), *Gleichschaltung unter Stalin?* pp. 242–48.

153. Note by V. M. Molotov, undated [4 January 1945 at latest], *Vostochnaia Evropa*, pp. 117–18; conversation I. V. Stalin–A. Hebrang, 9 January 1945, *Vos-*

tochnaia Evropa, pp. 118–33; Swain, "Stalin's Vision of the Postwar World," pp. 87–88; Smirnova, "'Grecheskii vopros' na parizhskoi mirnoi konferentsii," Chubar'ian (ed.), *Stalin i kholodnaia voina,* pp. 8–10; Stavrakis, *Moscow and Greek Communism,* pp. 26–40.

154. Stavrakis, *Moscow and Greek Communism,* pp. 49–50; Ivo Banac, *With Stalin Against Tito. Cominformist Splits in Yugoslav Communism* (Ithaca, NY, and London: Cornell University Press 1988), p. 33.

155. Büttner, "Volksdemokratie und Sowjetisierung," Creuzberger and Görtemaker (eds.), *Gleichschaltung unter Stalin?* pp. 378–87; Jukka Nevakivi, "The Soviet Union and Finland after the War," Francesca Gori and Silvio Pons (eds.), *The Soviet Union and Europe in the Cold War, 1943–52* (Basingstoke and London: Macmillan; New York: St. Martin's Press 1996), pp. 91–100; Alexander Fischer, *Sowjetische Deutschlandpolitik 1941–1945* (Stuttgart: Deutsche Verlagsanstalt 1975), p. 136.

156. Stavrakis, *Moscow and Greek Communism,* pp. 32–34.

157. I. Maiskii to V. M. Molotov, 11 January 1944, *SSSR i germanskii vopros, I,* pp. 333–60; *Vestnik Arkhiva Prezidenta Rossiiskoi Federatsii* (supplement to *Istochnik*), 4/1995, pp.124–44.

158. *FRUS. The Conferences at Malta and Yalta,* pp. 701–702f; *Sovetskii Soiuz, IV: Krymskaia konferentsiia,* p. 66.

159. See, inter alia, paper by V. M. Maiskii, 11 January 1944, *SSSR i germanskii vopros, I,* pp. 351–60. Top economist Evgenii Varga told the Kremlin that, by the very nature of the capitalist system, the United States had to seek financial exports and that, for this reason, Soviet acceptance of such exports would be a boon to its capitalists.

160. See the documents in *FRUS. The Conferences at Malta and Yalta,* pp. 611–16, 624–28, 656–58, 709, 936f, 947, 978. Cf. Yergin, *Shattered Peace,* pp. 64–65. For the Soviet position see I. V. Maiskii to V. M. Molotov, end of January 1945, *SSSR i germanskii vopros, I,* pp. 601–5.

161. See his remark in his conversation with General de Gaulle on 3 December 1944, "'Oshibki imeiutsia i u menia, i u moikh sotrudnikov'. Zapis' besedy I. V. Stalina i Sharlia de Gollia," *Vestnik,* 5/1996, p. 105.

162. See reports by F. T. Gusev and N. V. Ivanov, *SSSR i germanskii vopros, I,* pp. 605–6, 609–16, 617–19.

163. V. M. Molotov to F. T. Gusev, 24 March 1945, *SSSR i germanskii vopros, I,* p. 626.

164. Stalin's address of victory, 9 May 1945, *Die Sowjetunion auf internationalen Konferenzen während des grossen Vaterländischen Krieges 1941 bis 1945, published by the Ministry of Foreign Affairs of the USSR, Vol. VI: Die Potsdamer (Berliner) Konferenz der höchsten Repräsentanten der drei alliierten Mächte—UdSSR, USA und Grossbritannien (17 July–2 August 1945). Dokumentensammlung* (Moscow: Progress; [East] Berlin: Staatsverlag der DDR 1986), p. 354.

165. Characteristically, the atmosphere at Yalta was seen in Moscow to have had a distinctly "amicable character": I. V. Maiskii to V. M. Molotov, 15 February 1945, *SSSR i germanskii vopros, I,* pp. 606–8.

166. This underlying assumption would explain why he hastily initiated both measures (which were clearly designed for being taken over in all of Germany) in Berlin during the intermediate period of exclusive Soviet control.

3

Failure of Interallied Cooperation, 1945–1947

EUROPE AND THE ADJACENT REGIONS
AT THE END OF WORLD WAR II

As a result of his armistice with Finland in September 1944, Stalin was able to concentrate his forces against Berlin and, to a lesser extent, against Vienna. Soviet military success in spring 1945 was fostered by Anglo-Saxon willingness to allow him conquest of Berlin and Prague.[1] At the end of the war, all eastern and central European capitals were controlled by the USSR. To be sure, Berlin had been envisaged by interallied agreement to be an exclave occupied by the four victorious powers jointly. This city was both in the Kremlin's hands for a crucial initial period and had to accept permanently an exposed, dependent, and vulnerable position within Soviet-controlled territory. Stalin was determined to exploit this advantage as much as possible. He delayed entry of Berlin by Western troops to extend exclusive control and used the time for taking unilateral measures designed to prejudice domestic development of Germany as a whole. He also had the substantial industrial equipment in the city hastily dismantled and taken out for use in the USSR.

The decision to divide Germany by zones and its capital by sectors had been based on the assumption that the allied powers would reach agreement on policy toward the occupied country. Against the background of protracted conflict with the USSR, notably on Poland, and facing the Soviet policy of creating accomplished facts in Berlin, Churchill was not hopeful any longer that Stalin was willing for a policy of consensus on Germany as had been assumed when joint occupation and the interallied status of Berlin had been agreed upon. Given that the United States had occupied the crucial industrial and population centers of the prospective Soviet zone, he felt that this was a pawn to make the Kremlin comply. Churchill suggested to the U.S. president to make evacuation of these territories conditional on a Soviet pledge to accept common policy making on Germany. Truman, however, declined. He failed to appeal to the Soviet leader; his troops left their positions to the Red Army with no return service. When the modalities of Western entry to Berlin were negotiated, Eisenhower even failed to insist on a binding guarantee of permanently unimpeded transit through Soviet-controlled territory.[2]

As early as in November 1941, Stalin had planned to restore Austria as a separate state.[3] Since the Austrians had emphatically wanted to unite with Germany in the interwar period, he felt that separation had to be attractive for them. To this end, he agreed to give them the privileged status of a "liberated" country that would not share Germany's fate of international pariah. Nonetheless, Austria was subjected to quadripartite occupation, but there were fundamental differences. While, in the same way as Berlin, Vienna was both conquered by the Red Army and surrounded by Soviet-controlled territory, the Kremlin did not enforce sociopolitical transformation and installed a government whose head, social democrat Karl Renner, had much leeway not only to choose the cabinet members but to decide on domestic matters. He skilfully used his powers to the maximum extent even when Stalin was unhappy about this. To be sure, the communists had to be accepted as partners in an all-party coalition but only in a minor position. The Austrian government was accorded a fifth unoccupied sector in Vienna. In the other parts of the city, soldiers of the four powers jointly maintained public order. Stalin had clearly decided to take none of the steps by which he imposed socialism on Eastern Europe and his part of Germany. Neither had cadres been trained nor plans for transformation been devised in the USSR, and no bloc system was introduced to make the communists take a "leading position" and translate Soviet instructions into domestic policy.[4]

To be sure, Stalin had expected that the communists would play an important role in the government coalition and gain a position sufficiently strong to exercise decisive influence in the country after the United States would have withdrawn from Europe. Half a year after he had put Renner into office, free elections were held in all of Austria as had been agreed with the Western powers. The communists received only few votes and lost any considerable influence. Stalin acquiesced in this defeat and in the democratic orientation of the country. Unlike elsewhere, he allowed for his hope to be disappointed and made no effort to reverse the political situation, even though the communists would have liked to set up a separate state of their own and even were willing to seize power by a putsch. In the Kremlin's view, the country was strategically and geopolitically marginal. The Soviet leader could dispense with it and was satisfied as long as occupation allowed for material benefit by transfer of major economic assets alleged to be German property, notably the Zistersdorf oilfields.

In internal discussion, Stalin justified his restraint by saying that the Nazis had destroyed the communist party in Austria and killed its best cadres. So it was preferable to put a social democrat into power. He added that Renner's party deserved a more positive assessment than it had been previously accorded.[5] The argument is clearly unconvincing. It would have equally applied to Germany and to the East European countries (except for Bulgaria). There, however, Stalin did not spare any effort to impose socialist transformation.

Temporary Conflict in Scandinavia

As early as in December 1941, Stalin had demanded participation in control of the Danish Straits. In early 1944, the Soviet proposal for zonal division of Germany had envisaged the other waterway between the Baltic and the North Seas, the Kiel Canal, to be part of the territory that would be allotted to the USSR. But this demand was not put on the table, as the British offered an arrangement that, on the a whole, was even more favorable and Stalin decided to accept it. Feeling that agreement on this must not be jeopardized by seeking too much at one time, he rejected a proposal by the People's Commissariat of Foreign Affairs to seek additional inclusion of Schleswig-Holstein with the Kiel Canal in the Soviet zone.[6] But the Kremlin's interest in control of the Kiel Canal continued. In a subsequent draft, both it and the Danish Straits were envisaged to be under the authority of an international commission that would be dominated by the USSR.[7] As the end of war approached, the Red Army hastened to occupy the Canal region but British troops succeeded in being there first. At the Potsdam conference in July, after Churchill had rejected discussion on Soviet control of the Turkish Straits, Stalin refrained from initiating discussion on international control of the Kiel Canal and repeating the Danish Straits demand.

In spite of Denmark's neutral status (which had been violated by German occupation in 1940), the USSR occupied the island of Bornholm when the war had already been terminated. The Danes were told that the troops would stay "until the military question in Germany had been solved." While creation of a military base was advocated by leading circles in Moscow, the main purpose was apparently to put pressure on the government in Copenhagen to make concessions on the straits. But the Danes ignored the challenge. The Anglo-Saxons reinforced resistance to Soviet expansion in general. In 1946, the island was evacuated. In northern Scandinavia, there was another conflict. After Finland's change of sides in fall 1944, the Red Army had expelled the Germans from northern Norway and stayed there after the end of the war. Stalin claimed Norwegian coastal territory at the Arctic Sea including the Archipelago of Spitsbergen. Either annexation would have reinforced Soviet control of the northern maritime entrance. In September 1945, the Red Army withdrew, with no demand having been satisfied.[8]

On the basis of the 1944 armistice with the USSR, Finland had ceded territories at its Eastern border, including its only Arctic Sea harbor of Petsamo, and accepted a major military base in the close vicinity of the capital. This had been demanded by Stalin as a basis to allow Soviet troops both to use inner Finnish crucial roads and railways and to have an advantageous military position in the event of another war. In return, he did not press for immediate initiation of socioeconomic transformation. Nonetheless, the Kremlin was initially confident that Finland would take the same political road as Bulgaria, Hungary, and Romania.[9] Moscow apparently hoped for the Finnish communists to play a crucial role. While, during the early months, they had been on the rise and won a major (but not "leading") position in government, they were then increasingly losing power and influence.[10]

The Correlation of Power

The USSR was totally exhausted. Large parts of the country were in ruins; the losses of human lives were enormous. In stark contrast to this, the United States had unprecedented material resources. The Kremlin was well aware of this asymmetry. Despite the wartime alliance, its perception was shaped by the doctrine of class antagonism. American policy was shaped by the country being "in the highest stage of dynamic imperialism." Employment of the term *imperialism* implied that the United States was ascribed systemic hostility and expansionist designs. In all parts of the world, notably in Europe, it was seen to deliberately extend its power. The USSR had to cope with an "expansion of a new type": with "financial-economic" rather than "territorial expansion." As a weak economy, Britain had problems in defending the empire. It was therefore interested in stabilizing the status quo. Accordingly, it had reached the historical stage of "conservative imperialism." As a result, the two Anglo-Saxon powers were seen to be divided by conflict. But on the basis of systemic consensus and shared culture, they were also credited with an inclination to draw together. Against this background, it was expedient both to reinforce friendly relations with them and to exploit their mutual "contradictions." Contact with Britain must be emphasized as a political counterweight to the United States. The USSR would, it was hoped, attract all medium and small powers and the "genuinely democratic elements in these countries, particularly in Europe." Germany and Japan would have to be kept down "until the moment when and if these countries will show sincere endeavor to take the road of real democracy and socialism."[11]

While, seen from Moscow, U.S. economic expansionism essentially posed a threat, it did so less than did direct expansion. It also provided an opportunity for exploitation for the USSR's material benefit. The United States was interested in exporting capital. If appropriate conditions were negotiated to avoid negative implications notably on the political level, Soviet reconstruction might be greatly enhanced. As early as on 3 January 1945, the Kremlin wanted a six billion dollar credit from Washington. The United States had supported the Soviet war effort by massive land lease deliveries without payment, but the Senate had abruptly cancelled them immediately after Germany had surrendered. To be sure, the decision was revoked shortly afterward, but Soviet economic planning had already been put in disarray. In the Kremlin's perception, termination of wartime aid was an attempt to exert pressure. Stalin blamed the Americans for this and continued to seek big, long-term loans at favorable conditions. As late as in April 1947, the Soviet bid for the sum stated in 1945 was renewed. During the concluding talks, Washington was willing to consider fulfilment of the Kremlin's desire but made this conditional on termination of East European economic seclusion. Resumption of prewar exports from Hungary and elsewhere was vital for reconstruction of the western part of the Continent. But the Kremlin failed to permit free trade with the countries of its power sphere.[12]

Economic weakness was one of the reasons why Stalin did not consider war against the West despite the fact that the United States greatly weakened its position by massive withdrawal of troops from Europe immediately after the war. In the end, not much more than administrative personnel required for Germany and Austria remained. At the same time, the U.S. economy was adapted to peacetime requirements with no regard for maintenance of military power vis-à-vis the USSR. To be sure, the Americans continued to have a huge navy but this would be of little use in the event of land war.[13] If attacked by the Red Army, U.S. units would have no option but to evacuate as quickly as possible. Even though Soviet forces had been worn down by war with Germany and lacked elementary equipment, they would be able to occupy the Continent. Only after an extended period of rearmament would the U.S. military be able to return to launch a counteroffensive. Atomic monopoly did not prevent initial military inferiority. As a result, it was generally felt that Washington was bound to avoid conflicts that entailed a risk of war.[14]

For many years, however, the decision makers in Washington did not see disarmament as a source of weakness. They rather felt that, on this basis, relations with the Kremlin would be eased. But their attempt failed to persuade the Soviet side that this was part of a deliberate effort to come to meet its needs. Assertions that the United States was seeking mutual understanding met with disbelief and suspicion. The U.S. indication of willingness to reduce military capabilities, to eschew alliance with London, and to take a neutral position (which resulted in taking intermediate positions between Britain and the USSR to make them agree) did not elicit a positive response[15] but made Stalin feel that his view on American policy was correct. Given that he saw Washington take little interest in postwar Europe, he did not expect to face Western opposition worth major consideration when he sought to enforce crucial goals, notably in Eastern Europe and Germany. To be sure, he understood that he must practice some measure of restraint to allow for maintenance of cooperative relations with the Anglo-Saxon powers. He felt, however, that they would have to acknowledge that the Soviet-occupied territories were his "zone of security" where they had no right to interfere with his policy.[16]

On 14 November 1945, Stalin outlined his general situation assessment in a conversation with Polish communist leader Władysław Gomułka.

> Do not believe in divergencies between the English and the Americans. They are closely associated with each other. Their intelligence [service] conducts lively operations against us in all countries. In Poland, in the Balkans, and in China, everywhere their agents spread information that the war with us will break out any day now. I am completely certain that there will be no war, it is rubbish. They are not capable of waging war against us. Their armies have been disarmed by agitation for peace and will not raise their weapons against us. War is not decided by atomic bombs but by armies. First of all, they are trying to intimidate us and force us to yield in contentious issues concerning Japan, the Balkans, and the reparations. Secondly, [they want] to push us away from our allies—Poland, Romania, Yugoslavia, and Bulgaria. I asked them directly if they were starting the war against us. And they said: "No, of course not! No, of course not!" Whether in thirty years or so they want to have another war, is another issue. This would bring them great profit, particularly in the case of America which is beyond the oceans and couldn't care less about the effects of war. Their policy of sparing Germany testifies to this. He who spares the aggressor wants another war. To the statement that there are rumors in America that soon there will be an agreement between America and the Soviet Union, he [Stalin] said: "It is possible."[17]

Conflict on Soviet Bids to Extend Power

Ever since 1939, Stalin had wanted to extend his power to Turkey, particularly to gain control of its Straits which link the Black and the Aegean Seas and thereby open the sea lane to the Mediterranean.[18] Unaware of his far-reaching designs, the leaders of the United States and Britain agreed at Yalta in principle to revision of the 1923 Montreux Convention. With the Anglo-Saxon powers' apparent approval, the Kremlin felt that the time had come to press for its demand to be met. Molotov informed Ankara that "fundamental changes" resulting from war required that the regime of the straits was "improved." The Montreux Convention would be cancelled by the USSR at the end of the year. A new accord had to be concluded to guarantee free passage to the ships of all nations. The Turkish government responded by indicating willingness for international negotiations on regulations that would suit the other side's needs better. When, however, the Kremlin specified that it claimed transfer of sovereign rights at the straits, cession of the eastern provinces of Kars and Ardahan, and long-term lease of maritime and military bases, the proposal was rejected.[19] While the ambassador in Moscow was given the impression that the USSR would "not feel necessary to insist" on its demands if his country would "break away from its alliance with Britain," reports on Soviet troop movements along the Bulgarian frontier were spread to make the Ankara government accept Molotov's demands. The Greeks were told that it would be looked upon with great disfavor if they sought to unite with Turkey against Soviet claims to control of the straits.[20]

At the Potsdam conference, Stalin tried to make the Anglo-Saxon leaders put pressure on Turkey. Churchill declared that he was willing to allow for some change of the straits regime but opposed any consideration of Soviet bases.[21] The Soviet effort to gain control of the Turkish access to the Mediterranean Sea was complemented by an attempt to get hold of Libya at its southern coast. On Stalin's order, the Moscow People's Commissariat of Foreign Affairs had prepared a proposal for this former Italian colony to become a Soviet protectorate. When, in June 1945, the United States put the future status of the colonies on the international agenda, the Kremlin leader felt that the time had come to table the demand.[22] At the Potsdam conference, however, the British and the Americans avoided an argument on this by indicating that the problem had to be considered when the Italian peace treaty was discussed at the upcoming Council of Foreign Ministers.[23] When this met in London from 11 September 1945 onward, conflict developed over Romania, Bulgaria, and Soviet claims to Libya, or at minimum its western part, Tripolitania. On the basis of daily exchanges with Molotov, Stalin pressed hard to have all his demands fulfilled and not to allow for compromise. No agreement was reached: The Kremlin saw the Balkans as its sphere of exclusive control, and the Anglo-Saxon governments rejected a Soviet protectorate on Libya. As a result, the status quo—Soviet domination of the Balkans but exclusion from the Mediterranean region—continued.[24]

Italy's former colonies were on the agenda again when, in spring 1946, the four foreign ministers met in Paris. This time, Molotov declared that the USSR only wanted the use of Tripolitanian ports for its commercial fleet and was prepared to share the protectorate with other powers. While an allied, that is, Soviet representative would head the control commission, there might be an Italian deputy. This was rejected. U.S. Secretary of State

Byrnes bluntly asked what was Moscow's goal: security or expansion?[25] The Kremlin tried to make the Italian and French communists persuade their coalition partners to support its demand, which allegedly would serve the national interest of their countries by balancing British power in the Mediterranean. While the two parties may have complied, the Western governments did not change their attitudes.[26] Stalin vainly tried to make the UNO General Assembly accept that the USSR was entitled to take over former League of Nations mandates. He instructed Molotov to claim respect for his country as a great power whose attitude could not be ignored in any part of the world. While his interest focused on Europe, he saw recognition of great power status as prestigious and helpful for pressing all kinds of demands.[27] The attempt failed; Libya remained outside the sphere of Soviet power.

As early as in summer 1945, the Kremlin indicated interest to participate in discussion on former Italian territories designed to be put under a protectorate regime.[28] At the Paris session of foreign ministers, Molotov referred to the "Dodekanes problem" and blamed the Athens government for not having clarified its attitude on this. The statement referred to a Greek-inhabited archipelago that had been annexed by fascist Italy and, after the latter's defeat, was generally understood to be part of Greece. An *éclat* resulted when Bevin explained the background: The Soviet ambassador had pressed the government in Athens to concede a maritime base at one of the Dodekanes Islands. This would have complemented aspired control of the northern Aegean Sea entrance by control of its southern exit to the Mediterranean. General indignation in response to Bevin's statement made the Soviet foreign minister deny any such intention.[29] The Soviet attempt to extend power to the Mediterranean basin had failed again. But the Kremlin did not give up. Ever since 1943, it had cherished the hope that alignment with the Zionists would promote influence in the region, weaken Britain's position in the area, exacerbate its tensions with the United States, and enhance the status of the USSR among Jews around the world. It supported creation and maintenance of Israel politically and by military aid from 1947 through 1949 when the rising tide of domestic antisemitism in the Soviet empire put an end to the alliance.[30]

A major point of East-West conflict was Iran, which the allies had temporarily occupied during the war to protect oil supplies. The British had taken over the southern part of the country, whereas Soviet troops were deployed in the north. In the Azerbaijan oil region, the USSR had set up a communist satellite regime. At Yalta, the Kremlin leaders had succeeded in preventing discussion on military withdrawal. After the war had ended, the British forces duly left but the Red Army units remained. Moscow came under Anglo-Saxon criticism, which it sought to ward off.[31] In 1946, the Kremlin grew generally less uncompromising than during the year before.

The troops left Bornholm, and a less harsh attitude on Turkey was taken. In Iran, Stalin finally yielded to international pressure by evacuating Azerbaijan. Before this, he had imposed an agreement on the government in Teheran that provided for Soviet control of the oil production in this region. But when the Red Army had left and the communist satellite regime collapsed, the accord did not take effect. The Soviet negotiators had failed to notice that stipulated ratification by the Iranian *medshlis* within seven months was impossible given that this body had not been constituted yet and elections for it were not on the agenda. Stalin was furious when he learned about this.[32]

All Soviet attempts to extend power beyond the regions conquered by the Red Army ended in failure. Stalin clearly overplayed his hand when he tried to make Britain and the United States concede geostrategic positions to him that were within their sphere of power. His maritime capabilities were insignificant, and the Anglo-Saxon governments felt no need to allow him to set up military bases in areas where their fleets were in control. The USSR failed both to break out of its landlocked geographical position and to add a fundament for prospective sea power to its geostrategic superiority on the Eurasian continent. What resulted was simply a feeling of threat in the outside world. Greece and Turkey (which continued to be confronted with Moscow's claim for control over the straits all the time until Stalin's death) were effectively antagonized, which provided a psychological basis for their subsequent willingness to seek protection by participation in an anti-Soviet alliance. Conflict over Azerbaijan was a special case. There the Kremlin sought to exploit temporary occupation with a clear time limit for setting up a satellite regime and controlling foreign oil resources. When Stalin felt at last that the political price was too high in terms of indignation in not only Western but neutral capitals, he decided to abandon his Azerbaijan followers but maintain control of oil but then discovered that he had failed to attain his objective.

DEVELOPMENTS IN EASTERN EUROPE 1945–1947

At the end of World War II, the extent of East European progress along the Kremlin's line widely differed. In Poland, Romania, Bulgaria, and Hungary, socioeconomic transformation and a bloc system had been initiated. As a result, their governments were reliably controlled by the communists and the Soviet authorities behind them. In all these countries, however, there was latent opposition, which surfaced whenever the imposed political system ran into difficulties. While the Moscow leaders knew that the situation in Poland and potentially also in Romania was unstable, they felt that control, notably of Hungary, was unchallenged. They were caught by surprise

when, in fall 1945, elections there turned out a big noncommunist majority. From then on, they were increasingly cautious to allow for free expression of the people's will. But there were some more disappointments until,
contrary to the pledges made to the allies in the West, Moscow leaders at
last refused any meaningful elections.

When the Kremlin had planned to make Eastern Europe take the "road
to socialism," no functional substitute had been envisaged if the situation
would not allow for bloc politics to be imposed on all political parties in a
given country. This, however, was the problem in Poland when, on the basis of the 2 July 1945 agreement, groups from London exile were admitted
that then refused to join the communist-controlled bloc. In Romania, the
traditional parties, which had been ousted from government, were outside
the bloc and hence not obliged to define their positions on the basis of consensus with the communists. Bulgaria was subjected to exclusive control by
a communist-controlled front from the very start. Only later there were efforts to make the opposition join it. In all these cases, bloc politics failed to
work as a perfect instrument to impose discipline along Soviet lines. Underlying this were unforeseen adverse conditions that, for some while, prevented the occupation power from imposing the rules of bloc politics on
political forces outside the communist-dominated multiparty front. But
the Kremlin was not willing to allow independent positions and, as early as
appeared expedient, corrected the situation by taking recourse to direct
repression.

Soviet policy on Czechoslovakia was different. On the basis of pledges by
Beneš in December 1943, Stalin was confident that cooperation between
the "bourgeois" president and the communist party would initiate a process
of gradual but eventually total socialist transformation. He felt that, to allow for this to develop, political restraint was required for some time to
come. In December 1944, Stalin's aide Dimitrov instructed the leaders of
the Czechoslovak party accordingly.

> The question of sovietization of Czechoslovakia must not be put. At present,
> we cannot guess when the time will come to put the question of sovietization
> of Czechoslovakia. This is not so easy as many [people] think. The Czechs and
> the Slovaks must take the road to Soviet rule by themselves, by development of
> their own. And we, too, must lead up the people to socialism and Soviet rule
> by preparing it politically and ideologically. Those people in Slovakia who
> make too much haste with regard to Soviet rule, must be restrained. As Stalin
> has rightly said: One must take step by step, and before taking the next step,
> one must consolidate conquered positions.[33]

Communist leader Klement Gottwald received detailed instructions by
Stalin himself who, on 23 January 1945, talked with him at first in the
Kremlin (with the inclusion of Molotov) and then in his dacha (where no

one else was present).[34] On 10 March, Gottwald submitted a draft communist party program to Dimitrov in his function as head of the CPSU International Department and looked forward to one of the copies to be passed on to Stalin personally. In his accompanying letter, he emphasized that he was generally in agreement with Beneš and expected him to accept any point that would be important for the communists. Not only did he invite Soviet decision on the party program but asked for continuing "advice" from Moscow as well. In general, Dimitrov accepted the program and modified the wording only in formal respect. One change of substance, however, was made with regard to foreign policy. In the original text, the USSR and the Slavic countries were seen to be allies, while the version that resulted from Soviet editing indicated that the Kremlin looked forward to create a bloc of Slavic nations under its aegis.[35]

Beneš and his cabinet represented the only East European emigré government both permitted to return and acknowledged to represent the country. Characteristically, the Czechoslovak president went to Moscow before getting back home. When he arrived in the Soviet capital on 19 March 1945, he was met as an honored guest and handed a list of questions by the NKVD. The points on which he was expected to take a stand included organization of the Czechoslovak army, mutual relations between the USSR, Poland, and Czechoslovakia, and Soviet and Czechoslovak policy on Germany. In a conversation with Molotov on 21 March, Beneš explained that the British wavered on whether the Sudeten Germans should be transferred to Germany. The Soviet foreign minister responded by asking how many ethnic Germans his interlocutor wanted to be resettled. Beneš thought that 2.0 out of 2.8 million should be obliged to leave the country, and also 400,000 out of 600,000 Hungarians. On 21 and 24 March, reorganization of the Czechoslovak army was discussed. A strong force of ten well-equipped divisions was envisaged into which the army corps, which had fought side by side with the Red Army, would be included. Efficient radio communication with the USSR was to provide for close cooperation. Another point decided in Moscow was the composition of the future government. Stalin expressed his high esteem of Beneš by a giving a dinner in his honor before, in early April, his guest left for Prague.[36]

Development within the socialist camp indicated during the first postwar years already that, contrary to the myth of unfailing internationalist solidarity, relations between communist regimes were shaped by latent tension unless Soviet control provided for imposed conformity. Tito and his partisan leaders had taken instructions from Moscow during the war and, with a few significant exceptions, followed them. When victory was achieved, they hailed Stalin as their highest authority, with whom they felt to be in full agreement. But being aware that they owed their power to themselves rather than to the USSR, they based their decisions on priorities of their own and saw no reason to accept any outside instruction. They had far-reaching ambitions in the Balkans. This caused concern in neighboring countries, even communist-controlled countries, and also with Stalin who did not want to get involved in undesirable conflict and to have his exclusive authority infringed.

Struggle for Domestic Self-Determination in Poland

The 21 July 1945 agreement, on broadening the Lublin Committee government by exile leaders, had given rise to hope in Poland that communist dictatorship could be avoided. Admission of deviant parties was seen as a chance to enforce some measure of competition and to challenge the groups put into power by the USSR. Indeed, the political situation changed. As representatives of an alternative orientation, the London Poles, particularly Mikołajczyk who appealed to the country's peasant majority, elicited overwhelming support. Communist satellite party members joined exile leaders' pro-Western groups. The socialists, who had previously been aligned to the prewar regime, merged with them. When they tried to replace Edward Osóbka-Morawski and Józef Cyrankiewicz at their top, the Soviet authorities took preventive action. In spite of such protection, the two politicians felt they must satisfy their members' longing for a larger measure of independence. This created concern among the communist leaders that Osóbka-Morawski and Cyrankiewicz might escape control, draw close to Mikołajczyk's peasant-oriented People's Party, and provide him with a socialist label.[37]

On Soviet instructions, communist chairman Władysław Gomułka demanded the restoration of bloc politics to prevent overthrow of his regime. As he explained, the socialists faced a choice between "democracy" and "reaction." Unless they accepted a joint ticket with the communists, the "reactionary" Mikołajczyk might win prospective elections. Such an outcome would inevitably make the occupation power intervene. When this argument had been taken, Gomułka was seeking the People's Party acceptance of its inclusion in a multparty bloc. As a result, it would have renounced the option to present itself as an alternative to the communist regime. Negotiations failed when, in February 1946, Mikołajczyk did not accept a minor share of parliamentary seats in exchange for renunciation of competitive voting. While the socialists had accepted the common list, they did not agree that the People's Party was "reactionary" but held that it was a peasant party. The divergent views were put before Stalin, who saw it as a "front of the reaction against the government." Its preceding legalization had served the purpose to make its followers surface from the underground and thus to allow for effective persecution. He also decided that only one-fourth of parliamentary mandates might be offered to Mikołajczyk. If he would renounce organizational and propagandistic independence, he might be given more. He must accept the envisaged share of seats; otherwise, "repressions" and political isolation would ensue. Creation of a party bloc was imperative irrespective of whether he would join.[38]

The People's Party decided to maintain independence and continue opposition. When, on 30 June 1946, a national referendum was held on a minor issue, Mikołajczyk and his followers turned it into a plebiscite on government policy in general and won a resounding victory. While the communists saw their defeat as a technical problem that must be solved by improved propaganda, the socialists blamed them for having deviated from agreed policy by initiating a campaign against the People's Party, and they called for national reconciliation, presenting themselves as mediators between the political extremes. Gomułka saw the leading role assigned to the communists by the USSR put in jeopardy, rejected any agreement with the People's Party, and advised the socialists to ask Stalin for advice. When their representatives were received in the Kremlin, they were told that any compromise with Mikołajczyk was unacceptable and that unification of the two workers' parties was indispensable. As a result, the socialists entered a close alliance with the communists and joined them in their struggle against the People's Party as the "legal above-structure of the reactionary underground." But given strong resistance among socialist cadres and members, organizational unity was not put on the agenda yet.[39]

Persecution of noncommunist groups had continued unabated all the time. When national elections were held in fall 1946 at last, the People's Party, which had firmly resisted all pressure to renounce a ticket of its own, was exposed to open terror and thus denied any chance. The bloc of communists and socialists prevailed. Mikołajczyk lost all hope and left the country; his followers were subjected to unlimited ruthless persecution. Any legal basis for opposition was eliminated. The two partners of the bloc disagreed on distribution of government positions. Stalin again took the role of arbitrator. "Working class unity" was put on the agenda. The "United Workers Party" that resulted was controlled by Moscow cadres and monopolized power in state and society. A few remaining minor parties were retained as emasculated satellite organizations. The road to unbridled communist dictatorship was open.[40]

Stalin had succeeded at last in imposing his system and regime on Poland. Seeking to overcome overwhelmingly strong resistance in this country, he had eventually taken recourse with full-scale undisguised repression. This, however, had its vengeance: The Polish experience made the British lose any illusions about the Kremlin's policy and subsequently contributed to changing U.S. attitude. It is against this background that Anglo-Saxon performance in what was to become the Cold War must be seen. The major theater of the emerging confrontation was occupied Germany.

Conflict Over Communist Dictatorship in Romania and Bulgaria

Under the impression that there was no possibility for independent domestic policy making, a number of peasant and liberal leaders in Romania
joined the government bloc controlled by the communists in summer 1945
and thereby exposed themselves to blame for political submissiveness by
the members of their parties. A communist attempt to split the major opposition group, the National Peasant Party, over the issue of entering the
government failed: Maniu's plea to reject cooperation met with overwhelming support. With Western approval, King Mihai intervened by dismissing
the Groza government—a step to which he was entitled by the 1923 constitution, which continued to be officially in force. The Kremlin assured the
dismissed prime minister of its unflinching support. But the cabinet was divided by fundamental dissension. Notably the socialists, who were backed
by more than twice as many members as the communists, felt entitled to a
policy of their own. But their demand to include the two "bourgeois" opposition parties in the Bucharest leadership was treated as putting the
regime into jeopardy. Communist party leader Gheorghe Gheorghiu-Dej
responded by putting pressure on local socialist organizations to make
them disobey. At the same time, a show trial was initiated against members
of the resistance movement, which had begun to form in March. When, on
8 November, an annual ceremony in the king's honor took place, a brawl
developed between his followers and those of the government. The USSR
used the incident to accuse the opposition of organizing riots. Harsher measures against the opposition parties were declared to be necessary. But persecution of their leaders risked antagonizing major parts of the population.
To avoid public attention as much as possible, repression was primarily directed at lower party ranks. Final settlement of accounts at top levels was
postponed.[41]

The London session of the Council of Foreign Minsters in early fall provided an opportunity for Soviet attempts to make the Anglo-Saxon powers
abandon support of the opposition by extending recognition to the Groza
regime, but the United States and Britain declined.[42] So the controversy
continued. Discussion during the following meeting in Moscow was to no
avail either. But talking with Stalin, Byrnes felt that compromise was possible. It was agreed that, as a return service for Western approval of the Groza
cabinet, two opposition politicians would be included in it, elections held
at the earliest possible date, and free expression of opinion guaranteed. The
Kremlin, however, implicitly indicated that it was not prepared to accept
substantial concessions by not allowing the major opposition leaders—
Maniu, Brătianu, and Lupu—to enter the government.[43]

While the Soviet side continued to insist on abandonment of non-
recognition by the Anglo-Saxon powers, it prevented their observers from

monitoring political developments in Romania.[44] During the interparty negotiations, which were conducted in Bucharest as had been envisaged, Vyshinskii (who had again been sent from Moscow) rejected two successive proposals by denouncing suggested candidates as "fascists." Talking to Gheorghiu-Dej, he recommended direct repression and use of splitting tactics to eliminate the opposition altogether. An explicit ban had to be avoided as, given Anglo-Saxon attitudes, the effort at annihilation had to be veiled. To undermine the "bourgeois" membership basis, parties with similar labels were set up under communist control. The challenge resulting from the existence of an independent socialist party was eliminated by measures that caused it to split up.

Despite all this, the communists were not sure whether elections would produce acceptable results. A test was made by a number of local elections. The outcome was disastrous: The opposition parties defeated the communist-controlled bloc by a sizeable margin. Upon this, Molotov told Gheorghiu-Dej and Minister of the Interior Teohari Georgescu on 2 April 1946 that elections must be avoided before success was absolutely certain. In the following months, any conceivable pressure, initimidation, and manipulation was employed to guarantee "correct" voting. When, in November, elections in fulfilment of last year's pledge to the West were held at last, the government nonetheless suffered a resounding defeat. According to a U.S. Embassy estimate, 70 percent of the votes had been cast for Maniu's Peasant Party, while the ruling coalition received only 8 percent. The communists were shocked. When they asked for advice in Moscow, they were told that falsification of the result was the only way out. After forty-eight hours, a 70 percent victory of the bloc parties was announced. The Western powers protested sharply but refrained from further action. The Kremlin was determined to eliminate the opposition as soon as possible but waited until the allies had signed the Romanian peace treaty on 10 February 1947. Then the opposition was smashed. The socialists were forced to join a united "working class party" controlled by the communist leaders who established their monopoly of power.[45]

From the very start, the Bulgarian communists were in full control of the government. Occupation by the Red Army had allowed them to establish a regime which, for all practical purposes, had a one-party character. But as in all other countries of the Soviet power sphere, a multiparty bloc system was set up as a curtain to conceal "proletarian dictatorship." After the communist leaders had taken state power into their hands, they were confident that they would easily crush independent parties, notably the Agrarian Union. Stalin cautioned them that, given the international situation, rash action was not expedient. He explained that the Anglo-Saxon countries were paying much attention to developments in Bulgaria and must be persuaded that multiparty democracy was practiced. Two Agrarian Union ministers had to be included in the cabinet to create an appearance of all-party participation. As certain opposition politicians were absolutely unacceptable, the communists should decide whom they saw fit. The Soviet leader agreed with his Bulgarian followers that pressure and persecution must focus on crucial opposition representatives. Against the background of obvious unwillingness to accept opposition in Bulgaria, the Anglo-Saxon governments suspected that the outcome of elections would not express the people's opinion. When a voting date was fixed for August 1945, they protested and declared that they would not recognize the resultant government.

Upon this, Stalin made the communist regime in Sofia revoke the date and show regard for other parties but did not envisage genuine concessions. As he explained to the Bulgarian leaders, a legalized opposition was necessary since otherwise their domestic enemies would go underground. Permitting their political activities for an interim period of time would facilitate their eventual elimination. While willingness to come to meet their demands would have to be announced, they must not be permitted to work outside the framework of bloc politics. Accordingly, the Agrarian Union was excluded from participation in elections when it refused to be put on a joint ticket with the communists. It responded by an appeal to cast empty ballots. When the elections were held in November 1945, the communists were shocked by the number of empty ballots, as the British representative in Sofia reported to his government. These votes were officially declared invalid by the government. No count was published but an 88 percent approval announced. The United States and Britain refused to accept this alleged outcome as a basis of democratic legitimacy. As in Romania's case, they did not recognize the government but demanded genuine representation of the people's will.

Seeking to make the Anglo-Saxon governments accept policy in Bulgaria, Stalin wanted to create an appearance of willingness for compromise. He pressed the communists to provide for an all-party façade by allowing two minor opposition leaders to take unimportant cabinet positions. But the Agrarian Union politicians insisted on substantial concessions. Stalin and Molotov deemed their demands unacceptable and made the cadres in Sofia solve the problem by repression rather than bargaining. Britain and the United States, on their part, wanted to reach agreement and advised the opposition to be more accommodating. But the Agrarian Union insisted on a genuine compromise.

In June 1946, the communist leaders were instructed by Stalin that bloc politics had to be maintained to the full extent. Its multiparty front must spare no effort to come off as the leading force in the upcoming October elections. The opposition must be made to join the bloc. When the groups outside government set up a "federation" to challenge it, measures of persecution against them were increased further on orders from Moscow.

While action by the opposition parties was incredibly hampered—for example, many of their activists were put into jail, publication of newspapers was prevented for long periods of time, and followers were exposed to frequent attack by communist gangs—their election campaign was upheld. Under these miserable conditions, they were able to get 28 percent of the votes. In the resulting parliament, their leader, Nikola Petkov, won authority both at home and abroad by fearlessly castigating communist repression. On the assumption that the West would not seek conflict over Bulgaria, Stalin ordered action for gradual elimination of the opposition.[46]

Development of the Political System in Hungary and Czechoslovakia

At the end of war, the Red Army had taken full control of Hungary. It imposed socioeconomic transformation and the bloc system with a coalition government based on it. As a result, the communist party concentrated domestic power in its hands. Ruthless police organs were set up to persecute all "class enemies." In the Kremlin's view, political development took the right direction. A sizeable majority of the population, notably the poor and toiling "masses," were believed to support the regime. Competitive elections appeared acceptable; they would strengthen rather than jeopardize the communists' "leading role." The moment of truth came when, in October 1945, elections were held in Greater Budapest: The Smallholders Party, which represented peasant interest, won an absolute majority of 50.54 percent. In subsequent national elections, it even got 57 percent of the votes, which gave them 245 seats in parliament. The communists had only 70 and the social democrats 69. Soviet intervention, however, provided for a government that disregarded the leader of the victorious party and put the "power ministries" in communist hands. Restrictive and repressive measures were initiated, which gradually increased. In early 1947, the Smallholders Party was banned on grounds of the allegation that it had created a conspiratory network to topple the regime. This opened the road to unlimited introduction of the Soviet system.[47]

Given that Stalin saw agreement with Beneš as a starting point to make Czechoslovakia take the road to socialism, he did not set up an occupation regime there and withdrew his troops by the end of 1945. In his view, all political factors were there to make the country develop in the desired direction. The communist party, which was taken over by the leading cadres who had returned from Moscow, had firm roots in the "working class." Its well-trained elite was numerous, as was its membership, and there were hundreds of thousands of followers and sympathizers. Additionally, collaboration by the "bourgeoisie" appeared assured during the decisive stages of domestic change. All this was quite different from the situation in the other East European countries, where the socialist system had only few supporters when the Red Army conquered them. The Kremlin therefore felt that it could dispense with using military power to promote socialism and allow for the competitive democratic system of the interwar period to continue. No multiparty bloc was imposed, crucial positions of state power were not generally taken over by "reliable" cadres, and the executive and legislative branches of government retained their traditional structure and functions with little modification.

The communists were supported by the military units that had been part of the Red Army and took control of the ethnically cleansed regions by using their enormous assets for political purposes. They dominated the committees which, under the label of land reform, distributed agricultural property to small peasants, and they staffed the management of nationalized industrial enterprises. They were successful in entrenching themselves in a number of government agencies. At the top, the Ministries of the Interior, Agriculture, Information, and Education were turned into bases of their power. Ministries headed by other parties were penetrated to a considerable extent. Part of "bourgeois bureaucracy," the network of local administration, was replaced by somehow elected National Committees, which served to extend communist influence. A national front organization was set up to allow for the introduction of bloc politics at a later date.

Police personnel were selected by the communist-controlled Ministry of the Interior. While there were harsh sentences against several thousands of alleged "collaborators" and "traitors" to fortify the position of the communists and their leftist allies in state and society, there was generally no political repression for the time being. The communists did not control the army with President Beneš as its commander-in-chief. As a result of free elections in May 1946, they had 114 out of 300 seats. In the most highly industrialized regions, they even had an absolute majority. They exercised considerable but not decisive influence in parliament. Gottwald became head of an all-party coalition government and was confident that the next time he would win 51 percent of the votes. As the communists had proposed, a system of unified "societal organizations" was introduced, which more often than not allowed them to put their cadres at the top, notably in the crucial trade unions. The factory militias, which had been set up immediately after liberation, were another source of communist power.[48]

Incipient Conflict Among Communist Regimes

During wartime negotiations, Stalin had rejected Churchill's suggestion to federate countries in Eastern Europe. When, in the postwar period, the communists in Belgrade thought along similar lines as previously had the British leader, he suspected them to seek domination of the Balkans and to create a socialist power center besides the USSR. While this would be much inferior to the one in Moscow, it would allow for some measure of independence which, in Stalin's view, was unacceptable. His attitude to plans for a union of Yugoslavia and Bulgaria therefore depended on the underlying principles. If Bulgaria was envisaged to be a seventh federal state of Yugoslavia, he was willing to prevent implementation. If, however, the project was directed at creating a two-state union, it might foster Soviet control of the Belgrade leadership by the more "reliable" regime in Sofia.[49]

At the end of the war, Stalin had wanted the Greek communists to enter the Athens government and to exploit the influence thus accquired for loosening ties to Britain. Abortive insurrection in fall 1944 and, later on, failure of the new party leader Zakhariades to make his followers accept a coalition with the other parties, frustrated this hope. In the Kremlin's assessment, Greece was on the way to being firmly embedded in the Western power sphere. Stalin felt that this development had to be countered by the prevention of political consolidation. He did not object, therefore, when Yugoslavia and Bulgaria raised territorial claims for southern Macedonia including Saloniki, the second-largest Greek city and a major port at the Aegean Sea. Putting the leaders in Athens under pressure appeared helpful for destabilizing their country. He never contemplated supporting his allies in Belgrade and Sofia by practical action, nor did he expect that there was any prospect of success.[50] The British military presence in the disputed region was certain to prevent it. Additionally, it was unprecedented to seek change of the territorial status quo at the expense of a wartime ally.[51]

When Yugoslavia claimed Trieste, Stalin was in a dilemma. He was averse to straining relations with both the Anglo-Saxon leaders and the Italian communists who equally felt that the city, which had a clear Italian majority, rightly belonged to Italy. Such an arrangement offered itself all the more given that Trieste was occupied by Western troops. But at the same time, the Kremlin leader wanted to make his ally Tito feel supported. He tried to reconcile the two conflicting needs by verbally identifying with the Yugoslav demand to the full extent but doing little to enforce it. At the London meeting of foreign ministers, no agreement resulted. In Belgrade, this was attributed to lack of effective Soviet support.[52] To refute this blame, Stalin instructed Molotov at the following round of negotiations in spring 1946 to press hard for acceptance of the Yugoslav standpoint. If this attempt should fail despite sustained effort, he envisaged creation of a Free City as a fall back position. When, after heated controversy, the attempt to make the Anglo-Saxons accept annexation by Yugoslavia had predictably failed, Soviet negotiators acquiesced in an arrangement that gave the city to neither side.[53] To justify the agreement, the USSR argued that the compromise favored Yugoslavia. Additional Western concessions had been absolutely impossible; preservation of the status quo (which was the only alternative) would have been much worse. But Tito regarded any compromise as intolerable and felt that he had been let down.[54]

Conflict developed also over the course taken by the Greek communists. When Zakhariades was unable to make them enter the government coalition as recommended by the Kremlin and the Italian comrades, the leaders in Athens saw their communist compatriots to sustain their threat to the democratic order and initiated persecution. This provoked armed resistance, which was given a major boost by the Yugoslavs. Zakhariades tried to restrain his party by limiting its effort to mere defense, which would exclude active struggle against the government army. He advocated Greek neutrality to be guaranteed by the great powers. Under this protective shield, he wanted his party to be provided with arms and financial aid by the socialist countries. The Kremlin wavered for a short time and then declined.

In spite of lacking Soviet support, the wartime guerilla chieftains and General Markos as their commander took offensive action against the government in 1946, which was subsequently approved by a decision of the party. The military operations were supported by Tito, who sent weapons and other supplies. Most of these materials were channeled through Albania and Bulgaria, which by themselves provided only minor help. Stalin wavered again. In fall 1946, he felt that the insurrection was helpful in putting pressure on the British to leave Greece as being too burdensome financially and in weakening the Athens leadership by domestic turmoil. As it appears, he was confident that the insurgent communists were under safe control. At the end of the year, however, he accepted an American proposal to investigate Greek "frontier incidents," which indicated a willingness to put a brake on insurgency and to counter independent Yugoslav action. After the United States had firmly pledged support to Greece and Turkey in March 1947, Stalin changed his mind once more and approved aid to the Greek party.[55]

This was surprising. The Kremlin leader had always sought to avoid involvement in armed conflict, which might entail risk of armed clash with the Americans. He apparently felt that, given the "Truman Doctrine" of struggle against communist expansion which had just been proclaimed in Washington, political relations with the United States had been anyhow wrecked for the time being. In his view, this declaration was designed for domestic consumption as a mere justification of material aid to Greece and Turkey. Stalin wanted to demonstrate that he was not intimidated but willing to counter American support to the Athens regime. The Soviet leader failed to realize that the "Truman Doctrine" indicated a fundamental change of U.S. policy. He saw it as a statement designed for domestic justification of a specific action in the eastern Mediterranean region and, for this reason, felt that his response must be aimed to influence U.S. public opinion against involvement in Greece and Turkey.[56] At the same time, action to weaken Greece appeared useful. While the United States would certainly not risk military involvement, control of the insurgents by the Kremlin seemed assured by the power both to deliver or to withhold arms and the Soviet military presence in adjacent Bulgaria (which continued until the end of the year).

SOVIET POLICY ON GERMANY

Germany was crucial for postwar development of interallied relations. As the main enemy country and the single most important factor on the European Continent besides the USSR, it caught Stalin's attention more than anything else. It was there that the Soviet Union and the Western powers were jointly present and were in direct contact as a result of geographical vicinity and their task to agree on occupation policy. The framework for coping with this task was provided by the agreement to "reach [common] decisions on the chief questions affecting Germany as a whole," which had to be taken unanimously by the Allied Control Council. Zonal matters were to be decided by the respective commander.[57] No line of distinction had been drawn between the spheres of all-German and individual competence. This invited arbitrary delimitation. In the years to come, the USSR would justify any of its measures as having but zonal relevance and claim that any undesirable intention of the Western occupation partners affected the whole country and hence was susceptible to its veto. Political and socio-economic transformation was unilaterally initiated on Soviet-controlled territory with a clear intent to oblige all of Germany, but Britain and the United States were prevented from taking measures required for maintaining their zones.

Underlying this was the failure to agree on joint policy in occupied Germany. The "Big Three" had proclaimed common allegiance to denazification, demilitarization, decartellization, and democratization as proposed by the United States, but their views on what this meant in practice widely differed. As a result, the effort to implement these principles gave rise to continuing conflict. Initially, however, the major point of disagreement was reparations. The Kremlin insisted that, on the basis of the discussion at Yalta, it was entitled to massive deliveries. The equipment to be sent to the USSR had to be provided by dismantling factories under the label of "industrial disarmament." In all German territories occupied by the Red Army, this policy was immediately put into practice—and most radically at that. The Soviet side demanded that it was to receive similar shipments from the Western zones. In contrast to this, the Anglo-Saxon powers felt that it was impossible to exact such masses of equipment from devastated Germany into which millions of refugees were pouring from annexed eastern provinces and east central Europe, if mass starvation and general chaos were to be prevented. The conflict was aggravated by the Soviet insistence on fixation of an extremely low industrial production level that would not allow for any exports to pay for food imports. The Kremlin's veto against any increase beyond this level excluded any prospect of German economic self-sufficiency which, in London and Washington, was seen as indispensable.

The Potsdam Tripartite Conference

This situation had resulted as the "Big Three" had been unable to reach agreement at the Potsdam conference in summer 1945. There was a striking difference between the Soviet attitudes toward political and economic unity. When, in early June, Stalin had unilaterally authorized the formation of parties in Berlin, he had clearly looked forward to extending the political pattern thus created to the whole country. Accordingly, he wanted a united Germany. At Potsdam, he agreed with Churchill and U.S. President Truman that, "so far as practicable, there shall be uniformity of treatment of the German population." But when economic issues were raised, he pressed for satisfaction of his material demands with no consideration of German unity. As previously at Yalta, the British and the Americans were apprehensive that the occupied country would become a financial burden to them if the USSR would take goods out with no regard for requirements of the population's physical survival. Only if the resources of all 1937 territory and sufficient industrial potential to pay for imports were available on an equal basis for the whole country, people in their zones (which were densely populated and, in addition to this, overcrowded by eight million people expelled from the East) would be able to sustain themselves.[58]

Stalin saw no need to care for German supply and emphasized that appropriate reparations were indispensable to recompensate the USSR for the huge losses it had suffered. In his portrayal, Roosevelt's concession at Yalta that the Soviet ten billion dollar demand might be taken as a point of departure for future discussion was a final pledge to accept the Soviet claim. The only thing to be still discussed was implementation. In addition to reparations, "war booty" was declared to be justified. Under this label, not only military supplies and weapons but any financial and industrial assets were extracted from occupied territories. Whenever reparation claims were seen to be inexpedient, goods were taken away as war booty—a practice that permitted the USSR to seize any foreign property with no quantitative or qualitative limitation. When the Anglo-Saxons insisted that some industrial capacity in excess of minimum domestic needs was required to allow for payment of food imports, the Kremlin leaders declined, saying that this would help the Germans to retain a material war-making basis. They equally rejected the proposal that the German territory handed over to Poland which, before the war, had been a major agrarian surplus area, must continue its previous food deliveries. Also, Stalin was unwilling to implement German economic unity (which he advocated in theory) by accepting that available food resources must be shared among all zones. He even refused to supply the Western sectors of Berlin from the surrounding territory under his control. As a result, the three powers had to feed them by transports from their distant zones.[59]

Discussion of economic issues resulted in a decision that implicitly provided for economic division. Total Soviet industrial dismantlement of West Berlin before the Western troops had entered[60] made Byrnes expect radical removal of production capabilities by the USSR wherever possible. The United States and Britain would be unable to monitor, let alone prevent this. Even if agreement on a common reparation plan could be reached, there was no prospect to verify implementation. Such a scheme was therefore useless. The Soviet Union would take away as "war booty" whatever it wanted, and often the Western allies would not even know about it. To cope with the reparation problem nonetheless, Byrnes suggested that the USSR take its share from its own zone. While Eden rejected the proposal on the grounds that Germany would thus be divided into two separate reparation and, as a consequence, also economic zones, Molotov agreed but made approval conditional on additional delivery of industrial installations and equipments from the Ruhr District in the British zone at a value of two to three billion dollars. In the end, an accord was reached on the basis of what Byrnes had proposed: The USSR was to take its share from its zone and would get an additional 15 percent of the industrial equipment to be dismantled in the Western zones in exchange for food of equal value from Soviet-occupied Germany.[61]

The details were vague enough to result in subsequent controversy. Given different practices of implementation, the Soviet Union and the Anglo-Saxon powers remained deeply divided on the issues of reparations,[62] dismantlement, and level of industry. A clause that authorized the USSR to seize German property in occupied countries served to legitimize any Soviet seizure of industrial and other assets. The Kremlin was thus provided not only with invaluable material benefit but with a legal basis for control of East European economies by making key parts of it work for the USSR under Soviet management. When reparations from the Ruhr District were discussed, Molotov wanted this region to be internationalized as the backbone of German war potential. This demand had far-reaching political implications. If the Kremlin was allowed to participate in control of the Western zones' industrial heartland, it would have had a direct say in West German matters generally. Eden and Byrnes evaded an answer by saying that there were more pressing problems that had to be solved first.[63] In the years to come, the USSR repeated its demand again and again.[64] While Stalin saw the envisaged international regime as an instrument to project Soviet power on the Western zones, the French, who also advocated it, wanted the region to be separated from Germany as a sphere of predominant French influence. The Anglo-Saxon powers insisted that interallied agreement had recognized the Ruhr District to be part of the British zone.[65]

To extend Soviet influence on the occupied country as a whole, Molotov proposed that "German Central Administrations," headed by state secretaries and supervised by the Allied Control Council, should be set up. A few days before, such administrations had been secretly created in the Soviet Berlin sector to provide a nucleus of personnel and organization. Unaware of this, Bevin and Byrnes agreed in principle but felt that the time was not ripe for immediate implementation.[66] After the Potsdam conference (from which they had been excluded), the French raised violent objections, feeling that their demands for dismemberment, annexations, and a special Ruhr regime would be negatively prejudiced. Discussing the issue with them, the Soviet side became increasingly aware that central institutions would invite problems. Creation of an all-German economic department would entail renewed discussion on the Anglo-Saxon demand that the USSR accept requirements of economic unity. Existence of an all-zonal administration might also serve the British and the Americans to press for early termination of occupation and to demand sociopolitical transformation of the Soviet zone to be subjected to quadripartite reappraisal. In addition to this, the Soviet occupation authorities felt that there were not enough "reliable" cadres. The Kremlin concluded that German Central Administrations would have to be made conditional on Western compliance with the Soviet demands for reparations and "industrial disarmament," that is, removal of any industrial potential in excess of minimum civil supply.[67] What this meant in practice was controversial. While the USSR accepted but a very low level of production for domestic consumption, Anglo-Saxon powers felt that additional capabilities were required for export to pay for food imports necessary to prevent mass starvation. As a result of the Soviet refusal to allow for this, they paid the bill themselves.

General Traits of Soviet Occupation Policy in Germany

The Kremlin's policy in its German occupation zone basically resembled its policy in Eastern Europe. Native cadres brought back to their home country by the Red Army were assigned a crucial role. After they had been put on the "commanding heights," they were to reorganize public administration, take control of "societal organizations," and rebuild the party. As they were available only in comparatively small numbers (200–300), they had to rely on people who had not been trained in the USSR and hence were seen as potentially unreliable. This applied even to party members both at home and from Western exile who were badly needed for policy implementation, administrative services, and assessment of personnel.[68] But there were not enough of these comrades either. Administration had to be kept going by members and sympathizers of other parties recognized to be "antifascist," particularly by social democrats. Also, all kinds of politically untested "specialists" could not be dispensed with as long as no trainees were available from party schools, which were set up in big numbers.[69] To the extent that positions of public visibility had to be filled, the occupation authorities were careful to create an appearance of all-party representation. The persons on whom public attention would focus were selected to represent the respective sociopolitical environment. As a rule, the front man was a noncommunist, often a "bourgeois," chosen to project a democratic image. His deputy, generally a reliable cadre who received instructions from occupation authorities, actually controlled the apparatus, its performance, and policy. The heads of any crucial departments, notably those with competence for police, personnel, youth, and education, were also trusted communists. They were ordered not to seek the public limelight but to work behind the scenes.[70]

An influx of Moscow cadres had been under preparation since early February 1945. On 19 March, Stalin instructed Dimitrov to select personnel for employment in Germany. In late April, three "action groups" left the USSR for assisting Red Army officers to administer the occupied territory. As a result of the Kremlin's uncertainty on the kind of situation to be coped with, they did not receive detailed orders but had to report back and ask for instructions at any moment. A group headed by Ulbricht was sent to Berlin.[71] The Soviet occupation regime basically differed from the occupiers' performance in the Western zones. The German personnel were mere subordinates who served to create an appearance that, as in the West, domestic matters were largely put into the hands of natives who would simply ask the military authorities for approval. This allowed the Kremlin to pretend that imposed policy had essentially resulted from autochthonous will and was in accordance with the people's desire. The true origin of a given measure was carefully concealed; only those directly involved in its genesis would know. To this end, exchange was oral to the extent possible; German files were subsequently destroyed; and high-ranking communist leaders were reprimanded in those rare occasions when they had dropped any hints, if only to trusted comrades.[72]

The principal transmission belt for translation of Soviet will into German policy was the communist party. How it served this purpose has been described to a Soviet Central Committee commission by Major Nazarov, one of the officers in Colonel Tiul'panov's department, which was responsible for political guidance in the Soviet Military Administration of Germany (SMAG).

All the documents which are issued by the SED [as the communist party was termed by then], are practically worked out by us. When they have produced a document, it is looked through by us and all our remarks are inserted. There are no documents which we would have formulated and they would have failed to confirm, there are no such documents. A concrete example on religion. In [our] Department, we decided what kind of document must be prepared to take effect in the election campaign and deny the church the possibility of siding with the CDU [Christian Democratic Union]. We considered a number of problems. These problems were approved by Cde. Colonel [Tiul'panov]. I went to Pieck [the SED Chairman] and tell him that we have this opinion. It would be good if the SED would adopt a document in which the SED's point of view with regard to the church and to religion would be presented. Pieck says, this is alright; I have already talked [with our comrades] about this. Are there problems which you want to indicate? I tell him that we have some considerations, that this is not an order but that we have considerations. I have a preparatory document on which problems the decision should clarify. Pieck called [Anton] Ackermann and [Otto] Meier to me and says: Prepare such a document for the next session of the [SED] Secretariat. For not taking more of Pieck's time, we went to Ackermann and talked more broadly on the problem. On the next day, I come and say: Well, is the document ready? He says: Ready. On my instruction, he brings the document. In this document, Meier writes to Weisman who is the executive directly in charge. And he writes such a letter that he had a conversation with Major Nazarov today who had presented his view that it is currently necessary to make considerations with regard to religion. I tell Cde. Meier that it is inappropriate to refer to my name since the document may fall in someone's hands. Well, says Meier, I'll send my secretary at once, he will bring the document. They brought the document and eliminated it [Nazarov's name]. After this, they worked on all these instructions in a commission, and this commission worked out the problem.[73]

Soviet control of German policy makers differed in intensity. As the principal instrument to infuse Soviet measures, the communist party was subjected to strictest guidance and supervision. Like in Eastern Europe, its major task was to channel Soviet orders down to both the administrative apparatus and the other bloc parties pretending that these were initiatives of its own. It was logical that fulfilment of this task required previous approval not only of any policy decision but statement of position as well.[74] Orders on very minor problems would be given by the occupation authorities on their own. Whenever more important issues were involved, instructions had to be cleared with the CPSU Central Committee apparatus or even with Stalin himself. Proposals resulting from German communist initiative usually elicited detailed comment and correction from Moscow.[75]

The Soviet Military Administration of Germany (SMAG) limited supervision of other parties to general directives and implementation control. If statements or decisions deviated from the described line, reprimand and (notably against persons outside public attention) punishment (which often meant imprisonment, torture, and death) would ensue. Any manipulation and pressure was used to make dissenters comply. Intervention visible in public was avoided if possible.[76] Communists who failed to follow the Kremlin's line or demonstrated spontaneity (which was generally abhorred) suffered the same treatment.[77] Unconditional submission to the USSR was greatly enhanced by Soviet terror exercised notably by the secret police organization "Smersh," which used German auxiliary personnel selected on recommendation by local communists. All kinds of people alleged to be "fascists" and "war criminals" were detained, tortured, and killed. Among them, many had been but ordinary Nazi party members, had been seized by mere coincidence, or even had been Nazi opponents who refused to support communist policy.[78]

The occupation officers set up a "people's police" under their direct control. It was expressly assigned the task to contribute to the enforcement of sociopolitical transformation. In the initial period, an acute shortage of appropriate personnel prevented absolute reliability. Within one and a half years, however, the authorities succeeded in having a 90 percent portion of communist party members.[79] Soviet control extended to any aspect of public life: parties, administration, judiciary, economy, currency, and society. It was enforced by putting "disciplined" cadres into crucial positions and subjecting officials of party and state to a permanent threat of recall and punishment. Licentiation of "antifascist-democratic" parties was conditional on the acceptance of bloc consensus and hence the renunciation of deviating policy. The rules thus imposed were enforced by repression and terror. From the very start, the "bourgeois" parties were subjected to particular restrictions.[80] Organizations of social, professional, and other societal interest such as, notably, trade unions and associations for youths, women, writers, and others were put into an allegedly above-party framework to prevent political differentiation. Their respective apparatus was controlled by communist cadres.[81]

Initiation of the Political Process in the Soviet-Occupied Part of Germany

The Kremlin had agreed to the Anglo-Saxon proposal that political reconstruction in Germany must start from below. Local self-government would be introduced first, then regional representations were to be elected, and only after the population had proven political maturity, nationwide policy making by parties was envisaged.[82] Stalin, however, did not feel that this project continued to serve his purpose when he decided to advocate united Germany. The enforcement of sociopolitical transformation required quick action from "above" rather than a gradualist approach from "below." The Soviet conquest of Berlin and resulting exclusive control had created an opportunity to prejudice development of the country as a whole by determining decision making in the capital. Stalin used the time gained by delaying entrance of the Western garrisons to act unilaterally. Administrative and police structures were introduced to control political and social life in the German capital,[83] and the SMAG also used their authority to make the communists prevail in all sectors.[84] A big metropolitan media network was set up to disseminate propaganda, notably by radio broadcasts, to large parts of the country.[85]

The Soviet effort was also directed at creating accomplished facts to predetermine the fate of Germany as a whole. On 26 May 1945, Stalin ordered the SMAG to prepare for admission of parties and trade unions.[86] Licentiation would be based on fulfilment of Soviet demands. As in Eastern Europe, parties would have to accept bloc politics, while unified organization would apply to societal organizations. These conditions were defined unilaterally but expected to apply not only to Berlin and the Soviet zone but to all of Germany. This became clear by the suggestion that the party offices should claim to be *Reichsleitungen*, that is, leading bodies with authority in the country as a whole. They were made to take residence in the Soviet sector, which would allow the Kremlin to control them on a permanent basis. Even after the Western powers had taken possession of their parts of the city, Soviet supervision and guidance was bound to continue.[87]

To prepare the German communists for the envisaged step and the role assigned to them, Stalin called Ulbricht and other leading functionaries to Moscow. When they arrived on 4 June 1945, Pieck (who had remained in the Soviet capital as he had not been allowed yet to return home) told them that creation of "antifascist-democratic parties" had been envisaged. The communists must work out a document to serve as their political platform. Their task was to assure the working class and the people in general that they would open a way out of the current disaster. A conversation with Stalin, Molotov, Malenkov, and Kaganovich followed. Conclusions were written down by Anton Ackermann and then discussed with Pieck and Dimitrov. The talks also served to prepare decisions on KPD personnel and organization for submission to Soviet party officials. In a second session with Stalin and his aides on 7 June, the final decisions were taken.[88] A number of parties—notably social democrats, catholics, and liberals—would join the communists in a bloc but compete with them for people's support. By giving the communists both lead time and political backing, Stalin wanted to put them into a predominant position. They were instructed to commit the social democrats initially to "unity of action" and then to merge with them, after they had become capable of assimilating them. This, however, would take time.[89]

On the basis of Stalin's order, the SMAG Supreme Commander, Marschal Sokolovskii, announced on 10 June 1945 that "antifascist" parties, trade unions, and organizations would be admitted in the Soviet zone. The communists immediately started party activity. The manifesto, which had been worked out in Moscow, was published one day later. The German communists declared that they were committed to wage a "resolute struggle against militarism, imperialism, and imperialistic war" and emphasized:

> Together with annihilating Hitlerism, it is essential to complete the cause of Germany's democratization, the cause of bourgeois-democratic transformation which started in 1848, to eliminate the feudal remnants completely and to annihilate reactionary old-Prussian militarism with all its economic and political branches.
> We think that the way of imposing the Soviet system to Germany, would be wrong, as this way does not correspond to the present conditions of development in Germany. We rather think that the crucial interests of the German people prescribe another way, namely the way of establishing an antifascist, democratic regime of a parliamentary-democratic republic with all democratic rights and freedoms for the people.[90]

This advocacy of democratic transformation on the basis of bourgeois parliamentarism and explicit rejection of the Soviet system appeared to indicate an intention to take the road of Western democracy. Initiated cadres, however, realized that these sentences had another meaning. Enforcement of the Soviet system was premature since it did not accord to prevailing conditions for the time being. It should also be noted that, in Moscow's verbiage, adherence to "antifascism" implied not simply the rejection of Nazism but a willingness to side with the communists, who allegedly were the only political force to destroy the social roots of "fascism" (which was portrayed as an inherent orientation of the capitalist world generally). In sum, the manifesto carried the same message as Stalin's internal statements on "national roads to socialism" in occupied Eastern Europe.

It was also spelled out what the remarks on elimination of feudal remnants and destruction of the economic and political concomitants of Prussian militarism meant:

6. Expropriation of all property of the nazi bigwigs and war criminals, transfer of this property into the hands of people for disposal by the municipal and regional self-governments bodies.
7. Liquidation of the junkers', the counts' and the princes' big landed property and transfer of all their soil and also its livestock and inventory to the administrations of the provinces, respectively länder, for distribution to peasants ruined and deprived of their possessions by war. It goes without saying that these measures will by no means touch the landed property and the economy of big peasants.

8. Transfer of all enterprises that serve vital public needs (enterprises of transport, suppliers of water, gas, and electricity etc.), and also those enterprises where the proprietors have left, into the hands of the self-government bodies of the municipalities or provinces, respectively länder.[91]

While public ownership of supply works was understood as *per se* salutary and had to be introduced unconditionally, the owners of industrial enterprise and big landed property had allegedly supported Nazism and/or militarism. Struggle against these political forces therefore required depriving them of their economic basis. This, however, was mere pretense.[92] In internal communication, socioeconomic transformation along Soviet lines was declared to be a crucial, if implicit element of the denazificaction and democratization proposal designed for submission to the Western occupation partners.[93]

When, in 1944, the KPD commission had worked out the details of the Soviet action program for Germany, land reform had been envisaged only at a later date, presumably for the reason that an immediate effort to change agrarian ownership would increase chaos and want at the end of the war. The German communist leaders were therefore both surprised and concerned when, during the talks on the manifesto, Stalin told them to go ahead with land reform. They realized that implementing this measure before the collection of crops in the fall would result in enormous losses of food and entail additional hunger and starvation. But they felt unable to question Stalin's wisdom, let alone disobey.[94] As it appears, the Kremlin leader had concluded that it was expedient to exploit the general breakdown in Germany for ridding the country of any limitations to creating conditions for socialist transformation. He also hastened the creation of parties in Berlin to be finished before the Western powers entered the city. When Soviet willingness to allow for centralized party organizations was publicized on 10 June, not much time was left for their admission. While the communists were easily able to found their party and to seek licentiation as early as on 11 June, the other politicians had to precipitate application for admission without due preparation. On 20 June, Ulbricht reported to Marshal Sokolovskii that the first bloc session would be held four or five days ahead.[95]

Misery and want created by early land reform in the Soviet zone increased when bank and insurance company assets, values in safes, and private savings were confiscated without exception. This both transferred an estimated sum of ten billion prewar marks to the USSR and eliminated the major economic resources of the "bourgeoisie." Many firms, notably smaller ones, were deprived of their means to pay debts (which were not cancelled) and thus lost their basis for staying in business. Old and sick people, families with no one to earn money, and a large number of jobless people were left with no financial means to live on.[96] All private banks were closed. A centralist system of public banking was set up under political administration that did not allow for any autonomous business by local branches. The USSR used the money printing machine massively to exact reparations, to pay for occupation expenses, and to fund communist activities. The Western powers were unable to monitor, let alone influence Soviet money production. Galloping devaluation of German currency in all four zones resulted.[97]

Merger of the "Two Working Class Parties"

From the very start, the "restoration of working class unity" by unification of the two "working class parties" had been envisaged not only in Eastern Europe but in Germany as well.[98] In the long run, the personnel basis of the communist party had to be broadened and the social democratic competitor for the workers' allegiance eliminated. Nonetheless, a merger appeared inexpedient before communist preponderance had been asserted beyond doubt and the party had been turned into a Marxist-Leninist "combat organization" to assimilate members of different origin. Unification had to be enforced in this "correct" manner since the party would otherwise be unable to digest a massive influx of doctrinally "uneducated" and "undisciplined" social democrats.[99] Delaying the merger seemed useful also to facilitate relations with the Western occupation partners. Notably the British Labour government was expected to insist on revival of the social democratic party. It would therefore be set up in West Germany irrespective of Soviet attitude. If the two "working class parties" would merge in the East but remain separate in the West (with their major potential at the Ruhr), the Berlin *Reichsleitung* would be incapable of claiming all-German authority among the social democrats. If, however, members of the two parties would express their desire to unite at a later date, the social democrats of all the country would, hopefully, comply. For these reasons, the Moscow cadres in the East opposed immediate merger but wanted "unity of action" as a preparatory step to unification.[100]

Underlying this was the Soviet expectation that communist influence on the "masses" would prevail and put the party into a dominant position. But this was disproved by reality. In summer and fall 1945, the KPD increasingly fell back behind the SPD whose chairman in Berlin, Otto Grotewohl, claimed the leading role for his party. The Kremlin's plan was put in jeopardy by the prospect that the social democrats would demonstrate their talent to rally many more followers behind them when elections were held in 1946. This would not only undermine the communists' claim to political leadership but eliminate the basis for the Soviet practice of exercising indirect control by bloc politics. The SMAG would then be prevented from using the communists as an instrument to impose its policy covertly on the Germans. While the communists would no longer be in a position to make their claim to determine bloc politics appear democratic, the social democrats would not identify with Soviet orders and therefore fail to take the role of translating Soviet will into German policy. The SMAG officer responsible for party affairs, Colonel Tiul'panov, concluded in October 1945 that this had to be prevented. He suggested to his superiors in Moscow that it was crucial to eliminate the SPD before elections. This requirement had to take precedence; the task of digesting the social democratic element was secondary for the time being. The recommendation was supported by the Military Council, and Stalin approved it. The occupation authorities were instructed to concentrate their effort on making the two parties unify. "This fundamental idea" must be given absolute priority.[101] On 6 February 1946, Stalin explained to Ulbricht which steps the communists would have to take.[102]

The SMAG exploited all means of persuasion and compulsion at its disposal to enforce the envisaged merger. It faced both resistance by a big majority of social democrats who wanted to maintain organizational independence, and widespread opposition among the communist rank and file who felt that ideological purity would be put at risk. Preference for commitment to uncorrupted principle was castigated as unacceptable "sectarianism," and reluctant social democrats were accused of taking a "reactionary position." To make the SPD leadership comply, the Soviet side intervened. When, on 20 December 1945, the all-zonal party delegates had rejected organizational unification with an overwhelming majority, Tiul'panov's officers talked with them the whole night. As a result, there was a complete change of attitude: With but one exception, all delegates voted in favor.[103] Notably Grotewohl had been turned into a staunch advocate of the merger. But at lower levels, resistance continued to be strong. While the SMAG was seeking to make the opponents comply notably by subjecting them to prosecution, the advocates of the prospective "socialist unity party" pledged that it would not be oriented at the Soviet system and Marxist-Leninist doctrine. A Western organizational structure would be adopted. In the leading bodies, social democrats and communists would be represented on the basis of "parity." In analogy to the concept of "national roads to socialism" in Eastern Europe, Anton Ackermann proclaimed a "specifically German road to socialism."[104]

The Socialist Unity Party of Germany (Sozialistische Einheitspartei Deutschlands, SED) was set up on 20–21 April 1946. Contrary to the Kremlin's intent, it extended only to the Soviet zone. In West Germany, the social democrats had never accepted Grotewohl as their leader but rallied behind Kurt Schumacher who saw the communists as advocates of foreign interest. For this reason, the SPD in the West had opposed "unity of action" with the communists from the very start. Resistance to merger prevailed also among the social democrats in Berlin. While their chairman Grotwohl strongly advocated organizational unity with the KPD, four-power control of the city prevented the USSR from exercising overt pressure. The opponents succeeded in staging a referendum, which turned out a significant majority for rejection.[105] The Kremlin's attempt to exploit its position in Berlin to extend political influence to Western-occupied territory failed with the other parties as well. The CDU and LDP *Reichsleitungen* proved unable to project their authority onto West Germany. On their own initiative, indigenous leaders there had created regional branches and felt no need to submit to people who accidentally resided in the capital.[106] Soviet assumptions proved wrong that German centralist instincts would shape political development in their country. Regionalism was traditionally strong, and politicians in the eastern zone were suspected of not being able to express their own will. As a result, the political patterns in the Soviet power sphere were accorded recognition only where the Red Army was in control.

FOCUS ON THE SYSTEMIC CHARACTER OF EAST-WEST CONFLICT

More than anything else, discord between the Anglo-Saxon countries and the USSR on Soviet ruthless extraction of any resources from Germany, and Soviet insistence on extreme limitation of its industrial production with no regard for the population's German minimum supply, provided for conflict among the occupation powers. Given that the Kremlin justified its maximalist position largely by fear of renascent German military power, U.S. Secretary of State Byrnes concluded that firm commitment to prevent rearmament of the defeated country would allow for overcoming interallied disagreement. He therefore suggested a pact on long-term German demilitarization in September 1945. When the idea was discussed in the Kremlin, Stalin was favorably inclined but told Molotov not to express particular interest when talking with Byrnes. He felt that the project would be useful also as an instrument to exact concessions. Acceptance of such a treaty should be made conditional on American acceptance of Soviet participation in decision making on Japan, which had surrendered to the United States. In addition to this, Stalin wanted to make sure that an accord on German demilitarization would not serve as a basis for a continuing American presence in Europe. No justification must be allowed for the United States to play the same role there as the USSR. While all GIs would leave Germany soon, Soviet occupation must be maintained for a long time to come.

When, at the London session of the Council of Foreign Minsters in early fall 1945, the Soviet claim for a say in Japanese affairs was rejected by Byrnes and Bevin, Stalin saw this as "the climax of insolence." He told Molotov that assertion by the Anglo-Saxon powers to be allies was mere pretense given that they were unwilling "to listen to us as is proper." By "declin[ing] to discuss our statement," they demonstrated that they "have not even an elementary feeling of respect for their ally." As a result of this difference and other irreconcilable standpoints, negotiations failed completely.[107] In Moscow, the refusal to fulfill Soviet demands was seen as tantamount to forming a political front against the USSR.[108]

In a public speech on 9 February 1946, Stalin expressed belief that the Soviet Union was opposed to the West on grounds of principle. In the long run, the capitalist system was bound to generate war. Since it would inevitably split up into two hostile camps, armed confrontation within the "camp of imperialism" would result. In his perception, this was a law of history, as had been demonstrated by the outbreak of the two world wars in 1914 and 1939. Socialism was invariably promoted by military conflict between capitalist countries, which would eventually end up in a third world war.[109] The Washington State Department was startled by these statements and concluded that Stalin's policy was essentially determined not by pragmatic considerations such as the need for security against another German aggression or desires for recompensation of war damage. Shortly afterward, conflict over the project of a German demilitarization treaty provided further insight into the kind of attitudes that shaped Soviet policy toward the West.

Controversy on the Proposed German Demilitarization Treaty

On 14 February 1946, the Soviet government received a U.S. draft that was discussed with exceptional thoroughness and intensity. The text was submitted to thirty-eight high party, state, and military leaders who unanimously concluded that such a treaty did not accord to the USSR's interest and must be rejected, even though public reaction would be negative. If Germany were politically rehabilitated on the basis of mere compliance with demilitarization requirements, this would undermine Soviet policy and prevent sociopolitical transformation. The project was a very dangerous strategic ploy designed to terminate the Red Army's presence. If the project were implemented, it would eliminate the military fundament for a Soviet role in the future of Europe and, for this reason, had to be viewed as a long-term threat. As Marshal Zhukov surmised, the United States wanted to put an end to occupation of Germany and to make the Soviet troops leave as soon as possible. The Americans would then question the Soviet presence in Poland and also in the Balkans. It would be obnoxious for the USSR if military power would not be allowed to support competition for Germany.

Molotov's deputy Solomon Lozovskii added that the projected treaty would entail liquidation of the occupation zones, withdrawal of the Soviet troops, and unification of Germany. The country would be economically and politically united under U.S. leadership. This would result also in military revival and, after some years, allow for a German-British-American war against the USSR. Stalin agreed. To justify the Soviet position to the public, Molotov prepared a statement explaining that the proposal failed to pay attention to the requirements of both reparations to the USSR and democratization of Germany. Stalin approved the text but eliminated one sentence that said that there would be no need for occupation of German territory any longer, if the ten billion dollar reparation demand were met. As he explained, the international public must be allowed no doubt that the Soviet military presence was absolutely necessary to guarantee eradication of Nazism and militarism by fundamental transformation. The decision to reject the American proposal was taken on the assumption that the United States would withdraw also unilaterally and that, for this reason, there was no need for the USSR to reciprocate.[110]

In a letter to Byrnes on 19 April 1946, Molotov indicated that there were serious objections to the demilitarization treaty project in Moscow but declared willingness to have it put on the agenda of the session of the Council of Foreign Ministers in Paris.[111] When discussion there started, he explained that the draft required "amendment" and "correction." On Byrnes's offer to extend validity from twenty-five to forty years, he made clear that mere demilitarization was not sufficient. Besides the fulfilment of reparations demands, fundamental political, economic, and social restructuring of Germany was required.[112] A TASS commentary justified this by the argument that the military controls imposed on Germany by the 1919 Versailles Treaty had proven useless. The presence of occupation powers was the only means to protect the world from German aggression. The socioeconomic roots of "fascism" must be radically eliminated. In spite of this, TASS went on, the American proposal failed to make allied evacuation conditional on "complete fulfilment of the tasks the allies have undertaken to achieve through this occupation." By pretending that "simple willingness of the German authorities to accept demilitarization" guaranteed peaceful behavior, the United States wanted to rid itself of its commitment to promote lasting eradication of "militarism" and "fascism." The proposed treaty was a "paper curtain" designed to conceal "withdrawal from obligations previously taken or at least to circumvent these decisions."[113]

Soviet argument at the negotiating table conformed to this line. The tone became increasingly aggressive. The Western governments were accused of protecting rather than eradicating German militarism and refusing enforcement of "denazification," "demilitarization," "decartellization," and "democratization" as stipulated at Potsdam and practiced in East Germany.

They were obliged to follow the Soviet example by initiating political, economic, and social transformation: Thus "militarism" and "fascism" would be unrooted and "democratization" achieved. Only if the draft were amended accordingly would the USSR be able to accept it. Predictably, the Western powers failed to comply. The Kremlin responded by blaming them for support of "fascist" tendencies in the defeated country.[114]

Soviet Assessment of U.S. Policy and the World Situation

The Kremlin was frustrated by the occupation partners' refusal to come to meet its systemic demands. This Soviet feeling was underlying when the ambassador in Washington, Nikolai Novikov, assessed mutual relations in a paper which, in Molotov's judgment, was a source of crucial guidance. The author pointed out that, "in the postwar period, the foreign policy of the USA which expresses the imperialistic tendencies of the American monopol capital, is characterized by the endeavor [to dominate the] world." The U.S. had greatly strengthened its economic position throughout the world. Given that war-ridden countries needed supplies, a "perspective of huge good deliveries and capital imports" had opened to its "monpol-capitalistic" leadership. But Washington's calculation had proved wrong that devastation caused by German invasion would greatly weaken the USSR and make it dependent on aid. The Soviet Union had not only preserved its independence but accquired an international position much more stable than previously. "As a result of the historical victories of Soviet weaponry, the Soviet forces are on the territory of Germany and other former enemy countries and provide a guarantee that these countries can't be used for another attack against the USSR." "Transformation on the basis of democratic principles," had created regimes in Bulgaria, Finland, Hungary, and Romania, which had put their stakes in "strengthening and supporting friendly relations with the Soviet Union." The Slavic countries Poland, Czechoslovakia, and Yugoslavia had been liberated by the Red Army and with its support had created "democratic regimes" that cultivated relations with the USSR based on agreements of friendship and mutual assistance.

American policy was shaped by motives of expansion and world domination as was clearly demonstrated by the existence of military bases on islands in the Atlantic and Pacific, part of them at a distance of ten to twelve thousand kilometers from the homeland. In the West, Britain was the only power that had retained some significance. While it competed with the United States, it was also dependent on it, notably in economic respects. London therefore had to support Washington whenever essential. As a result, only the Soviet Union was an obstacle to the enforcement of U.S. designs. For this reason, it had become the major target of American enmity. Novikov emphasized that the Truman Administration departed from Roosevelt's policy of seeking cooperation and understanding between the three allied powers. Influence by "the most reactionary circles of the Democratic Party" had increased. Under the label of bipartisan foreign policy, an evil "unofficial bloc between reactionary Southern Democrats and the Old Guard of Republicans" had been created. The president's decision to choose James Byrnes as secretary of state reflected an anti-Soviet orientation. The ambassador stated:

The "firm" policy with regard to the USSR proclaimed by Byrnes after the rapprochement of the reactionary [part of the] Democrats with the Republicans, is currently the crucial impediment on the road to cooperation between the great powers. It mainly implies that, in the postwar period, the United States does no longer pursue a policy of strengthening cooperation among the Big Three (or Four) but, on the contrary, seeks to undermine unity among these powers. The objective which has been posed, consists of imposing the will of other countries on the Soviet Union.

In pursuit of this policy, the United States would like to abolish the veto in the UNO Security Council for the purpose of anti-Soviet bloc-building and to transform the United Nations into an Anglo-Saxon domain.

The current policy of the American government with regard to relations with the USSR is also directed at limiting or pushing aside Soviet influence in neighboring countries. The USA seek to implement this policy at various international conferences or directly in the respective countries by taking measures which, on the one hand, express support for reactionary forces in former enemy or neighboring countries in order to create impediments for the processes of democratizing these countries and, on the other hand, to secure positions for penetrating American capital into their economies. This policy aims at weakening and undermining the democratic governments at power which are friendly to the USSR and subsequently to replace them by new governments which would pursue a submissive policy dictated by the USA. With regard to this policy, the USA are fully supported by English diplomacy. One of the most important elements of general USA policy directed at limiting the role of the USSR in the postwar world, is its policy relating to Germany. The measures [designed] to strengthen reactionary forces in order to counter democratic transformation which run parallel with completely insufficient demilitarization measures, are taken by the USA in Germany with particular persistence. The American occupation policy fails to seek liquidation of the remnants of German fascism and transformation of German political life on democratic fundaments to make Germany cease being an aggressive force. The USA does not take measures to liquidate monopolistic associations of industrialists on which German fascism relied when preparing for aggression and warfare. No agrarian reform is carried through to liquidate the big landowners who were another reliable pillar of Hitlerism. Additionally, the USA looks forward to terminate allied occupation of German territory prior to fulfilment of the main tasks of occupation which are demilitarization and democratization of Germany. This would create the preconditions for revival of imperialistic Germany which the

USA wants to use on its side in future war. One cannot fail to see that such a policy has a sharply anti-Soviet cutting edge and poses a serious danger to the cause of peace.

Novikov felt that the United States was contemplating war against the USSR and had initiated a campaign to "create an atmosphere of war psychosis among the broad masses" designed to allow maintenance of a big war potential. Looking forward to combat against the Soviet Union, the U.S. imperialists were planning to establish foreign military bases all over the world and exploit German and Japanese military potential.[115]

Intensification of Conflict on Germany

The Kremlin was aware that its public argument to denounce the U.S. demilitarization treaty proposal was not helpful to make the Germans support the Soviet cause. After all, opposition to Eastern sociopolitical transformation was very strong among them. So it was more promising to challenge the West on another issue. Advocacy of centralization (which would challenge the U.S. concept of federalization and French demand for dismemberment), possibly to be complemented by the initiation of a referendum, was expected to attract an enormous majority of the population. Another divisive issue among the occupation powers resulted from previous agreement to hold elections. In January 1946, the SMAG rejected the British proposal to seek agreement on common procedures. Only general principles without practical detail were felt to be acceptable.[116] Against this background, Soviet zone elections were held in the fall. The military authorities were determined to provide for an outcome that would support the SED claim to a "leading role." To this end, a plan of measures had been worked out.[117]

After massive Soviet intervention, the communists won by a very narrow margin. Success resulted from the votes in the countryside where not only repression of opponents was particularly pronounced but also political competition had been altogether prevented by denying registration to the local and district branches of CDU and LDP. In the cities, where there were fewer restrictions, the SED suffered defeat almost anywhere. In Berlin, notably in the Western sectors, voting resulted in complete disaster. The SMAG saw the outcome as most disappointing and employed even more massive pressure and manipulation.[118] Escape from practical implications was sought by transferring administrative control from institutions with parliamentary legitimation to bodies created on the basis of "equal representation," which allowed multiplying the communists' presence by including their comrades at the top of "societal organizations." In addition to this, the central administrations set up in East Berlin in 1945 were equipped with additional powers expressly to facilitate measures of sociopolitical transformation and coordination of economic control.[119] All Soviet zone institutions, notably the police, were subjected to successive centralization from fall 1946 onward.[120] All these measures intensified structural differences between Eastern and Western Germany and ran counter to previous allied agreement.

The principal issue of discord among the four powers, the direction of economic policy in the defeated country, became more acute when the Anglo-Saxon leaders lost hope that shortages of food in their zones might be eased by deliveries from Soviet-occupied territory, let alone regions under Polish administration. This resulted in increased emphasis on the need for a level of German industry that would allow exports to pay for imports. The USSR, however, continued to insist on extremely low production levels, arguing that "economic disarmament" had to take precedence. The view expressed by Stalin at Potsdam, that German suffering was well-deserved and must be ignored, was not shared by the British and American leaders who felt that one could not allow for mass starvation. As long as the policy makers in Washington felt, or at least deemed possible, that Soviet attitudes resulted from genuine fear of German military revival, they were reluctant to side with the British but took an intermediate position to allow for compromise.[121] When, however, Molotov rejected their offer of a guarantee for long-term German demilitarization, they began to reappraise their stance. They increasingly saw a need to put an end to allowing the USSR to make the United States and Britain pay the bill for Soviet reparations and Soviet restrictive policy on Germany. Resentment against the Kremlin increased.[122]

Stalin did not realize that an emotional potential was accumulating. He failed to understand the humanitarian motive underlying food deliveries to West Germany. In his view, the two governments simply wanted to woo the Germans and implant in them an anti-Soviet attitude. British and American exasperation about the need to send food to the defeated country at their own expense was seen as a mere pretense.[123] The Anglo-Saxon demand for economic unity was but an instrument to justify claiming control of the Soviet zone economy.[124] In this perception, maintenance of an uncompromising attitude appeared as a wise policy: Why should the USSR help its Western rivals to save costs for buying German sympathy? This may explain why the Kremlin missed the opportunity to placate Britain and the United States when, in March 1946, it began to substitute dismantlement in its zone by increasing industrial production for reparations. The plants in which Moscow was interested were left in place but taken out of the German economic process and subjected to Soviet management. In the Kremlin's view, this did not interfere with "industrial disarmament."[125] A similar arrangement might have been worked out to allow for major West German production for export required for import of food. The governments in

London and Washington were incensed when the USSR provided for excess production to satisfy its appetite for reparations but continued to reject production for payment of food bills. Another source of exasperation was the Kremlin's failure to accept any proposal for German currency reform, which would have been indispensable for economic recovery. A major Soviet motive was its unwillingness to acquiesce in quadripartite currency control, which was bound to stop unilateral use of the money-printing machine.[126]

Britain and the United States decided to join their efforts in defending their interests against the USSR. The tone was set by Byrnes in his Stuttgart speech of 6 September 1946. He emphasized that the United States did not intend to deny the Germans "the possibility to improve their lot by hard work over the years." Both their well-being and European well-being were interrelated. He assured the audience of U.S. continuing "interest in the affairs of Europe."[127] In Moscow, particular attention was internally paid to Byrnes's statement that the United States was committed to Europe. This was interpreted as a U.S. desire to exploit, under the pretense of a "democratic mission," material superiority for international predominance. Europe had allegedly been assigned a crucial role in this endeavor, while Germany had been chosen as a basis of struggle against the USSR. In this view, the principal U.S. objective was to undercut Soviet influence by both preventing stable rapprochement between the USSR and "democratic Germany" and restoring the defeated country "on a reactionary basis."[128] On 2 December 1946, the United States and Britain signed an agreement on economic fusion of their zones for joint management of the food supply.[129] Stalin internally declared that the accord was contrary to "the common interests of the German people" and served "the special interests of the American monopolist capital" which was "determined to subdue German economy and to exploit it as a basis for expansion in Europe." The Anglo-Saxon "unification of zones" had to be seen as a "unification of occupyers" which left the Germans outside and pertained but to the economic sphere. Hence the needs of genuine unification were declared unmet.[130]

EAST-WEST RELATIONS
ON THE EVE OF OVERT CONFRONTATION

In early 1947, the USSR was increasingly inclined to abandon its regard for cooperation with the West. In the Soviet zone, there was a progressive process of marginalizing the "bourgeois" parties and centralizing the administration to make both political forces outside the SED and elements of federation irrelevant. In Eastern Europe, after peace treaties had been concluded with the former enemy countries, the opposition essentially liquidated, and fundamental steps toward socialism enforced, the Kremlin leaders sought to strengthen control by the communist regimes. They faced a major problem in Czechoslovakia where, in the absence of bloc politics and nationwide socioeconomic transformation, their followers did not have a position of unassailable dominance that would have allowed them to impose socialism on the country. The crucial challenge to the Soviet effort, however, was Germany. Contrary to the original program of action, merger of the "two working class parties" had been prematurely enforced. As a result, a situation had emerged that, at the all-national level, increased rather than reduced antagonism between communists and social democrats. Continuing existence of the SPD as a hostile party in the West denied the SED leaders in the East a powerful instrument to promote Moscow's policy in all of Germany. In the Kremlin's assessment, the adverse situation could be reversed, if the "united working class party" would extend to the Western zones. The message to the workers there, notably in the Ruhr District, that they must support and join an undivided class organization, was seen to be crucial. At the same time, it seemed necessary that the German desire for national unification was satisfied by a strong political force.

Soviet Pressure on Foreign Communists on the Eve of the Cold War

As early as in fall 1946, Moscow had begun to doubt the wisdom of proclaiming "national roads to socialism" and offered as substitution for "class struggle" the phrase "peaceful development." In Eastern Europe, this increased the problem to justify overt repression of opposition groups. Also, the conclusion of peace treaties with the former enemy countries implied a loss of Soviet occupation rights. In Stalin's view, this opened the prospect that national communist leaders would claim a larger measure of more autonomy than he deemed appropriate. When, in late summer 1946, the Hungarian party wanted to convene a conference of the Danube countries, the Kremlin raised objections.[131] In early February 1947, the Soviet party apparatus supported an ordinary Czech party member's suggestion (which may have been initiated by someone higher up) to revive the Comintern and explained that this would be useful for curbing self-willed policy by foreign communists.[132] Shortly before this, a leading apparatchik in Bucharest who had been a Soviet agent for a long time, Emil Bodnăraş, reported to Moscow that deviators in the party were opposing Secretary-General Gheorghiu-Dej. It was necessary to strengthen his position in order to allow him enforcement of envisaged policy.[133] One month later, "nationalistic mistakes within the Romanian communist party" were ascribed to Gheorghiu-Dej and other high-ranking functionaries.[134]

The Central Committee in Moscow also received information by Bodnăraş against his co-leaders Gheorghiu-Dej and Gheorghe Maurer. The final conclusion was that, due to the two leading cadres' attitude, the situation was critical. They were seeking to bolster the ailing economy by developing relations with the United States and Britain. Notably Maurer had gone much further than was acceptable and was disloyal to the USSR. According to Bodnăraş, both had complained about the costs caused by the Soviet occupation troops. Gheorghiu-Dej was even accused of taking open issue with colleagues who, in defense of Soviet performance, disagreed with his policy. It was held in Moscow that the leeway provided by the concept of different "national roads to socialism" had resulted in intolerable deviation. In Hungary, the Kremlin saw a similar situation: The communist leaders there were blamed for often having taken "narrowly nationalist positions."[135]

Early in 1947, the Kremlin generally pressed for overtly enforcing communist dictatorship. Molotov ordered Hungarian party head Rákosi to take a "line of more pronounced class struggle."[136] Elimination of the Small Landowners' Party was finished by May.[137] In Bulgaria, general terrorization and prosecution of the opposition began in February 1947. Stalin was aware that repression was bound to provoke protest among the Western allies but expected simply that short-lived tension would result.[138] In Romania, creation of a "united working class party" to provide a basis for the exercise of exclusive communist power was initiated in February 1947 but, as a result of stubborn resistance among the socialists, a final decision was delayed until early 1948.[139] In Poland, public opposition had been essentially crushed by the end of 1946 but underground activity continued for some time to come.[140]

A major object of Soviet concern was Czechoslovakia. Hope in Moscow was waning that people would rally behind the communist party and enable it to win absolute majority in the upcoming 1948 elections. Instead, the communists increasingly faced rejection and isolation. The Kremlin was concerned and sent an envoy in May 1947 to examine the situation. He came back to report that, with Anglo-Saxon support, the "reactionary elements" intensified their effort, displayed hostility against both communists and the USSR, and praised the virtues of Western democracy. The communist party concentrated its energy on winning a majority in parliament but failed to take decisive action against the opponents' positions in the state apparatus, in the army, in the countryside, among the middle classes, and so on, and to mobilize its human and organizational potential as would have been necessary to counter the effort by the adversaries of people's democracy.[141]

In the Soviet zone, pledges to accept the social democrats as equal partners in the SED had not prevented communist exploitation of cadre superiority and covert bureaus to assert intraparty predominance.[142] Nonetheless, the Kremlin felt that there were far too many Western-democratic elements, and it did not see the SED as a Marxist, let alone Leninist organization.[143] At the same time, it resented the remains of regional administra-

tive autonomy as not being compatible with the Soviet system. These defi-
ciencies had to be overcome as early as the domestic and international situations would allow. The time for this was seen to have come in early 1947.
On 4 February, Stalin approved guidelines for transforming the SED into a
"party of a new [Stalinist] type." As a first step, the parity principle for communists and previous social democrats in leading party positions was not
obligatory any longer.[144] Administrative centralization gained additional
momentum.[145] The police were expressly instructed to support the "antifascist-democratic order" and to "protect" sociopolitical transformation.[146]

The West European communists came under increasing Soviet pressure.
When, in spring 1947, they were thrown out of government in Brussels,
Paris, and Rome, the Kremlin saw this as a failure of its policy of domestic
cooperation with Western democracies. On behalf of the Moscow leadership, Zhdanov turned to French party leader Thorez and expressed deep
concern. Indicating that there were "contradictory and insufficient" press reports, he asked for more detailed information. "Top secret" copies of this
letter were sent to the East European leaders. As previously in relations with
the parties of Czechoslovakia, Hungary, Romania, and Bulgaria, the Kremlin felt that the concept of "national roads to socialism" had become a
source of serious concern. As a result, it appeared doubtful that this aspect
of "compromise" with the West was worth continuing.[147]

Soviet Appeal to German National Feeling

In the Soviet view, advocacy of unity was crucial for making the Germans
side with the USSR (and implicitly the Soviet system) against the West. This
was "class politics" in "national form."[148] As early as in his conversation
with the KPD leaders on 4 June 1945, Stalin had underlined that the bid for
German unity was crucial.[149] The USSR invariably claimed to defend German unity against Western "splitting policies." The East Berlin leaders appealed to "all patriots" to join this struggle.[150] Under Colonel Tiul'panov's
guidance, an SED commission provided guidelines for structures depicted
as reflecting determination to unite all of Germany. In internal exchange,
however, creation of a separate zonal state was equally considered.[151]
The communist party apparatus complemented the effort by preparing
and publishing a draft constitution, which was also designed for a dual
purpose.[152]

Stalin and his SED clients felt that the idea of state centralization was popular among the Germans and planned to exploit this to discredit the West as
an enemy of national unity. If the issue of centralist unity were put before the
people in a referendum, most of them would drop their objections against
proposals of communist origin. At least 60 percent would then vote in support. This outcome might be exploited to claim that it implied approval of

Soviet zone policy. As a result, all-German economic departments would have to be created under supervision by the Allied Control Council. They would be obliged to implement the Potsdam Agreement which, in Moscow's interpretation, envisaged "denazification," "decartellization," "demilitarization," and "democratization" as was already practiced in the Soviet zone. It was also felt that centralist rather than federated structures were helpful in the struggle against the "property-owning classes," notably the "bourgeois," the landlords, and other "reactionaries."[153]

While a separate zonal organization was being prepared to provide for the contingency that the Western powers would not allow for a Soviet-type all-national state, German unification was advocated in public.[154] The SED had to point out that, in contrast to the United States, the USSR was committed to national interest. Stalin explained:

> Germany with its 70-million population cannot be thrown out of history. It equally cannot be excluded from the world market. America is presently making an unsound proposal since one can't do without Germany. The Americans think that they alone can cope with the world market. This is an illusion. They won't cope with it.

After vehement polemics against the United States, Stalin continued that he did not want a weak and dismembered Germany that would become a hotbed of revenge and war (as it had been after World War I).

> This is undesirable for us. This is the kind of the considerations from which we start, not to mention [our] relations of comradeship [with the German communists]. We are very sorry that the German workers are suffering. For the German proletariat to live better, it is necessary to pursue the line which I have outlined here. We think that we as comrades should help the German workers. This is our line [of policy]. But Germany cannot be built without a German government. A government is required to plan taxes [and] laws and to direct the administration. Without political unification of Germany, German economic unification will be a unification of occupiers, with no Germans. The sooner we will create a central government, the better. This is why we are against federalism. If federalism will be practised, then this will lead fairly soon to revenge and war, and the slogan of German unity will pass from our hands into the hands of the bourgeoisie. This is disadvantageous for us. This slogan must not fall out of our hands. If it is not possible to create a central government soon, then it is temporarily necessary to create a central administration. Comrade Stalin thinks that the allies are against a central administration.

After having blamed the Western powers for seeking German unity in words but not deeds, Stalin nonetheless felt that agreement with them might be possible on both central administrations and a body of coordination. This was the position the USSR would defend firmly.[155] In pursuit of his instructions, the SED subsequently claimed championship of German unity and demanded a referendum.[156]

In conformity with Stalin's instruction that argument must appeal to the "masses," emphasis was put on national slogans, not on postulates of "class struggle." The underlying political premise was that most people, notably the workers, would naturally sympathize with the demands raised by the Eastern side but had to be taken out of "reactionary" domination. In accordance with this, "insufficient" communist representation in West German parliaments was explained by restrictions not based on "democracy."[157] Stalin also felt that former Nazis and other rightists must not be neglected as a factor in the struggle for German allegiance. He asked the SED leaders: "Are there many fascist elements in Germany? How many percent? What strength do they represent? Can one approximately tell? Particularly in the Western zones?" Underlying was his supposition that these people might have a major, possibly even decisive, impact in all-German elections. Grotewohl answered affirmatively but expressed the opinion that, given their allegiance to the bourgeois parties, they had to be written off as "reactionaries." Stalin disagreed.

"Can't they be split up?" Grotewohl answers that this can be done on the basis of the referendum. Comrade Stalin remarks: "Before voting?! For example, in the Soviet zone there are its fascists. Can't they be permitted to organize their party under another name? For the purpose of not driving all of them to the Americans." Comrade Stalin says that, with regard to the fascists, they (the SED leaders) have taken course on [their] annihilation. Perhaps it is necessary to complement this course by another course [directed] at attracting [them] so as not to drive all former fascists into the adversaries' camp? Grotewohl objects that as long as nazis are in leading positions in the Western zones, such an SED course would not be understandable to the working people masses in the West. Comrade Stalin says that one would have to do this at home, in the Soviet zone, in order to make the fascists in the Western zones understand that one will not annihilate all of them. Pieck objects that this is impossible. Comrade Stalin remarks: "Impossible? It seems to me that it is possible." Pieck says that, up to now, the SED has made a difference between nominal nazis and active nazis. Against the active nazis, a struggle has been waged. Comrade Stalin asks: [make a difference between] "Not very active nazis and very active nazis?!" Pieck says that such an approach would be very difficult for the SED. Comrade Stalin says that this would not be bad. There had been, after all, patriotic elements in the fascist party. It is necessary to enlist these on our side. Perhaps one can take someone from the medium level of the former nazi party or [someone] of [its] former leaders. Such people are likely to be there.

Ulbricht argued that, notably among young Nazis, many had believed the socialist promise of their party. This should be exploited to split them up after the upcoming Moscow session of the Council of Foreign Ministers had been held. Upon this, Stalin explained that he did not think of making former fascists join the SED. Instead, they must be allowed

> to organize their party on condition that this party will operate in a [common] bloc with the SED. Pieck mentions that many former nazis have already entered the bourgeois parties which exist in the Soviet zone—the CDU and the LDP. Comrade Stalin says that for former nazis some party must be created which would attract the patriots and the inactive elements of the former National-Socialist Party. Then they would not be apprehensive [any longer] that the socialists will annihilate them. Among former fascists there is fear. One must neutralize them. This is a problem of tactics. This implies no surrender of principles. And if another line is taken with regard to the former fascists, it will provide good results. Pieck says that, in the Soviet zone, the nazis have voted for the bourgeois parties. Comrade Stalin answers that this is absolutely [true]. The nazis are afraid of their being annihilated. But one has been eliminating them already sufficiently. One has to relieve those who have not sold themselves [to the bourgeois parties yet] and who can be turned around to [form] a coalition [with the SED]. One must not forget that elements of nazism exist not only in bourgeois strata but within the working class and the petty bourgeoisie as well. Pieck expresses doubt how the Soviet Military Administration in Germany might admit such a party. Comrade Stalin smiles. He, Comrade Stalin, will see to it that they will admit such a party. It might be called "national-democratic party" or somehow else, the name is not important. But the old name must not be given. In this way, one can break up the camp which rallies behind the English and the Americans. Now all of them [i.e., all former nazis] are afraid that in the Soviet zone allegedly all are imprisoned and eliminated. But we will say that this not true. Look here, they have even organized their own party! Perhaps one can build this up. There is nothing unacceptable about it.[158]

Stalin's Plan for "Working Class Unity" in Germany

Stalin had always felt that a united communist, respectively working class, party was crucial for achievement of German state unity after the country had been divided.[159] This implied that creation of the SED in the Soviet zone was a major political deficiency. He therefore argued that it "would be good to have the SED in West Germany," notably in the Ruhr District with its big working class population. "This would be very good. The earlier the better." Stalin expected leftists among the social democrats to follow the example set by East Germans and seek merger with the communists. His SED interlocutors did not share this view: The SPD leaders opposed unification and the Western occupation powers were unwilling to license a "united working class party." The Kremlin leader, however, declared that this situation was not unchangeable.

There [in the West] they are still reading the old program of the communists which says that everything must be destroyed [and] reversed, [that] dictatorship of the proletariat must be set up etc. This frightens many people, also workers. The SED has another platform. The SED's platform look forward to the next objectives of the party, it encompasses the period immediately ahead. Very little is said on the party's final goals. For [attainment of] socialism and communism, the existence of [but] one party is required. This [concealment of final goals] makes entering the party easier for those people who are prejudiced against communism.

Stalin asked the East German communist leaders whether the Western powers demanded that the SPD must be admitted in the Soviet zone. The answer was that they did, even though the social democrats there had merged with the KPD. Upon this, the Kremlin leader confronted the SED triumvirate with a most unexpected suggestion:

"One must admit it [the SPD]. What are you afraid of, ay? Will the unity party break apart?!" The SED Chairman raised the objection that the social democrats would "organize anti-Soviet campaigns." Stalin did not accept this argument saying "that, if the SPD were admitted, it would have a right to criticize only within the limits of what is digestible. Criticism on minor questions is possible but in such a way that one could digest it. There is nothing to be afraid of." He also failed to be impressed by the prospect of SPD election boycott. When he was told that the SED would break apart, he retorted that it "would be very difficult to break the SED up there [i.e. in the Soviet zone]" and emphasized that, in his view, a split in the party would indicate weakness, and added that being afraid of this, meant weakness. He blamed his interlocutors for lack of political manliness and for inclination "to lean on the occupation authorities" rather than to try hard themselves. Their task was to combat "enemy propaganda" by organizing "counterpropaganda." Stalin insisted: "If you can't stand firm, then you are weak altogether," and took the view that prohibiting the SPD would miss the goal. "As long as this group is prohibited, it has an aureole; only if it is admitted, it will have no aureole."[160]

Stalin's plea to legalize the social democratic party in the Soviet zone and to accept the political risks involved can be plausibly ascribed to two motives. With regard to politics in Germany as a whole, the Soviet leader apparently saw direct SED access to the workers in the West, notably in the Ruhr District, as crucial for state unification under Eastern auspices. If this is correct, he must have thought that, while most workers there did not prefer the communists to the social democrats, they would vote for a "united working class party" if given the choice. Recurrent abortive communist attempts to create such a party, at least fictionally,[161] support the assumption. Awareness that the social democratic and communist vote combined was at 46.6 percent in all of Germany, and that the communists greatly surpassed the SPD in membership,[162] may have added to Stalin's feeling that "working class unity" was necessary. With regard to politics in the Soviet zone, the Kremlin leader seems to have believed that, with Soviet support, the communists were sufficiently strong to cope with the social democratic challenge. His remarks can be understood to express contempt for the East German communists if, under these favorable conditions, they would not "stand up against Schumacher," the anticommunist SPD leader. Their aversion did not prevent the Kremlin from instructing the SMAG to prepare for legalization of the social democrats.[163]

Against the background of the upcoming Moscow session of the Council of Foreign Ministers, Soviet diplomats hinted to their Western counterparts that readmission of the SPD was on the agenda.[164] Legalization of a social democratic party in East Germany depended on admission of the SED by the Western powers in their zones. Underlying this was an expectation that some agreement at the prospective Moscow session of the Council of Foreign Ministers would confirm cooperation with the Anglo-Saxon powers, notably Britain (which was in control of the Ruhr District).[165]

The Abortive Moscow Conference

After the allied powers peace treaties had been concluded with all other enemy countries in 1946, the Kremlin insisted that the time had come to reach agreement also on the conditions to be imposed on Germany. Besides enforcement of the reparation and Ruhr demands, it wanted creation of a national government to provide for political unity.[166] As occupation would continue, this implied that Soviet claims to decide on domestic matters not only of its own zone but for Germany as a whole would be confirmed by international accord. Molotov expected the negotiations with the Western allies on this to be difficult and lengthy. The formation of the government could not be achieved at once but only on the basis of a step-by-step approach. A start should be made by creating central administrations. If the USSR would propose to set up a central coalition caucus at the same time, it was doubtful whether the Western powers would agree.[167]

During the Moscow session of the Council of Foreign Ministers on 10 March–24 April 1947, it became clear that decisions on central government and a peace treaty depended on agreement on economic problems. Therefore, discussion focused on the issues of reparations, Ruhr control, the level of industry, export-import plans, the standard of living, currency reform, and economic unity in general. The principal objective of the Anglo-Saxon side was restoration of German economic viability on the basis of self-sufficiency to unburden the taxpayers at home and to make German industrial potential contribute to European recovery. At the same time, a common basis for democratic reconstruction and long-term demilitarization of the defeated country was sought.[168] The USSR took a punitive approach, looked forward to delaying rather than accelerating economic rehabilitation, demanded unconditional fufilment of all reparation claims, and wanted progress toward nationwide socioeconomic transformation. The Potsdam principles of demilitarization, denazification, decartellization, and democratization were once again interpreted as obliging the West to follow the Soviet zone's example. In particular, land reform and control of industry by the central government were required to make Germany a "democratic" and "peaceloving" country.[169]

To provide for German self-sufficiency, Secretary of State Marshall and Bevin wanted accords on food deliveries to their zones, higher levels of industry, joint management of exports and imports, priority for both payment of imports and maintenance of a minimum living standard, termination of production equipment removals, limitation of Soviet reparation claims, and free movement of people, goods, and ideas across zonal borders. Quadripartite control of the German economy, which would neither exclude the Soviet zone nor provide for a special Ruhr regime, was equally deemed indispensable. Molotov uncompromisingly rejected all these demands and insisted that his position had to be accepted to the full extent. He blamed the British and the Americans for having violated the Potsdam obligation on economic unity by the merger of their zones. Marshall and Bevin retorted that they were willing to give it up (bizonia, that is, the unification of the U.S. and British zones) if the USSR would allow for economic unity in all of the country. Marshall tried in vain to make Stalin realize in a personal conversation that the United States could not possibly abandon its position on Germany. Molotov, on his part, posited that the American three to six billion dollar credit under discussion must not be conditional on the Kremlin's willingness to pay its debts under the wartime land lease arrangement.[170]

To overcome the impasse on Germany, Marshall offered a compromise. With Bevin's consent, he was willing to accept reparations from current production contrary to the stipulations at Potsdam, if the USSR would accept higher levels of industry. Increased production would allow for payment of necessary food imports, fulfilment of Soviet reparation demands, and a major contribution to European recovery. This accord would enter into force once a united German administration had been set up. The U.S. foreign minister advocated political and economic unity under a democratic government to guarantee human rights and fundamental freedoms. Molotov was prepared to discuss the proposal only if the United States and Britain would commit themselves to "liquidation of German war potential" (which, in the Kremlin's view, implied strict "economic disarmament"), quadripartite Ruhr control (which would be imposed with no reciprocation by any Western say in East German matters), "decartellization" (a Soviet

code word for eliminating private ownership of industry), and land reform. He also rejected a treaty on long-term German demilitarization as
a guarantee of Soviet security and insisted that, prior to the conclusion
of peace and troop withdrawal, all reparation and "other" demands (allegedly) agreed at Potsdam must be fulfilled. All this was absolutely unacceptable for the Anglo-Saxon power. No compromise resulted even on
minor questions.[171]

Molotov proposed German unification on the condition that, as in the
Soviet zone, "formation and activity of all democratic political parties, and
also of the professional organizations and other societal democratic organizations and institutions" must be permitted all over the country.[172] He privately hinted that, as a reward for the West, readmission of the SPD in East
Germany might be possible.[173] For Marshall and Bevin, agreement on reparations and level of industry was the basis of any accord. When they realized that the USSR was definitely unwilling to accept a compromise on
these issues, they deemed further discussion useless. The Moscow conference ended in total failure.

NOTES

1. General Eisenhower sent a message to Stalin saying that he left conquest of
Berlin to him (Alan Bullock, *Hitler und Stalin—Parallele Leben. Überarbeitete Neuausgabe* (Berlin: Siedler 1999), p. 1157. He also ordered General Patton to refrain from
marching to Prague, which was within his immediate reach (cf. V. V. Mar'ina, "Sovetskii Soiuz i Chekhoslovakiia. 1945 god," *Novaia i noveishaia istoriia*, 3/2005, p. 23).

2. See, inter alia, Gerhard Wettig, *Das Vier-Mächte-Abkommen in der Bewährungsprobe. Berlin im Spannungsfeld von Ost und West* ([West] Berlin: Berlin Verlag 1982,
2nd ed.), pp. 12–25.

3. Aleksej Filitov, "Sowjetische Planungen zur Wiedererrichtung Österreichs
1941–1945," Stefan Karner and Barbara Stelzl-Marx (eds.), *Die Rote Armee in
Österreich. Sowjetische Besatzung 1945–1955. Vol. I: Beiträge* (Vienna: Oldenbourg
2005), pp. 27–28; Peter Ruggenthaler, "Warum Österreich nicht sowjetisiert werden sollte," Karner and Stelzl-Marx (eds.), *Die Rote Armee in Österreich*, pp. 73–76.
It was only for propaganda purposes that maintenance of "Greater Germany" was
advocated when the National Committee Free Germany was put into operation.
The involved Soviet personnel were controlled by the Ministry of Internal Affairs,
which was in no position to make statements on foreign policy: *SSSR i germanskii
vopros 1941–1949. Dokumenty iz Arkhiva vneshnei politiki Rossiiskogo Federatsii*,
ed. Historico-Archival Department of the Russian Ministry of Foreign Affairs
and the Potsdam Center for Contemporary Historical Research, *Vol. I: 22 iiunia
1941 g.–8 maia 1945 g.* (Moscow: "Mezhdunarodnye otnosheniia" 1996),
pp. 126, 301–303; Jörg Morré, *Hinter den Kulissen des Nationalkomitees. Das Institut 99 in Moskau und die Deutschlandpolitik der UdSSR 1943–1946* (Munich: Oldenbourg 2001), pp. 76–82.

4. Natal'ja Lebedeva, "Österreichische Kommunisten im Moskauer Exil," Karner and Stelzl-Marx (eds.), *Die Rote Armee in Österreich*, pp. 46–60; Ruggenthaler, "Warum Österreich nicht sowjetisiert werden sollte," pp. 65–70, 76–78; Stefan Karner and Peter Ruggenthaler, "Unter sowjetischer Kontrolle," Karner and Stelzl-Marx (eds.), *Die Rote Armee in Österreich*, pp. 104–48; Gerald Stourzh, *Um Einheit und Freiheit. Staatsvertrag, Neutralität und das Ende der Ost-West-Besetzung Österreichs 1945–1955* (Vienna: Böhlau 1998), pp. 11–34; Oliver Rathkolb, "Sonderfall Österreich? Ein peripherer Kleinstaat in der sowjetischen Nachkriegsstrategie 1945–1947," Stefan Creuzberger and Manfred Görtemaker (eds.), *Gleichschaltung unter Stalin?Die Entwicklung der Parteien im östlichen Europa 1944–1949* (Paderborn: Schöningh 2002), pp. 353–73.

5. V. V. Kariagin, *Diplomaticheskaia zhizn' za kulisami i na stsene* (Moscow: "Mezhdunarodnye otnosheniia" 1994), pp. 107–8.

6. Jochen Laufer, "Die UdSSR und die Zoneneinteilung Deutschlands (1943/44)," *Zeitschrift für Geschichtswissenschaft*, 4/1995, pp. 324–30.

7. Donal O'Sullivan, *Stalin's "Cordon Sanitaire." Die sowjetische Osteuropapolitik und die Reaktion des Westens 1939–1949* (Paderborn: Schöningh 2003), pp. 274–75.

8. Sven G. Holtsmark, *A Soviet Grab for the High North and Northern Norway 1920–1953* (Oslo: Institutt for Forvarsstudier 1993), pp. 57–64; Sven G. Holtsmark, "The Limits of Soviet Influence: Soviet Diplomats and the Pursuit of Strategic Interests in Norway and Denmark, 1944–47," Francesca Gori and Silvio Pons (eds.), *The Soviet Union and Europe in the Cold War 1943–53* (Basingstoke: Macmillan; New York: St. Martin's Press 1996), pp. 106–24; Bent Jensen, "Sowjetische Okkupation neuen Typs. Die lange Befreiung der dänischen Insel Bornholem 1944 bis 1946," *Osteuropa*, 4/1999, pp. 397–416; "Vvedenie," *SSSR i germanskii vopros. Vol. II: 9 maia 1945 g.—3 oktiabria 1946 g.* (Moscow: "Mezhdunarodnye otnosheniia" 2000), p. 46; Elena Semënova and Boris Chavkin (eds.), "Aus den persönlichen Tagebüchern des sowjetischen Diplomaten V. S. Semenov," *Forum für osteuropäische Ideen- und Zeitgeschichte*, 2/2004, p. 252; Norman M. Naimark, "Stalin and Europe in the Postwar Period 1945–53: Issues and Problems,"*Journal of Modern European History 2*, no. 1 (2004), pp. 36–38.

9. In the first postwar years, Finland was already seen to follow the same political direction as the East European satellite countries, cf. N. V. Novikov to V. M. Molotov, 27 September 1946, *Sovetsko-amerikanskie otnosheniia 1945–1948. Rossiia XX vek. Dokumenty pod obshchei redaktsiei Akademika A.N. Iakovleva* (Moscow: Izdatel'stvo "Materik" 2004), p. 313.

10. Hermann Beyer-Thoma, *Kommunisten und Sozialdemokraten in Finnland 1944–1948* (Wiesbaden: Harrassowitz 1990), pp. 24–47.

11. As a characteristic Soviet evaluation of the international situation see the comprehensive memorandum by I. M. Maiskii for V. M. Molotov, 11 January 1944, *SSSR i germanskii vopros*, I, pp. 355–60.

12. John Lewis Gaddis, *We Now Know. Rethinking Cold War History* (Oxford: Clarendon Press 1998), p. 41; O'Sullivan, *Stalin's "Cordon Sanitaire,"* pp. 284, 289; V. Batiuk and D. Evstaf'ev, *Pervye zamoroski. Sovetsko-amerikanskie otnosheniia v 1945–1950 gg.* (Moscow: Rossiiskii nauchnyi fond 1995), pp. 91–100; N. V. Novikov to J. F. Byrnes, 15 March 1945, *Sovetsko-amerikanskie otnosheniia 1945–1948,* pp. 175–76; N. V. Novikov to D. Acheson, 17 May 1946, *Sovetsko-amerikanskie*

otnosheniia 1945–1948, pp. 229–30; conversation V. M. Molotov–W. Bedell Smith, 30 December 1946, *Sovetsko-amerikanskie otnosheniia 1945–1948*, pp. 357–60; conversation V. M. Molotov–W. Bedell Smith, 5 April 1947, *Sovetsko-amerikanskie otnosheniia 1945–1948*, p. 393; conversation V. M. Molotov–W. Bedell Smith, 9 April 1947, *Sovetsko-amerikanskie otnosheniia 1945–1948*, p. 395; conversation I. V. Stalin–G. K. Marshall, 15 April 1947, *Sovetsko-amerikanskie otnosheniia 1945–1948*, pp. 407–408; N. V. Novikov to D. Acheson, 25 April 1947, *Sovetsko-amerikanskie otnosheniia 1945–1948*, p. 421; conversation N. V. Novikov–W. L. Clayton, 15 July 1947, *Sovetsko-amerikanskie otnosheniia 1945–1948*, pp. 430–32 (in retrospect).

13. I. M. Maiskii for V. M. Molotov, 11 January 1944, *SSSR i germanskii vopros, I*, p. 359.

14. Cf. I. V. Bystrova, "Voenno-ekonomicheskaia politika SSSR: ot 'demilitarizatsii' k gonke voruzhenii," A. O. Chubar'ian (ed.), *Stalinskoe desiatiletie kholodnoi voiny. Fakty i gipotezy* (Moscow: "Nauka" 1999), pp. 171–87 (notably pp. 171–82).

15. Cf. report by V. D. Sokolovskii and V. S. Semënov on their conversation with W. Bedell Smith on 28 March 1946, *Sovetsko-amerikanskie otnosheniia 1945–1948*, pp. 188–90.

16. I. M. Maiskii to V. M. Molotov, 25 November 1945, *SSSR i germanskii vopros, II*, p. 295.

17. Report on conversation I. V. Stalin–W. Gomułka (English transl.), 14 November 1945, *Cold War International History Project Bulletin* 11 (Winter 1998), p. 136.

18. M. M. Litvinov to V. M. Molotov, 15 October 1943, *SSSR i germanskii vopros, I*, p. 316.

19. *Keesings Archiv der Gegenwart, Vol. XV (1945)* (Frauenfeld: Huber and Co, undated [1946]), 147A, 166B, 299B; *Sto sorok besed s Molotovym. Iz dnevnika F. Chueva* (Moscow: "Terra" 1991), pp. 102–3.

20. Peter J. Stavrakis, *Moscow and Greek Communism, 1944–1949* (Ithaca, NY, and London: Cornell University Press 1989), pp. 61–62.

21. *Foreign Relations of the United States [FRUS]. Diplomatic Papers, The Conference of Berlin (The Potsdam Conference) 1945* (Washington D.C.: Government Printing Office 1960), pp. 265–66, 301–5, 312–14, 365–67, 372–73.

22. Vladimir Pechatnov, ed., "'Soiuzniki nazhimaiut tebia dlia togo, chtoby slomit' u tebia voliu . . .' (Perepiska Stalina s Molotovym i drugimi chlenami Politbiuro po vneshnepoliticheskim voprosam v sentiabr–dekabr 1945 g.)," *Istochnik*, 2/1999, p. 72.

23. *Germany 1947–1949. The Story in Documents*, Department of State Publication 3556 (Washington D.C.: Government Printing Office 1950), pp. 47–57 (see pp. 54–55).

24. Conversation V. M. Molotov–D. F. Byrnes, 14 September 1945, *Sovetsko-amerikanskie otnosheniia 1945–1948*, pp. 13–15; Pechatnov, "'Soiuzniki,'" pp. 70–74; G. K. Agafonova, "Diplomaticheskii krizis na Londonskoi sessii SMID," A. O. Chubar'ian, *Stalin i kholodnaia voina* (Moscow: Institut vseobshchei istorii RAN 1997), pp. 68–72; *Sto sorok besed*, p. 103.

25. Vladimir Pechatnov, "'Na ètom voprose my slomaem antisovetskoe uporstvo . . .' (Iz perepiski Stalina s Molotovym po vneshnepoliticheskim delam v 1946 godu)," *Istochnik*, 3/1999, pp. 92–93.

26. Pechatnov, "'Na étom voprose,'" p. 93.

27. Pechatnov, "'Na étom voprose,'" pp. 100–101.

28. A. A. Gromyko to E. R. Stettinius, 23 July 1945, *Sovetsko-amerikanskie otnosheniia 1945–1948*, pp. 26–27.

29. N. D. Smirnova, "'Grecheskii vopros' na Parizhskoi mirnoi konferentsii," Chubar'ian, *Stalin i kholodnaia voina*, pp. 10–12.

30. Laurent Rucker, *Moscow's Surprise. The Soviet-Israeli Alliance of 1947–1949*, Cold War International History Project, Working Paper No. 46 (Washington D.C.: Woodrow Wilson International Center for Scholars, July 2005).

31. N. Egorova, "'Iranskii krizis' 1945–1946 gg.: Vzgliad iz rossiiskikh arkhivov," M. M. Narinskii (ed.), *Kholodnaia voina. Novye podkhody, novye dokumenty* (Moscow: Institut vseobshchei istorii RAN 1995), pp. 294–314; V. M. Molotov to W. A. Harriman, 29 November 1945, *Sovetsko-amerikanskie otnosheniia 1945–1948*, pp. 118–20.

32. Egorova, "'Iranskii krizis,'" p. 99.

33. Quoted by Mar'ina, "Sovetskii Soiuz i Chekhoslovakiia," Chubar'ian, *Stalin i kholodnaia voina*, p. 11.

34. Mar'ina, "Sovetskii Soiuz i Chekhoslovakiia," p. 11.

35. Mar'ina, "Sovetskii Soiuz i Chekhoslovakiia," pp. 11–12, 20.

36. Mar'ina, "Sovetskii Soiuz i Chekhoslovakiia," pp. 12, 21–24.

37. Harald Moldenhauer, "'Ihr werdet Euch dem Sozialismus ohne blutigen Kampf annähern.' Kommunistische Blockpolitik und 'Gleichschaltung' der Parteien in Polen," Creuzberger and Görtemaker (eds.), *Gleichschaltung unter Stalin?* pp. 102–7. See, inter alia, conversation I. V. Stalin–W. Gomułka and G. Mints, 14 November 1945, *Vostochnaia Evropa I v dokumentakh rossiiskikh arkivov 1944–1953 gg.*, ed. Rossiiskaia Akademiia Nauk/Institut slavianovedeniia i balkanistiki/Rossiiski Tsentr khraneniia i izucheniia dokumentov po noveishei istorii/Gosudarstvennyi arkhiv Rossiiskoi Federatsii, Vol. I (Moscow and Novosibirsk: "Sibirskii khronograf" 1997), pp. 301–3.

38. Moldenhauer, "'Ihr werdet Euch dem Sozialismus ohne blutigen Kampf annähern,'" Creuzberger and Görtemaker, *Gleichschaltung unter Stalin?* pp. 108–9, 115; conversation I. V. Stalin–B. Bierut, E. Osóbka-Morawski, 24 May 1946, *Vostochnaia Evropa, I*, pp. 443–63.

39. Moldenhauer, "'Ihr werdet Euch dem Sozialismus ohne blutigen Kampf annähern,'" pp. 109–14; conversation I. V. Stalin–E. Osóbka-Morawski, St. Szwalbe, Ju. Cyrankiewicz, 19 August 1946, *Vostochnaia Evropa, I*, pp. 505–13.

40. Moldenhauer, "'Ihr werdet Euch dem Sozialismus ohne blutigen Kampf annähern,'" pp. 114–20; N. V. Petrov, "Rol' MGB v sovetizatsii Pol'shi: referendum i vybory 1946–1947 gg.," Chubar'ian, *Stalinskoe desiatiletie kholodnoi voiny*, pp. 102–24.

41. Ulrich Burger, "Von der Zusammenarbeit über die Konfrontation zur Auflösung. Die Strategie der Kommunisten in Rumänien zur Gleichschaltung des Parteiensystems zwischen 1944 und 1948," Creuzberger and Görtemaker (eds.), *Gleichschaltung unter Stalin?* pp. 145–49. See also the documents in T. V. Volokitina, G. P. Murashko, and A. P. Noskova (eds.), *Tri vizita A.Ia. Vyshinskogo v Bukharest 1944–1946. Dokumenty rossiiskikh arkhivov* (Moscow: ROSSPĖN 1998), p. 116–228; *Vostochnaia Evropa, I*, pp. 88–94, 109–11, 162–70, 196, 207–9, 212–13, 246–48, 252–54, 320–25, 365–68.

42. A. Ia. Vyshinskii to W. A. Harriman, 10 September 1945, *Sovetsko-amerikanskie otnosheniia 1945–1948*, pp. 9–11; A. Ia. Vyshinskii to W. A. Harriman, 11 September

1945, *Sovetsko-amerikanskie otnosheniia 1945–1948*, pp. 11–15; V. M. Molotov to J. F. Byrnes, 16 September 1945, *Sovetsko-amerikanskie otnosheniia 1945–1948*, pp. 20–25; conversation V. M. Molotov–J. F. Byrnes, 19 September 1945, *Sovetsko-amerikanskie otnosheniia 1945–1948*, pp. 28–33; conversation V. M. Molotov–J. F. Byrnes, 20 September 1945, *Sovetsko-amerikanskie otnosheniia 1945–1948*, pp. 33–35; Pechatnov, "'Soiuzniki,'" pp. 71–72.

43. Conversation I. M Maiskii–W. A. Harriman, 12 December 1945, *Sovetsko-amerikanskie otnosheniia 1945–1948*, p. 124; conversation V. M. Molotov–J. F. Byrnes, 18 December 1945, *Sovetsko-amerikanskie otnosheniia 1945–1948*, pp. 130–36; Burger, "Von der Zusammenarbeit über die Konfrontation zur Auflösung," Creuzberger and Görtemaker (eds.), *Gleichschaltung unter Stalin?* p. 149.

44. A. Ia. Vyshinskii to V. M. Molotov, 1 January 1946, *Sovetsko-amerikanskie otnosheniia 1945–1948*, pp. 139–40; report by A. Ia. Vyshinskii to Moscow, 8 January 1946, *Sovetsko-amerikanskie otnosheniia*, pp. 141–42; V. G. Dekanozov to G. F. Kennan, 17 January 1946, *Sovetsko-amerikanskie otnosheniia*, pp. 146–47.

45. Burger, "Von der Zusammenarbeit über die Konfrontation zur Auflösung," Creuzberger and Görtemaker (eds.), *Gleichschaltung unter Stalin?* pp. 149–63. See, inter alia, conversation V. M. Molotov and G. M. Malenkov–G. Gheorghiu-Dej and T. Georgescu, 2 April 1946, *Vostochnaia Evropa*, *I*, pp. 399–402, and the documents in Volokitina, Murashko, and Noskova (eds.), *Tri vizita A.Ia. Vyshinskogo*, pp. 116–228.

46. Marietta Stankova, "Das parteipolitische System in Bulgarien 1944–1949. Äussere Einflüsse und innere Faktoren," Creuzberger and Görtemaker (eds.), *Gleichschaltung unter Stalin?* pp. 189–212; conversation V. M. Molotov–J. F. Byrnes, 18 December 1945, *Sovetsko-amerikanskie otnosheniia 1945–1948*, pp. 130–36; N. V. Novikov to J. F. Byrnes, 7 March 1946, *Sovetsko-amerikanskie otnosheniia 1945–1948*, pp. 174–75.

47. Bela Zhelitski, "Postwar Hungary, 1944–1946," Norman Naimark and Leonid Gibianskii (eds.), *The Establishment of Communist Regimes in Eastern Europe 1944–1949* (Boulder, CO: Westview 1997), pp. 76–91; János M. Rainer: "Der Weg der ungarischen Volksdemokratie. Das Mehrparteiensystem und seine Beseitigung 1944–1949," Creuzberger and Görtemaker (eds.), *Gleichschaltung unter Stalin?* pp. 326–45. See, inter alia, K. E. Voroshilov to I. V. Stalin and V. Molotov, 22 October 1945, *Vostochnaia Evropa*, *I*, pp. 271–75; K. E. Voroshilov to I. V. Stalin and V. M. Molotov, 13 November 1945, *Vostochnaia Evropa*, *I*, pp. 299–301; K. E. Voroshilov to I. V. Stalin and V. M. Molotov, 14 November 1945, *Vostochnaia Evropa*, *I*, pp. 303–5.

48. Paul E. Zinner, *Communist Strategy and Tactics in Czechoslovakia, 1918–48* (New York and London: Praeger 1963), pp. 117–86; JiYí Kocian, "Vom Kaschauer Programm zum Prager Putsch. Die Entwicklung der politischen Parteien in der Tschechoslowakei in den Jahren 1944–1948," Creuzberger and Görtemaker (eds.), *Gleichschaltung unter Stalin?* pp. 303–13; Igor Lukes, "The Czech Road to Communism," Naimark and Gibianskii (eds.), *The Establishment of Communist Regimes*, pp. 248–50.

49. Ivo Banac, *With Stalin Against Tito. Cominformist Splits in Yugoslav Communism* (Ithaca, NY, and London: Cornell University Press 1988), pp. 31–32.

50. Note by V. M. Molotov, undated [4 January 1945 at latest], *Vostochnaia Evropa,*
I, pp. 117–18; conversation I. V. Stalin–A. Hebrang, 9 January 1945, *Vostochnaia*
Evropa, I, pp. 118–33; Geoffrey Swain, "Stalin's Vision of the Postwar World," *Diplo-*
macy and Statecraft 7, no. 1 (March 1996), pp. 87–88; N. D. Smirnova, "'Grecheskii
vopros' na parizhskoi mirnoi konferentsii," Chubar'ian, *Stalin i kholodnaia voina,* pp.
8–10; Stavrakis, *Moscow and Greek Communism,* pp. 26–40.
51. Stavrakis, *Moscow and Greek Communism,* pp. 15–20. To be sure, the USSR had
annexed territories from both Poland and Czechoslovakia which were recognized to
be members of the wartime alliance. This, however, was officially seen as voluntar-
ily ceded: The Polish government had accepted to cede the Eastern parts of the country in exchange for being given German provinces in the West, and President Beneš
was willing to give up the Ukrainian-inhabitated region not only to come to meet
Soviet desires but to get rid of an ethnic group he saw as a liability for his nation
state.
52. L. Ia. Gibianskii, "Stalin i triestskoe protivostoianie 1945 g.," Chubar'ian,
Stalin i kholodnaia voina, pp. 44–62; G. K. Agafonova, "Diplomaticheskii krizis na
Londonskoi sessii SMID," Chubar'ian, *Stalin i kholodnaia voina,* pp. 63–68.
53. Directives for the Soviet delegation to the Paris session of the Council of For-
eign Ministers, 19 April 1946, *Sovetsko-amerikanskie otnosheniia 1945–1948,* p. 206;
conversation V. M. Molotov–J. F. Byrnes, 21 June 1946, pp. 268–69; conversation
V. M. Molotov–J. F. Byrnes, 24 June 1946, pp. 271–75; conversation V. M.
Molotov–J. F. Byrnes, 25 June 1946, pp. 276–80; conversation V. M. Molotov–J. F.
Byrnes, 2 July 1946, pp. 281–85; conversation V. M. Molotov–J. F. Byrnes, 25
November 1946, pp. 335–38 (all citations from the volume *Sovetsko-amerikanskie*
otnosheniia 1945–1948); Pechatnov, "'Na etom voprose,'" pp. 93–102.
54. Leonid Gibianskii, "The Soviet-Yugoslav Split and the Cominform,"
Naimark and Gibianskii (eds.), *The Establishment of Communist Regimes,*
pp. 291–92.
55. Banac, *With Stalin Against Tito,* pp. 34–36; Stavrakis, *Moscow and Greek Com-*
munism, pp. 138–59.
56. Ia. M. Lomakin to A. Ia. Vyshinskii, 19 April 1947, *Sovetsko-amerikanskie*
otnosheniia 1945–1948, pp. 414–17.
57. On Soviet interpretation and implementation: A. Ia. Vyshinskii to V. M.
Molotov, 5 July 1945, *SSSR i germanskii vopros, II,* pp. 175-78.
58. This position resulted from bad experience after World War I when economic
burdens imposed on Germany had both politically destabilized the country and
eventually forced the British and notably the Americans to help out by granting major credits and arranging for alleviated long-term repayment schedules.
59. Gisela Biewer, "Zur Einführung," *Dokumente zur Deutschlandpolitik,* ed. by the
Federal Ministry of the Interior, Series II, 1/1 (Kriftel: Metzner 1992), pp. xix–xxiii.
Cf. the documents in FRUS. *The Potsdam Conference,* pp. 218, 262, 383–84, 388–91,
and the explanations by Norman M. Naimark, *Fires of Hatred. Ehtnic Cleansing*
in Twentieth Century Europe (Cambridge, MA: Harvard University Press 2001),
pp. 109–13. For the number pouring into the British and American zones
see Bernd Lindner, "Trennung, Sehnsucht und Distanz. Deutsch-deutsche
Verwandtschaftsverhältnisse im Spiegel der Zeitgeschichte," *Deutschland Archiv,*
6/2004, p. 902.

60. Cf. K. I. Koval', "Rabota v Germanii po zadaniiu GKO," *Novaia i noveishaia istoriia*, 2/1995, pp. 104–5.

61. Biewer, "Zur Einführung," *Dokumente zur Deutschlandpolitik, II, 1/1*, pp. xxiii–xxv.

62. For the Soviet position on reparations see W. A. Harriman to V. M. Molotov, 7 September 1945, *Sovetsko-amerikanskie otnosheniia 1945–1948*, pp. 17–20; A. Ia Vyshinskii to G. F. Kennan, 16 September 1945, *Sovetsko-amerikanskie otnosheniia 1945–1948*, pp. 15–17; message by the Soviet government to the U.S. government, 27 February 1946, *Sovetsko-amerikanskie otnosheniia 1945–1948*, pp. 170–72; V. M. Molotov to M. I. Dratvin and V. S. Semënov, 26 March 1946, *Sovetsko-amerikanskie otnosheniia 1945–1948*, pp. 186–87; conversation V. M. Molotov–J. F. Byrnes, 12 July 1946, *Sovetsko-amerikanskie otnosheniia 1945–1948*, pp. 287–90.

63. Biewer, "Zur Einführung," *Dokumente zur Deutschlandpolitik, II, 1/1*, p. xxv. For the Soviet demand of quadripartite control of the Ruhr district see directive to the Soviet delegation at the Paris session of the Council of Foreign Ministers, 13 May 1946, *Sovetsko-amerikanskie otnosheniia 1945–1948*, p. 228; preparatory paper by M. M. Litvinov, 5 July 1945, *SSSR i germanskii vopros, II*, pp. 171–74.

64. Paper by M. M. Litvinov, undated [early September 1945], *SSSR i germanskii vopros, II*, p. 233; I. M. Maiskii to V. M. Molotov, 29 November 1945, *SSSR i germanskii vopros, II*, pp. 295–96; paper by M. M. Litvinov, 15 December 1945, *SSSR i germanskii vopros, II*, p. 303; K. V. Novikov, A. A. Smirnov, S. P. Kozyrev to V. M. Molotov, V. G. Dekanozov, 31 January 1946, *SSSR i germanskii vopros, II*, pp. 354–61; F. E. Bokov to V. M. Molotov, 16 March 1946, *SSSR i germanskii vopro, II*, pp. 394–407; directives for the Moscow session of the Council of Foreign Ministers, 1 February 1947, *SSSR i germanskii vopros, Vol. III: 6 oktiabria 1946 g.–15 iiunia 1948 g.* (Moscow: "Mezhdunarodnye otnosheniia" 2003), pp. 264–65.

65. See in particular Pechatnov, "'Na ètom voprose,'" pp. 96–97.

66. A. A. Smirnov and V. S. Semënov to A. Ia. Vyshinskii, 4 July 1945, *SSSR i germanskii vopros, II*, pp. 169–71; "Vvedenie" [with reference to related documents], *SSSR i germanskii vopros, II*, pp. 60–65; Frank Zschaler, "Die Entwicklung einer zentralen Finanzverwaltung in der SBZ/DDR 1945–1949/50," Hartmut Mehringer (ed.), *Von der SBZ zur DDR. Sondernummer Schriftenreihe der Vierteljahreshefte fuer Zeitgeschichte* (Munich: Oldenbourg 1995), p. 102; Jochen Laufer, "Konfrontation oder Kooperation? Zur sowjetischen Politik in Deutschland und im Alliierten Kontrollrat," Alexander Fischer (ed.), *Studien zur Geschichte der SBZ/DDR* (Berlin: Duncker and Humblot 1993), p. 68; Biewer, "Zur Einführung," *Dokumente zur Deutschlandpolitik II, 1/1*, pp. xviii–xix.

67. Report on conversation V. M. Molotov–G. Catroux, 24 August 1945, pp. 220–27; V. S. Semënov to A. A. Sobolev, 16 October 1945, pp. 264–65; A. A. Smirnov to V. M. Molotov, 27 October 1945, pp. 278–79; A. A. Smirnov to V. M. Molotov, 3 December 1945, pp. 300–301; V. S. Semënov to G. K. Zhukov, 18 December 1945, pp. 310–12; A. A. Smirnov to V. G. Dekanozov, 23 January 1946, pp. 347–48 (all citations from the volume *SSSR i germanskii vopros, II*); Gunther Mai, *Der Alliierte Kontrollrat in Deutschland 1945–1948. Alliierte Einheit—deutsche Teilung?* (Munich: Oldenbourg 1995), pp. 106–10.

68. "Einführung," Gerhard Keiderling (ed.), *"Gruppe Ulbricht" in Berlin April bis Juni 1945. Von den Vorbereitungen im Sommer 1944 bis zur Wiedergründung der KPD im Juni 1945. Eine Dokumentation* (Berlin: Berlin Verlag 1993), pp. 64–82; Wolfgang

Leonhard, *Die Revolution entlässt ihre Kinder* (Cologne: Kiepenheuer and Witsch 1955), pp. 381–89; Friederike Sattler, "Bündnispolitik als politisch-organisatorisches Problem des zentralen Parteiapparats der KPD 1945/46," Manfred Wilke (ed.), *Die Anatomie der Parteizentrale. Die KPD/SED auf dem Weg zur Macht* (Berlin: Akademie Verlag 1998), pp. 119–212.

69. Peter Erler, "Zur Sicherheitspolitik der KPD/SED 1945–1949," Siegfried Suckut and Walter Süss (eds.), *Staatspartei und Staatssicherheit. Zum Verhältnis von SED und MfS* (Berlin: Ch. Links 1997), p. 82; Thomas Lindenberger, "Die Deutsche Volkspolizei (1945–1990)," Torsten Diedrich, Hans Ehlert, Rüdiger Wenzke (eds.), *Im Dienste der Partei. Handbuch der bewaffneten Organe der DDR* (Berlin: Ch. Links 1998), pp. 97–98; Monika Tantzscher, "Vorläufer des Staatssicherheitsdienstes," *Jahrbuch für Historische Kommunismusforschung*, 1998, pp. 134–37. See also I. A. Serov to S. N. Kruglov, 26 June 1946, GARF, 9401, 2, 138, pp. 49–57; P. M. Mal'kov to M. G. Gribanov, 19 August 1947, AVPRF, 0457a, 4, 19, 48, pp. 24–35.

70. For a particularly vivid account see Leonhard, *Die Revolution*, pp. 355–58 (quotation on p. 358).

71. Morré, *Hinter den Kulissen des Nationalkomitees*, pp. 156–69; Laure Castin-Chaparro, *Puissance de l'URSS, misères de l'Allemagne. Staline et la question allemande, 1941–1955* (Paris: Publications de la Sorbonne 2002), pp. 114–28; Pieck's notes on talks with, and instructions by, high-ranking Soviet representatives: Rolf Badstübner and Wilfried Loth (eds.), *Wilhelm Pieck—Aufzeichnungen zur Deutschlandpolitik 1945–1953* (Berlin: Akademie Verlag 1994), pp. 137–43, 147–51, 161–89. For correspondence with Dimitrov and other high-ranking officials see Keiderling (ed.), *"Gruppe Ulbricht,"* pp. 296–301, 312–16, 318–19, 323, 327–28, 331–35, 338, 340–44, 348–54, 359, 361–62, 369–72, 374–77, 385–88, 402–3, 405–14, 416–17, 430–31, 435–40, 470–72.

72. Alexei Filitov, "The Soviet Administrators and Their German 'Friends,'" Naimark and Gibianski (eds.), *The Establishment of Communist Regimes*, pp. 111–22; Gerhard Wettig, "Die sowjetische Besatzungsmacht und der politische Handlungsspielraum in der SBZ," Ulrich Pfeil (ed.), *Die DDR und der Westen. Transnationale Beziehungen 1949–1989* (Berlin: Ch. Links Verlag 2001), pp. 39–62; Gerhard Wettig, "Autonomy and Dependence. The East German Regime's Relationship with the USSR, 1945–1949," Laurence McFalls and Lothar Probst (eds.), *After the GDR. New Perspectives on the Old GDR and the Young Länder* (Amsterdam and Atlanta, GA: Rodopi 2001), pp. 49–75; Alexandr Haritonow, *Ideologie als Institution und soziale Praxis. Die Adaption des höheren sowjetischen Parteischungssystems in der SBZ/DDR (1945–1965)* (Berlin: Akademie Verlag 2004), pp. 5–8, 58, 77–79, 157, 160, 163; Johannes Raschka, "Kaderlenkung durch die Sowjetische Militäradministration in Sachsen," Rainer Behring and Mike Schmeitzner (eds.), *Diktaturdurchsetzung in Sachsen. Studien zur Genese der kommunistischen Herrschaft 1945–1952* (Cologne: Böhlau 2003), pp. 51–78; report on the SED Party Board plenum, 19–20 June 1946, Bernd Bonwetsch [Bonvech], Gennadij Bordjugov, and Norman M. Naimark (eds.), *Sowjetische Politik in der SBZ 1945–1949. Dokumente zur Tätigkeit der Propagandaverwaltung (Informationsverwaltung) der SMAD unter Sergej Tjul'panov* (Bonn: Dietz Nachf. 1998), p. 41.

73. Protocol of session of the Soviet Central Committee commission set up for investigation of Colonel Tiul'panov's Administration for Propaganda (excerpts), 19

September 1946, Bernd Bonvech, Gennadij Bordiugov, and Norman Neimark (eds.), *SVAG. Upravlenie propagandy (informatsii) i S. I. Tiul'panov. 1945–1949* (Moscow: "Rossiia molodaia" 1994), pp. 182–83.

74. Norman Naimark, "Die SMAD und die Frage des Stalinismus," *Zeitschrift für Geschichtswissenschaft*, 4/1995, p. 306. Cf. Pieck's notes on conversation with Marshal Bokov, 23 January 1946, Badstübner and Loth (eds.), *Wilhelm Pieck*, pp. 63–65; "information" by I. A. Serov, 7 August 1946, Badstübner and Loth (eds.), *Wilhelm Pieck*, pp. 77–79; "information" provided by A. G. Russkikh, 3 November 1948, Badstübner and Loth (eds.), *Wilhelm Pieck*, p. 242; "information" provided by M. A. Suslov, 28 January 1949, Badstübner and Loth (eds.), *Wilhelm Pieck*, p. 274.

75. Cf. S. I. Tiul'panov to M. A. Suslov (excerpt), 27 September 1947, Bonvech, Bordiugov, and Neimark, *SVAG.*, pp. 87–95; preparation of the statements to be presented by SED leaders during their stay in Moscow on 16–18 September 1949, Badstübner and Loth (eds.), *Wilhelm Pieck*, pp. 293–309. This document has also been printed in *Aus Politik und Zeitgeschichte. Beilage zur Wochenzeitung "Das Parlament,"* B 5/91, 25 Jan. 1991, pp. 12–14.

76. For details see Siegfried Suckut (ed.), *Blockpolitik in der SBZ/DDR. 1945–1949. Die Sitzungsprotokolle des zentralen Einheitsfrontausschusses* (Cologne: Wissenschaft und Politik 1986), pp. 53–568; Brigitte Kaff (ed.), *"Gefährliche politische Gegner." Widerstand und Verfolgung in der scwjetischen Zone/DDR* (Düsseldorf: Droste 1995); Michael Richter and Martin Rissmann (eds.), *Die Ost-CDU. Beiträge zur Entstehung und Entwicklung* (Weimar: Böhlau 1995); Ulf Sommer, *Die Liberal-Demokratische Partei Deutschlands. Eine Blockpartei unter der Führung der SED* (Münster: Agenda Verlag 1996), pp. 29–33, 42–49; Manfred Wilke, *Die SBZ-CDU 1945–1947. Zwischen Kriegsende und Kaltem Krieg* (Munich: Herbert Utz Verlag Wissenschaft 1998); Gerhard Wettig, "Der Konflikt der Ost-CDU mit der Besatzungsmacht 1945–1948 im Spiegel sowjetischer Akten," *Historisch-Politische Mitteilungen*, 6 (1999), pp. 109–37; Ralf Thomas Baus, *Die Christlich-Demokratische Union Deutschlands in der sowjetisch besetzten Zone 1945 bis 1948. Gründung—Programm—Politik* (Düsseldorf: Droste 2001). For examples see report by I. V. Skliarenko, 1 August 1945, *SSSR i germanskii vopros, II*, pp.190–94; A. G. Kotikov to A. A. Sobolev, 5 October 1945, *SSSR i germanskii vopros, II*, pp. 250–58; V. S. Semënov to A. A. Smirnov, 16 November 1945, *SSSR i germanskii vopros, II*, p. 287.

77. "Einführung," Keiderling (ed.), *"Gruppe Ulbricht,"* pp. 64–82; Leonhard, *Die Revolution*, pp. 381–89; Sattler, "Bündnispolitik," Wilke (ed.), *Die Anatomie*, pp. 119–212.

78. Vladimir Vladimirovič Sacharov, Dmitrij Nikolaevič Filippovych, and Michael Kubina, "Tschekisten in Deutschland. Organisation, Aufgaben und Aspekte der Tätigkeit der Sowjetischen Sciherheitsapparate in der Sowjetischen Besatzungszone Deutschlands (1945–1949)," Wilke (ed.), *Die Anatomie*, pp. 293–335; Jens Gieseke, *Mielke-Konzern. Die Geschichte der Stasi 1945–1990* (Stuttgart: Deutsche Verlags-Anstalt 2001), pp. 26–38; Peter Erler, "Berliner Sozialdemokraten und die Internierungspraxis des NKWD/MWD in der Nachkriegszeit," Klaus Schroeder (ed.), *Geschichte und Transformation des SED-Staates. Beiträge und Analysen* (Berlin: Akademie Verlag 1994), pp. 71–84; Günter Buchstab (ed.), *Verfolgt und entrechtet. Die Ausschaltung ChristlicherDemokraten unter sowjetischer Besetzung und SED-Herrschaft 1945–1961. Eine biographische Dokumentation* (Dusseldorf: Droste 1997);

Jörg Morré, "Das Speziallager Bautzen als Instrument sowjetischer Herrschaftssicherung," Behring and Schmeitzner, *Diktaturdurchsetzung in Sachsen*, pp. 79–100.

79. Peter Erler, "Zur Sicherheitspolitik der KPD/SED 1945–1949," Siegfried Suckut and Walter Süss (eds.), *Staatspartei und Staatssicherheit. Zum Verhältnis von SED und MfS* (Berlin: Ch. Links 1997), p. 82; Thomas Lindenberger, "Die Deutsche Volkspolizei (1945–1990)," Torsten Diedrich, Hans Ehlert, Rüdiger Wenzke (eds.), *Im Dienste der Partei. Handbuch der bewaffneten Organe der DDR* (Berlin: Ch. Links 1998), pp. 97–98; Tantzscher, "Vorläufer des Staatssicherheitsdienstes," pp. 134–37. See also I. A. Serov to S. N. Kruglov, 26 June 1946, GARF, 9401, 2, 138, pp. 49–57; P. M. Mal'kov to M. G. Gribanov, 19 August 1947, AVPRF, 0457a, 4, 19, 48, pp. 24–35.

80. See S. I. Tiul'panov's accounting report on his handling the CDU and LDP: Trëkhletnyi opyt raboty Upravleniia informatsii SVAG (oktiabr' 1945–oktiabr' 1948 gg.), Berlin 1948, GARF, 7317, 19, 1, pp. 65–96; papers by V. I. Semënov, 10 July 1946 and 1 August 1946, *SSSR i germanskii vopros, II*, pp. 638–41, 666–69; report on conversation S. I. Tiul'panov–J. Kaiser, 29 April 1947, *SSSR i germanskii vopros, II*, pp. 373–80; report on conversation S. I. Tiul'panov–W. Külz, 8 May 1947, *SSSR i germanskii vopros, II*, pp. 380–85; report on conversation S. I. Tiul'panov–CDU leaders, 19 July 1947, *SSSR i germanskii vopros, II*, pp. 466–69; Haritonow, *Ideologie*, pp. 25, 34.

81. Ulrich Mählert, *Die Freie Deutsche Jugend 1945–1949. Von den "antifaschistischen Jugendausschüssen" zur SED-Massenorganisation: Die Erfassung der Jugend in der Sowjetischen Besatzungszone*, (Paderborn: Schöningh 1995).

82. As late as in summer 1945, the USSR verbally agreed that "representative and elective principles" be introduced "into regional, provincial, and state (land) administration as rapidly as may be justified by the successful application of these principles in local government" (Protocol of the Proceedings of the Berlin [Potsdam] Conference, 1 August 1945, *Documents on Germany 1944–1985*, Department of State Publication 9446 [Washington D.C.: Government Printing Office 1985], p. 57).

83. Stefan Winckler, "Ein Markgraf als williger Vollstrecker des Totalitarismus. Die Biographie des deutschen Berufssoldaten Paul H. Markgraf (SED) unter besonderer Berücksichtigung seiner Amtszeit als Berliner Polizeipräsident 1945–48/49," Heiner Timmermann (ed.), *Die DDR—Analysen eines aufgegebenen Staates* (Berlin: Duncker and Humblot 2001), pp. 343–53.

84. For the enduring effort to control all of Berlin see information letter by V. S. Semënov, 9 March 1946, pp. 382–83; information letter by V. S. Semënov, 17 March 1946, pp. 412–14; information letter by V. S. Semënov, 2 April 1946, pp. 443–47; information letter by V. S. Semënov, 22 April 1946, pp. 461–66, 470–73 (all citations from *SSSR i germanskii vopros, II*).

85. Heinrich Maetzke, *Der Union Jack in Berlin. Das britische Foreign Office, die SBZ und die Formulierung britischer Deutschlandpolitik 1945/47* (Konstanz: Universitätsverlag 1996), pp. 39–40. Cf. SMAG Order No. 29 to set up a Sector of Propaganda and Censorship, 18 August 1946, *Sovetskaia voennaia administratsiia v Germanii 1945–1949. Politika SVAG v oblasti kul'tury, nauki i obrazovaniia: Tseli, metody, rezul'taty. Sbornik dokumentov pod obshchei redaktsiei Kh. Mëllera [H. Möller]*

i A. O. Chubar'iana (henceforth: *Dokumenty SVAG*) (Moscow: ROSSPĖN 2006), pp. 90–91; SMAG Order No. 45 to supply information to provincial newspapers, 31 August 1945, *Dokumenty SVAG*, pp. 91–92; S. I. Tiul'panov to G. M. Malenkov, 28 October 1945, *Dokumenty SVAG*, pp. 97–98; report by the Sector of Propaganda on activities 15 July–15 October 1945, *Dokumenty SVAG*, pp. 98–102.

86. For the decision and its subsequent implementation see "Vvedenie," *SSSR i germanskii vopros*, II, pp. 25–26.

87. Cf. paper by I. Turaginov, 17 October 1945, *SSSR i germanskii vopros*, II, pp. 269–76; V. S. Semënov to G. K. Zhukov, 17 December 1945, *SSSR i germanskii vopros*, II, pp. 309–10; paper by V. S. Semënov, 1 August 1946, *SSSR i germanskii vopros*, II, pp. 660–63.

88. A. Ackermann, "Für den Fernsehfilm zur Geschichte der deutschen Arbeiterbewegung," 30 September 1966, SAPMO-BArch, NY 4109/5, pp. 140–42; "Genauer Terminkalender zur Juni-Beratung in Moskau" [written down by Anton Ackermann], 11 April 1969, SAPMO-BArch, NY 4109/5, pp. 151–52.

89. Pieck notes on conversation I. V. Stalin (with some of his aides)–W. Pieck, W. Ulbricht, A. Ackermann, and G. Sobottka, 4 June 1945, Badstübner and Loth (eds.), *Wilhelm Pieck*, pp. 50–53; "Einleitung," Peter Erler, Horst Laude, and Manfred Wilke (eds.), *"Nach Hitler kommen wir." Dokumente zur Programmatik der Moskauer KPD-Führung 1944/45 für Nachkriegsdeutschland* (Berlin: Akademie Verlag 1994), pp. 121–22.

90. Appeal by the KPD Central Committee, 11 June 1945, *"Nach Hitler kommen wir,"* pp. 390–97 (quotation on p. 394).

91. Appeal by the KPD Central Committee, 11 June 1945, *"Nach Hitler kommen wir,"* p. 396.

92. Even families whose members had resisted Hitler and lost their lives, were disowned and prosecuted.

93. A. Ia. Vyshinskii to V. M. Molotov, 5 July 1945, *SSSR i germanskii vopros*, II, pp. 175–78.

94. "Vvedenie" [with reference to related documents], *SSSR i germanskii vopros*, II, pp. 35–38; Jochen Laufer, "Die UdSSR und die Einleitung der Bodenreform in der Sowjetischen Besatzungszone," Arnd Bauernkämper (ed.), *"Junkerland in Bauernhand"? Durchführung, Auswirkungen und Stellenwert der Bodenreform in der Sowjetischen Besatzungszone, Beiheft 20 zu den Historischen Mitteilungen der Ranke-Gesellschaft* (Stuttgart: Steiner Verlag 1996), pp. 22–23; Monika Kaiser, "Sowjetischer Einfluss auf die ostdeutsche Politik und Verwaltung 1945–1970," Konrad Jarausch and Hannes Siegrist (eds.), *Amerikanisierung und Sowjetisierung in Deutschland 1945–1970* (Frankfurt/Main: Campus Verlag 1997), pp. 116–17; Sattler, "Bündnispolitik," Wilke (ed.), *Die Anatomie*, pp. 143–66.

95. W. Ulbricht to Marshal Sokolovskii, 20 June 1945, *Dokumenty SVAG*, pp. 87–88.

96. "Vvedenie" [with reference to related documents], *SSSR i germanskii vopros*, II, pp. 40–43; Frank Zschaler, "Die vergessene Währungsreform. Vorgeschichte, Durchführung und Ergebnisse der Geldumstellung in der SBZ 1948," *Vierteljahrshefte für Zeitgeschichte*, 2/1997, pp. 198–99; Fritz Schenk, "Mit Geheimbefehl Nr. 01 wurden 1945 die Tresore ausgeplündert," *Frankfurter Allgemeine Zeitung*, 2 June 1998.

97. Laufer, "Die UdSSR und die deutsche Währungsfrage 1944–1948," pp. 457–62.

98. See the relevant passage in the 21 October 1944 action program envisaged for the prospective "Bloc of Militant Democracy": Keiderling, *"Gruppe Ulbricht,"* p. 131; Erler, Laude, and Wilke, *"Nach Hitler kommen wir,"* p. 266.

99. Lecture by W. Pieck at the KPD Party School near Moscow, 31 October 1944, *"Nach Hitler kommen wir,"* pp. 272–80; statement by W. Pieck during a conversation with KPD members in Moscow, 27 June 1945, Keiderling, *"Gruppe Ulbricht,"* pp. 594–95; "Zur programmatischen Arbeit der Moskauer KPD-Führung 1941–1945," p. 75.

100. S. I. Tiul'panov, Trëkhletnyi opyt raboty Upravleniia informatsii SVAG (oktiabr' 1945–oktiabr' 1948 gg.), Berlin 1948, GARF, 7317, 19, 1, pp. 22–23.

101. Memorandum by S. I. Tiul'panov (excerpt), 14 March 1946, Hermann-Josef Rupieper (ed.), *Die Zwangsvereinigung von KPD und SPD. Einige ausgewaehlte SMAD Dokumente, 16. Januar–7. Juni 1946* (Halle/Saale: Gesellschaft für Demokratie- und Zeitgeschichte, University of Halle 1997), pp. 5–7; testimony by S. I. Tiul'panov to the CC Investigation Commission (excerpt), 16 September 1946, Bonvech, Bordiugov, and Neimark (eds.), *SVAG*, p. 158; "Vvedenie," *SSSR i germanskii vopros, II*, pp. 20–28.

102. See Pieck's notes on conversation with Stalin, 6 February 1946, Badstübner and Loth (eds.), *Wilhelm Pieck*, p. 68.

103. Gert Gruner and Manfred Wilke (eds.), *Sozialdemokraten im Kampf um die Freiheit. Die Auseinandersetzungen zwischen SPD und KPD in Berlin 1945/46. Stenografische Niederschrift der Sechziger-Konferenz am 21./22. Dezember 1945* (Munich: Piper 1981).

104. Anton Ackermann, "Gibt es einen besonderen deutschen Weg zum Sozialismus?" *Einheit. Organ zur Vorbereitung der Vereinigung der Arbeiterparteien*, 9 February 1946, pp. 22–32.

105. Manfred Wilke, "Schumachers sozialdemokratischer Führungsanspruch und die Gründung der SED," Wilke, *Die Anatomie*, pp. 214–18, 222–27.

106. Hans-Otto Kleinmann, *Die Geschichte der CDU 1945–1982* (Stuttgart: Deutsche Verlags-Anstalt 1993), pp. 15–79.

107. Pechatnov, "'Soiuzniki,'" pp. 74–78; N. D. Smirnova, "'Grecheskii vopros' na Parizhskoi mirnoi konferentsii," Chubar'ian, *Stalin i kholodnaia voina*, p. 10.

108. Cf. circular letter by V. M. Molotov to all Soviet ambassadors and chargés d'affaires (excerpt), 10 October 1945, *Vneshniaia politika Sovetskogo Soiuza. 1946 god* (Moscow: Gosudarstvennoe izdatel'stvo politicheskoi literatury 1952), pp. 260–63.

109. Stalin's speech in his Moscow constituency, 9 February 1946, *Vneshniaia politika Sovetskogo Soiuza. 1946 god*, pp. 27–42 (particularly pp. 28–30).

110. Pechatnov, "'Na ètom voprose,'" p. 96; "Obsuzhdenie v SSSR amerikanskogo predlozheniia o zakliuchenii dogovora o razoruzhenii i demilitarizatsii Germanii (1945–1947 gg.)," *Mezhdunarodnaia zhizn'*, 8/1996, pp. 69–73; G. K. Zhukov, V. D. Sokolovskii, V. S. Semënov to V. M. Molotov, undated [February/March 1946], "Obsuzhdenie v SSSR," pp. 74–76; Agafonova, "Diplomaticheskii krizis," Chubar'ian (ed.), *Stalin i kholodnaia voina*, pp. 76–77; "Vvedenie" [with reference to related documents], *SSSR i germanskii vopros, II*, pp. 75–77; Hanns Jürgen Küsters, *Der Integrationsfriede. Viermächte-Verhandlungen über die Friedensregelung mit Deutschland 1945–1990* (Munich: Oldenbourg 2000), pp. 271–73.

111. V. M. Molotov to J. F. Byrnes, 15 March 1945, *Sovetsko-amerikanskie ot-nosheniia 1945–1948*, p. 203.

112. "Vvedenie," *SSSR i germanskii vopros, II*, pp. 80–81; "Obsuzhdenie v SSSR," pp. 72–73.

113. Text: *Izvestiia*, 4 May 1946. In the abridged German version of *Tägliche Rund-schau*, 4 May 1946, essential passages were omitted.

114. See, inter alia, Molotov's press declaration, 26 May 1946, and his statements at the Paris session of the Allied Council of Foreign Ministers, 9 and 10 July 1947, W. M. Molotov, *Fragen der Aussenpolitik. Reden und Erklärungen April 1945–Juni 1948* (Moscow: Verlag für fremdsprachliche Literatur 1949), pp. 39–74; commentary by TASS, 16 June 1946, *Izvestiia*, 18 June 1946 [inaccurate German translation in *Tägliche Rundschau*, 18 June 1946]; "Vvedenie," *SSSR i germanskii vopros, II*, pp. 77–81, 87; "Obsuzhdenie," p. 72. Cf. the underlying ideological explanation published under Fred Oelssner's name: "Unser Kampf gegen den Militarismus," *Neues Deutschland*, 18 July 1946. Cf. Küsters, *Der Integrationsfriede*, pp. 276–78, 281–83, 285–88.

115. V. N. Novikov to V. M. Molotov, 27 September 1946, *Sovetsko-amerikanskie otnosheniia 1945–1949*, pp. 312–22.

116. A. A. Sobolev to G. K. Zhukov, 29 January 1946, *SSSR i germanskii vopros, II*, pp. 351–52.

117. S. I. Tiul'panov to V. S. Semënov, 22 May 1946, *SSSR i germanskii vopros, II*, pp. 513–17.

118. Creuzberger, *Die sowjetische Besatzungsmacht*, pp. 44–154.

119. Tantzscher, "Vorläufer des Staatssicherheitsdienstes," pp. 137–43; Jochen Laufer, "Die Ursprünge des Überwachungsstaates in Ostdeutschland," Bernd Flo-rath, Armin Mitter, and Stefan Wolle (eds.), *Die Ohnmacht der Allmächtigen* (Berlin: Ch. Links 1992), pp. 150–51.

120. Laufer, "Die Ursprünge des Überwachungsstaates in Ostdeutschland," pp. 154–63; Stefan Creuzberger, "Klassenkampf in Sachsen," *Historisch-Politische Mitteilungen*, II (1995), pp. 119–30; Erler, "Zur Sicherheitspolitik," Suckut and Süss (eds.), *Staatspartei und Staatssicherheit*, pp. 83–86; Torsten Diedrich, "Die Gren-zpolizei der SBZ/DDR (1946–1961)," Torsten Diedrich, Hans Ehlert, Rüdiger Wen-zke (eds.), *Im Dienste der Partei. Handbuch der bewaffneten Organe der DDR* (Berlin: Ch. Links 1998), p. 201; Verordnung über die Deutsche Verwaltung des Innern, ap-proved by General Kurochkin, undated [May 1947], BArchB, MdI 7/1, pp. 19–28.

121. As an illustrative example see the following report on negotiations in a Commission under the Allied Control Council's authority: B. U. Ratchford and M. W. D. Ross, *Berlin Reparations Assignmment* (Chapel Hill: University of North Car-olina Press 1947); K. I. Koval', *Poslednii svidetel'. "Germanskaia karta" v kholodnoi voine* (Moscow: ROSSPÉN 1997), pp. 192–94.

122. Küsters, *Der Integrationsfriede*, pp. 283–84, 340.

123. Cf. N. V. Ivanov and M. G. Gribanov to V. M. Molotov, 20 June 1947, AVPRF, 06, 9, 43, 632, pp. 16–17.

124. Report by V. S. Semënov, 25 May 1946, *SSSR i germanskii vopros, II*, pp. 524–25.

125. "Vvedenie," *SSSR i germanskii vopros, III*, pp. 41–42; directives for the Soviet delegation to the Paris session of the Council of Foreign Ministers, 19 April 1946, *Sovetsko-amerikanskie otnosheniia 1945–1948*, p. 228.

126. "Vvedenie," *SSSR i germanskii vopros, II*, pp. 41–43; V. D. Sokolovskii to V. M. Molotov, 17 May 1946, *SSSR i germanskii vopros, II*, pp. 505–9; V. M. Molotov to A. I. Mikoian and I. V. Stalin, 26 July 1946, *SSSR i germanskii vopros, II*, pp 647–49; "Vvedenie," *SSSR i germanskii vopros, III: 6 oktiabria 1946 g. – 15 iiunia 1948 g.* (*Moscow: "Mezhdunarodnye otnosheniia" 2003*), pp. 50–54; Laufer, "Die UdSSR und die deutsche Währungsfrage," pp. 457–76.

127. Address by Secretary of State Byrnes in Stuttgart, 6 September 1946, *Documents on Germany 1944–1985*, pp. 91–99.

128. S. I. Kavtaradze to V. M. Molotov, 9 September 1946, pp. 694–95; A. G. Bogomolov to V. M. Molotov, 10 September 1946, pp. 695–97; G. M. Pushkin to V. M. Molotov, 10 September 1946, pp. 697–99; N. V. Novikov to V. M. Molotov, 10 September 1946, pp. 697–703 (all citations refer to *SSSR i germanskii vopros, II*).

129. Memorandum of Agreement Between the United States and the United Kingdom on Economic Fusion of Their Respective Zones of Occupation in Germany, 2 December 1946, *Documents on Germany 1944–1985*, pp. 110–13.

130. Conversation I. V. Stalin–W. Pieck, O. Grotewohl, W. Ulbricht, and M. Fechner, 31 January 1947, *SSSR i germanskii vopros, III*, p. 250.

131. V. S. Lel'chuk and E. I. Pivovar, *SSSR i kholodnaia voina* (Moscow: Mosgorarkhiv, 1995), p. 89.

132. Lel'chuk and Pivovar, *SSSR i kholodnaia voina*, p. 82; Z. Rejchl to I. V. Stalin, 20 September 1946, *Vostochnaia Evropa, I*, p. 527; M. A. Suslov to I. V. Stalin (recommendation by the Section of Foreign Relations of the VKP (b)), 7 February 1947, *Vostochnaia Evropa*, pp. 572–79.

133. Conversation D. G. Iakovlev–E. Bodnăraş, 2 January 1947, *Sovetskii faktor v Vostochnoi Evropy 1944–1953. Dokumenty*, ed. T. V. Volokitina et al., Vol. I: *1944–1948* (Moscow: ROSSPÈN 1999), pp. 389–92.

134. Conversation I. V. Stalin–G. Gheorghiu-Dej and A. Pauker, 2 February 1947, *Vostochnaia Evropa*, pp. 564–68; V. Moshetov and I. Medvedev to M. A. Suslov, 7 February 1947, *Vostochnaia Evropa*, pp. 572–79; Conversation I. V. Stalin–G. Gheorghiu-Dej, 10 February 1947, *Vostochnaia Evropa*, pp. 579–83.

135. Lel'chuk and Pivovar, *SSSR i kholodnaia voina*, pp. 83–84.

136. T. V. Volokitina, "Stalin i smena strategicheskogo kursa Kremlia k kontse 40-kh godov: ot kompromissov k konfrontatsii," Chubar'ian (ed.), *Stalinskoe desiatiletie kholodnoi voiny. Fakty i gipotezy* (Moscow: "Nauka" 1999), p. 17.

137. János M. Rainer, "Der Weg der ungarischen Volksdemokratie. Das Mehrparteiensystem und seine Beseitigung 1944–1949," Creuzberger and Görtemaker (eds.), *Gleichschaltung unter Stalin?* pp. 341–44.

138. Marietta Stankova, "Das parteipolitische System in Bulgarien 1944–1949. Äussere Einflüsse und innere Faktoren," Creuzberger and Görtemaker (eds.), *Gleichschaltung unter Stalin?* pp. 211–15.

139. Burger, "Von der Zusammenarbeit über die Konfrontation zur Auflösung," Creuzberger and Görtemaker (eds.), *Gleichschaltung unter Stalin?* pp. 159–63.

140. Harald Moldenhauer, "'Ihr werde euch dem Sozialismus ohne blutigen Kampf annähern.' Kommunistische Blockpolitik und 'Gleichschaltung' in Polen, 1944–1948," Creuzberger and Görtemaker (eds.), *Gleichschaltung unter Stalin?* pp. 122–24.

141. Volokitina, "Stalin i smena, " Chubar'ian (ed.), *Stalinskoe desiatiletie*, p. 20.

142. Michael Kubina, "Der Aufbau des zentralen Parteiapparats der KPD 1945/46," Manfred Wilke (ed.), *Die Anatomie der Parteizentrale. Die KPD/SED auf dem Wege zur Macht* (Berlin: Akademie Verlag 1998), pp. 49–147; Michael Kubina, "Die Schaffung von strukturellen Voraussetzungen für die Westarbeit im zentralen Parteiapparat von KPD/SED in den ersten Nachkriegsjahren," Gerhard Wettig (ed.), *Die sowjetische Deutschland-Politik in der Ära Adenauer* (Bonn: Bouvier 1997), pp. 37–47.

143. S. I. Tiul'panov to M. A. Suslov (excerpt), 4 July 1946, Bonvech, Bordiugov, and Neimark (eds.), *SVAG*, pp. 77–79; S. I. Tiul'panov to I. V. Shikin (excerpt), 20 July 1946, Bonvech, Bordiugov, and Neimark (eds.), *SVAG*, pp. 55–57; S. I. Tiul'-panov to M. A. Suslov (excerpt), 25 July 1947, Bonvech, Bordiugov, and Neimark (eds.), *SVAG*, pp. 48–51; note of information by the SMAG Administration for Propaganda (excerpt), 9 September 1947, Bonvech, Bordiugov, and Neimark (eds.), *SVAG*, pp. 83–85; situation assessment by the Soviet CC Investigation Commission (excerpt), 16 September 1946, Bonvech, Bordiugov, and Neimark (eds.), *SVAG*, pp. 158, 160; A. Paniushkin, K. Kazakov, M. Burtsev to A. A. Zhdanov (excerpt), 11 October 1946, Bonvech, Bordiugov, and Neimark (eds.), *SVAG*, pp. 185–86. Cf. Andreas Malycha, *Partei von Stalins Gnaden? Die Entwicklung der SED zur Partei neuen Typs in den Jahren 1946 bis 1950* (Berlin: Dietz 1996), p. 81; Monika Kaiser, "Die Zentrale der Diktatur. Struktur und Kompetenzen der SED-Führung 1946 bis 1952," Jürgen Kocka (ed.), *Historische DDR-Forschung. Aufsätze und Studien* (Berlin: Akademie Verlag 1993), pp. 60–67.

144. Haritonow, *Ideologie*, pp. 52–54.

145. Ministerstvo inostrannych del, Istorichesko-diplomaticheskoe upravlenie: Germanskii vopros vo vzaimootnosheniiakh SSSR, SShA, Anglii i Frantsii v period Berlinskoi konferentsii do obrazovaniia dvukh germanskikh gosudarstv (1945–1949 gg.). Obzor podgotovil G. P. Kynin, chast' III (henceforth: Obzor Kynina), AVPRF, Arkhivno-operativnaia biblioteka (henceforth: AOB), 11zh, 71, 19, p. 597; SMAG deputy head Colonel General Serov, Vremennoe polozhenie o nemetskom upravlenii Vnutreenikh del von Sovetskoi zone okkupatsii Germanii, 13 January 1947, AVPRF, 0457a, 4, 19, 48, pp. 40–47; [East German] decree on the German Administration of the Interior, confirmed by deputy SMAG head Colonel General Kurochkin, May 1947, BArchB, MdI 7/1, pp. 19–28.

146. Vremennoe polozhenie o nemetskom upravlenii Vnutrennykh del v Sovetskoi zone okkupatsii Germanii (order by SMAG Deputy Commander Col.-Gen. I.S. Serov), 13 January 1947, AVPRF, 0457a, 4, 19, 48, pp. 40–47 / BArchB, MdI 7/1, pp. 131–41.

147. Lel'chuk and Pivovar, *SSSR i kholodnaia voina*, pp. 81–82.

148. S. I. Tiul'panov to V. S. Semënov, 12 May 1949, AVPRF, 0457a, 7, 39, 10, pp. 1–14; S. I. Tiul'panov to V. S. Semënov, 24 May 1949, AVPRF, 0457a, 7, 39, 10, pp. 28–46.

149. Pieck notes on conversation I. V. Stalin (with some of his aides)–W. Pieck, W. Ulbricht, A. Ackermann, G. Sobottka, 4 June 1945, Badstübner and Loth (eds.), *Wilhelm Pieck,* pp. 50–51.

150. Internal statement by O. Grotewohl, 14 November 1946, cited by Dietrich Staritz, "Einheits- und Machtkalküle der SED (1946–1948)," Elke Scherstjanoi (ed.), *"Provisorium auf längstens ein Jahr . . ."* (Berlin: Akademie Verlag 1993), pp. 18–19.

151. Transcript of session, 16 September 1946, RGASPI, 17, 128, 149, pp. 144–95; transcript of session, 17–18 September 1946, RGASPI, 17, 128, 149, pp. 1–143.

152. "Entwurf einer Verfassung für die Deutsche Demokratische Republik," 14 November 1946, *Dokumente der Sozialistischen Einheitspartei Deutschlands, Vol. I* ([East] Berlin: Dietz 1951), pp. 114–37; A. A. Smirnov to V. A. Zorin, 19 August 1948, AVPRF, 06, 35, 171, 75, p. 1; Obzor Kynina, AVPRF, AOB, 11zh, 71, 20, pp. 611–12; Walter Ulbricht, *Zur Geschichte der deutschen Arbeiterbewegung, Aus Reden und Aufsätzen, Vol. III* ([East] Berlin: Dietz 1961), pp. 137–56; Creuzberger, *Die sowjetische Besatzungsmacht,* pp. 124–25; Jochen Laufer, "Verfassungsgebung in der SBZ 1946–1949," *Aus Politik und Zeitgeschichte. Beilage zur Wochenzeitung "Das Parlament,"* B 32–33/98, 31 July 1998, pp. 30–33; Staritz, "Einheits- und Machtkalküle," pp. 18–19.

153. V. D. Sokolovskii, V. S. Semënov to V. M. Molotov, 28 January 1947, *SSSR i germanskii vopros, III,* p. 238; conversation I. V. Stalin–W. Pieck, W. Ulbricht, O. Grotewohl, M. Fechner, 31 January 1947, *SSSR i germanskii vopros, III,* pp. 245–50. Cf. the notes inserted by Suslov into the SED report on the situation in Germany that had been transmitted to him in advance, *Vierteljahrshefte für Zeitgeschichte,* 2/1994, pp. 294–98 (German translation based on the original Russian text in the file RGASPI, 17, 128, 1091).

154. Notes inserted by Suslov into the SED report on the situation in Germany, *Vierteljahrshefte für Zeitgeschichte,* 2/1994 p. 296.

155. Conversation I. V. Stalin–W. Pieck, W. Ulbricht, O. Grotewohl, M. Fechner, 31 January 1947, *SSSR i germanskii vopros, III,* pp. 260–61. Cf. Suslov's summary of Stalin's statements, *Vierteljahrshefte für Zeitgeschichte,* 2/1994, pp. 304–5.

156. S. I. Tiul'panov to V. S. Semënov (report on SED Central Committee plenum), 17 February 1947, *SSSR i germanskii vopros, III,* pp. 271–75.

157. Conversation I. V. Stalin–W. Pieck, W. Ulbricht, O. Grotewohl, M. Fechner, 31 January 1947, *SSSR i germanskii vopros, III,* pp. 249–50. In a number of *länder,* the communists had received less than 5 percent of the vote and thus failed to meet a clause in the electoral law that stipulated this as a minimum requirement for representation in parliament.

158. Conversation I. V. Stalin–W. Pieck, W. Ulbricht, O. Grotewohl, M. Fechner, 31 January 1947, *SSSR i germanskii vopros, III,* pp. 250–52. Cf. the notes inserted by Suslov, *Vierteljahrshefte für Zeitgeschichte,* 2/1994, p. 297.

159. Notes by Pieck on conversation with Stalin, Molotov, and Zhdanov on 4 June 1945, Badstübner and Loth (eds.), *Wilhelm Pieck,* p. 50. The remark that, "despite allied unity," "two Germanies" would emerge, has occasionally been understood to mean that Stalin predicted creation of two states. Morré, *Hinter den Kulissen des*

Nationalkomitees, p. 170, has rightly pointed out that he referred to the emergent zones, which he is known to have seen as basically two regions.

160. Conversation I. V. Stalin–W. Pieck, W. Ulbricht, O. Grotewohl, M. Fechner, 31 January 1947, *SSSR i germanskii vopros*, *III*, pp. 257–58. See also notes by Suslov, *Vierteljahrshefte für Zeitgeschichte*, 2/1994, p. 299.

161. Conversation V. D. Sokolovskii–W. Pieck, O. Grotewohl, W.Ulbricht, M. Fechner, 25 April 1947, *SSSR i germanskii vopros*, *III*, pp. 370–71; Udo Vorholt and Volker Zaib, "Zur Deutschlandpolitik der SED in den Jahren 1947/48. Die SED-Gründungskomitees in der britischen Besatzungszone," *Deutschland Archiv*, 12/1995, pp. 1279–91; Staritz, "Einheits- und Machtkalküle," pp. 21–23; Patrick Major, "Big Brother—Little Party. Zum Verhältnis SED-KPD 1946–1950," Scherstjanoi (ed.), *Provisorium*, p. 156; transcript of the 12th session of the SED Party Leadership, 1–3 July 1947, SAPMO-BArch, DY 30/IV 2/1/22, pp. 7–51.

162. Conversation I. V. Stalin–W. Pieck, W. Ulbricht, O. Grotewohl, M. Fechner, 31 January 1947, *SSSR i germanskii vopros*, *III*, pp. 253–54, 256–57. Cf. notes inserted by Suslov, *Vierteljahrshefte für Zeitgeschichte*, 2/1994, pp. 297–98. The counts referred to all of Germany, i.e., the election results and the membership numbers of the Soviet zone were included.

163. S. I. Tiul'panov to N. V. Ivanov, 20 March 1947, *SSSR i germanskii vopros*, *III*, pp. 318–21.

164. Hans-Peter Schwarz, *Vom Reich zur Bundesrepublik. Deutschland im Widerstreit der aussenpolitischen Konzeptionen in den Jahren der Besatzungsherrschaft 1945–1949* (Neuwied: H. Luchterhandt 1966), p. 264.

165. In February 1947, Stalin had even offered a military alliance to Britain (Gaddis, *We Now Know*, p. 43).

166. Conversation V. M. Molotov–J. F. Byrnes, 25 November 1946, *Sovetsko-amerikanskie otnosheniia 1945–1948*, p. 335.

167. Suslov's summary of remarks by V. M. Molotov during the conversation I. V. Stalin–W. Pieck, W. Ulbricht, O. Grotewohl, M. Fechner, 31 January 1947, *Vierteljahrshefte für Zeitgeschichte*, 2/1994, pp. 299–300.

168. *FRUS. Diplomatic Papers 1947, Vol. II: Council of Foreign Ministers; Germany and Austria, Department of State Publication 8530* (Washington D.C.: Government Printing Office 1972), pp. 139–278 (notably letter by G. Marshall to H. Truman and D. Acheson, 13 March 1947, on pp. 249–51).

169. V. M. Molotov to I. V. Stalin, 7 March 1947, *SSSR i germanskii vopros*, *III*, pp. 285–89; V. M. Molotov to I. V. Stalin, 8 March 1947, *SSSR i germanskii vopros*, *III*, pp. 289–95; Soviet proposal for directives by the Council of Foreign Ministers, 11 March 1947, *SSSR i germanskii vopros*, *III*, pp. 296–300; A. A. Smirnov to V. M. Molotov (with attachment), 13 March 1947, *SSSR i germanskii vopros*, *III*, pp. 303–12 (quotation on p. 309); Soviet proposal for directives by the Council of Foreign Ministers, 26 March 1947, *SSSR i germanskii vopros*, *III*, pp. 322–28; N. V. Novikov and B. E. Shtein to V. M. Molotov, 26 March 1947, *SSSR i germanskii vopros*, *III*, pp. 328–30; additional directive to the Soviet delegation at the Council of Foreign Ministers, 29 March 1947, *SSSR i germanskii vopros*, *III*, pp. 330–31; Soviet proposal for directives by the Council of Foreign Ministers, 3 April 1947, *SSSR i germanskii vopros*, *III*, pp. 331–33; Küsters, *Der Integrationsfriede*, pp. 327–47.

170. See the documents in *FRUS 1947, II*, pp. 278-385. For conversation G. Marshall-I. V. Stalin, 15 April 1947 (*FRUS 1947, II*, pp. 337-44) see also the Soviet protocol (*Sovetsko-amerikanskie otnosheniia 1945-1948*, pp. 406-13).

171. See the documents *FRUS 1947, II*, pp. 344-502; Conversation V. M. Molotov-E. Bevin (quotations), 25 April 1947, *SSSR i germanskii vopros, III*, pp. 364-69; answer by the Soviet delegation to the U.S. proposal to demilitarize Germany, 24 April 1947, *Sovetsko-amerikanskie otnosheniia 1945-1948*, pp. 418-19; Küsters, *Der Integrationsfriede*, pp. 348-63.

172. Project of Directives to the Soviet delegation, 26 March 1947, *SSSR i germanskii vopros, III*, p. 323.

173. For reference to Molotov's proposal cf. G. Marshall to H. Truman and D. Acheson, 13 March 1947, *FRUS 1947, II*, p. 251.

4

Outbreak and Culmination of the Cold War, 1947–1949

CHANGE OF RELATIONS WITH THE WEST

At the Moscow conference, disagreement over economic issues had resulted in termination of the negotiations before the divergent views on systemic problems had been discussed in any detail. It was logical, therefore, that the point of departure for subsequent East-West confrontation was economics. In the Anglo-Saxon view, there was both a pressing need to make the Western zones pay the costs of their food supply and to provide for recovery of distressed Europe in general. Economic reconstruction would protect the continent's "free societies" against the communist threat. The inclusion of West Germany was indispensable as its industrial potential, notably in the Ruhr District, would contribute essentially to recovery of the other countries. Given that there was little prospect that the Kremlin might join the program, the governments in Washington and London concluded that they had to act on their own with no regard for Soviet objections. Their patience had run out. Moscow's veto could not possibly be taken into account any longer; there was no choice but to accept a handicap to relations with the USSR.

Stalin did not expect this but felt that Britain and the United States would be as indulgent as before and looked forward to business as usual.[1] Inter alia, he continued to be hopeful that the Western occupation authorities in Germany would permit a "unified socialist party" to extend SED activities to their zones.[2] He was therefore unprepared when, on 5 June 1947, Secretary of State Marshall announced willingness to start a recovery program for Europe. The United States offered aid to put an end to misery by initiating economic development. All European countries were invited to join.

Stalin's Reaction to the Marshall Plan

The Soviet ambassador in Washington saw the U.S. initiative as being directed at creating an anti-Soviet bloc and strengthening the position of American capital in Europe and Asia.[3] Stalin nonetheless felt that the USSR should take the offer. To be sure, he was far from trusting U.S. policy makers but initially felt that their willingness to extend help to foreign countries might be exploited. He hoped that a massive loan might finally materialize, while negative political implications would be warded off.[4] So he initially wanted to accept the offer, and he explicitly permitted his client countries to participate in the negotiations on the modalities of implementing the offer. But members of his establishment felt that the selfish motive allegedly underlying the Marshall Plan already predetermined the outcome to favor the antagonist on the other side of the Atlantic.[5] Top economist and academician Evgenii Varga submitted a paper on 24 June that not only concurred to the view that the formation of an anti-Soviet "bourgeois front" in Europe was a major purpose but explained that the United States had an urgent need to prevent economic crisis by selling products to other countries on credit. The USSR must neither join this saving operation nor take part in a political venture designed for exploitation prejudicial to its interests.[6]

Stalin concluded that negotiations must be directed at denying the Americans any material and political benefit. In particular, they must not be allowed any economic control of recipient countries, notably the USSR and Eastern Europe. Only aid with no conditions attached (as previously under land lease) was to be taken into account. The Soviet delegation to the preparatory meeting in Paris was instructed accordingly. When intelligence information was received in Moscow that both credits would be made conditional on willingness to accept economic cooperation under U.S. supervision and that Germany, respectively its Western part, would be included, Stalin realized that Washington wanted to rebuild the West European economy and get the Western zones on their feet again with no regard for Soviet objections. As a result, he would be unable to continue exercising influence on West Germany. For some while, he felt that his best option was seeking to kill, or at minimum hamper, the scheme by destructive participation.

His confidence, however, that he would be capable of spoiling the enemy's game was shattered when Molotov reported from Paris that the Anglo-Saxons insisted that the recovery program did not allow for major modification. Another source of concern was the Czechoslovak eagerness to accept the U.S. invitation, as well as indications of a similar Polish attitude. Stalin now suspected that the client countries were willing to defy him by accepting U.S. conditions. He dreaded losing control of Eastern Europe more than anything else. On 7 July, he called Molotov back.[7]

The Kremlin justified performance in Paris by declaring that, from the very beginning, it had not particularly trusted the American venture but sent delegates to clarify the conditions for credit. The United States had refused to provide information but demanded that participation in the committee, which would control crucial economic resources of the countries involved, must be accepted without knowing the implications. The Soviet delegation felt that this meant intervention in internal affairs and hence was unable to agree. "Given this serious divergence between the Anglo-French position and the Soviet position," agreement was impossible.[8]

Subsequent Soviet statements indicated that the USSR was looking forward to confrontation with the West. The United States was both a "fascisizing" power and the "center of worldwide reaction and anti-Soviet activity." All countries aligned to it were enemies. In Moscow's view, the Marshall Plan was a cunning ploy to eliminate Soviet influence. Communist ouster from the Belgian, French, and Italian coalition governments in spring was retrospectively ascribed to alleged U.S. messages that this was a condition for aid. According to this view, interallied cooperation was a total failure. The USSR displayed absolute hostility against all Western countries and declared that "marshallization" must be resisted and prevented by any means. The communist parties in Western Europe, notably in France and Italy, were to make a maximum effort to sabotage implementation of the Marshall Plan. The "enemy" embassies in Moscow were exposed to isolation, their personnel denied contact even with Soviet officials. Rare diplomatic exchange was reduced to formalities.[9]

Formation of an Anti-Western Bloc of Communist Parties

Soviet reaction to the Marshall Plan had major implications for the communist regimes in Eastern Europe. The leaders in Warsaw complied with the Kremlin's policy without raising objections. But Czechoslovak Foreign Minister Jan Masaryk and other Prague leaders who had enthusiastically greeted the U.S. offer did not want to yield. Only when discussing their divergent position with Stalin did they realize that they would not be allowed participation in the U.S. recovery program under any circumstance. They returned from Moscow with a feeling of having been made satellites with no claim to decisions of their own.[10] The two countries' desire to join the West Europeans in accepting American aid reinforced Stalin's feeling that tighter controls were required to provide for reliable satellites. Existing mechanisms were insufficient since they did not work smoothly and failed to guarantee full control. As early as in April 1945, Tito had proposed to set up an international center again to coordinate communist policies.[11] In spring 1947, Stalin made Gomułka invite the parties of Eastern Europe,

Italy, and France but did not inform him of the underlying purpose.[12] At the time, the Central Committee Foreign Policy Department in Moscow received instruction to prepare a founding conference at which, under the postulate of inexorable struggle against the United States and the Marshall Plan, foreign communists' attitudes would be subjected to severe criticism.[13]

All major European communist parties, except for the SED, were invited to send delegations to a conference at Szklarska Poręba on 22–27 September 1947. On orders by Stalin, the sessions were chaired by Andrei Zhdanov, who was in permanent radio contact with the Kremlin leader and being provided with additional instructions all the time. Both the conference schedule and the reports by Soviet participants had been prepared by the Moscow party apparatus under Stalin's personal guidance.[14] At the beginning of the conference, Politburo member Georgii Malenkov presented the CPSU report to set the tone.

As a result of the victorious war against fascism, the position of socialism and democracy has been strengthened and that of the imperialist camp has been weakened. One of the most important results of the Second World War is the strengthening of the USSR and the establishment of new democratic regimes led by the working class. The defeat of Germany and Japan signifies a weakening of the camp of imperialism and a further deepening of the crisis of the capitalist system. Among the capitalist countries, the U.S.A. has emerged considerably strengthened from the war, but its partners, Great Britain and France, have been weakened. In conditions in which its principal competitors— Germany and Japan—have been eliminated, and Great Britain and France have been weakened, the U.S.A. has gone over to a new, openly expansionist policy aimed at establishing its domination of the world. In these new postwar conditions, a change has taken place in the relations of yesterday's military allies who cooperated in the war against fascist Germany and imperialist Japan. Two opposing tendencies have emerged in international politics. The one policy is being pursued by the Soviet Union and the countries of new democracy. The foreign policy of the Soviet Union and the democratic countries is directed at undermining imperialism, securing a lasting democratic peace among the peoples and strengthening in every way friendly cooperation between peaceloving nations. In doing so, our foreign policy is based on the growing international importance of the Soviet state and the countries of new democracy. The other tendency in international politics is dominated by the ruling clique of the American imperialists. Seeking to consolidate the position occupied by American monopolist capital in Europe and Asia during the war, this clique has taken the road of overt expansion, enslavement of the weakened capitalist countries of Europe and the colonial and dependent countries, the road of preparing new plans for war against the USSR and the countries of new democracy under the banner of struggle against "the communist danger." This orientation of the American capital's policy has found its clearest and most concrete expression in the Truman and Marshall Plans. These are the two tendencies in present-day international politics. Stalin's wise Soviet foreign policy, both before the war and in the course of it, has enabled us to exploit correctly the contradictions within the camp of imperialism, and this was one of the main reasons for our victory in the war.

Malenkov continued by pointing out that the USSR understood that dualism between the two opposing systems would persist for some time to come. While it desired good-neighborly relations, it had to rebuff the discriminatory, hostile policies it had to face. He accused the Anglo-Saxon powers of having changed their previous attitude by supporting any anti-communist and anti-Soviet forces.

The VKP(b) clearly and distinctly recognizes the danger of this reorientation which is currently taking place on the side of certain former USSR allies in war. In our view, the game of the U.S.A. and Great Britain [is] fraught with great danger to repudiate obligations taken in World War II, to seek new allies among the antidemocratic circles in Germany and Japan, antidemocratic Turkey and monarchofascist Greece, to display indulgence to Franco's Spain, to encourage the Dutch imperialists in Indonesia, to support the reactionary regime in China etc., wheras they pursue a terroristic policy of persecution and discrimination, unceremonious coercion and interference in internal affairs, open support of antidemocratic, antigovernment elements within these countries etc., with regard to genuinely democratic states which greatly contributed to the defeat of fascism such as Yugoslavia and Poland. . . . As antagonistic classes have been liquidated in the USSR and moral-political unity of Soviet society has been achieved, intensified class struggle has shifted [from] the USSR to the international arena. There two systems are competing, the capitalist system and and the socialist system. Here our party has to test its weapon in conflicts with hard-line representatives of bourgeois business. The VKP(b) devotes much attention to the problems of foreign policy and takes particular care to select and train cadres capable of promoting the Party's line in this sphere.

Malenkov concluded by indicating that links with the "fraternal communist parties" were insufficient and failed to provide a reliable basis for exchange of information on each other, for coordination of mutual action, and for elaboration of common policies. Definite steps had to be taken to cope with this "abnormal situation."[15]

Declaration of Political War

Assessing the international situation, Zhdanov explained that the force correlation in international politics had fundamentally changed. He portrayed treacherous Western policy in 1938–1939, which had turned against its authors, as the starting point of this development.

The main outcome of World War II was the fact of military defeat of Germany and Japan, the two most militaristic and aggressive capitalist countries. The reactionary imperialist elements throughout the world, notably in the U.S.A., in Britain and France, had put particular hope on Germany and Japan, primarily on Hitlerite Germany—firstly as a force most capable of striking a blow at the Soviet Union if not to destroy, then at least to weaken it and to undermine its influence, and secondly as a force capable of smashing the revolutionary working class and democratic movement in Germany itself and in all target countries of Hitlerite aggression and thereby to consolidate the situation of capitalism generally. This was one of the principal reasons of the so-called Munich policy of "appeasement" and stimulation of fascist aggression—a policy which was consistently pursued by the ruling imperialist circles of Britain, France, and the U.S.A. But the hopes put on the Hitlerites, were frustrated. The Hitlerites proved weaker and the Soviet Union and the freedom-loving peoples [proved] strong than the politicians of [the] Munich [Agreement] had thought. As a result of World War II, the main forces of militant international fascist reaction were smashed and put out of action for a long time. In this context, the world capitalist system as a whole has been given yet another serious blow. The most important result of World War I had been that the united imperialist front had broken apart by removal of Russia from the world capitalist system. As a result of the triumph of the socialist system in the USSR, capitalism ceased to be the only and all-embracing system of world economy. World War II and defeat of fascism, the weakening of capitalism's world positions and the strengthening of the antifascist movement has resulted in a number of Central and South Eastern Europe countries breaking away from the imperialist system. In these countries, new democratic people's regimes have emerged. The great example of the Patriotic War of the Soviet Union and the Red Army's liberating role was complemented by an upsurge of the freedom-loving peoples' national liberation struggle against the fascist predators and their hirelings. . . . Within a very short period of time, the new democratic power in Yugoslavia, Bulgaria, Romania, Poland, Czechoslovakia, Hungary, and Albania supported by the mass of the people, has proved capable of carrying out progressive democratic changes which the bourgeois democracies are unable to achieve. Agrarian reform has transferred the land to the peasants and led to liquidation of the landlord class. Nationalization of both big industry and banking, and confiscation of the property of traitors who collaborated with the Germans, have radically undermined the position of monopolist capital in these countries and freed the masses from imperialist servitude. Along with this, the basis was laid for state ownership by the whole people, and a new type of state was created, the people's republic where power belongs to the people, [where] big industry, transport, and the banks belong to the state, and the leading force is a bloc of all classes of the working population under working class leadership. As a result, the peoples of these countries have not only been freed from the clutches of imperialism but have also laid the fundament for transition to the road of socialist development.

Zhdanov emphatically denounced the Marshall Plan and U.S. policy.

Prior to World War II, the most influential reactionary circles of American imperialism stuck to the policy of isolationism and refrained from active intervention in the affairs of Europe or Asia. Under the new postwar conditions, however, the bosses of the Wall Street have gone over to a new policy. They have presented a program for utilizing all American military and economic power not only to preserve and consolidate the positions abroad won during the war but also to extend them as much as possible in order to take the place of Germany, Japan, and Italy on the world market. A sharp decline of the other capitalist countries' economic potential has created the possibility of speculating on exploitation of their postwar difficulties which facilitate submission of these countries to American control and, in particular, exploitation of Great Britain's economic difficulties. The U.S.A. has proclaimed a new openly predatory, expansionist course. This new openly expansionist course of the U.S.A. has been directed at establishing world domination by American imperialism. In the interests of consolidating monopolist position on the markets which has resulted from elimination of the two major competitors, Germany and Japan, and impairment of its capitalist partners, Great Britain and France, the new course of U.S. policy relies on a broad program of military, economic, and political measures which are designed to establish political and economic U.S. domination in all countries which are objects of U.S. expansion, to reduce these countries to the status of U.S. satellites, and to set up in them domestic regimes which would eliminate any working class and democratic movement resistance to exploitation of these countries by American capital. The U.S.A. tries to extend this new political course not only to yesterday's war enemies and to neutral states but also to an ever increasing degree to its military allies.

Zhdanov argued that the USSR was the principal impediment standing in the way of American expansion and that, for this reason, the United States had initiated an anti-Soviet and anticommunist campaign that ascribed aggressive intent to the Soviet Union. It was willing to support any country against the alleged threat. As Zhdanov explained, the underlying motive was to frighten them into submission and to prepare for their further political and economic enslavement. He also depicted the Marshall Plan in great detail as the "American plan for enslavement of Europe." The East-West confrontation that had come into the open in mid-1947 must therefore be seen as caused by U.S. expansionism. Intensified political battles between irreconcilable antagonists resulted.

A new alignment of forces has emerged. The further we are removed from the end of war, the more clearly do the two basic directions emerge which relate to the division of the political forces in the world arena into basically two camps—the imperialist and antidemocratic camp on the one hand, and the antiimperialist and democratic camp on the other. The fundamental leading force of the imperialist camp is the U.S.A. Allied to the U.S.A. are England and

France. That there is the Labour Attlee-Bevin government in England and the socialist Ramadier government in France does not prevent both countries to follow as satellites the lead of U.S. imperialist policy. Such colonial countries as Belgium and Holland, countries with reactionary antidemocratic governments as Turkey and Greece, and countries politically and economically dependent on the U.S.A. as the Middle East countries, South America, and China also support the imperialist camp. The fundamental objective of the imperialist camp is to strengthen imperialism, to prepare a new imperialist war, to fight against socialism and democracy, and to provide comprehensive support to reactionary and antidemocratic profascist regimes and movements. To solve these tasks, the imperialist camp is prepared to rely on reactionary and antidemocratic regimes in all countries and to support yesterday's military adversaries against their military allies. The antiimperialist and antifascist forces constitute the other camp. The fundament of this camp are the USSR and the countries of the new democracy. It includes also those who have broken with imperialism and have firmly taken the road of democratic development, countries such as Romania, Hungary, and Finland. Close to the antiimperialist camp are Indonesia and Vietnam; India, Egypt, and Syria sympathize with it. The antiimperialist camp is based on the workers and democratic movement in all countries, on the fraternal communist parties in all countries, on the fighters of the national liberation movement in all colonial and dependent countries, and on support by all progessive democratic forces in every country. The objecitve of this camp is to struggle against the threat of new wars and imperialist expansion, for consolidation of democracy and eradication of fascism.[16]

The essence of Zhdanov's speech was the so-called two-camps theory: Socialism and "imperialism" were facing each other as enemies on the levels of power politics, systemic orientation, and resultant policy. This was written into the declaration adopted at the end of the meeting.[17] The Kremlin was confident to prevail in the struggle against the West. As Molotov told the Moscow City Soviet in November 1947, victory was ahead. "In all developed countries, the matter has ripened for establishment of socialism."[18]

Castigation of the Italian and French Communist Parties

The conference at Szklarska Poręba also served to impose discipline on the parties in Western Europe. This was first hinted by Zhdanov on 30 June, who indicated that the communists must abandon coalition policy, notably if it resulted in "excessive loyalty to partners."[19] But neither this statement, which had been made in an internal context, nor any other indication of the topics on the agenda had been transmitted to foreign conference participants. Even Gomułka did not know anything. As a result, all delegations, with the sole exception of the Soviet one, were totally unprepared. Only after their arrival at the conference site, they learned that foreign policy coordination was on the agenda.[20] Even then no foreign delegate was aware that this would include harsh criticism of communist policy in Western Europe.

Zhdanov castigated the parties in Italy and France for "incorrect, harmful, and essentially unnatural" collaboration with their domestic antagonists. They had failed to realize that, in spite of national frameworks of operation, the communist movement had common tasks and interests. For fear of being blamed for taking orders from Moscow, they had ignored the requirement of maintaining international contact and consulting each other on matters of mutual concern. If this would continue, "extremely harmful consequences for the development of the brother parties' work" would result. Zhdanov added that "the need for consultation and voluntary coordination of action between different parties" had currently become more imperative than ever. Rather than joining the rival parties in "acting as agents of the imperialist circles of the U.S.A.," the communists had to play a "historical role—to take the lead of the resistance to the American plan for the enslavement of Europe and to unmask all domestic accomplices of American imperialism." The communists had to stand firm in defending national independence and sovereignty against the United States.[21]

On the next day, many participants (who may have been instructed by the Soviet as their arguments seem to indicate) vehemently attacked their Italian and French comrades for distasteful "bourgeois opportunism" that had made them collaborate with other parties and take part in government coalitions dominated by other forces. Yugoslav accusations, which surpassed all other reproaches, apparently were made on their own. The Italian and French chief delegates, Luigi Longo and Jacques Duclos, were prevented by tacit communist rule from pointing out that Stalin had instructed their parties in 1944 to renounce opposition strategy and seek broad cooperation. They were thus obliged to repent for fundamentally incorrect political orientation.[22] Such professions of guilt implied that the collective of communist parties, in fact the Kremlin, had an unlimited right to intervene at will in any member's internal affairs. In his report to Stalin, Zhdanov noted with satisfaction that all Eastern delegations had unanimously supported all his statements and accusations.[23]

Implications for the West European Communists

Stalin clearly wanted the communists in Western Europe to fight against the Marshall Plan and against reconstruction of their countries. The French delegates transmitted this message to their party.

Duclos declares that he and Fajon [the other delegate sent to Szklarska Poręba] did not know until the beginning of the discussion what its real purpose was. Discussion took place in accordance with the will of the Soviet delegates.

Zhdanov demonstrated his power and imposed a real *diktat*. On the political plane, he directed a real accusation against the French and Italian communist parties. He said that it is of no interest whether the communists are in government or in opposition—a problem with which these parties have been excessively occupied. The only objective is to destroy capitalist economy and to unite systematically the live national forces [who are willing to enter a common political front with the communists]. He insisted that the effort which has been made to unite the masses, had been insufficient. From now on, it will not matter to the Kremlin whether the communists will be in government or not, but the parties will have to wage struggle against against U.S. aid which is always possible, and they will have to increase the [party] cells and to unite the masses. He insisted on the necessity to prevent any stabilization of government and recommended free choice of the means which must be employed on the national level emphasizing that, for the Kremlin, only [achievement of] the objective has decisive importance.

Duclos added that the Communist Information Bureau (Cominform) in Belgrade, which had been set up at the conference, was to serve "the purpose of avoiding the mistakes of the past." Inter alia, it was to provide "new methods of propaganda and organization." He also emphasized that, through the Cominform, Moscow would take complete control of the French communist party's activities. Malenkov had justified this by saying that the parties in the West could no longer hope to rally the masses on the basis of Marxist faith.[24]

Soviet criticism of the French and Italian parties had implicitly been directed at the communists of all Western Europe. The French passed Duclos's message on to their fellow parties in Belgium and Britain and also informed Spanish communist underground leaders. In Szklarska Poręba, struggle against U.S. presence and influence in Western Europe by any means including sabotage had been declared necessary. The communist leaders in Rome and Paris asked themselves whether this meant that they must also prepare for armed revolt. While Zhdanov had criticized them for having chosen collaboration rather than independent action, he failed to express a clear attitude on this point. Did he and Stalin agree with the statement by the Yugoslavs that the comrades in Italy and France should have conquered state power at the end of war as they had, and that they must correct their failure as soon as possible?[25]

To clarify the problem, French communist leader Thorez went to Moscow. Talking with Stalin, he expressed his gratitude that his party's flaws had been exposed at Szklarska Poręba and asked for additional "direction and advice." Upon this, he was instructed that, in the present situation, the French had to choose between "peace and war," between "the advocates of peace and the advocates of war." No wavering permitted. After discussion on the domestic situation in France, Stalin made clear that the struggle against the Marshall Plan had to be waged under the slogan of national independence. The communists were to argue that credits were fine but conditions must be compatible with the country's sovereignty. They had to unite all domestic forces willing to fight for this. Thorez then justified his party's failure to wage armed struggle for power in 1944 saying that this must be attributed to "a number of reasons of international character." The FCP had wanted to contribute to military victory over Germany and to take into account that the area was controlled by Anglo-Saxon forces. Stalin agreed that it would have been a hopeless endeavor for the French communists to seek power by armed struggle in 1944. Even if they had managed to seize it, they would have lost it again given the U.S. and British military presence.

Stalin failed to clarify what kind of action was recommendable under present conditions once the foreign troops had left. He expressed surprise that the French communists had never asked for Soviet aid but did not specify what precisely he had in mind, and then he questioned whether they needed arms. As another internal statement seems to indicate, he started from the assumption that, faced with the prospect of immediate confrontation, the communists in Western Europe would have to prepare for clandestine action. Thorez avoided a statement on whether weapons were required by saying that two leading party cadres were studying the problem. Stalin argued that military equipment and organization were necessary. The French communists must not be unarmed when confronted with the enemy. They might be attacked and should then offer resistance. In case of need, the USSR might provide them with arms. He suggested permanent links of communication to be set up between the PCF and the party apparatus in Moscow. The two communist leaders agreed that the French army was weak. Stalin failed to state clearly whether the parties in the West should, in addition to defending themselves if attacked, engage in armed struggle on their own initiative.[26]

The Italian communists also wanted clear orientation. One of their prominent cadres, Secchia, went to Moscow and told Zhdanov that party leader Palmiro Togliatti hesitated to embark on civil war, while members widely expected armed conflict with rightist forces. Stalin supported Togliatti's view but emphasized that the Italian comrades must be prepared for any contingency: "We maintain that an insurrection should not be put on the agenda, but one must be ready in case of an attack by the enemy." He failed to explain his attitude further. As a result, there was no precise directive on the course to be followed. While civil war must not be initiated, radicals within the party were not discouraged from provoking it. Togliatti concluded that he had to prepare for any provocations by the enemy. He even felt that major armed clashes might result which, however, he wanted to avoid.

The Italian communists wanted to achieve a political breakthrough in the national elections of April 1948. Togliatti asked the USSR to support them by pledging financial help and food deliveries in the event that they and their leftist allies would win a majority to take office. Without this promise, they would be unable to offer an alternative to the Marshall Plan and hence be put at a disadvantage. But the Kremlin declined. When the Italian party leader sought Soviet approval of his position that armed struggle must be sought only in extreme circumstances, he succeeded. On behalf of the Kremlin, Molotov agreed. Only if "reactionary forces" launched a military attack should the communists resort to armed struggle. Insurrection would be a dangerous adventure. Yugoslav advice should not be heeded. Contrary to their apprehension, the communists did not come under military attack. Contrary to their hope, the elections turned out a democratic majority; Italy took the road of permanent stabilization.[27]

Policy on Eastern Europe

Less conspicuous than Zhdanov's castigation of the communists in the West was his criticism of the East European parties. They, too, were blamed for cooperation with other political groups even though they had assumed absolute leadership in all the countries except for Czechoslovakia. The essential but implicit reason for criticism was that noncommunists were allowed any influence at all. After the open clash with the West, Stalin saw no more need to concede even insignificant limitations of communist dictatorship and Soviet control. As he internally argued in early January 1948, it was logical for both the West and the USSR to impose their respective systems on the countries they had occupied.[28] He also may have felt that confrontation required the "socialist camp" to be a political fortress with no opposition inside. The Cominform provided him with a new instrument to make the client regimes conform. In the context of undisguised East-West confrontation, the idea of "national roads to socialism," and substitution of "class struggle" by "peaceful development" on the basis of cooperation with dependent other forces, no longer appeared suitable. Change was called for. To this end, the satellite parties, notably in Hungary, Czechoslovakia, and Poland, were blamed for "nationalistic aberration."[29]

In all of Eastern Europe, regard for a democratic appearance (which until then had continued to shape domestic policies at least to some extent) was fully abandoned. When, in August 1947, elections were held in Hungary and, in spite of heavy pressure, the parties outside the government bloc unexpectedly received almost 40 percent of the votes, all-out repression set out to liquidate any independent political forces.[30] In the same month, total annihilation of the opposition in Bulgaria began on the basis of continuing instructions by Soviet cadres who had penetrated party and state. The

Agrarian Union was dissolved. Its fearless leader Petkov was put to trial as a "traitor," convicted, sentenced to death, and executed after he had refused to beg for mercy. In November, the socialists, as the other noncommunist party, were prohibited as well. In February 1948, the multiparty Patriotic Front was made a monolithic organization. By May, the opposition was totally crushed. As a result of strong pressure during the following ten months, the social democrats (who were already tied to the communists by "unity of action") accepted full merger in the end. As a last step, all noncommunist groups in the multiparty bloc were liquidated with the exception of an agrarian representation. While there was harsh repression throughout the country, major noncommunist politicans aligned to the communists were blamed for lacking appreciation of the USSR's helpful role. Unless they repented and submitted unconditionally, they were tried and mostly executed.[31] Given that the situation in Poland continued to be most difficult even after elimination of the opposition, the Kremlin felt that it was necessary to maintain an appearance of all-party participation in government. As before, noncommunist bloc parties with pretended autonomy were allowed to exist.[32]

DEVELOPMENTS AT THE FRINGES OF THE SOVIET EMPIRE

A few East European countries had not been subjected to Soviet occupation authority and thus avoided subjugation. Finland had remained outside the Soviet empire altogether. The armistice of September 1944 had deprived it of its military defenses against the USSR but spared it the Red Army presence all over the country. Domestic autonomy was largely retained. Most importantly, the democratic order remained intact. The Finns were naturally obliged to accept the communists (who had been outlawed until then) as partners of an all-party government coalition but in a junior position and without imposed bloc politics. In spite of this, Finland was seen in Moscow to be one of the countries that was "on the road to socialism."[33] Accordingly, the Kremlin had not put up with the continuing existence of democracy.

Soviet relations with Czechoslovakia were different. While there as well the democratic system had not been eliminated by bloc politics, the communists had won a very strong position on the basis of free elections. Socioeconomic transformation had been initiated as Beneš had promised to Stalin in 1943, in most cases, however, only in the regions previously inhabited by ethnic Germans. While the USSR exercised dominant influence in the country, it was unable both to eliminate major "bourgeois" positions in traditional administration and among the military and to prevent people's increasing dissatisfaction with communist policy, which jeopardized the party's success in the upcoming 1948 national elections.

Quite another challenge to Soviet control arose in Yugoslavia. The communist leaders were even more eager to introduce Stalinism in their country than was the Kremlin leader himself, who wanted them to be more cautious in both their domestic and foreign policy. He repeatedly counseled more consideration of the international situation, notably of the requirement to maintain cooperation with the Anglo-Saxon powers. While his aureole as the adored leader of world communism peaked in Belgrade, he felt his control to be potentially threatened by Yugoslav self-willed performance. When, at the Cominform founding conference, foreign parties were attacked for alleged political deviation, one of the targets was the Tito leadership, if only by implication. The underlying purpose was to prevent the Yugoslavs from ignoring "the general interests of the democratic forces," which they were seen to do by seeking a "leadership role in the Balkans."[34] The reproach referred to the scheme of unification with Bulgaria, to aspirations concerning Albania, and to massive support of the Greek communists' second insurrection.

Decision on Finland

When the Finnish communists were blamed by the Kremlin for failure to exploit their opportunity to seize power, they prepared for a putsch. Their situation, however, was complicated. To be sure, they controlled the ministry of the interior and the security forces under its command, but they were marginalized in government and had to face military resistance if they would attack the constitutional order. The Soviet side gave them instructions all the time but did not trust them after they had not lived up to expectation both during the Winter War of 1939–1940 and in the postwar period. The major reproach was that they had been unable either to make the social democrats join a common front against "bourgeois" policy or else to undermine their influence and power. In contrast to the parties in Soviet-controlled countries, their party apparatus appears not to have been systematically penetrated by Moscow cadres. The difficulties for seizing power by force increased when the key figure of any armed action, Minister of the Interior Leino, was ordered by the Kremlin to resign from party leadership at the very moment when a putsch was being considered. Loss of party function usually implied withdrawal from government. But the communists anticipated that they would not be allowed another minister of the interior. So they decided to conceal Leino's resignation for the time being. However, as the Soviet leaders did not trust him, they refused to authorize any action while he remained.

Given the poor prospect of success, the Finnish communists were not keen to initiate action. The army's commitment to the constitutional order, the people's general support of it, and the political strength of the staunchly anticommunist social democratic party made insurrection an incalculable adventure. The communists saw themselves isolated in society—a feeling that was increased further when the USSR obliged them to take unpopular measures. At the same time, they were not quite sure what the Kremlin really wanted them to do. When they asked for clarification, it took several months until they were invited to receive instructions in Moscow. Having arrived there in early January 1948, they were criticized for having failed to propose a pact with the USSR and to exercise decisive domestic influence at home.

After their return to Helsinki, the communist leaders vainly tried to make the government seek a treaty of military assistance. In close coordination with Soviet representatives in Helsinki, they began to prepare for "brisk action" which, as the party members were told, was taken to prepare for elections in summer but in fact also might create conditions for a putsch. It became increasingly clear that an attempt to seize power might succeed only if actively supported by the USSR. Otherwise, resistance by the army was insuperable. Awareness that direct Soviet involvement would be required seems to have made the Kremlin shrink back from support. Instead, Stalin proposed to President Paasiviki a pact analogous to the treaties with Hungary and Romania. Only a few Finnish parliamentarians were inclined to accept such an arrangement. To exercise domestic pressure the communists initiated a campaign that was not limited to demonstrations and strikes but included secret background operations. Talks between them and Soviet representatives were envisaged to promote victory in elections by exposing "enemies of democracy" and making preparations for punitive action against them.

Shock groups were covertly created. One of them cruelly suppressed a meeting of a tiny "radical party." Rumors were spread about a pro-Western conspiracy that involved government members. An official complaint about this allegation was answered by the Soviet side saying that there was no smoke without fire. A glance around would make clear what was happening. Leino hinted to the army commander that rightist conspiracies might surface. Both the military and the social democrats were concerned over prospective communist action and took precautions for the contingency of attack from both within and outside.

Against this background, Paasiviki concluded that Finland had to meet the Kremlin's demand for a pact. Against the will of a parliamentary majority, he accepted on 9 March Stalin's proposal to enter negotiations. This step deprived the communists of the justification underlying their campaign. In ensuing talks with the Soviet side, the Finns managed to secure conditions that provided for domestic independence and permitted maintenance of military neutrality unless the USSR was attacked by Germany and countries allied to it. The president's acceptance was supported by the army leaders who felt that, given Soviet military traffic across national territory to the Porkkala base, Finland would anyhow get involved in war on the USSR's side. This view was made known to Stalin, who saw Finnish military reliability assured. In the final stages of the negotiations, the communists started a press campaign to discredit right-wing social democratic leaders. But the attempt to isolate them failed; unity of their party was not undermined. After the pact had been concluded, the Kremlin put an end to communist anti-government policy.[35]

Communist Putsch in Czechoslovakia

For some time, the Kremlin had been uneasy about developments in Czechoslovakia. In the Soviet assessment, the communists were in deep crisis for having failed to exploit their strong position to make the country take the road to socialism. After they had achieved relative majority in the 1946 national elections and their party chairman had become prime minister as a result, they had done little to assert comprehensive political leadership. To be sure, they had deprived the traditional administration of major functions by transferring local and regional government to newly established committees in which they largely dominated. They had, however, failed to eliminate "bourgeois" influence in both the army under President Beneš's command and the central bureaucracy that decided on national policy. Expropriation of industrialists and big landowners had not been imposed on Czech and Slovak "bourgeois." The communists and their leftist allies therefore had won major economic power positions only where German and, to some extent also Hungarian, citizens had been forced to leave and to abandon their property.[36]

In the Kremlin's view, failure to impose socioeconomic transformation was a crucial political deficit generally that in part explained that Czechoslovakia did not advance on the road to socialism. To be sure, parties outside the "National Front," which obliged its members to have cooperative relations, were excluded from government and thus deprived of the chance to participate in national decision making but allowed to exist and operate. In principle, both intra-government dissent and advocacy of alternative positions in public were possible. But ministers who expressed divergent minority views had to be careful not to opt out of what was recognized as an accepted consensus. No party wanted to lose the right to be in government by voicing views that fundamentally deviated from the official line. In contrast to countries occupied by the Red Army, however, there were no Soviet occupation authorities whom the communists could rely on to assert their "leading role." Their opponents were therefore hopeful that success in recurrent competitive elections would allow them to limit communist ambition.[37] For Moscow, these political conditions were unsatisfactory, particularly as, during 1947, the communists were losing popularity. A 40 percent vote as in 1946, let alone an absolute majority as then expected by Gottwald, was unlikely to result. The party was in political retreat. This sharply contrasted to the doctrinal concept that the proponents of socialism were bound to advance. Against this background, it is logical that developments in Czechoslovakia were seen not only as embarrassing but unacceptable.

On instructions from Moscow, the communists took the political offensive in late fall 1947. Open conflict broke out early on 5 February 1948 when they chose a minor issue as a test case of struggle with the trade unions on one hand and their opponents on the other. Discussion in government resulted in rejection of their position. Upon this, the communists started a massive campaign against the decision taken by seeking to mobilize the "masses." Communist trade-union organizers made a great effort to create an atmosphere of solidarity and militancy so as to intimidate and silence any opponents. Client organizations of industrial workers and poor peasants were made to sabotage the public order and to threaten action including use of arms against the "enemies of the people." The police, controlled by a communist minister, was presented to the public as the friend of the "people" who would invariably take its side. The commander of the security police in Bohemia (which includes Prague) issued an instruction that all regional officers had to be replaced by communists. To be sure, the government decided against the measure but did not succeed in enforcing compliance. Equally, its protest against communist action generally failed to achieve the desired result.[38]

The crisis culminated when, on 20 February, two ministers asked Gottwald whether the police order in Bohemia had been rescinded. After having received an evasive answer, they and some others resigned. Their expectation that the prime minister could not but follow their example proved wrong: he stayed in office. With the cabinet absent as a collective body, the communists, actively supported by Soviet agents, used their ministries to seize power with no regard for government authority. The Ministry of the Interior organized and equipped a workers' militia under the communist party presidium's direct control; the Ministry of Communication took all media into its hands. At the same time, the ministries held by the democratic parties were "secured" by communist-directed "action committees"; both the respective ministers and noncommunist employees were prevented from entering their offices. Beneš, who as the nation's president commanded the military, remained inactive and capitulated at last when, on 24 February, the communists had taken all positions that they needed for exclusion of the other parties from power and the creation of one-party dictatorship.[39] From then on, the Kremlin was in full control of Czechoslovakia.[40]

Development of Conflict with Yugoslavia

In September 1947, the Yugoslav leadership approved a plan that envisaged to increase the forces of the communist insurgents in Greece to 50,000 men for "liberation" of Macedonia including Saloniki. The Belgrade-based section of the party pledged to assist the operation by underground armed activity and sabotage. When time went on, however, it proved difficult to enlist the required "freedom fighters." When Zakhariades also needed more weapons, he turned to the Kremlin complaining that substantial supplies were received only from Yugoslavia and Albania while Bulgaria failed to be much help. Before this, Tito and Dimitrov had agreed to form the closest possible alliance between their countries and to resolve the issue of Bulgarian Pirin Macedonia. In Moscow, this had been understood as a preparatory step for an offensive directed at Northern Greece. Stalin was unwilling to support such a venture which he felt was now overly risky given firm U.S. resolve for counteraction.

Soviet displeasure increased when, during the fall, Belgrade tried to take control of the Albanian economy and prepared for the deployment of two divisions in Southern Albania close to the border of Greece. The communists felt encouraged to set up a provisional "democratic government." Upon this, the Kremlin concluded that ambition and adventurism of the Yugoslavs must be stopped. Their delegation, which had been summoned to Moscow in early January 1948, was surprised by Stalin's appeal to "swallow Albania." In the light of the attitude taken by the Soviet leader afterward, this was a ruse designed for making Tito and his entourage avow their expansionist designs in order to allow for subsequent denunciation of their political course.[41]

In a following conversation with Dimitrov and the Yugoslav leaders on 10 February, Stalin insisted that their federation project must be stopped. Turning to the delegates from Belgrade, he castigated them for their support of the insurrection in Greece and rebuffed their argument that communist success was still possible. "No, they have no prospect of success at all. What do you think, that Great Britain and the United States—the United States, the most powerful state of the world—will permit you to break their line of communication in the Mediterranean Sea! Nonsense." As it appears, he allowed for some measure of military aid to the comrades in Greece but clearly rejected seeking socialist transformation of their country. As Moscow sources indicate, Stalin wanted to continue exploiting civil war as a means of preventing domestic stabilization. But he raised strong objections against the Albanian "adventure" arguing that it "would give the Americans an excuse for attack" precisely when the USSR (allegedly) sought an arrangement with them that would provide "some sort of peace." Shortly after this, Molotov vainly tried to make Kardelj (who had come to Moscow in Tito's stead) sign a treaty that would have obliged Yugoslavia to consult the USSR on all foreign policy matters. After these disputes, the leaders in Belgrade decided not to submit to the Kremlin but to abide by its policies on Albania and Greece. They also took the unprecedented step to stop providing Moscow with internal information.[42]

The Rift with Tito

Stalin saw noncompliance with his demands as indicating distrust and hostility. Having failed to make Tito yield by vehement accusation, he decided to increase pressure. As early as on 22 February, a Yugoslav request for economic aid had been turned down. On 18 March, all Soviet advisers were called back in a deliberate effort to complicate civil and military reconstruction. This step was tantamount to an open declaration of conflict. While support of the Greek communists and attack on Albanian integrity by Yugoslavia were the immediate causes of disagreement, more fundamental issues were underlying: Belgrade's independent foreign policy and its willingness to extend power in the Balkans by militant action, if it felt this to be expedient. Stalin did not permit taking risks he had not authorized and required that his instructions must be unconditionally followed. Tito, on his part, resented that his country was treated as "small change."[43] In an internal CPSU assessment, he and his associates were portrayed as guilty of having adopted an anti-Marxist position in domestic and foreign policy—the worst thing that a communist could imagine. They were also condemned for overestimation of their achievement, offensive adventurism against other countries, and hegemonic aspirations in the Balkans. Tito was personally ascribed an attitude of ignoring the teachings of Marx, Engels, and Lenin on policy making and accused of opportunism with no correct idea of "class struggle" requirements. In many respects, his position was said to resemble Bukharin's who, in the thirties, had been convicted as a traitor to the socialist cause.[44]

In spite of these attacks, Tito was willing to normalize relations but did not accept the accusation that he had displayed an unfriendly attitude toward the USSR. For Stalin, this amounted to a refusal to demonstrate the required repentence. This appeared all the more annoying as all-out confrontation with the West had increased the need for communists to rally behind Stalin and to accept his control. On 27 March, he and Molotov sent a letter to Belgrade that officially repeated all accusations. It was also distributed to the other Cominform members who duly responded by taking the Soviet view. The conflict escalated. While the Yugoslavs continued to be prepared to admit "some" mistakes, Stalin insisted on unconditional capitulation and demanded that they account for their performance at a Cominform conference in Bucharest. This was rejected in mid-June. Stalin responded by having the Yugoslav party expelled from the Cominform on 19–23 June 1948.[45] A pro-Soviet putsch in Belgrade failed; a plan to assassinate Tito was not implemented.[46]

The wisdom of intensifying conflict with another communist regime and making it an issue of principle did not meet with general approval in the Soviet bloc. Gomułka voiced open criticism, and Dimitrov indicated reservation.[47] Stalin naturally abided by his position and employed all kinds of pressure to make Tito yield, but due, inter alia, to economic aid and political support by the United States,[48] Yugoslavia successfully defended its independence. The price was abandonment of anti-Western militancy and even acceptance of limited alignment with the West. As a result, the fronts in the Cold War ceased to be strictly bipolar but gave way to a more complicated pattern of relations.

Implications for the Communist Parties in the Soviet Bloc

The rupture between Moscow and Belgrade had a dimension that transcended pragmatic power politics: The Kremlin's claim to exclusive ideological authority was put in jeopardy. This explains why Stalin saw a need to reassert communist orthodoxy in Soviet-controlled Eastern Europe. Even before his clash with Tito, he had already felt that declarations on "national roads to socialism" and advisability of a "parliamentary approach" had become undesirable. After, as a result of the overt Cold War, regard for Anglo-Saxon sensitivities was not required any longer and satellite regimes had taken power in dependent Eastern Europe, these slogans served to defend communist autonomy against the USSR. The defection of Yugoslavia had shown the consequences of such "nationalistic aberrations." To prevent this, a most vehement campaign against "Titoism" was initiated throughout the Eastern bloc. Agents of both the West and Tito (who was alleged to be its willing servant) were everywhere seen to engage in subversive activity. Underlying this was Stalin's feeling that Tito's "betrayal" was not an isolated phenomenon but a symptom of widespread inclination among communist state leaders. Once they had firmly asserted domestic control with Soviet support, they wanted to be more independent.

To cope with centrifugal tendencies, Stalin ordered the conversion of the Cominform into an instrument to monitor and control internal affairs of the other parties.[49] He also contemplated turning this organization into a tribunal for sentencing high-ranking deviators but then dropped the idea as impractical. Instead, he decided to exploit conflict among communist party leaders. Soviet cadres who had penetrated party and state of the European countries were instructed to accord priority to intraleadership conflict in their reports; rival top functionaries were encouraged to transmit information against one another.[50] A continuous stream of accusations on "nationalistic deviations," "insufficient appreciation of the USSR's role," entertainment of "links with Tito," and even "espionage for Yugoslavia" resulted that entailed persecution of many major party cadres in all dependent countries including East Germany.[51] The highest party functionaries got involved. In many of these cases, the outcome of their trials changed not only their power position and personal fate but their party's orientation of policy.

The first country to put the new approach into practice was Albania. The communist leaders in Tirana were traditionally divided over attitudes toward Belgrade. Against the background of Soviet indifference, the critics of the pro-Yugoslav orientation suffered total defeat in 1947. In despair, their spokesman Nako Spiru committed suicide. But when, in the course of spring 1948, the Kremlin made clear that it wanted the Albanian party to take sides against Tito, its chairman Enver Hoxha changed his course.[52] In Poland, Gomułka was challenged by his intraparty rivals Bolesław Bierut and Jakub Berman, who blamed him for undue willingness for reconciliation with Yugoslavia, wrong views on communist attitudes to national independence, and a serious right-wing nationalistic tendency. Their reaffirmation of these reproaches in conversations with Stalin and Molotov resulted in Gomułka's deposition as party secretary-general in early September 1948 and subsequently in his being put into jail as well.[53]

In Bulgaria, a longtime Red Army officer who served in the country's forces as general and the supreme Soviet military advisor reported to Moscow that party secretary Traicho Kostov had claimed liberation from the old regime to have been achieved by indigenous effort and concluded that this position was precisely what had caused Tito's betrayal. When Kostov duly repented, the case against him appeared to have been dropped. Then, however, Stalin got word that, in Sofia, Kostov was envisaged to be the man at the top of the party after Dimitrov's death (which had to be expected soon). As a result, no Moscow cadre, but a communist who had remained in his country during World War II, would be the leader. This prospect appeared intolerable. In June 1949, Stalin ordered the arrest of Kostov, who was sentenced to death on 14 December and then executed. A number of other high-ranking functionaries who belonged to the same category were put into prison for many years.[54]

Prior to the open outbreak of conflict with Tito, in March 1948, the CPSU party apparatus prepared a report on the Hungarian party in which Secretary-General Rákosi and some of his associates were blamed for nationalistic tendencies and malappreciation of the USSR. This indicated the Soviet intent to make them targets of political attack. The Kremlin politicians were surprised when, three months later, they received information according to which the views ascribed to the party head were held by a member of the leadership whom they highly trusted, László Rajk. What they did not know was that this was an allegation originating from Rákosi who redirected attack to his major rival. In May 1949, he made the secret police in Prague arrest Noël Field who, on grounds of having sympathized with communists in Western exile and supported them by finance from a U.S. charitable organization, had many contacts in East European capitals. Rajk was one them. After Field had been transferred to Hungarian custody, he was made to confess that he had enlisted Rajk as an American agent. On the basis of this testimony, Rajk was arrested at the end of the month. After the case had aroused controversial discussion in the Kremlin, Stalin summoned Rákosi to Moscow. In their conversation on August 20, the Soviet leader got convinced that the accusation was correct. A show trial was staged in Budapest. At its end in October, Rajk was sentenced to death and executed. Those who had been put on trial with him had to serve long terms of imprisonment. In the following years, Rákosi transmitted more slanderous information to Moscow on the basis of which he was able to arrest more top cadres.[55]

Since Field had met many prominent communist emigrés during World War II and had been in postwar Budapest and Warsaw for extended periods of time, there were many leaders in Eastern Europe liable of accusation of being connected to this alleged U.S. secret service agent. As a result, not only former emigrés in Western Europe but major postwar East European party cadres were candidates for accusation of treacherous activities and designs. Given that Stalin was apparently interested, Rákosi was intensely busy with "unmasking" more and more agents of the international espionage network allegedly set up by Field. While national communist leaders sought to eliminate intraparty rivals, Stalin exploited the opportunity to rid himself of undesirable followers. After Israel had changed sides to the United States, he notably wanted to reduce the large number of cadres of Jewish origin. Within one year, almost all East European parties were affected. For some while, Czechoslovakia was spared, but increasing insight into Field's numerous contacts was bound to produce accusations against Prague functionaries. The most prominent victim among them was the party secretary-general, Rudolf Slánský. A show trial was staged against him and those seen to be his associates. In November 1951, Slánský was executed; the others had to serve long terms of imprisonment.[56] In East Germany, a show trial against a top functionary seen as a rival by Ulbricht was only in the first stages of preparation when Stalin died in early March 1953. Until then, only second-rank cadres had been imprisoned.[57]

STRUGGLE FOR GERMANY

The major battlefield of the Cold War was, naturally, Germany, where the USSR and the three Western powers faced each other. The ongoing political struggle between them was primarily directed at the country's Western part.

While the United States and its European allies needed its participation in economic and political reconstruction, the Soviet Union saw it as the territory that would allow for extension of influence and power to the remaining continent. If the West Germans would espouse the "antifascist-democratic" Soviet zone system and regime and thus undermine Western occupation, the Americans would lose their territorial basis on the Continent and any prospective Western alliance there would be deprived of its major component. In this, the Kremlin had to face a most difficult problem. As early as in 1945, a vast majority of Germans had been inclined to prefer Western to Soviet occupation. Prevailing rejection of the USSR and its communist supporters was subsequently reinforced by the frequent "disppearance" of persons, large-scale persecution of noncommunists, and poor living conditions in the Soviet zone. Additional antipathy was created by brutal Red Army excesses that for a long time had been officially encouraged as a way to take revenge for German crimes in the USSR. The best known phenomenon was the rape of millions of women that continued during the following weeks and months.[58] An element that also greatly influenced public opinion was the fact that, as a result of conquest by the USSR, large provinces east of Oder and Neisse had been taken away from Germany. A major part of the inhabitants was killed, and more than a dozen million were expelled from there and the Czech Sudeten territories to pour into the overcrowded four zones. This created significant antipathy.

Policy in the Soviet Zone of Germany

Undisguised confrontation with the West had two implications for Soviet policy on Germany. The termination of allied cooperation allowed the Soviets to disregard Western objections to policy in the Soviet zone.[59] For the foreseeable future, the evacuation of Germany and Europe by the United States, and also Western acquiescence in the extension of East German measures to the remaining country, had become unlikely on a voluntary basis. To combat the inclination to allow for leniency in waging both the international and the intra-German "class struggle," the Soviet occupation authorities initiated a campaign in the SED for ideological purity, vigilance, and militancy.[60] Ruthless control of political discipline was enforced, large-scale cleansing of cadres put on the agenda, and socialist transformation and communist repression intensified. Reinforced orientation at unilateralism in the Soviet zone went along with blaming the West for undermining the Allied Control Council by failing to accept Soviet objections to policy in the Western zones.[61] Stalin was more anxious than ever to make the German population support him in his struggle for their country. He was aware, however, that most people were "bourgeois"-minded and averse to socialism. So he wanted the Soviet zone regime to appear as but an "antifascist-democratic order." Measures such as expropriation of industrial enterprise had to be depicted as punishment of individuals who had failed to fulfill their obligations.[62]

In the Kremlin's view, the SED had to assert ideological and organizational strength by adopting the Soviet model. This would make the party prevail also in the western parts of the country.[63] Such hope was based on the assumption that the West's anticommunist and anti-Soviet front was bound to collapse sooner or later.[64] On instructions from Moscow, the SED was subjected to fundamental restructuring at its Second Congress in September 1947. Marxist-Leninist orientation and organizational patterns of "democratic centralism" were deemed indispensable for a "party of combat" in its effort to impose "class postulates" on society and thus serve the "struggle for German unity." Only the "organized working class," that is, a Marxist-Leninist party, was declared capable to defend Germany's true interest. Its pro-Soviet, anti-Western policy line allegedly expressed the will of the working masses in the whole country and created the only possible basis of national unity and political reconstruction. Accordingly, public administration and the apparatus of the judiciary had to be subjected to "people's control" by the party.[65] Administrative centralization was accelerated.[66]

At the same time, the Kremlin reinforced the instruments of repression and began to transfer a larger measure of responsibility to the SED regime. The ban that had prevented setting up an indigenous secret police organization was lifted. Under the occupation power's strict control, personnel who had already rendered auxiliary services to the Soviet secret police, and new recruits of "proletarian origin," were given responsibility to punish or pardon previous Nazis, to reintegrate them into society, and to keep an eye on personnel in the state apparatus. Training in Soviet methods of observation, interrogation, and "penetrating and handling" administrative networks was introduced.[67] While propaganda denounced nonexisting Western plans to "remilitarize West Germany," high-ranking Soviet military officers began highly secret talks in late summer 1947 with a few selected East German political and military cadres including Ulbricht about an army to be set up under the disguise of police units.[68]

Against this background, Grotewohl complained during a talk between Stalin and the SED leaders on 26 March 1948 that the Soviet zone police was poorly armed.

Stalin asks whether these people are reliable. Grotewohl answers that there are 90% party comrades. The [land] ministers of the interior are all our people. Stalin asks: And at the center? Grotewohl answers: Also. Stalin asks, don't you feel that the police must be strengthened and well kept. Grotewohl says that this is, of course, the crucial issue. Stalin asks which help is needed from us. Grotewohl talks about desirability of assistance in training the police. Stalin asks whether they have good cadres who might train the police. Grotewohl answers that there are generally few cadres for the police. Stalin says that they may perhaps be taken from prisoners of war. Grotewohl says that part of the police cadres is from the [1943] Committee "Free Germany," and he mentions in particular the head of the Berlin police, Colonel [Paul] Markgraf, and the deputy of one of the *land* ministers of the interior [Bernhard] Bechler. Stalin says that if people from the prisoners of war are required, one may take them. He asks whether a number [of military professionals] has been fixed which may be taken into the police. Semënov answers that, as much as he remembers, no agreement has been fixed given differing views on this question in the Control Council. Stalin says if armament is required, you can use German weaponry which we possibly have. Stalin emphasizes that the police is a very serious thing which must be seriously discussed.[69]

In 1947–1948, Soviet occupation authorities paid increasing attention to the "bourgeois" parties.[70] The CDU and LDP came under pressure to identify fully with the positions taken by the communists. At a number of occasions, they had to choose between adaptation (tantamount to surrender) and resistance (with likely punitive reaction), which served to split them up into "progressive" and "reactionary" forces.[71] For example, they were required in fall 1947 to support the creation of a "new people's control organ" in industry, which was clearly designed to allow the communists additional exercise of power.[72] This probe was followed by the issue of participation in the SED-controlled German People's Congress. This was accepted by the LDP. The CDU refused and took a pro-Western position by supporting the Marshall Plan. The occupation authorities responded by putting pressure on lower party levels to project an image that Christian Democratic members largely disagreed with their leaders. The underlying purpose was to implant a split in the party ranks, to discredit independent leaders, and to prepare for their replacement.

Colonel Tiul'panov's department also employed any means short of imprisonment and liquidation to make regional CDU representatives oppose their zonal chairman Jakob Kaiser and his deputy Ernst Lemmer who would have to be replaced by more "progressive" personnel. It took some time until the occupation officer felt that he could risk initiating the dismissal of the two politicians. Despite all pressure and intervention, however, he repeatedly failed to win a majority. In the end, he unilaterally appointed a new leadership but did not dare to make this public. Only some time after Kaiser and Lemmer had been forced to leave for West Berlin, his candidate Otto Nuschke was officially installed. But it was not before August 1948 that a party conference was convened to have him legitimized by a statutory vote. In the meantime, satellization had been systematically enforced by means of manipulation, initimidation, and repression. Nonetheless, it was difficult for Tiul'panov to succeed. From then on, opposition was usually absent in the higher and medium levels but continued among the rank and file for years to come. The LDP, which was less obstinate, was similarly subjected to forceful repression until all its organizations were unconditionally obedient. The Kremlin might have dispensed with the "bourgeois" parties altogether but, as internal statements indicate, it allowed them to continue their existence since it wanted to exploit their relations with their "bourgeois" counterparts in the Western zones to promote German unity along Soviet lines.[73]

Satellization of the "bourgeois" parties did not prevent their continued exposure to distrust and enmity. Even after they had been subjugated fully, the CDU and LDP were seen as "class enemies" who, as Stalin put it, had to be "undermined."[74] In conformity with an explanation of his to the SED leaders in January 1947, the Soviet authorities began to initiate a "national-democratic" party (NDPD) in summer 1948 as an organization to deprive the CDU and LDP of political support among the "bourgeoisie." The new "bourgeois" party, which was controlled by covert communists, expressly served the purpose of rallying the former Nazis and professional military behind the SED.[75] In parallel to this, a peasant party, the DBP, was set up by communist cadres. The two parties also served as a basis for the attempt to make West German "fascists," military professionals, and peasants feel that their political home was in the Soviet zone which, in contrast to the West, provided them with parties of their own.[76] To weaken the CDU and LDP still further, the basis for cooperation in the "antifascist-democratic bloc" was changed by introducing the model of "equal" representation that had already been applied at the German People's Congress. All political parties and a very large number of "democratic mass organizations" were accorded one vote each in the bloc that was set up. As the SED leaders controlled all the alleged nonparty organizations, they were able to multiply their representation and to reduce the CDU and LDP to a tiny minority.[77] The political emasculation of the two parties culminated when, in May 1949, one list of bloc candidates preselected by the communist leaders was submitted to the electorate.[78]

Appeal to German Desire for Unity

When challenged by the Marshall Plan, the Kremlin insisted that previous agreements obliged the Western powers to drop it. In particular, the inclusion of West German in its implementation was incompatible with the 1945 Potsdam decisions on German economic unity.[79] The Anglo-Saxon decision to restore the economy in the Western zones was seen to be directed at creating a basis for an extended stay of American troops in Europe and the imminent formation of an anti-Soviet military bloc that would include West Germany.[80] To prevent this, the Soviet authorities and their East

German clients increased their efforts to mobilize people against national partition, which was allegedly initiated by the "splitting politicians" in the West.[81] In June 1947, the idea emerged in East Berlin that a congress should be convened with delegates from political parties, trade unions, regional parliaments, administrative bodies, industrial institutions, and "anti-fascist organizations" all over the country to discuss steps to set up central administrations. This proposal would have to be justified by referring to the respective decision at Potsdam. An all-zonal referendum on the issue was envisaged. If the Western powers opposed, the population of the Soviet zone would be called to the polls to demonstrate German support. But this was rejected by the Kremlin as unpromising.[82] For several months after disruption of relations with the West, no instructions were forthcoming from Moscow. As a result, the a priori abortive attempt continued to make the Western occupation authorities accept extension of the SED.[83]

While there was little hope that the United States and Britain were willing to change their position, the best thing was to put pressure on them by maintaining any previous demand and appealing to the German public for support. To this end, propaganda claimed that Soviet insistence on enforcement of the Potsdam accords (which also implicitly postulated socioeconomic transformation) was directed at both political and economic unification of Germany. Identification with it was therefore justified on grounds of German national interest. A mass movement was required to support the demands raised by the USSR. In accordance with this concept, the Soviet delegation at the London session of the Council of Foreign Ministers in late fall was instructed to abide by the position taken at the preceding spring session in Moscow. Only concerning discussion tactics were a few minor variants envisaged.[84]

Against the background of failure to reach agreement in London, the Germans were appealed to that they must protest against the Western powers' "imperialist splitting policies" and demand conclusion of a peace treaty that was alleged to result automatically in unification.[85] They were declared to be entitled to "unity and a just peace." To enforce these demands, "authoritative representatives" from all parts of Germany were to assemble and send a request to London.[86] The foreign ministers there must be confronted with demands for the instant creation of a countrywide government, urgent conclusion of a peace treaty, and subsequent withdrawal of the occupation troops. By advocating these steps, the USSR presented itself as the only power to defend the defeated nation's interest in unification.[87] This program served the purpose of putting pressure on the Anglo-Saxon powers to accept the immediate creation of an all-German government and to enter negotiations on a peace treaty. The fulfilment of either demand was bound to prevent implementation of the Marshall Plan. If a goverment were set up, it would include the Soviet zone whose representatives were certain to veto

any step not authorized by the Kremlin. Negotiating necessarily implied renunciation of any measure not commonly agreed upon by all four powers.

At the same time, the advocated evacuation of Germany by the occupation troops did not reflect the Kremlin's real policy. Long-term deployment
of Soviet troops in the defeated country was seen as an indispensable condition to create "irreversible facts," that is, to provide for the road to socialism to be taken permanently.[88] For this reason, any agreement on terminating the Red Army's presence in Central Europe was rejected.[89] The fact
that propaganda differed from actual intent did not embarrass the policy
makers in Moscow. After all, it was clear that the West would decline. Therefore, the USSR did not risk being taken at its word.

The SED and its satellite organizations duly adopted the Soviet program of
action but pretended that, in the German national interest, they acted on their
own initiative. According to their argument, the Western effort to split the
country had created a challenge that required all parties and groups to unite in
supporting the USSR in its struggle for unification. The appeal met with rejection by all politicians in the Western zones, naturally except for the communists. Also, the CDU in Eastern Germany refused support. Thus the attempt to
make it appear as an all-party initiative failed. Upon this, the SED declared on
instructions from Moscow that it was willing to fulfill its obligation to the German people and to organize the assembly on behalf of "all patriots."[90]

A "German People's Congress" was convened in East Berlin on 6–7 December 1947. The participants from the Soviet zone were recruited by the
SED and its client organizations; a KPD committee that also pretended to
represent the social democrats selected a minor number of West German
delegates.[91] As was officially claimed, people of all political and social strata
in all the four zones were present. On the basis of a Soviet draft, a resolution was worked out and sent to the four foreign ministers in London.[92] A
second German People's Congress met on 17–18 March 1948. On the basis of detailed Soviet planning, reliable delegates ostensibly representing
both parts of the country were selected. The proceedings followed a preconceived plan of speeches and discussions. At the end, a permanent German People's Council was elected on the basis of a proposal submitted by
the SED organizers. A minor number of cadres from the Western zones were
included to substantiate the claim that all of Germany was represented.

The People's Council set up a number of committees to prepare a constitution and other documents for a prospective state. In an appeal to the public, it was argued that "national emergency" entailed a need for "self-help"
by initiating a "movement of national resistance" designed to create a
"bourgeois-democratic" state in the tradition of 1848. Both the feudal order that had then been the antagonist and the current national partition
would thus be overcome.[93] This was to "mobilize the masses and make
them close ranks" against the Western powers.[94] The resultant "German

Democratic Republic" was said to extend to all of Germany but the centralized administration simultaneously set up provided a basis for a separate state.[95] Stalin told the SED leaders that the prospective constitution was also to serve propaganda functions.

> He [Stalin] says that it would be good if some organ of the People's Congress would work out a constitution of Germany and would submit it to discussion in both West and East Germany. This constitution must not be very democratic so as not to intimidate people, but it must be also sufficiently democratic that the best elements of West and East can accept it. This would be very good. The whole population must be drawn into the discussion of the constitution. This will create a psychological basis for enforcement of Germany's unity.

In the Soviet leader's view, more than mere advocacy of national unification was required.

> People must be made to get involved in the process of its being achieved. Elaboration of the constitution was one of the crucial levers for preparing the German population for unity. One must not repeat words on unity all the time. They will listen several times but then all of them will be bored. One has to submit a concrete scheme and to involve the population in working out this document. One has to do this as soon as possible. It is not a matter of putting the constitution into practice. This will not be soon. One must make it a lever for preparing the masses for unification of Germany. The English and the Americans will make an effort to buy the Germans by putting them in a privileged position. The only means against this is preparing people's minds for unity. The constitution is a means [to this end]—it is a very good means, a remarkable means. . . . The commission [of the People's Congress] must work out the constitution but the Congress will discuss and ratify it, then it will put it before the people. This will be a lengthy process. If it will take several years, you will profit by it. If the minds are prepared for this idea, then unity can't be destroyed. Then the Americans will surrender. If you take this advice, it will be good. Grotewohl remarks that they [the SED leaders] have the same opinion, and that this will provide a possibility for concrete propaganda. Stalin confirms this. The whole people expects this and will get the material. And no America whatever will be able to do anything about it. You will thus associate people with the [People's] Congress. Its authority must be increased. Stalin says that unification of Germany will not result immediately. But one must fight for unifaction of Germany by [both] simplified and sophisticated propaganda.[96]

The two People's Congresses were followed by propaganda appeals to "all patriots" to support the demand for the immediate creation of a united state and conclusion of a peace treaty. Communist cadres were sent from the Soviet zone to the West to set up a German People's Congress network as "solid bases" for "patriotic" political work. In fact, however, these regional and local committees were intended to provide a substitute for an SED party apparatus.

They claimed to represent "patriots" with no party affiliation but were firmly controlled by the East German regime. Their principal, if unavowed task was to split the SPD by recruiting "social democratic workers" and isolating Schumacher's followers. "Working class unity" continued to be seen as the condition of creating national unity. To be sure, "bourgeois" nationalists were also given attention but not ascribed major importance despite their being more amenable than the social democrats.[97] As the Western occupation authorities did not accept a party organization based on the pretense that it had been set up by both communists and social democrats, an attempt was made to make the KPD appear as representing the "working class" as a whole by renaming it "socialist people's party."[98]

THE BERLIN BLOCKADE

During the first months of 1948, it became increasingly clear that both massive propaganda and all organizational effort had failed to mobilize the West Germans against the Western powers. With very few exceptions, they saw Anglo-Saxon occupation as their protection against the Soviet threat and understood that the Marshall Plan provided a basis for economic reconstruction. While they continued to desire allied agreement on national unification, they were both suspicious of Soviet intent and in favor of receiving U.S. aid to cope with their miserable material situation. The communist leaders of East Germany were aware that their propaganda was rather unsuccessful. While Pieck claimed in his report to Stalin that the "bourgeoisie" had been defeated [in the Soviet zone as he should have added], he had to admit that the attempt to mobilize the West Germans against their occupiers had failed. Support for the SED in East Germany was waning—a problem that he ascribed to powerful enemy propaganda from West Berlin.[99] The Kremlin had already realized that its policy did not prevent the Western zones from being transformed into a state within the Western sphere of power. As a first step, a separate currency reform was expected in the second half of 1948 to provide a basis for economic recovery. As early as in late fall 1947, the Soviet side had begun to prepare for a similar measure that would be implemented immediately afterward to make the public believe that this was a direct response to the "provocation" in the West.[100]

The Kremlin was determined to take no passive look at economic and political consolidation of the Western zones. Given that the Germans had failed to allow themselves to be persuaded by Eastern advocacy of unification and a peace treaty, the Anglo-Saxon powers on whose backing they relied had to be exposed as being weak and unable to provide protection. This would teach people that they had no option but to join the USSR. To this end, it appeared necessary to inflict a major defeat on the West.[101] Exploitation of its vulnerable position in Berlin would serve the purpose. Action to "annul the Berlin zone and integrate it into the Soviet zone" was envisaged as a reprisal for refused compliance with the demand to abstain from creating the West German state. As the United States would not risk threatening war in defense of its position in Berlin, it could not but accept a major political defeat. It would either have to renounce the creation of a separate state in the Western part of the country or abandon the position in Berlin when the access routes would be closed.[102] Underlying this was a willingness to shatter German confidence in support by the West.

Stalin's Decision to Block Western Access to Berlin

In the Soviet view, the Western presence in Berlin was based not on the right of aquisition by victory but on agreement with the USSR. The argument that the Americans (and their associates) had violated almost any quadripartite accord on Germany[103] therefore invited the conclusion that they did not enjoy corresponding rights. On 11 January 1948, public warning that Western "splitting policies" would inevitably affect the status of Berlin[104] indicated that the Kremlin wanted to operate on the basis of this rationale.

The prospective introduction of a separate currency would provide an opportunity to claim that all four sectors must accept the currency which, under the pretense that this measure had only been provoked by the preceding step in the West,[105] would then be circulated in the surrounding Soviet zone. The argument that geography did not allow for another arrangement after the split had been caused by the other side would justify enforcement of this demand by closing the access routes. The West would then have to take the onus of being guilty of the resulting conflict. If the Western powers were prepared to authorize circulation of the Eastern currency in their sectors to buy access, they would undermine their presence since this would mean not only economic but political control by the Soviet zone. Alternatively, the Western powers would have to accept defeat by giving up their plan for a West German state and allowing Soviet developments within their zones. The Kremlin was confident that this strategy was bound to entail victory.

Early in 1948, the United States, Britain, and France actively prepared for a West German state. On 23 February through 6 March, they and the Benelux countries discussed the problem and decided to go ahead. The Soviet Union protested that this was an initiative by "aggressive circles" directed at undermining the agreements on the Allied Control Council and the Council of Foreign Ministers. It did not serve peace but entailed the danger of Germany's revival as an "aggressive power." The decisions that had resulted failed to have "legal power and international authority."[106] On 17 March, Britain, France, and the Benelux states concluded a treaty on mutual assistance. The Kremlin saw any military arrangement of other countries on the Continent to be directed against the USSR and reacted accordingly. On 15 March, Stalin assessed the situation and envisaged countermeasures. He ordered successive tightening of Soviet zone border controls to place restrictions on Western access to Berlin and approved a schedule of successive action. After a West German state had been created, the foreign ministers of the USSR and East European countries were to meet to denounce this as illegal and to issue a demand for a quadripartite conference on Germany. The Western governments would have to choose between acceptance and rejection. If they, as Stalin expected, failed to comply, they would thereby admit violation of their contractual obligation to take decisions on Germany in cooperation with Moscow. The Soviet Union would then announce that their right of presence in, and access to, Berlin had been deprived of its legal basis and would not be respected any longer.[107]

The Kremlin started its political offensive by making the Soviet supreme commander in Germany leave the Allied Control Council on 20 March. Taking this step, he pointed out that, in violation of allied agreements on the common exercise of authority in Germany, his colleagues had failed to account for the measures taken in the Western zones. These were incompatible with contractual obligations and could "not be recognized as legal." Refusal by the three powers to discuss issues such as demilitarization, democratization, reparations, and dissolution of emigré organizations indicated that they did not take interallied control of Germany seriously but used it as an umbrella to conceal unilateral action. The Control Council had ceased to exist for all practical purposes.[108] In a conversation with the SED leaders shortly afterward, Stalin gave the impression that he was still undecided on how to cope with the unsatisfactory situation. When Pieck expressed the opinion that negative influence from Berlin might be eliminated by making the Western powers leave the city, he answered, "Let's try through common efforts, perhaps we will drive them out."[109]

Stalin expected his attempt to succeed but did not exclude unforeseen friction. The game had not been won yet.[110] A major factor to consider was the correlation of military forces. The Soviet army possessed superior strength at the places of possible combat but was not prepared for an offensive and long-term war. To be sure, the United States, like the other Western countries, had disbanded most of its troops and was largely inferior in the European theater but it had impressive deterrent capabilities, notably the atomic bomb monopoly and an immensely superior economic potential that, if with delay, could be mobilized for military purposes. In contrast to this, the USSR was exhausted, and its political and industrial centers were unprotected against the threat of atomic devastation. Predictable victory in Europe during the early stages would not prevent massive destruction and ultimate defeat. For this reason, any risk of war had to be avoided.[111] Stalin saw himself in a favorable position against West Berlin but he knew that he must be cautious.[112] It was necessary to probe the U.S. reaction to any step of escalating pressure. By successively restricting Western access to the city from 1 April onward, he retained the option of moderating his course in response to unforeseen risks.

Initiation of the Berlin Blockade

When Soviet action against surface traffic gained momentum in late spring, the United States warned that any attempt to dislocate the Western garrisons by force would be answered by military counteraction. Violation of obligations under the air corridor agreement (which was the only written accord on access rights) would not be tolerated either. Upon this, Stalin abandoned the plan to block air traffic. Closure of only the surface lanes—roads, railway lines, and canals—was envisaged. The Kremlin did not see the prospect of final victory jeopardized. This assessment was reinforced by reports that the West Germans were already losing confidence in U.S. protection.[113]

Limitation of the intended blockade to access on land was not seen as a major concession by the Kremlin leaders. To be sure, the Western garrisons would not be forced to surrender at once. They even could hold out satisfying their own needs by air transport for a long period of time. But given that it was generally believed impossible to supply 2.4 million inhabitants by aircraft, the West Berliners would inevitably turn to the Eastern side of Germany for the goods necessary for survival. As a result, the Western occupiers' position would become untenable; they would have to leave. While they would not have to withdraw immediately and directly, they would be unable to defend their presence in the long run. Only willingness to accept Soviet conditions, notably the restoration of the correlation of power that existed in Germany before the Marshall Plan, might spare them dislocation. In spring 1948, the Kremlin leaders did not recognize that major delay of victory entailed major disadvantage. They realized only in the course of the blockade that Western success to resist pressure for some time was apt to enhance German anti-Soviet and pro-Western feeling.

On 16 June 1948, a major step of conflict escalation was taken. The Soviet commander of Berlin left the quadripartite *Komendatura* saying that joint control of the city had lost its basis.[114] Two days later, the Western governments informed the USSR that they would circulate a new currency in West Germany on 23 June. The Kremlin was caught by surprise. It had expected the measure to be taken two months later; Soviet intelligence had provided no indication to the contrary. At an East-West meeting of financial experts on 22 June, Moscow's representative insisted that the Western zone currency must not be introduced in any part of Berlin. Only the circulation of Soviet zone money would be permitted. Otherwise, "economic and administrative sanctions" would result. As the Western powers had destroyed German unity, Berlin had lost its function as the location of quadripartite control of Germany. As he argued, this raised the question about what need there was any longer for the Western occupation authorities to be present there. On the following day, the USSR closed all surface access routes.[115]

At the suggestion of his air commander in Berlin, the British military governor in Germany, General Robertson, recommended initiation of an airlift as an emergency operation. His U.S. colleague, General Clay, felt that this was a promising way to resist Soviet pressure, and he convinced his military and political superiors in Washington that the effort was worthwhile. When the airlift developed, it gradually involved all available U.S. and other Western air transport capabilities and required unprecented organizing skills.[116]

The introduction of Western currency reform prior to the expected date resulted in the disarray of Stalin's schedule. The denunciation of Western willingness to create a West German state as a violation of interallied agreement and the presentation of a list of maximum demands (such as quadripartite Ruhr control and acceptance of any reparation claims) at the envisaged communist foreign ministers' meeting failed to precede the Soviet blockade but followed only later. It was postulated that a "provisional, democratic, peaceloving all-German government" must be set up to include "democratic political parties and organizations." Equally, the domestic issues of unification were to be decided exclusively by representatives of the East and West German authorities on the basis of parity.[117] Termination of occupation was also posited. This, however, was propaganda since the Kremlin was determined to retain both its army and regime in Germany as an indispensable means to enforce and maintain socioeconomic transformation.[118]

Negotiations on Berlin

Feeling that it was impossible to separate Berlin permanently from the surrounding territory, the Western powers introduced the West German currency in their sectors only provisionally. They were apparently willing to allow for their financial association with the Soviet zone provided that this would not imply economic and political control by the USSR that was bound to undermine their presence. As they did not want to risk military confrontation for surface access,[119] they sought to negotiate a mutually acceptable agreement. Underlying this was the assumption that an accord was possible that would make extension of the East German currency to all of

Berlin compatible with the maintenance of Western occupation in the Western sectors. It was also held that the airlift would allow for but a breathing spell. The Western governments therefore felt that the time that had been won should be used to solve the conflict by negotiations. So they indicated their willingness that, given appropriate conditions, they would allow for introduction of the East German currency in the Western sectors in exchange for Soviet lifting of the blockade.[120]

After preceding Soviet-U.S. exchange on conflict over Berlin,[121] Ambassador Bedell Smith emphasized on behalf of his British and French colleagues (who were present) to Stalin on 2 August 1948 that the Western presence in Berlin resulted from German surrender and hence did not depend on joint exercise of occupation authority. The need for access resulted from the need to safeguard supply. Stalin retorted that Western military presence in a city in the midst of the Soviet zone was "understandable" only as long as Germany had been one country. But since it had been split up and a West German state was emerging with Frankfurt as its capital, Berlin had lost its function as capital of Germany. The Western presence had thus been deprived of its juridical basis. Nonetheless the USSR did not intend to force the Western troops out. This would apply even if the Western powers would not return to the quadripartite decisions on Germany. But he demanded transfer of the city's supply. If this condition were met, the USSR would tolerate the three powers' stay in Berlin in spite of lacking legal fundament. The current measures to "restrict transport" had been taken as a tactical device to defend Berlin against penetration by alien currency. Stalin left no doubt that he saw the blockade as a means to counter the creation of a West German state.

The Kremlin leader proposed to promote a solution of the Berlin problem by introducing the Soviet zone currency in the Western sectors. He made lifting of transport restrictions conditional on both deferring implementation of the London six-power decisions to create a state in the West and on starting quadripartite negotiations on the German problem. He declared that he did not insist absolutely on such a four-power conference but wanted "the emphatic interest of the Soviet government in postponing solution of the problem of a West German state" to be taken into account. The Western ambassadors answered that they would report to their governments.[122] On 6 August, they submitted a draft communiqué that, in exchange for cancellation of all restrictions at the access routes, expressed willingness to introduce the Soviet zone currency in the Western sectors if its flow and use were subjected to joint supervision by the four powers. When Molotov instantly wanted Stalin's proposal to defer creation of a West German state to be included, they declined. The draft that he tabled in return added this point and failed to mention that Western acceptance of the currency demand had been made conditional on quadripartite control. The ambassadors retorted that agreement on this basis was impossible. They argued that restriction of access must not be linked to the problem of currency reform, respectively reconstruction of West Germany, as it had been initiated before. They also felt that, when Stalin had referred to negotiations on Germany, this had not been a condition for opening the transit routes. In their portrayal, four-power supervision of the currency in Berlin did not impair Soviet currency control outside the city.[123]

In another conversation on 23 August, Stalin and the three ambassadors discussed the controversial Soviet draft and a directive to the four commanders in Germany who would have to work out practical details on how the East German currency would be extended to West Berlin. Stalin indicated that it would be good if deferment of the London decisions' implementation were mentioned as an obligation. If, for reasons of prestige, the Western powers did not want to say so in public, this might be fixed by a private exchange of letters. Supported by his French colleague, the U.S. ambassador suggested a compromise formula that, however, was rejected by the British side. The Western governments were asked to provide a new draft. With regard to the directive, Stalin advocated the control of money circulation by the Soviet zone bank that would operate under supervision by a four-power commission. The American ambassador objected that the Western governments were thus far not in agreement on the bank being assigned such a function. He also made clear that a joint commission must not have some vague supervisory function but effective control authority to take decisions on currency in Berlin. On this basis, the bias of the Soviet proposal that an Eastern bank was envisaged to be in charge might thus be corrected at least partially. Upon this, debate focused on the competences to be accorded to the financial commission. While the ambassadors wanted it to be an instrument of quadripartite control of money circulation, Stalin felt it must simply rubberstamp Soviet zone bank decisions. Nonetheless, the two sides declared in the end that they agreed "basically."[124]

The resultant directive charged the four governors in general terms with "providing adequate safeguards to prevent the use in Berlin of the German mark of the Soviet zone from leading to disorganizing currency circulation or disrupting the stability of currency in the Soviet zone."[125] In subsequent negotiations, the Soviet side insisted on the narrowest possible interpretation. The crucial issue was which powers must be accorded to the quadripartite financial commission. The Western position was that it must have "supreme authority" to control all Soviet zone bank activities "with regard to money exchange and further circulation of money in Berlin." The Soviet side rejected this as absolutely unacceptable. It also declined to make the Soviet supreme commander in Germany lift all restrictions of access and allow for full control of all Soviet zone bank operations relating to Berlin if negotiations with him were to continue. As was alleged, this demand was based on a one-sided interpretation of the preceding agreement. For their part, the Western governments were not willing to renounce currency control fully. Otherwise, the USSR would be in control of their sectors.[126]

Failure of the Berlin Blockade

The Kremlin supported its claim to control Berlin as a whole by a putsch. On 6 September 1948, supposedly "outraged citizens"—in fact, a crowd mobilized by the SED youth organization FDJ—stormed the city hall in the Eastern sector. The election-based city government was routed; its democratic members had to leave and were replaced by communists and their clients. But the objective of taking over all of Berlin and thereby undermining the Western occupation was missed. The representatives of the democratic parties went to West Berlin and set up a city government there. As a result, the city was divided also on the level of German administration.[127] Ernst Reuter, who had been elected mayor as early as in 1946 but prevented from taking office by a Soviet veto, took over. He appealed to his citizens to defend freedom fearlessly and to the "free world" to support them in their struggle for democracy. The resonance was enormous. Never had there been assembled as many people in the city as when they listened to him; among both governments and the public in the Western countries, notably the United States, a strong feeling of solidarity with the heroic Berliners reinforced determination not to leave them alone.

For some time, the Kremlin maintained confidence in victory. On 6 November 1948, Molotov only felt that the attempt to reassert influence in the Western zones had failed.[128] When the SED leaders reported to Stalin in mid-December, they admitted to having suffered a political defeat but argued that this was but a temporary setback. Their struggle for a "democratic city government," an "assembly of representatives for Berlin as a whole on a bloc basis," and "introduction of one single currency and of a democratic economic order" would continue. Stalin concluded that, for the time being, West Berlin had managed to defend independence against him.[129] His continuing expectation that the airlift would fail to provide the Western sectors with sufficient supply during the winter period was equally disappointed.

The blockade also increasingly produced highly detrimental effects. Public sentiment took an anti-Soviet and anticommunist turn not only in West Berlin and West Germany. In Western countries, a feeling of threat from the East and a resultant awareness of the need for joint resistance were spreading. The three occupation powers that until then had largely seen their task in preventing the Germans to become a danger to the world again were impressed by the West Berliners' courage and willingness to accept hardship and risk and by emerging German identification with their political orientation. The growing sense of common challenge created a basis for growing mutual trust and more cooperative relations. The perception that Moscow was a source of mortal danger to "freedom" extended to the neutral countries of Europe. There was increasing willingness among them to commit themselves to a joint defense of democracy. As the United States was the backbone of any effective effort to halt Soviet expansion, the Benelux countries, Denmark, Norway, and Italy, decided to become members of the North Atlantic alliance that was under negotiation in winter 1948–1949. The treaty on its formation concluded on 4 April 1949. This implied U.S. determination to defend Western Europe—the very thing that Stalin had always sought to avert. To prevent further deterioration of his position, he indicated willingness to lift the blockade. To save face, he made an agreement that was reached on 5 May, conditional on a quadripartite conference on Germany.[130]

The USSR was on the defensive when the delegations of the four powers met in Paris on 23 May—20 June 1949. Foreign Minister Vyshinskii, however, took an offensive stand. In public sessions, he reasserted all previous positions with no regard for predictable rejection by his Western interlocutors. After all, the postulated restoration of unlimited joint control of Berlin and Germany, including the Ruhr District, was precisely the outcome that had been prevented by the United States, Britain, and France during the preceding two years. The demands for fulfilment of all Soviet reparation claims, for creation of both an All-German State Council and a Berlin City Authority on the basis of parity between East and West German authorities, and for a "bloc of parties and [communist-controlled] social organizations" to allow for elections in Berlin, were equally unacceptable. In private exchanges, Soviet diplomats admitted that their superiors did not hope for Western approval and expressed their expectation that no agreement on all-German issues would result. Serious negotiations focused on Berlin where, for obvious practical reasons, some degree of consensus was necessary. But even there Soviet insistence on unlimited quadripartite control that would have provided the Kremlin with a veto on any decision and denied any autonomous action to the Germans (who were privately blamed for hating the USSR) did not allow for an accord on the city as a whole. The only result of negotiating was Soviet acquiescence in the *status quo ante*. The Kremlin restored the previous practice of Western access but avoided recognition of such a right.[131]

STATE-BUILDING IN EAST GERMANY

When Stalin refused to put the issue of German reunification on the political agenda, he acted on the assumption that partition necessarily implied the creation of two states. As early as in spring 1948, he felt that the organization of the Western zones as a state was likely and concluded that then similar action was required on the Soviet side. From 1946 onward, the zonal administration had been continuously reinforced. The German Economic Commission and the German Administration of the Interior had emerged as major centers to execute the occupation power's policy. Police and judiciary had also been transformed into unified organizations designed to cope primarily with "political crimes."[132]

When, in 1949, Soviet attempts to inflict defeat on the Western occupation powers had resulted in failure, it was clear that the allegedly all-German constitution prepared in the framework of the People's Council was going to be used for setting up a "German Democratic Republic" confined to the Eastern part of the country. This had been envisaged as a possibility from the very start. In March 1948, Stalin explained to the SED leaders that he expected a zonal state to result for the time being. He agreed with Grotewohl that the prospective East German state must be announced only after a West German state had been created first. For this reason, the constitution had simply been discussed but not put into effect. It would be ratified and implemented (in the Soviet zone as was implied) only later. To be sure, the current effort was directed at the zonal state as an immediate result but more than this must be sought. The task was also to provide "a substitute or rather germs (embryos) of an all-German parliament and government." As Stalin made clear, the separate state was to be the nucleus of future unification.[133]

Wilfried Loth has argued that Stalin invariably sought a united Germany on a democratic basis. But due to a lack of comprehension or will of subordinate functionaries in East Berlin, notably Tiul'panov and Ulbricht, a separate communist state was set up against his will. He could not but accept it as an accomplished fact but tried to get rid of it afterward.[134] This thesis is incompatible with any available evidence on internal and public statements by Stalin and on preparations for setting up the East German state. The only Eastern source referred to by Loth are notes taken by KPD/SED Chairman Pieck. They are used only selectively, that is, when they appear to fit the author's purpose. In addition to this, interpretation is based on the assumption that the term *democracy* in Soviet statements has the same meaning as in the West. It is certainly correct that, after March 1945, Stalin advocated German unity, but he did so on the premise that it would take the road to socialism. Otherwise, he preferred partition. Another flaw in this thesis is the implication that he was allegedly utterly unable to monitor, let alone control, major decisions by his subordinates. Actors on the third or fourth level of the Soviet hierarchy are believed to have enforced a policy that was rejected by their boss. Loth sees this as an inexplicable "mystery of German postwar history."[135] This would indeed have been most mysterious given the usual unconditional subordination to Stalin as a godlike unfailing leader who ruthlessly punished even minor deviation. The discipline thus imposed used to make subordinates prefer inaction to taking necessary but unauthorized steps.

Preparations for Setting up an East German State

The committees of the German People's Council on constitution, peace treaty, economy, judiciary, culture, agriculture, and social problems worked out texts in accordance with instructions from Moscow. The first step of Soviet guidance was that the SED key cadres who controlled the process of formulation were provided with outlines of the intended texts. When, on this basis, drafts had been worked out, these were secretly submitted to the responsible Soviet agencies for detailed comment and correction. When their response had been received, modification to make the text conform was suggested by the SED liaison cadres who pretended that they had reached the conclusions on their own. After this, another check ensued to make sure that the wording fully corresponded to Soviet intent. As a result of the procedures employed to conceal guidance, the committee members were made to feel that they prepared the texts on their own. When the texts had been completed by the inclusion of all successive amendments, they were submitted to the plenum of the German People's Council for formal discussion and approval.[136]

As Stalin had previously told the SED leaders, the wording of the constitution and the other texts was designed to appear acceptable to communists and "bourgeois"-minded people alike. This was achieved by use of ideological terminology that created a Western-democratic image among the uninitiated but provided for interpretation and implementation along Soviet lines. Notably the constitution was designed to create a positive impression among the general public. The claim to both "bourgeois democratic" orientation and all-German legitimacy was expressed by the term *German Democratic Republic* (GDR). Allegation that it was based on "bourgeois democratic" principles was justified by claiming that the democratic pre-Nazi Weimar Republic constitution was the underlying model. But a few modifications had been made to extend political democracy to the socioeconomic sphere. This referred to the measures of socialist transformation introduced in the Soviet zone since 1945. All-German legitimation was derived from the assertion that the People's Congress was an assembly with delegates from all four zones which, for this reason, represented the nation as a whole. The government that it would create was envisaged to have zonal authority but receive "approval by a national organ."[137]

Democratic pretense went along with an effort to liquidate "bourgeois" administration and to persecute independent-minded personnel. The SED leaders prided themselves with having "smashed" the "old state apparatus" but felt that the "class enemy" continued to be strongly entrenched in positions of state, economy, and administration. The instruments of repression therefore required further development to meet the challenge.[138] They appealed to the occupation power to enlarge their powers to support their regime by police organizations. On 28 December 1948, the Politburo in Moscow approved their plans for a secret police in conformity with the Soviet model.[139] The existing nuclei of a secret police subjected to direct operational control by the occupation power were enlarged and reorganized. The higher-ranking cadres were sent to the USSR for training.[140]

On Stalin's order, formation of East German military units started in July 1948. Expressly designed to avoid "problems" with interallied legislation on demilitarization,[141] they were labelled police alert units (*Polizeibereitschaften*). Both former Wehrmacht professionals and communists with military experience served as cadres. "Regular military training" was provided with an accent on street and bush fighting. Armament consisted of German World War II "automatic and other weapons." After an initial period of training in basic military skills, officer schools and mixed formations were set up to prepare for combined-weapons combat with infantry, artillery, tank, and engineering elements. In 1950, approximately 50,000 men were under arms. In the course of this year, navy cadres were also set up.[142] As previously in the Red Army when cadres from czarist forces had been deemed unreliable, a command chain for the control of military officers by representatives of the communist party was introduced. An additional network of control was provided by a hierarchy of Soviet "advisors" who actually took the function of supreme military authority.[143]

Political Mimicry as a Crucial Instrument of Struggle for Germany

Stalin continued to seek political support in the Western zones but realized that the USSR and the SED regime were unpopular. He therefore felt it was tactically expedient that the West German communists denied ties to their East German masters and took precautions not to be seen as "Russian agents." This would deprive the Western enemy of a political weapon that to date had caused much damage. Stalin told the SED leaders that the KPD must officially cut its links with them but continue to underlie their full control.[144] This was part of a broader political strategy.

Comrade Stalin asks whether one can't arrange to make some good communists join the SPD in the West and renounce communism who then will start to undermine the SPD from within. Is such tactics acceptable? Comrade Stalin feels that the German communists wage the struggle too openly. The old Teutons went to the battle with the Roman naked and suffered defeat. It seems to Comrade Stalin that the German communists somewhat resemble the Teutons in this respect for they wage the struggle too openly. But this way [of doing it] requires many victims and does not always achieve its objective. It is necessary to mask oneself, since there is an intensified struggle under most complicated conditions. . . . Comrade Stalin emphasizes that we are confronted with such enemies against whom such tricks are acceptable. In time of war, they are [generally] applied. And we have real war. Experience demonstrates that such tricks are necessary. It is not always advantageous to go to war naked. Bravery is good. But in the event of war, bravery alone does not achieve good results.[145]

For reasons of tactical expediency, the SED must disavow the goal of people's democracy and pretend to pursue an "all-democratic" course. Measures aimed at socialism must not be enforced unless they would appear as punishment of illegal behavior by individuals. The "group of capitalists" and law-abiding "big peasants" must "not be touched." It was essential to take into account that the situation in Germany was basically different from conditions in Eastern Europe: Soviet power was present in but one part of the country. Partition, however, provided a basis for an effort to mobilize people by promising national unification.

Comrade Stalin continues that presently one must not focus the German people's attention on those problems which pose themselves in the countries of people's democracy but on the problems of German unity, on the peace treaty, on lowering of prices, on rise of wages, and on better nourishment. This will unite all of Germany, and this is the most important thing. It is around these problems that all work must be done, and on this appropriate noise has to be made. The capitalists must be pressured on a legal basis.

Stalin explained to his East German comrades that an "opportunistic policy" was a more effective way to fight the enemy than open struggle. The road to socialism must not be taken "directly but in zigzags and by detour movements, since conditions in Germany are difficult and dictate a more cautious policy."[146] Accordingly, it was premature to accept the SED as a member of the Cominform. Restraint for tactical reasons did not imply restraint in crucial matters. The SED must organize as a Marxist-Leninist "party of struggle," as a "party of a new type" that would be both consolidated internally and protected from penetration by "enemy elements." A detailed party program along the lines of the model provided by the CPSU was required.[147] The West German communists were blamed for having failed to rally major support behind them. This was seen to have been caused by both insufficient political effort and "sectarianism," that is, failure to apply mimicry and zigzag tactics and to seek alliances for exploitation of cooperation partners. The leading cadres who were thus criticized duly repented and pledged absolute obedience.[148]

Proclamation of the German Democratic Republic

A third German People's Congress was convened on the basis of single list elections in the Soviet zone. Despite heavy pressure, no more than two-thirds of the population had voted for it. As an assembly allegedly based on the people's will, the Congress was declared to be a provisional parliament that, having co-opted West German members, claimed an all-national character.[149] To make the official thesis appear credible that the co-opted personnel represented the West German population, the KPD was ordered to collect signatures in support of the Eastern position on unity. The action was largely unsuccessful[150] but the claim was maintained. After the Federal Republic of Germany had been set up in the West, procedures aimed at proclaiming the Soviet zone state were initiated. In early October 1949, the German People's Council was transformed into the "Provisional German People's Chamber" that, allegedly on behalf of the whole nation, founded the GDR, put the prepared texts of the constitution and several fundamental laws into effect, and appointed the "Provisional German Government."[151]

While the SED leaders had submitted proposals, the Soviet Ministry of Foreign Affairs prepared recommendations on any major matter of personnel and organization for Stalin, who took the final decisions.[152] The USSR government applauded the willingness of the "German democratic circles" to take national reunification "on a democratic and peaceful basis" into their own hands and accepted their binding commitment to the Potsdam obligation to enforce sociopolitical transformation as an immutable fundament of domestic policy and unification effort. But contrary to SED expectation, it refused reward by granting autonomy. The East German state was accorded but "administrative" authority, or power to execute instructions.[153] As before, the Soviet exercise of the occupation regime was not limited by any legal or political regulation. The USSR also continued its previous penetration of administrative, military, and secret police structures.[154] As a result, there was little change of control by the occupation regime.

In a congratulatory telegram, Stalin emphasized that the creation of a "German Democratic peace-loving Republic" was a "turning point in the history of Europe." Based on the tacit assumption that the GDR was identical with future Germany as a whole, he predicted that the "existence of a peaceloving democratic Germany on the side of the existing peaceloving Soviet Union" would no longer allow for the "possibility of new wars in Europe." This put an end to "bloodshed in Europe"; "enslavement of European countries by the global imperialists was rendered impossible." As he underlined, it was a great achievement for all of Europe that the fundament of a "united democratic and peace-loving Germany" had been laid.[155] On 6 November 1949, his favorite aide Malenkov hailed the GDR's foundation as the starting point of a development that would allow the "forces of people's democracy" in close cooperation with the USSR to gain the upper hand in Germany. In the Eastern part of the country, all opponents had been deprived of power; "basic democratic transformations" were enforced. This would provide essential preconditions for "solution of the German problem on a democratic fundament."[156]

NOTES

1. Cf. Conversation G. Marshall–I. V. Stalin, 15 April 1947, *Foreign Relations of the United States. Diplomatic Papers 1947 (henceforth: FRUS), Vol. II: Council of Foreign Ministers; Germany and Austria, Department of State Publication 8530* (Washington D.C.: Government Printing Office 1972), pp. 343–44.

2. Conversation V. D. Sokolovskii–W. Pieck, O. Grotewohl, W. Ulbricht, and M. Fechner, 25 April 1947, *SSSR i germanskii vopros 1941–1949. Dokumenty iz Arkhiva vneshnei politiki Rossiiskoi Federatsii*, ed. by Istoriko-Dokumental'nyi Departament MID Rossii / Zentrum für Zeithistorische Forschung Potsdam, *Vol. III: 6 oktiabria 1946 g.–15 iiunia 1948 g.* (Moscow: "Mezhdunarodnye otnosheniia" 2003), pp. 370–71.

3. N. V. Novikov to V. M. Molotov, 9 June 1947, *Sovetsko-amerikanskie otnosheniia 1945–1948. Rossiia XX vek. Dokumenty pod obshchei redaktsiei Akademika A. N. Iakovleva* (Moscow: Izdatel'stvo "Materik" 2004), pp. 429–30.

4. John Lewis Gaddis, *We Now Know. Rethinking Cold War History* (Oxford: Clarendon Press 1998), p. 41.

5. M. M. Narinskii, "SSSR i 'plan Marshalla,'" M. M. Narinskii (ed.), *Kholodnaia voina. Novye podkhody, novye dokumenty* (Moscow: Institut vseobshchei istorii RAN 1995), pp. 172–74.

6. E. Varga to V. M. Molotov, 24 June 1947, *Sovetsko-amerikanskie otnosheniia 1945–1948*, pp. 433–35.

7. Narinskii, "SSSR i 'plan Marshalla,'" pp. 174–80; M. M. Narinskii, "The Soviet Union and the Marshall Plan," Antonio Varsori and Elena Calandri (eds.), *The Failure of Peace in Europe 1943–48* (Houndmills and New York: Palgrave 2002), pp. 275–96; Anna Di Biagio, "The Cominform as the Soviet Response to the Marshall Plan," Vasori and Calandri (eds.), *The Failure of Peace in Europe*, pp. 300–301; Friederike Sattler, "Die Gründung der DDR begann in Prag," *Zeitschrift des Forschungsverbunds SED-Staat*, 6/1998, p. 97.

8. Declaration by the government of the USSR, 5 July 1947, *Sovetsko-amerikanskie otnosheniia 1945–1948*, pp. 437–38.

9. N. I. Egorova, "Evropeiskaia bezopasnost' i 'ugroza' NATO v otsenkakh stalinskogo rukovodstva," A.O. Chubar'ian (ed.), *Stalinskoe desiatiletie kholodnoi voiny. Fakty i gipotezy* (Moscow: Institut vseobshchei istorii RAN 1999), pp. 58–59; Georges Catroux, *J'ai vu tomber le rideau de fer a Moscou 1945–1948* (Paris: Hachette 1952), pp. 247–60.

10. Conversation I. V. Stalin–J. Masaryk and K. Gottwald, 9 July 1947, *Sovetskii faktor v Vostochnoi Evrope 1944–1953. Dokumenty, Vol. I* (Moscow: ROSSPÈN 1999),

pp. 462–65; Karel Krátký, "Czechoslovakia, the Soviet Union, and the Marshall Plan," Odd Arne Westad, Sven Holtsmark, and Iver B. Neumann (eds.), *The Soviet Union in Eastern Europe 1945–89* (New York: St. Martin's Press 1994), pp. 9–25.

11. Cf. Csaba Békés, "Soviet Plans to Establish the Kominform in Early 1946: New Evidence from Hungarian Archives," *Cold War International History Project Bulletin*, 10 (March 1998) (Washington D.C.: Woodrow Wilson International Center for Scholars), pp. 135–37.

12. Grant M. Adibekov, *Das Kominform und Stalins Neuordnung Europas* (Frankfurt/Main: Peter Lang 2002), pp. 54–68.

13. Di Biagio, "The Cominform as the Soviet Response to the Marshall Plan," Vasori and Calandri (eds.), *The Failure of Peace in Europe*, pp. 299–302.

14. Adibekov, *Das Kominform*, pp. 59–86.

15. Statement by G. M. Malenkov (Russ. orig. and Engl. transl.), 22 September 1947, Giuliani Procaccio (ed.), *The Cominform. Minutes of the Three Conferences 1947/1948/1949* (Milan: Feltrinelli Editore 1994), pp. 64–94 (quotations on pp. 88, 90, 92, 94).

16. Statement by A. A. Zhdanov (Russ. orig. and Engl. transl.), 25 September 1947, Procaccio (ed.), *The Cominform*, pp. 216–50 (quotations on pp. 216, 218, 224–27).

17. Declaration of representatives of the communist parties at the meeting in Poland (Russ. orig. and Engl. transl.), undated [27 September 1947], Procaccio (ed.), *The Cominform*, pp. 378–83.

18. Egorova, "Evropeiskaia bezopasnost'," Chubar'ian (ed.), *Stalinskoe desiatiletie kholodnoi voiny*, p. 57.

19. T. V. Volokitina, "Stalin i smena strategicheskogo kursa Kremlia k kontse 40-kh godov: ot kompromissov k konfrontatsii," Chubar'ian (ed.), *Stalinskoe desiatileite kholodnoi voiny*, p. 17.

20. Grant Adibekov, "How the First Conference of the Cominform Came About," Procaccio, *The Cominform*, pp. 3–9; Nataliia I. Egorova, "Stalin's Foreign Policy and the Cominform, 1947–1953," Francesca Gori and Silvio Pons (eds.), *The Soviet Union and Europe in the Cold War, 1943–53* (Basingstoke: Macmillan; New York: St. Martin's Press 1996), p. 197.

21. Statement by A. A. Zhdanov (Russ. orig. and Engl. transl.), 25 September 1947, Procaccio (ed.), *The Cominform*, pp. 248–51.

22. Protocol of discussion (Russ. orig. and Engl. transl.), 26 September 1947, Procaccio (ed.), *The Cominform*, pp. 270–371. See also Anna Di Biagio, "The Marshall Plan and the Founding of the Cominform, June–September 1947," Gori and Pons (eds.), *The Soviet Union and Europe in the Cold War*, pp. 214–16.

23. V. S. Lel'chuk and E. I. Pivovar, *SSSR i kholodnaia voina* (Moscow: Mosgorarkhiv 1995), p. 85.

24. Protocol of the report given to the FCP Politburo in the Russian version which was submitted to Stalin, Lel'chuk and Pivovar, *SSSR i kholodnaia voina*, pp. 87–88.

25. Silvio Pons, "Stalin, Togliatti, and the Origin of the Cold War in Europe," *Journal of Cold War Studies* 3, no. 2 (Spring 2000), pp. 16–18; Stéphane Courteois, "Thorez, Stalin und Frankreichs Befreiung im Lichte von Moskauer Archiven,"

Jahrbuch für Historische Konfliktforschung, 1998, pp. 82–83; M. M. Narinskii, "I. V. Stalin i Moris Torez," *Istoricheskii arkhiv,* 1/1996, pp. 5–6.

26. Report on conversation I. V. Stalin–M. Thorez, 18 November 1947, *Istoricheskii arkhiv,* 1/1996, pp. 6–21. For Stalin's assessment of the communist situation in Western Europe see his remarks to Finnish party leaders in January 1948 as cited by Kimmo Rentola, "1948: Which Way Finland?" *Jahrbuch für Historische Kommunismusforschung,* 1998, p. 102.

27. Pons, "Stalin, Togliatti," pp. 18–21.

28. Milovan Djilas, *Conversations with Stalin* (New York: Harcourt 1962), pp. 152–53.

29. Lel'chuk and Pivovar, *SSSR i kholodnaia voina,* pp. 88–89, 92–96.

30. Rainer, "Der Weg der ungarischen Volksdemokratie. Das Mehrparteiensystem und seine Beseitigung 1944-1949," Stefan Creuzberger and Manfred Görtemaker, *Gleichschaltung unter Stalin? Die Entwicklung der Parteien im östlichen Europa* (Paderborn. Schöningh 2002), pp. 344–52; Doral O'Sullivan, "'Wer immer ein Gebiet besetzt. . . .' Sowjetische Osteuropapolitik 1943-1947/48," Creuzberger and Görtemaker, *Gleichschaltung unter Stalin?* pp. 70–71.

31. Marietta Stankova, "Das parteipolitische System in Bulgarien 1944–1949. Äussere Einflüsse und innere Faktoren," Creuzberger and Görtemaker, *Gleichschaltung unter Stalin?* pp. 212–15.

32. Harald Moldenhauer, "'Ihr werdet Euch dem Sozialismus ohne blutigen Kampf annähern,' Kommunistische Blockpolitik und 'Gleichschaltung' der Parteien in Polen, 1944-1948," Creuzberger and Görtemaker, *Gleichschaltung unter Stalin?* pp. 119–22.

33. Statement by A. A. Zhdanov (Russ. orig. and Engl. transl.), 25 September 1947, Procaccio (ed.), *The Cominform,* pp. 226–27.

34. Anna Di Biagio, "The Cominform as the Soviet Response to the Marshall Plan," Varsori and Calandri (eds.), *The Failure of Peace in Europe,* pp. 299–302.

35. Kimmo Rentola, "1948: Which Way Finland?" *Jahrbuch für Historische Kommunismusforschung,* pp. 99–123. Cf. Hermann Beyer-Thoma, *Kommunisten und Sozialdemokraten in Finnland 1944–1948* (Wiesbaden: Harrassowitz 1990), pp. 416–510.

36. Memorandum by the International Relations Section of the VKP(b) on the economic and political situation in Czechoslovakia, undated [September 1947], *Sovetskii faktor, I,* pp. 496–503; Report by N. V. Guliaev on the situation in Czechoslovakia, undated [22 June 1947 at latest], *Vostochnaia Evropa v dokumentakh rossiiskikh arkhivov 1944-1953 gg.,* ed. by Rossiiskaia Akademiia Nauk / Institut slavianovedeniia i balkanistiki / Rossiiskii Tsentr khraneniia i izucheniia dokumentov po noveishei istorii / Gosudarstvennyi arkhiv Rossiiskoi Federatsii, *Vol. I* (Moscow and Novosibirsk: "Sibirskii khronograf" 1997), pp. 649–56; R. Slánský to the International Relations Section of the VKP(b) (excerpt), undated [27 June 1947 at latest], *Vostochnaia Evropa, I,* pp. 661–64; report by S. A. Shmeral' on the situation in Czechoslovakia, 26 December 1947, *Sovetskii faktor, I,* pp. 514–32; Donal O'Sullivan, *Stalins "Cordon Sanitaire." Die sowjetische Osteuropapolitik und die Reaktionen des Westens 1939–1949* (Paderborn: Schöningh 2003), pp. 348–49; Paul E. Zinner, *Communist Strategy and Tactics in Czechoslovakia, 1918–1948* (New York and London: Praeger 1963), pp. 158–95.

37. Jiří Kocian, "Vom Kaschauer Programm zum Prager Putsch. Die Entwicklung der politischen Parteien in der Tschechoslowakei in den Jahren 1944–1948," Creuzberger and Görtemaker (eds.), *Gleichschaltung unter Stalin?* pp. 311–14.

38. Marietta Stankova, "Das parteipolitische System in Bulgarien," Creuzberger and Görtemaker (eds.), *Gleichschaltung unter Stalin?* pp. 197–204; Lel'chuk and Pivovar, *SSSR i kholodnaia voina*, pp. 80–81.

39. Report by N. G. Novikov on development of the government crisis in Czechoslovakia, 27 February 1947, *Sovetskii faktor, I*, pp. 539–52; Report by Polish party delegates on their visit to Czechoslovakia of 21 through 27 February 1948, undated [8 March 1948 at latest], *Vostochnaia Evropa, I*, pp. 770–75; Lel'chuk and Pivovar, *SSSR i kholodnaia voina*, p. 81; G. N. Sevostianov (ed.), *Fevral' 1948. Moskva i Praga. Vzgliad cherez polveka. Materialy vtorogo zasedaniia komissii istorikov i arkhivistov Rossii i Chekhii, Moskva, 26–30 aprelia 1997 g.* (Moscow: Institut slvavianovedeniia i balkanistiki RAN 1998); Kocian, "Vom Kaschauer Programm zum Prager Putsch," Creuzberger and Görtemaker (eds.), *Gleichschaltung unter Stalin?* pp. 315–17; O'Sullivan, *Stalins "Cordon Sanitaire,"* pp. 350–51; Igor Lukes, "The Czech Road to Communism," Norman M. Naimark and Leonid Gibianskii (eds.), *The Establishment of Communist Regimes in Eastern Europe 1944–1949* (Boulder, CO: Westview 1997), pp. 252–65; Andrzej Paczkowski, "The Polish Contribution to the Victory of the 'Prague Coup' in February 1948," *Cold War International History Project Bulletin*, 11 (Winter 1998), pp. 141–48.

40. Cf. Recommendation by the Fourth European Department of the Soviet Ministry of Foreign Affairs, 2 March 1947, *Sovetskii faktor, I*, pp. 552–53.

41. Milovan Djilas, *Jahre der Macht. Kräftespiel hinter dem Eisernen Vorhang. Memoiren 1945–1966* (Munich: Molden-Seewald 1983), pp. 171–220; Ivo Banac, *With Stalin Against Tito. Cominformist Splits in Yugoslav Communism* (Ithaca, NY, and London: Cornell University Press 1988), pp. 37–40; Peter J. Stavrakis, *Moscow and Greek Communism, 1944–1949* (Ithaca, NY, and London: Cornell University Press 1989), pp. 160–68.

42. Stavrakis, *Moscow and Greek Communism*, pp. 168–70; Banac, *With Stalin Against Tito*, pp. 40–42; N. D. Smirnova, "Stalin i Balkany v 1948 g. Problemy natsional'noi bezopasnosti SSSR," Chubar'ian (ed.), *Stalinskoe desiatiletie*, pp. 37–44; Volokitina, "Stalin i smena," Chubar'ian (ed.), *Stalinskoe desiatiletie*, pp. 18–19; Lel'chuk and Pivovar, *SSSR i kholodnaia voina*, p. 89; Leonid Gibianskii, "The Soviet-Yugoslav Split and the Cominform," Naimark and Gibianskii (eds.), *The Establishment of Communist Regimes*, pp. 292–300. In contrast to Gibianskii, Smirnova emphasizes that, on 10 February 1948, Stalin did not reject any support for the Greek insurgents but wanted it to be limited to a level that was not prone to risk. This was as unacceptable to Tito as total renunciation of support would have been. Additional evidence is provided by the fact that, in a letter to Hungarian party head Rákosi, a Soviet party apparatchik whose opinion invariably reflected Stalin's intent, Mikhail Suslov advocated military aid to the Greek insurgents but did not want recognition of their leaders as the country's government.

43. Lel'chuk and Pivovar, *SSSR i kholodnaia voina*, p. 89; Jose Pirjevec, "Vittorio Vidali and the Cominform, 1947–53," Gori and Pons (eds.), *The Soviet Union and Europe in the Cold War*, pp. 266–67; Leonid Gibianskii, "The Beginning of the

Soviet-Yugoslav Conflict and the Cominform," Procacci (ed.), *The Cominform,*
pp. 468–78; Volokitina, "Stalin i smena strategicheskogo kursa Kremlia v konce
40-kh godov: ot kompromissov k konfrontatsii," pp. 19–20; Adibekov, *Das Kominform,* pp. 149–51.
    44. Memorandum by the Foreign Relations Section of the VKP(b), 18 March
1948, *Vostochnaia Evropa,* pp. 787–800; Gibianskii, "The Soviet-Yugoslav Split,"
Naimark and Gibianskii (eds.), *The Establishment of Communist Regimes,* pp. 293–98;
Lel'chuk and Pivovar, *SSSR i kholodnaia voina,* pp. 89–92.
    45. Lel'chuk and Pivovar, *SSSR i kholodnaia voina,* pp. 97–98; Adibekov, *Das Kom-
inform,* pp. 151–81; Gibianskii, "The Beginning of the Soviet-Yugoslav Conflict and
the Cominform," Procacci (ed.), *The Cominform,* pp. 478–80; A. F. Noskova (otv.
red.), *Moskva i vostochnaia Evropa. Stanovlenie politicheskikh rezhimov sovetskogo tipa.
1949–1953. Ocherki istorii* (Moscow: ROSSPĖN 2002), p. 496.
    46. "Stalin's Plan to Assassinate Tito," *Cold War International History Project Bul-
letin,* 10 (March 1998) (Washington D.C.: Woodrow Wilson International Center for
Scholars), p. 137.
    47. Noskova, *Moskva i vostochnaia Evropa,* pp. 499–500.
    48. Beatrice Heuser, *Western "Containment" Policies in the Cold War. The Yugoslav
Case, 1948–1953* (London and New York: Routledge 1989), pp. 43–102.
    49. Leonid Gibianskii, "The Last Conference of the Cominform," Procaccio (ed.),
The Cominform, pp. 645–49; Gibianskii, "The Soviet-Yugoslav Split," pp. 298–302,
303–8.
    50. Noskova, *Moskva i vostochnaia Evropa,* p. 501.
    51. Noskova, *Moskva i vostochnaia Evropa,* pp. 514–15.
    52. Noskova, *Moskva i vostochnaia Evropa,* pp. 501–5.
    53. Noskova, *Moskva i vostochnaia Evropa,* pp. 505–11.
    54. Noskova, *Moskva i vostochnaia Evropa,* pp. 515–19.
    55. Noskova, *Moskva i vostochnaia Evropa,* pp. 519–27, 537–38.
    56. Noskova, *Moskva i vostochnaia Evropa,* pp. 527–37.
    57. Gennadij Bordjugov, "Das ZK der KPdSU(B), die sowjetische Militäradminis-
tration in Deutschland und die SED (1945–1951)," Ulrich Mählert and Hermann
Weber (eds.), *Terror. Stalinistische Parteisäuberungen 1936–1953* (Paderborn: Schöningh 1998), pp. 302–8; Ulrich Mählert, "'Die Partei hat immer recht!' Parteisäuberungen als Kaderpolitik in der SED (1948–1953)," Mählert and Weber (eds.), *Terror. Stalinistische Parteisäuberungen 1936–1953,* pp. 388–439.
    58. Norman M. Naimark, *The Russians in Germany. A History of the Soviet Zone
of Occupation 1945–1949* (Cambridge, MA: Harvard University Press 1997),
pp. 69–141; M. M. Semiriaga, *Kak my upravliali Germaniei* (Moscow: ROSSPĖN
1995), pp. 155–80, 311–27.
    59. A. A. Smirnov and V. S. Semënov to V. M. Molotov, 1 November 1947, *SSSR
i germanskii vopros, III,* pp. 518–20.
    60. *Tägliche Rundschau,* 29 September 1947.
    61. I. V. Ivanov to V. M. Molotov and A. A. Smirnov, 20 June 1947, *SSSR i ger-
manskii vopros, III,* p. 408.
    62. See Stalin's explanations to the SED leaders, 18 December 1948, V. K. Volkov,
Uzlovye problemy noveishei istorii stran Tsentral'noi i Iugo-Vostochnoi Evropy (Moscow: Izdatel'stvo "Indrik" 2000), pp. 134–35.

63. V. M. Molotov to M. I. Dratvin, V. E. Makarov, and V. F. Razin, 17 November 1947, ibid., p. 545. Cf. speech by O. Grotewohl, 15 October 1947, Otto Grotewohl, *Im Kampf um die einige Deutsche Demokratische Republik. Reden und Aufsätze, Vol. I* ([East] Berlin: Dietz 1959), p. 147.

64. Soviet policy paper, undated [late August or early September 1947], Rolf Badstübner and Wilfried Loth (eds.), *Wilhelm Pieck—Aufzeichnungen zur Deutschlandpolitik 1945–1953* (Berlin: Akademie Verlag 1994), pp. 161–62; Egorova, "Evropeiskaia bezopasnost'," p. 57.

65. V. S. Semënov to V. M. Molotov, 15 July 1947, *SSSR i germanskii vopros, III*, pp. 431–33; S. I. Tiul'panov to V. S. Semënov, 1 August 1947, AVPRF, 0457a, 6, 32, 25, pp. 49–57; report on a SED Executive Body meeting, 20–21 August 1947, SAPMO, DY 30/IV 2/1/025, p. 2; report on a SED Executive Body meeting, 16 September 1947, SAPMO, DY 30/IV 2/1/26, p. 4; Lieutenant General V. Makarov to the CPSU CC (Kusnetsov), 14 October 1947, RGASPI, 17, 128, 358, pp. 74–91; Gyptner's information on Soviet instructions, 26 July 1947, Soviet report on a regional party conference, 19 August 1947, conversation Marshall Sokolovskii–SED leaders, 28 August 1947, a letter addressed to Stalin, undated, and conversation Lieutenant General Makarov–SED leaders, 8 September 1947, as reflected in notes taken by W. Pieck, Badstübner and Loth (eds.), *Wilhelm Pieck*, pp. 130, 131–34, 137–43, 147–49, 149–51, 162–72, 173–74. For details of the measures see Werner Müller, "Entstehung und Transformation des Parteiensystems der SBZ/DDR 1945–1950," *Materialien der Enquete-Kommission "Aufarbeitung von Geschichte und Folgen der SED-Diktatur in Deutschland"* (Baden-Baden: Nomos; Frankfurt/Main: Suhrkamp 1999), Vol. II/2, pp. 2350–59; Semiriaga, *Kak my upravliali Germaniei*, p. 59; Andreas Malycha, *Partei von Stalins Gnaden? Die Entwicklung der SED zur Partei neuen Typs in den Jahren 1946 bis 1950* (Berlin: Dietz 1996), pp. 81–85; Monika Kaiser, "Die Zentrale der Diktatur. Struktur und Kompetenzen der SED-Führung 1946 bis 1952," Jürgen Kocka (ed.), *Historische DDR-Forschung. Aufsätze und Studien* (Berlin: Akademie Verlag 1993), pp. 67–75. Major Party Congress materials have been published: Walter Ulbricht, *Zur Geschichte der neuesten Zeit, Vol. III* ([East] Berlin: Dietz 1961), pp. 140–88; Walter Ulbricht, "Der deutsche Plan" (policy paper provided by the Soviet side), *Neues Deutschland*, 2 September 1947.

66. Verordnung über die Deutsche Verwaltung des Innern, undated [July 1947], BArchB, MdI 7/1, pp. 29–33; General Lieutenant Dratvin, Polozhenie. O nemetskom Upravlenii Vnutrennikh Del v Sovetskoi zone Germanii, undated [summer 1947], AVPRF, 0457a, 4, 19, 48, pp. 48–56; K. Fischer to Colonel Lieutenant Dollada (in Russian), 12 August 1948, BArchB, MdI 7/42, pp. 34–35; Major General Mal'kov to M. G. Gribanov, 19 August 1947, AVPRF, 0457a, 4, 19, 48, pp. 24–35; K. Fischer to Major General Gorokhov, 29 September 1948, BArchB, MdI 7/42, p. 61; S. Gorokhov to K. Fischer, 16 December 1948 [date of translation], BArchB, MdI 7/42, pp. 88–90; Colonel Dollada to K. Fischer, 11 October 1949, BArchB, MdI 7/42, pp. 100–104; S. Gorokhov to K. Fischer, 24 June 1949, BAAP, MdI 7/45, pp. 262–63; S. F. Gorokhov to K. Fischer (with enclosure), 11 July 1949, BArchB, MdI 7/42, pp. 182–97; S. F. Gorokhov to K. Fischer, 12 August 1949, BArchB, MdI 7/42. pp. 271–72.

67. A. A. Vyshinskii to Marshal Sokolovskii (with text of SMAG Order No. 201 attached), 29 July 1947, AVPRF, 06, 9, 43, 639, pp. 3–7; SMAG Order No. 201 (German

transl.), 16 August 1947, BArchB, MdI 7/421, pp. 14–18; handwritten comments by Erich Mielke on Order 201, undated [late August 1947], BStU, SdM No. 1405, pp. 7–13; circular letter by E. Mielke to the DVdI department heads, 31 October 1947, BArchB, MdI 7/421, pp. 53–55; report on a conversation with E. Mielke, undated [November 1947], BArchB, MdI 7/421, p. 65; records of Saxon Crime Investigation Department, K 5, on amendment and correction of *land* instructions concerning Order No. 201, 25 November 1947, BArchB, MdI 7/421, pp. 80–83; lecture by DVdI Vice President Mielke, 19 January 1948, BStU, SdM, pp. 65–78 (quotation on p. 41); lecture on Order No. 201 [by E. Mielke?], undated [mid-1948], BStU, SdM, pp. 27–32; statements by E. Mielke during a meeting at the Higher Police School, 1 July 1948, BStU, SdM, pp. 15–26; report on session of the SED Central Secretariat, 26 August 1947, SAPMO, DY 30/IV 2/2.1/120, p. 4. Cf. Stefan Creuzberger, *Die sowjetische Besatzungsmacht und das politische System der SBZ* (Weimar: Böhlau 1996), p. 31; Naimark, *The Russians,* pp. 360, 354; Alexandr Haritonow, *Sowjetische Hochschulpolitik in Sachsen 1945–1949* (Cologne: Böhlau 1995), p. 155; Jochen Laufer, "Ursprünge des Überwachungsstaates in Ostdeutschland," Bernd Florath, Armin Mitter, and Stefan Wolle (eds.), *Die Ohnmacht der Allmächtigen* (Berlin: Ch. Links 1992), pp. 161–64; Monika Tantzscher, "Vorläufer des Staatssicherheitsdienstes," *Jahrbuch für Historische Kommunismusforschung,* 1998, pp. 137–54; Wilfriede Otto, *Erich Mielke—Biographie* (Berlin: Dietz 2000), pp. 103–7, 109–13; Jens Gieseke, "Das Ministerium für Staatssicherheit (1950–1990)," Torsten Diedrich, Hans Ehlert, and Rüdiger Wenzke, *Im Dienste der Partei. Handbuch der bewaffneten Organ der DDR* (Berlin: Ch. Links 1998), pp. 373–74.

68. Deutsches Armeemuseum (ed.), *Ich schwöre. Eine Bilddokumentation* ([East] Berlin: Ministry of National Defense 1969), p. 251 [testimony by Army General Heinz Hoffmann].

69. Conversation I. V. Stalin–W. Pieck and O. Grotewohl, 26 March 1948, *SSSR i germanskii vopros, III,* p. 629. Both Markgraf and Bechler were Wehrmacht professionals who had received political training in the USSR. Recollection by the SED leadership member Gniffke (who subsequently defected to the West) that, in fall 1947, he heard about a secret visit to Moscow for discussion with Stalin on military forces (Erich W. Gniffke, *Jahre mit Ulbricht* [Cologne: Wissenschaft und Politik 1966], p. 262) may actually relate to the above conversation.

70. Cf. report by S. I. Tiul′panov, 9 June 1947, *SSSR i germanskii vopros, III,* pp. 401–2; S. I. Tiul′panov to V. S. Semënov, 19 August 1947, *SSSR i germanskii vopros, III,* pp. 466–69.

71. See, inter alia, internal CDU report by Robert Tillmanns, 1 July 1947, Siegfried Suckut (ed.), *Blockpolitik in der SBZ/DDR 1945–1949. Die Sitzungsprotokolle des Zentralen Einheitsfront-Ausschusses* (Cologne: Wissenschaft und Politik 1986), pp. 210–12; SED declaration of principle concerning bloc politics, 14 August 1947, Suckut (ed.), *Blockpolitik,* pp. 228–30.

72. Report on the 30th Joint Session of the United Front of Anti-Fascist Democratic Parties, 31 October 1947, Suckut (ed.), *Blockpolitik,* p. 243.

73. A. A. Smirnov to V. S. Semënov, 26 January 1948, AVPRF, 0457a, 5, 28, 8, pp. 26–33; S. I. Tiul′panov to the Ministry of Foreign Affairs, 19 March 1948, AVPRF, 0457a, 5, 28, 8, p. 61; paper on the situation in the CDU, 19 March 1948, AVPRF, 0457a, 5, 28, 8. pp. 63–70; Lieutenant General Guliaev to V. S. Semënov, 4 Decem-

ber 1948, AVPRF, 0457a, 5, 28, 8, pp. 297–99; Colonel Radionov to V. S. Semënov, 6 January 1949, AVPRF, 0457a, 7, 39, 11, pp. 1–6; S. I. Tiul'panov to V. S. Semënov, 28 February 1949, AVPRF, 0457a, 7, 39, 11, pp. 11–42; report by S. I. Tiul'panov on the CDU in the Soviet zone and in Berlin, 3 May 1948, RGASPI, 17, 128, 568, pp. 62–93; S. I. Tiul'panov to L. S. Baranov, 28 April 1948, RGASPI, 17, 128, 569, pp. 3–34; M. G. Gribanov to A. A. Smirnov, 14 February 1948, AVPRF, 0457a, 5, 28, 8, p. 36; S. I. Tiul'panov, Trëkhletnii opyt raboty Upravlenija informatsii SVAG (oktiabr' 1945–oktiabr' 1948 gg.), October 1948, GARF, 7319, 19, 1, pp. 81–87, 90–96; S. I. Tiul'panov to V. S. Semënov, 2 November 1948, AVPRF, 0457a, 5, 28, 8, pp. 214–31. See also Semiriaga, *Kak my upravliali Germaniei*, pp. 61–64; Michael Richter, *Die Ost-CDU 1948–1952. Zwischen Widerstand und Gleichschaltung* (Dusseldorf: Droste 1991), pp. 32–153; Ulf Sommer, *Die Liberal-Demokratische Partei Deutschlands. Eine Blockpartei unter Führung der SED* (Münster: Agenda Verlag 1996), pp. 49–56; Wolfgang Schollwer, *Potsdamer Tagebuch 1948–1950. Liberale Politik unter sowjetischer Besatzung*, 2 vols. (Munich: Oldenbourg 1988); Bernard Bode, *Liberal-Demokraten und "deutsche Frage." Zum Wandel einer Partei in der Sowjetischen Besatzungszone und in der DDR zwischen 1945 und 1961* (Frankfurt/Main: Peter Lang 1997), pp. 72–82, 94–103, 113–22; Gerhard Wettig, "Der Konflikt der Ost-CDU mit der Besatzungsmacht 1945–1948 im Spiegel sowjetischer Akten," *Historisch-Politische Mitteilungen*, 6 (1999), pp. 124–33; Ralf Thomas Baus, *Die Christlich-Demokratische Union Deutschlands in der sowjetisch besetzten Zone 1945 bis 1948* (Düsseldorf: Droste 2001), pp. 353–460.

74. Pieck's notes on conversation I. V. Stalin–W. Pieck, W. Ulbricht, and O. Grotewohl, 18 December 1948, Badstübner and Loth (eds.), *Wilhelm Pieck*, p. 261.

75. V. S. Semënov to the Ministry of Foreign Affairs (forwarded to Stalin), 10 August 1947, *SSSR i germanskii vopros, III*, pp. 456–58.

76. S. I. Tiul'panov to L. S. Baranov, 7 May 1948, RGASPI, 17, 128, 568, pp. 103–5; S. I. Tiul'panov to V. S. Semënov, 7 May 1948, AVPRF, 0457a, 5, 28, 8, pp. 99–102; Burzhuaznye partii sovetskoj zony okkupatsii Germanii (po materialam PV GSOV v Germanii), 24 May 1948, RGASPI, 17, 128, 568, pp. 127–35; S. I. Tiul'panov to V. S. Semënov, 25 May 1948, AVPRF, 0457a, 5, 28, 8, p. 113; S. I. Tiul'panov to L. S. Baranov, 28 May 1948, RGASPI, 17, 128, 568, pp. 136–38; S. I. Tiul'panov to V. S. Semënov, 7 May 1948, *SSSR i germanskii vopros, III*, pp. 674–76; S. I. Tiul'panov to V. S. Semënov, 31 May 1948, *SSSR i germanskii vopros, III*, pp. 682–88; S. I. Tiul'panov to L. S. Baranov, undated [end of May 1948], RGASPI, 17, 128, 568, pp. 140–45; S. I. Tiul'panov to L. S. Baranov, 12 June 1948, RGASPI, 17, 128, 568, pp. 146–57; S. I. Tiul'panov to V. S. Semënov, 16 September 1948, AVPRF, 0457a, 5, 28, 8, pp. 185–89; Major Mamontov [Tiul'panov's deputy] to V. S. Semënov, 6 September 1948, AVPRF, 0457a, 5, 28, 8, pp. 183–84; S. I. Tiul'panov to V. S. Semënov, 29 September 1948, AVPRF, 0457a, 5, 28, 8, pp. 190–95; S. I. Tiul'panov to V. S. Semënov, 9 February 1949, AVPRF, 0457a, 7, 39, 13, pp. 1–4; S. I. Tiul'panov to V. S. Semënov, 25 March 1949, AVPRF, 0457a, 7, 39, 13, pp. 71–80; S. I. Tiul'panov to V. S. Semënov, 13 April 1949, AVPRF, 0457a, 7, 39, 13, pp. 53–61; S. I Tiul'panov, Trëkhletnii opyt raboty Upravlenija informatsii SVAG (oktiabr' 1945–oktiabr' 1948gg.), October 1948, GARF, 7319, 19, 1, pp. 97–107. See also Theresia Bauer, *Blockpartei und Agrarrevolution von oben. Die Demokratische Bauernpartei Deutschlands 1948–1963* (Munich: Oldenbourg 2003), pp. 67–295.

77. W. Ulbricht to M. A. Suslov, 12 December 1947, RGASPI, 17, 128, 1098, p. 7.

78. See Pieck's preparatory notes for a meeting with V. M. Molotov on 11 May 1949, Badstübner and Loth (eds.), *Wilhelm Pieck*, p. 279. Cf. "Einleitung," Suckut (ed.), *Blockpolitik*, p. 42.

79. Marshal Sokolovskii to General Clay, 9 September 1947, *Sovetsko-amerikanskie otnosheniia 1945–1948*, pp. 448–49; M. Gribanov to the members of the Allied Control Council, 9 September 1947, *Sovetsko-amerikanskie otnosheniia 1945–1948*, pp. 449–53.

80. Information paper by A. A. Smirnov, 15 June 1947, *SSSR i germanskii vopros*, *III*, pp. 689–92; M. M. Narinskii, "Berlinskii krizis 1948–1949 gg. Novye dokumenty iz rossiiskikh arkhivov," *Novaia i noveishaia istoriia*, 3/1995, p. 18.

81. Conversation V. S. Semënov–W. Pieck and O. Grotewohl, 27 October 1947, *SSSR i germanskii vopros*, *III*, pp. 514–17.

82. N. V. Ivanov and M. G. Gribanov to V. M. Molotov, 20 June 1947, AVPRF, 06, 9, 43, 632, Bl. 16–20.

83. Report on session of the SED Executive Body, 1–3 July 1947, SAPMO-BArch, DY 30/IV 2/1/22, pp. 7, 25; report by F. Oelssner and subsequent discussion at session of the SED Executive Body, 20/21 July 1947, as reported by S. I. Tiul'panov, 26 July 1947, RGASPI, 17, 137, 92, pp. 3–10; transcript of session of the SED Central Secretariat (with attachment), 16 September 1947, SAPMO-BArch, DY 30/IV, 2/2 January /127, pp. 2, 4; transcript of session of the SED Central Secretariat, 18 September 1947, SAPMO-BArch, DY 30/IV 2/2.1/130, p 2; attachment to transcript of session of the SED Central Secretariat, 6 October 1947, SAPMO-BArch, DY 30/IV 2/2.1/137, pp. 1–14.

84. V. M. Molotov to I. V. Stalin, 2 November 1947, *SSSR i germanskii vopros*, *III*, pp. 521–22; instructions to the delegation at the London session of the Council of Foreign Ministers, November 1947, *SSSR i germanskii vopros*, *III*, pp. 526–31; instructions to the delegation at the London session of the Council of Foreign Ministers, November 1947, *SSSR i germanskii vopros*, *III*, pp. 531–36; A. A. Smirnov and V. S. Semënov to V. M. Molotov, November 1947, *SSSR i germanskii vopros*, *III*, pp. 537–42.

85. Manifesto to the German people, 13 November 1947, *Dokumente der Sozialistischen Einheitspartei Deutschlands. Beschlüsse und Erklärungen des Parteivorstandes*, *Vol. III* ([East] Berlin: Dietz 1951), pp. 254–56; G. N. Goroshkova, *Dvizhenie nemetskogo narodnogo kongressa za edinstvo i mirnyi dogovor* [acknowledged as quasi-official by the Soviet Ministry of Foreign Affairs] (Moscow: Izdatel'stvo Institut mezhdunarodnykh otnoshenii 1959), p. 49.

86. Obzor Kynina, AVPRF, AOB, 11zh, 71, 19, p. 340.

87. See the paper by the Third European Department of the Soviet Ministry of Foreign Affairs, 2 March 1948, quoted by Narinskii, "Berlinskii krizis," p. 21.

88. Conversation V. S. Semënov–W. Pieck and O. Grotewohl, AVPRF, 06, 9, 44, 660, pp. 24–27. Cf. Jochen Laufer, "Die UdSSR und die Ursprünge der Berliner Blockade," *Deutschland Archiv*, 4/1998, pp. 569, 574.

89. W. Pieck to V. S. Semënov, 11 July 1950, Federal Ministry of the Interior (ed.), *Dokumente zur Deutschlandpolitik*, Series II, Vol. 3/2 (Munich: Oldenbourg 1997), p. 867.

90. L. Baranov to M. A. Suslov, 25 October 1947, RGASPI, 17, 128, 1097, p. 1; S. I. Tiul'panov to M. A. Suslov, 15 November 1947, RGASPI, 17, 128, 329, pp. 207–17.

91. See reports on the following SED Central Secretariat sessions: 24 November 1947, SAPMO-BArch, DY 30/IV 2/2.1/147, p. 2; 26 November 1947, SAPMO-BArch, DY 30/IV 2/2.1/148, p. 1; 26 November 1947 (2nd session), SAPMO-BArch, DY 30/IV 2/2.1/149, pp. 1–7; 30 November 1947, SAPMO-BArch, DY 30/IV 2/2.1/150, pp. 1–2; 1 December 1947, SAPMO-BArch, DY 30/IV 2/2.1/151, p. 1; 2 December 1947, SAPMO-BArch, DY 30/IV 2/2.1/152, p. 1; 4 December 1947, SAPMO-BArch, DY 30/IV 2/2.1/153, pp. 1–3; Obzor Kynina, AVPRF, AOB, 11zh, 71, 20, p. 606; appeal to join, resp. support, the German People's Congress for Unity and a Just Peace, 26 November 1947, *Dokumente der Sozialistischen Einheitspartei Deutschlands*, Vol. I ([East] Berlin: Dietz 1951), p. 260; Goroshkova, *Dvizhenie nemetskogo narodnogo kongressa*, p. 50; S. I. Tiul'panov to M. G. Gribanov, 8 December 1947, AVPRF, 082, 34, 154, 79, pp. 99–108; W. Pieck to M. A. Suslov, 12 December 1947, RGASPI, 17, 128, 1098, p. 2; report on meeting of the SED Central Secretariat, 7 December 1947, SAPMO-BArch, DY 30/IV 2/2.1/154, pp. 1–5.

92. Transcript of SED press conference, 26 November 1947, RGASPI, 17, 128, 1097, pp. 109–26. On the Soviet origin of the initiative see S. I. Tiul'panov to M. A. Suslov, 9 December 1947, RGASPI, 17, 128, 331, p. 95; L. S. Baranov to M. A. Suslov, 30 January 1948, RGASPI, 17, 128, 1166, p. 68; Obzor Kynina, AVPRF, AOB, 11zh, 71, 20, pp. 606–12.

93. Obzor Kynina, AVPRF, AOB, 11zh, 71, 20, pp. 608–10; A. A. Smirnov to V. M. Molotov, 3 February 1948, *SSSR i germanski vopros, III*, pp. 574–75; A. A. Smirnov to V. M. Molotov, 12 March 1948, *SSSR i germanski vopros, III*, pp. 601–3; conversation I. V. Stalin–W. Pieck and O. Grotewohl, 26 March 1948, *SSSR i germanski vopros, III*, pp. 618–19; M. G. Gribanov to A. Ia. Vyshinskii, 27 March 1947, *SSSR i germanski vopros, III*, pp. 633–45; Goroshkova, *Dvizhenie nemetskogo narodnogo kongressa*, pp. 73–80.

94. S. I. Tiul'panov to L. S. Baranov, 24 March 1948, RGASPI, 17, 128, 568, pp. 22–24.

95. V. M. Molotov to I. V. Stalin, 6 January 1948, *SSSR i germanskii vopros, III*, pp. 567–68; P. M. Mal'kov to M. G. Gribanov, 28 January 1948, *SSSR i germanskii vopros, III*, pp. 571–72; "Vvedenie," *SSSR i germanskii vopros, III*, pp. 45–47; Jan Foitzik, *Sowjetische Militäradministration in Deutschland (SMAD) 1945–1949. Struktur und Funktion* (Berlin: Akademie Verlag 1999), pp. 364–88; André Steiner, "Die Deutsche Wirtschaftskommission—ein ordnungspolitisches Machtinstrument?" Dierk Hoffmann and Hermann Wentker (eds.), *Das letzte Jahr der SBZ. Politische Weichenstellungen und Kontinuitäten im Prozess der Gründung der DDR* (Munich: Oldenbourg 2000), pp. 85–105; Jens Gieseke, "Von der Deutschen Verwaltung des Innern zum Ministerium für Staatssicherheit 1948 bis 1950," Hoffmann and Wentker (eds.), *Das letzte Jahr der SBZ*, pp. 137–43; Hermann Wentker, "Das Jahr 1948 als Auftakt zu Zentralisierung, Politisierung und Sowjetisierung des Justizwesens," Hoffmann and Wentker (eds.), *Das letzte Jahr der SBZ*, pp. 149–67; Gerhard Wettig, "All-German Unity and East German Separation in Soviet Policy, 1947–1949," *Jahrbuch für Historische Kommunismusforschung*, 1994, pp. 129–33.

96. Conversation I. V. Stalin–W. Pieck and O. Grotewohl, 26 March 1948, *SSR i germanskii vopros, III,* pp. 631–32.

97. Report on meeting of the SED Central Secretariat, 7 December 1947, SAPMO-BArch, DY 30/IV 2/2.1/154, pp. 1–5; Obzor Kynina, AVPRF, AOB, 11zh, 71, 20, pp. 606–8; report by S. I. Tiul'panov, 8 December 1947, AVPRF, 082, 34, 154, 79, pp. 99–108; S. I. Tiul'panov to M. A. Suslov, 9 December 1947, RGASPI, 17, 128, 331, pp. 92–93; W. Ulbricht to M. A. Suslov, 12 December 1947, RGASPI, 17, 128, 1098, pp. 6–7; S. I. Tiul'panov to L. S. Baranov, 24 March 1948, RGASPI, 17, 128, 568, pp. 8–9; "Vvedenie," *SSR i germanskii vopros, III,* pp. 34–37; Goroshkova, *Dvizhenie nemetskogo narodnogo kongressa,* pp. 53, 58–72.

98. Application by Max Reimann (KPD Chairman) to General Robertson (Commander of the British zone), 18 May 1948, SAPMO-BArch, DY 30/3538, pp. 1–3.

99. Conversation I. V. Stalin–W. Pieck and O. Grotewohl, 26 March 1948, *SSR i germanskii vopros, III,* pp. 616–26 (quotation on p. 623).

100. V. D. Sokolovskii to V. M. Molotov, 23 December 1947, *SSR i germanskii vopros, III,* pp. 558–63; V. M. Molotov to I. V. Stalin, 14 May 1948, *SSSR i germanskii vopros, III,* pp. 677–80; "Vvedenie," *SSR i germanskii vopros, III,* pp. 53–54; Narinskii, "Berlinskii krizis," pp. 19–20; Jochen Laufer, "Die UdSSR und die deutsche Währungsfrage," *Vierteljahrshefte für Zeitgeschichte,* 3/1998, pp. 476–80; Laufer, "Die UdSSR und die Ursprünge der Berliner Blockade," *Deutschland Archiv,* 4/1998, pp. 570–73.

101. A. A Smirnov to A. Ja. Vyshinskii, 12 January 1948, AVPRF, 06, 21, 16, 219, p. 1; Dietrich Staritz, "Einheits- und Machtkalküle der SED," Elke Scherst-janoi (ed.), *"Provisorium auf längstens ein Jahr"* (Berlin: Akademie Verlag 1993), p. 29; Siegfried Suckut, "'Wenn die Nation erhalten bleibt, werden alle administrativen Spaltungsnahmen eines Tages zergehen und zerfallen.' Zur Vorgeschichte der DDR-Gründung," *Die Deutschlandfrage von Jalta und Potsdam bis zur staatlichen Teilung Deutschlands 1949, Studien zur Deutschlandfrage Vol. 12* (Berlin: Duncker and Humblot 1993), pp. 120–21; Laufer, "Die UdSSR und die Ursprünge," p. 572.

102. Laufer, "Die UdSSR und die Ursprünge," p. 569.

103. Assessment of U.S. policy on Germany by the Soviet Ministry of Foreign Affairs, 18 November 1947, *Sovetsko-amerikanskie otnosheniia 1945–1948,* pp. 468–82.

104. Hannes Adomeit, *Die Sowjetmacht in internationalen Krisen und Konflikten* (Baden-Baden: Nomos 1983), p. 100.

105. In fact, the USSR was similarly preparing for a separate currency reform which, for reasons of propaganda, was envisaged for implementation only after this measure had been taken in West Germany (Laufer, "Die UdSSR und die Währungsfrage," p. 480).

106. A. S. Paniushkin to G. Marshall, 6 March 1948, *Sovetsko-amerikanskie otnosheniia 1945–1948,* pp. 532–38.

107. Laufer, "Die UdSSR und die Währungsfrage," pp. 573–75; Narinskii, "Berlinskii krizis," pp. 20–21; Egorova, "Evropeiskaia bezopasnost'," pp. 63, 73.

108. Statement by Marshal Sokolovskii, 20 March 1948, *Documents on Germany 1944–1985,* Department of State Publication 9446 (Washington D.C.: Government Printing Office 1985), p. 142; telephone report by Marshal Sokolovskii and V. S. Semënov to the Ministry of Foreign Affairs, 20 March 1948, *Sovetsko-amerikanskie ot-*

nosheniia 1945–1948, pp. 538–39. For preceding Soviet decision making see "Vvedenie," *SSSR i germanskii vopros, III,* p. 76.

109. Conversation I. V. Stalin–W. Pieck and O. Grotewohl, 26 March 1948, *SSSR i germanskii vopros, III,* pp. 616–26 (quotation on p. 623).

110. Laufer, "Die UdSSR und die Ursprünge," pp. 576–77.

111. For Soviet assessment of the military situation see Victor Gobarev, "Soviet Military Plans and Actions during the First Berlin Crisis, 1948–49," *The Journal of Slavic Military Studies,* 10, no. 3 (September 1997), pp. 1–24.

112. Gobarev, "Soviet Military Plans and Actions during the First Berlin Crisis, 1948–49," pp. 1–24 (notably pp. 5–7); M. M. Narinskii, "Berlinskii krizis," p. 24. For Soviet defense planning in fall 1946 see M. A. Garelow [pseudonym for M. A. Gareev], "Woher droht Gefahr?" *Einheit,* 6/1989, pp. 573–89.

113. "Vvedenie," *SSSR i germanskii vopros, III,* pp. 76–77; V. S. Semënov to the Ministry of Foreign Affairs, 23 April 1948, *SSSR i germanskii vopros, III,* pp. 661–62; A. A. Smirnov to V. M. Molotov, 15 June 1948, *SSSR i germanskii vopros, III,* pp. 689–92; Narinskii, "Berlinskij krizis," pp. 21–23; Laufer, "Die UdSSR und die Ursprünge," pp. 573–77. On Soviet successive measures at the access routes 1 April–17 June 1948 see *FRUS 1948, II,* Department of State Publication 8660 (Washington D.C.: Government Printing Office 1973), pp. 885–908.

114. *FRUS 1948, II,* p. 941; Frank Howley, *Berlin Command* (New York: Putnam 1950), pp. 177–84.

115. Berlinskii vopros v 1948–1959 gg. Spravka po materialam Arkhiva MID SSSR, sostavl. G. P. Kyninym, 23 April 1959, AVPRF, 0742, 4, 34, 60, pp. 8–14.

116. Bernd von Kostka, "Die Berliner Luftbrücke 1948/49. Krisenmanagement am Beginn des Kalten Krieges," Michael Bienert, Uwe Schaper, and Andrea Theissen (eds.), *Die Vier Mächte in Berlin. Beiträge zur Politik der Alliierten in der besetzten Stadt* (Berlin: Landesarchiv Berlin 2007), pp. 81-92.

117. Declaration of the foreign ministers of USSR, Albania, Bulgaria, Czechoslovakia, Yugoslavia, Poland, Romania, and Hungary, 24 June 1948, *Vneshniaia politika Sovetskogo Soiuza. Dokumenty i materialy. 1948 god. Chast' pervaia: Ianvar'–iiun' 1948 goda* (Moscow: Gosudarstvennoe izdatel'stvo politicheskoi literatury 1950), pp. 238–48. This position implied that, in contrast to the USSR, which totally controlled Soviet zone authorities, the Western powers were prevented from having any say on the system and regime of united Germany.

118. Laufer, "Die UdSSR und die Ursprünge," pp. 573–74 (reference to Foreign Ministry paper of 23 February 1948).

119. Before this, a recommendation by General Clay, to send an armed convoy to Berlin to threaten enforcement of access by military force, had been rejected in Washington.

120. Note of the United States to the USSR, 6 July 1948, *Documents on Germany 1944–1985,* pp. 156–58.

121. S. A. Paniushkin to G. Marshall, 14 July 1948, *Sovetsko-amerikanskie otnosheniia 1945–1948,* pp. 593–96; conversation V. M. Molotov–W. B. Smith, 31 July 1948, *Sovetsko-amerikanskie otnosheniia 1945–1948,* pp. 598–600.

122. Conversation V. M. Molotov–3 Western ambassadors, 2 August 1948, *Sovetsko-amerikanskie otnosheniia 1945–1948,* pp. 600–611. Cf. Berlinskii vopros v 1948–1959

gg. Spravka po materialam Arkhiva MID SSSR, sostavl. G. P. Kyninym, 23 April 1959, AVPRF, 0742, 4, 34, 60, pp. 14–15; W. B. Smith to G. Marshall, 31 July 1948, *FRUS 1948, II*, pp. 996–98; W. B. Smith to G. Marshall, 3 August 1948, *FRUS 1948, II*, pp. 999–1004; Walter Bedell Smith, *My Three Years in Moscow* (Philadelphia and New York: Lippincot 1950), pp. 238–52.

123. Conversation V. M. Molotov–3 Western ambassadors, 6 August 1948, *Sovetsko-amerikanskie otnosheniia 1945–1948*, pp. 612–27; Berlinskii vopros v 1948–1959 gg. Spravka po materialam Arkhiva MID SSSR, sostavl. G. P. Kyninym, 23 April 1959, AVPRF, 0742, 4, 34, 60, pp. 15–16; Western draft of four-power communiqué, 6 August 1948, *Documents on Germany 1944–1985*, p. 163; U.S. documents in *FRUS 1948, II*, pp. 1004–1060.

124. Conversation I. V. Stalin–3 Western ambassadors, 23 August 1948, *Sovetsko-amerikanskie otnosheniia 1945–1948*, pp. 631–44; Berlinskii vopros v 1948–1959 gg. Spravka po materialam Arkhiva MID SSSR, sostavl. G. P. Kyninym, 23 April 1959, AVPRF, 0742, 4, 34, 60, pp. 17–18; W. B. Smith to G. Marshall, 23 August 1948, *FRUS 1948, II*, pp. 1061–65; W. B. Smith to G. Marshall, 24 August 1948, *FRUS 1948, II*, pp. 1065–68; W. B. Smith to G. Marshall, 24 August 1948, *FRUS 1948, II*, pp. 1069–71.

125. Four Power Directive to the Military Governors in Berlin, 30 August 1948, *Documents on Germany 1944–1985*, pp. 168–69.

126. Conversation V. M. Molotov–3 Western ambassadors, 30 August 1948, *Sovetsko-amerikanskie otnosheniia 1945–1948*, pp. 647–60; Aide-Mémoire of the Western Powers to the Soviet Union, 14 September 1948, *Documents on Germany 1944–1985*, pp. 169–71; Berlinskii vopros v 1948–1959 gg. Spravka po materialam Arkhiva MID SSSR, sostavl. G. P. Kyninym, 23 April 1959, AVPRF, 0742, 4, 34, 60, pp. 19–23; U.S. documents in *FRUS 1948, II*, pp. 1072–1197.

127. Protest by the democratic majority parties of the Berlin City Parliament, 8 September 1948, Deutsche Gesellschaft für Auswärtige Politik / Senate of [West] Berlin (eds.), *Dokumente zur Berlin-Frage 1944–1963* (Munich: Oldenbourg 1963), pp. 97–98.

128. Address by V. M. Molotov, 6 November 1948, *Bol'shevik*, 21/1948, pp. 12–13. A similar statement is contained in "SSSR v avangarde bor'by za prochnyi mir" (editorial), *Bol'shevik*, 23/1948, pp. 2–5.

129. Answers by the SED leaders to the questions that had been submitted to them prior to their conversation with Stalin on 18 December 1948, Badstübner and Loth (eds.), *Wilhelm Pieck*, pp. 247–48; notes by Pieck on conversation I. V. Stalin–W. Pieck, W. Ulbricht, and O. Grotewohl, 18 December 1948, and for oral report on it to the SED Central Secretariat, 27 December 1948, Badstübner and Loth (eds.), *Wilhelm Pieck*, pp. 260, 266.

130. See the documents in *Foreign Relations of the United States (FRUS) 1949, II*, Department of State Publication 8752 (Washington D.C.: Government Printing Office 1974), pp. 694–818.

131. See U.S. documents in *FRUS 1949, II*, pp. 856–1057; Soviet documents (to the extent of their having been publicized at the time) in *Vneshniaia politika Sovetskogo Soiuza. 1949 god* (Moscow: Gosudarstvennoe izdatel'stvo politiceskoi literatury 1953), pp. 366–427; Dean Acheson, *Strengthening the Forces of Freedom. Selected Speeches February 1949–April 1950*, Department of State Publication 5852 (Washington D.C.: Government Printing Office 1950), pp. 124–27; Gerhard Wettig, *Poli-*

tik im Rampenlicht. Aktionsweisen moderner Aussenpolitik (Frankfurt/Main: Fischer Bücherei 1967), pp. 74–78; Hanns Jürgen Küsters, *Der Integrationsfriede. Viermächte-Verhandlungen über die Friedensregelung mit Deutschland 1945–1990* (Munich: Oldenbourg 2000), pp. 399–429.

132. Vremennoe polozhenie o kriminal'noi politsii Sovetskoi zony okkupatsii Germanii, signed by S. Gorokhov on 17 May 1949, BArchB, MdI 7/1, p. 154; S. Gorokhov to K. Fischer (in German transl.), 14 July 1949, BArchB, MdI 7/45, pp. 240–41; S. Gorokhov to K. Fischer (in German transl.), 24 June 1949, BArchB, MdI 7/45, pp. 262–63.

133. Conversation I. V. Stalin–W. Pieck and O. Grotewohl, 26 March 1948, *SSSR i germanskii vopros, III*, pp. 629–30.

134. Wilfried Loth, *Stalins ungeliebtes Kind. Warum Moskau die DDR nicht wollte* (Berlin: Rowohlt 1994). See notably the conclusions on pp. 223–31.

135. W. R. Smyser, *From Yalta to Berlin. The Cold War Struggle Over Germany* (Houndmills and London: Macmillan 1999), p. 39. William Smyser shares Loth's view but notes that there is a contradiction he can't explain and hence feels to be mysterious.

136. Obzor Kynina, AVPRF, AOB, 11zh, 71, 20, pp. 608–18; S. I. Tiul'panov to L. S. Baranov, 24 March 1948, RGASPI, 17, 128, 568, pp. 22–25; A. A. Smirnov to V. A. Zorin, 19 August 1948, AVPRF, 06, 35, 171, 75, pp. 1–3; V. S. Semënov to V. M. Molotov, 6 October 1948, AVPRF, 06, 10, 36, 488, p. 1; letter to I. V. Stalin, undated [21 October 1948?], AVPRF, 06, 10, 36, 488, pp. 39–41; V. M. Molotov to I. V. Stalin, 21 October 1948, AVPRF, 06, 36, 187, 40, Bl. 1–12; Lieutenant Colonel Guliaev to V. Semënov, 10 December 1948, AVPRF, 0457a, 5, 28, 8, pp. 300–310; M. G. Gribanov to A. A. Smirnov, 25 January 1949, AVPRF, 082, 10, 36, 488, Bl. 39–41; M. G. Gribanov to A. Ia.Vyshinskii, undated [August 1949], AVPRF, 082, 36, 187, pp. 82–83.

137. Report on conversation I. V. Stalin–W. Pieck, W. Ulbricht, and O. Grotewohl (excerpt), 18 December 1948, Volkov, *Uzlovye problemy*, pp. 135–36.

138. Answers by the SED leaders to the questions that had been submitted to them prior to their conversation with Stalin on 18 December 1948, Badstübner and Loth (eds.), *Wilhelm Pieck*, p. 247.

139. Jens Gieseke, "Erich Mielke (1907–2000). Revolverheld und oberster Tschekist," Dieter Krüger and Armin Wagner (eds.), *Konspiration als Beruf. Deutsche Geheimdienstchefs im Kalten Krieg* (Berlin: Ch. Links 2003), p. 246.

140. Tantzscher, "Vorläufer," pp. 143–55; Monika Tantzscher, "'In der Ostzone wird ein neuer Apparat aufgebaut.' Die Gründung des DDR-Staatssicherheitsdienstes," *Deutschland Archiv*, 1/1998, pp. 50–51; Jens Gieseke, "Das Ministerium für Staatssicherheit (1950–1990)," Krüger and Wagner (eds.), *Konspiration als Beruf*, pp. 374–77; Otto, *Erich Mielke*, pp. 109–30.

141. See Ulbricht's statement on this and other documents in "Dokumente und Materialien. Sicherheits- und militärpolitische Konzepte der SED in der SBZ von 1948. Eine Dokumentation," *Beiträge zur Geschichte der Arbeiterbewegung*, 4 (1992), pp. 58–71.

142. Obzor Kynina, AVPRF, AOB, 11zh, 71, 20, pp. 602–3 (with reference to AVPRF, 06, 10, 40, 530, pp. 2–3); Major Liul'ka to M. G. Gribanov, 15 July 1948, AVPRF, 0457a, 5, 33, 27, p. 165; A. A. Smirnov to V. M. Molotov, 20 January 1949,

AVPRF, 06, 11, 12, 174, pp. 1–3; Pieck's notes on conversation I. V. Stalin–W. Pieck, W. Ulbricht, and O. Grotewohl, 18 December 1948; Badstübner and Loth (eds.), *Wilhelm Pieck*, p. 261; S. Gorokhov to K. Fischer, 8 May 1949, BArchB, MdI 7/45, pp. 49–50; S. Gorokhov to K. Fischer, 9 May 1949, BArchB, MdI 7/45, pp. 67–68; Mayer to K. Fischer, 25 May 1949, BArchB, MdI 7/45, pp. 72–76; K. Fischer to S. Gorokhov, 17 June 1949, BArchB, MdI 7/45, p. 78; Hans Ehlert, "Die Hauptverwaltung für Ausbildung (1949–1952)," Diedrich, Ehlert, and Wenzke, *Im Dienste der Partei*, pp. 253–58, 260–75; Gerhard Wettig,"Neue Erkenntnisse aus sowjetischen Geheimdokumenten über den militärischen Aufbau in der SBZ/DDR 1947–1952," *Militärgeschichtliche Mitteilungen*, 53, no. 2 (1994), pp. 402–6. Cf. the biographical evidence in Hans Ehlert and Armin Wagner (eds.), *Genosse General! Die Militärelite der DDR in biographischen Skizzen* (Berlin: Ch. Links 2003).

143. V. Chuikov to K. Fischer, 26 April 1949, BArchB, MdI 7/45, pp. 45–46; V. D. Sokolovskii to V. Chuikov, 8 August 1949, AVPRF, 0458, 264ss, 314, 0036, p. 11; "Dokumente und Materialien. Sicherheits- und militärpolitische Konzepte," *Beiträge zur Geschichte*, pp. 58–71; Ehlert, "Die Hauptverwaltung," pp. 258–59; Wettig, "Neue Erkenntnisse,"pp. 412–19.

144. Report on conversation I. V. Stalin–W. Pieck, W. Ulbricht, and O. Grotewohl (excerpt), 18 December 1948, Volkov, *Uzlovye problemy*, pp. 133; Patrick Major, "Big Brother and Little Brother: Das Verhältnis SED-KPD 1948–1951," Scherstjanoi (ed.), *"Provisorium auf längstens ein Jahr,"* pp. 156–57.

145. Report on conversation I. V. Stalin–W. Pieck, W. Ulbricht, and O. Grotewohl (excerpt), 18 December 1948, Volkov, *Uzlovye problemy*, pp. 133–34.

146. Report on conversation I. V. Stalin–W. Pieck, W. Ulbricht, and O. Grotewohl (excerpt), 18 December 1948, Volkov, *Uzlovye problemy*, pp. 134–35.

147. Pieck's notes for report on conversation I. V. Stalin–W. Pieck, W. Ulbricht, and O. Grotewohl on 18 December 1948 to the SED Central Secretariat, 27 December 1948, Badstübner and Loth (eds.), *Wilhelm Pieck*, pp. 269–72.

148. S. I. Tiul'panov to V. S. Semënov, 12 May 1949, AVPRF, 0457a, 7, 39, 10, pp. 1–14; S. I. Tiul'panov to V. S. Semënov, 24 May 1949, AVPRF, 0457a, 7, 39, 10, pp. 28–46; S. I. Tiul'panov to V. S. Semënov, 29 July 1949, AVPRF, 0457a, 7, 39, 10, pp. 72–81; protocol of the SED West Commission session, 26 September 1949, SAPMO-BArch, DY 30/IV 2/1/73, pp. 126–29; protocol of the SED West Commission session, 14 October 1949, SAPMO-BArch, DY 30/IV 2/1/73, pp. 131–36; protocol of the SED West Commission session, 18 October 1949, SAPMO-BArch, DY 30/IV 2/1/73, pp. 137–39; protocol of the SED West Commission session, 22 October 1949, SAPMO-BArch, DY 30/IV 2/1/73, pp. 142–43; protocol of the SED West Commission sessions, 2 November 1949, SAPMO-BArch, DY 30/IV 2/1/73, pp. 144–47; protocol of the SED West Commission session, 11 November 1949, SAPMO-BArch, DY 30/IV 2/1/73, pp. 148–52; protocol of the SED West Commission session on 24 November 1949, SAPMO-BArch, DY 30/IV 2/1/73, pp. 153–60; protocol of the SED West Commission session, 29 November 1949, SAPMO-BArch, DY 30/IV 2/1/73, pp. 161–63.

149. Cf. Pieck's notes in preparation of a letter to I. V. Stalin and/or a conversation with V. M. Molotov (on 11 May 1949), Badstübner and Loth (eds.), *Wilhelm Pieck*, p. 279. The need for co-optation was justified by saying that the population

of the Western zones had been prevented from taking part in elections for the People's Congress.

150. Goroshkova, *Dvizhenie nemetskogo narodnogo kongressa,* pp. 73–181.

151. *Dokumente der Sozialistischen Einheitspartei Deutschlands, Vol. II* ([East] Berlin: Dietz 1952), pp. 351–81.

152. A. A. Gromyko to I. V. Stalin, 6 October 1949, AVPRF, 07, 22a, 10, 138, pp. 4–9; A. A. Gromyko to I. V. Stalin, October 1949 [8 October 1949 or shortly afterward], AVPRF, 07, 22a, 10, 138, pp. 1–3; A. A. Gromyko to I. V. Stalin (with attachments), 20 October 1949, AVPRF, 07, 22a, 10, 138, pp. 10–12; I. I. Il'ichëv to M. G. Gribanov (with attachments), 18 October 1949, AVPRF, 082, 36, 183, 12, pp. 14–24.

153. Declaration by Marshal V. I. Chuikov, 10 October 1949, *Dokumente zur Deutschlandpolitik, Series II, Vol. 3/2,* pp. 236–38; Alexandr Haritonow, *Ideologie als Instiution und soziale Praxis. Die Adaption des höheren sowjetischen Parteischulungssystems in der SBZ/DDR (1945–1956)* (Berlin: Akademie Verlag 2004), pp. 117–18. For preceding SED expectations see the outlines of envisaged government declaration, 8 September 1949, Siegfried Suckut, "Zur Vorgeschichte der DDR-," *Vierteljahrshefte für Zeitgeschichte,* 1/1991, pp. 157–58.

154. Gerhard Wettig, "Abhängigkeiten und Handlungsspielräume der SBZ/DDR im Verhältnis zur UdSSR 1945–1955," Deutscher Bundestag (ed.), *Materialien der Enquete-Kommission "Überwindung der Folgen der SED—Diktatur im Prozess der deutschen Einheit" (13. Wahlperiode des Deutschen Bundestages), Vol. VIII/3: Das geteilte Deutschland im geteilten Europa* (Baden-Baden: Nomos; Frankfurt/Main: Suhrkamp 1999), pp. 2587–2619.

155. *Dokumente zur Deutschlandpolitik der Sowjetunion, Vol. I* ([East] Berlin: Rütten and Loening 1957), pp. 238–39.

156. *Pravda,* 7 November 1949.

5

"Struggle for Peace," 1949–1953

THE SLOGAN OF PEACE AS AN INSTRUMENT
OF SOVIET PROPAGANDA

After World War II had devastated large parts of the Continent, the Europeans abhorred military conflict. The USSR and Germany were among the countries that had suffered most. Their people felt a particularly strong need to maintain peace. This was a major consideration underlying Soviet policy making. The Marxist-Leninist thesis that the promotion of socialism was the only way to create peace provided a rationale for linking political objectives, notably control of West Germany and U.S. withdrawal from Europe, with the popular desire for peace. The claim that war was impossible once the socialist system was adopted allowed for condemnation of any opponents of "progress" toward socialism as "enemies of peace" and "warmongers." Since the United States and its allies were willing to resist expansion of the socialist system and the Kremlin's power, they were denounced as the camp of war. Any armament, even if minor, on their side was "militarism," that is, an expression of willingness to make war. Military preparations in socialist countries, however big, were bound to serve the "defense of peace." According to Soviet doctrine, militarism was a fundamental ingredient of the capitalist system which, in its current stage of development, was tantamount to "imperialism." On this premise, any armament effort in the West was denounced as testifying to "militaristic" intent and creating a threat to peace.[1]

As early as at the Cominform founding conference in September 1947, the Kremlin had taken the view that communist peace propaganda was a major political weapon. In Zhdanov's program of action, anti-Western mobilization of people for peace and international security played a prominent role. To persuade the public that peace and socialism were interconnected, the Cominform bulletin was termed "For a Lasting Peace, for a People's Democracy." The slogan of peace was also used to propagate Soviet policy on Germany: Negotiations on a peace treaty were depicted as a suitable method to overcome East-West conflict in Central Europe by agreement. The real motive underlying the argument was a willingness to extend the USSR's influence to West Germany and to press for evacuation of U.S. troops. Western rejection of the Soviet offer to "make peace" was ascribed to aggressive intent.

When, in early 1949, the United States, Canada, and ten West European countries including Britain, France, and Italy negotiated and concluded the North Atlantic Treaty, the Kremlin felt that public advocacy of peace was becoming even more important. To be sure, the Western alliance by then merely provided for U.S. political commitment to the allies' security and did not entail preparation of effective military defenses. Nonetheless, the Moscow leaders saw this as a threat to their ambitions in Europe. They sought to meet the challenge by sustained effort to discredit the Atlantic alliance as a military bloc devised to antagonize the countries and to seek war against the "peaceloving" states of socialism. The prime target of denunciation was the United States. The communists in Western Europe were instructed to undermine their countries' governments by organizing a "movement of partisans of peace."

Initiation of Peace Propaganda

On 6 January 1949, the USSR issued an appeal for a world peace congress designed "to mobilize the societal forces which defend peace and to rein in the warmongers." As the main dangers to be averted, it pointed to the March 1948 Brussels Pact between France, the Benelux countries, and Britain; the emergent North Atlantic Alliance; and the atomic bomb in U.S. hands. The congress was held from 20 to 25 April 1949. The Soviet side wanted it "to contribute as much as possible to including the broad masses and the democratic circles of all countries in a campaign of struggle for secure peace." To this end, a manifesto on the peace struggle would have to be addressed to all peoples. This appeal and other resolutions had been fully worked out before the congress.[2]

As another channel to disseminate the message, the Cominform was activated. At its third conference on 16–19 November 1949, "defense of peace and struggle against the warmongers" was the first and foremost point on the agenda. The representatives of the participating parties stated that they had intensified their efforts to create a "broad front of struggle for peace" as posited by the USSR. The "Anglo-American imperialists and their henchmen" were denounced as enemies of peace. "Bourgeois" groups, the social democrats, the Catholic Church hierarchy, a major, "not [class-]conscious" part of the peasantry, and "enemy agents" in communist parties were alleged to be accomplices of the U.S. and British "warmongers." To combat their influence, peace committees must be set up all over Europe. Also, the collection of signatures was envisaged as a means to express protest against the Western threat to peace.[3]

With special regard to the German public, previous appeals to support the Soviet policy of national unification was complemented by peace slogans. The West's alleged splitting effort was portrayed as an effort to make war. Attainment of national unification was therefore closely linked to attainment of peace. Both objectives would only be achieved if the "warmongers" in the West would be defeated and forced to conclude a peace treaty with Germany. To this end, national and pacifist forces had to join their efforts. To propagate this thesis, the SED leaders used an organizational network in West Germany which, besides the KPD and the "bourgeois" satellites in the East German "National Front," included all kinds of committees and a number of World Peace Council offspring directed at different audiences. They were to influence their respective addressees and to recruit followers among them.[4] Not only sympathy but active support was sought. For example, the collection of signatures was designed not just to make people simply express positive attitudes but to involve them in the "struggle for peace."

Obstacles to Propaganda in West Germany

The change of emphasis from unification to peace did not change the underlying strategic concept. As before, class categories shaped Soviet policy on Germany. In the Kremlin's view, control of the working class and creation of a united workers party continued to be crucial. Weakening the social democrats, and allowing the communists to take their role, was seen as the principal means to shift the correlation of domestic forces. SPD Chairman Schumacher was blamed for splitting the nation by his anti-Soviet attitude. This was to little avail. His followers failed to oppose their leader, let alone change their party affiliation. Somewhat easier was recruiting "patriots" among other groups. At least a few "bourgeois" allowed themselves to be persuaded that partition might be ascribed to Western policy and should be overcome by a search for agreement with the USSR. Against their ideological belief, the policy makers in Moscow and East Berlin had little choice but to direct their effort increasingly at "bourgeois" circles, notably nationalists and rightists.

However, the dogma was not questioned that the "working class" attitude was decisive. Much effort was wasted on futile attempts at "liberating" industrial workers from "social democratic error" and on seeking to re-educate them accordingly. The expectation that the German social democrats, with their tradition of advocating liberal democracy and rejecting Russian autocracy, might enter an alliance with the Soviet dictatorship against the West was illusory from the very start. In contrast to this, conservative nationalists occasionally indulged in positive reminiscences of past cooperation with czarist Russia or the USSR. This might have become a major political factor if it had not been for the Red Army's previous excesses, the repressive system of government in the GDR, and Soviet treatment of German prisoners of war. Against this background, unity and peace along Soviet lines met with almost general opposition. While there was much sympathy for a neutral but democratic Germany along Western lines, an overwhelming majority was terrified by any prospect of being subjected to the SED regime and to Soviet control.[5] The Western side increasingly emphasized the systemic source of East-West conflict. At U.S. and social democratic initiative, a most successful campaign for reunification "on the basis of free elections" was started in early 1950. Soviet and East German propaganda was put on the defensive.

At the same time, the communist claim to promote peace was challenged by an innovative Western peace concept: that the nations of Europe were called upon to cooperate and to unite on a permanent basis. But attainment of this goal was difficult since, as a result of its experience in World War II, Germany as a crucial component was largely seen as a potential threat to national security in the neighboring countries. To cope with this problem, integration into a common economic and political framework was suggested. Arrangements to provide for mutual participation in each other's affairs would eliminate Germany's capacity for unilateral action and tie it to the community of Western nations. Antagonism would thus be overcome. Whereas the international order after World War I had humiliated, burdened, and discriminated against the defeated countries and thus given rise to revanchist ambition, the concept of integration of the early 1950s basically provided for creating peace on the basis of nondisriminatory, mutually obliging relations.[6]

The Kremlin rightly saw this as a challenge to its claim that peace must be achieved by joining the socialist camp as the only hope for a peaceful world. Therefore, the USSR responded in a most hostile manner when, as a major step toward integration, France proposed the "Schuman Plan" on 9 May 1950 for joint control of coal and steel industries as a scheme to prevent use of crucial war-making capabilities by individual countries. Underlying this was the idea that such an arrangment was bound to create lasting peace among traditional antagonists in Europe. The Federal Republic was to be integrated in the West firmly on a basis designed to eliminate both national control of resources to wage war and resulting fears of threat by Germany. Intra-Western tension, which allowed for exploitation by the Soviet Union, would be greatly reduced.

Stalin's Instructions on Political Struggle for German Unity

A few days before Robert Schuman outlined his integration initiative in public, Stalin explained to the SED leaders his idea of peace for a divided Germany. Struggle for its national unity must be linked to struggle for "democratic freedoms." "Democratization" (as practised in the GDR) presupposed restoration of German unity which, for this reason, was a crucial objective. Activities by a "movement for peace" were more promising than efforts by the East German "National Front" which, despite its claim to all-party representation, was widely suspected of being communist-inspired. Accordingly, peace committees to be set up, besides the "National Front" network, had the task of persuading the Germans that the USSR was the very champion of peace with whom they had to unite for the restoration of national unity.

> Stalin says that this is good but nonetheless the main thing is to conduct a broad peace campaign. Germany remembers war well and has lost much by it. The Germans don't want war. When a broad peace campaign will be developed in Germany, then the German people's movement for peace won't allow to antagonize West Germany with East Germany. The Germans now have two roads [before them]: war or peace. The Americans seek to draw Germany into war by claiming that this is the only means of restoring a strong Germany. The peace campaign demonstrates that the road of war leads to Germany's destruction and that the only way to restore a strong Germany is peace and cooperation among the peaceloving peoples. When the whole German population will be drawn into a campaign of struggle for peace, then all plans of the U.S.A. to draw Germany into war will be liquidated.[7]

When the SED rapporteur was skeptical about the chance to influence West German attitudes, Stalin disagreed. While parties, trade unions, the press, and similar organizations might not be amenable, the correlation of forces in the Federal Republic must not be assessed on this basis.

> He, Comrade Stalin, can tell what happened in the history of the bolshevist [that is, Lenin's] party before the revolution. All organizations were hostile against the bolsheviks. The impression was created that there was no breakthrough for the bolsheviks. But one had only to move down and to turn to the masses, then it became clear that everything was boiling. The leaders of the other parties and organizations who talked about the struggle being unfeasible, had actually lost contact with the people. One had only to throw a spark— and everything looked different. . . . It seems to me, says Comrade Stalin, that the attitude of the people's masses in West Germany must be different from

what it appears to the West German party and trade-union organizations. Why? For all actions by the Americans point into this direction: long-term occupation, frustration of the peace treaty, dismantling [of industry], mass unemployment, the workers and their families being left with no means to live on. Unwillingly, the Americans and the British are themselves teaching the German people resistance. You want that everything will sharply change at once? This will not happen. The population of West Germany fears the Americans. One has to keep this in mind. But the population is waking up. Comrade Stalin says that he has advised the West German communists to continue their internal work. To entertain and reinforce contact with the humble folk (prostoi narod). To shout less. To explain more. The people might possibly have risen already but it is fearful and remains silent but on occasion such people's silence is more dangerous than open demonstrations. For this reason, one must not look only at what can be deduced from speeches by politicians. One has to see what is not visible at a simple glance. Among the people, there is a growing hatred against the imperialists who are now being viewed in West Germany more as occupiers than as imperialists. For this reason, the perspectives in West Germany are better than expressed in Grotewohl's report [which had been given on behalf of the SED].[8]

Subsequent exchange focused on economic competition between the two opposing systems in Germany. Stalin and his SED interlocutors agreed that supply of the GDR population must be made to compare favorably with the Federal Republic and that dependence on West German imports had to be eliminated. It was crucial to create an impression of socialist systemic superiority. With a view at the East German elections in October, Stalin expressed willingness to alleviate imposed burdens. While the voters would not have a choice among a number of party tickets, there might be massive abstentions if people were dissatisfied. It was deemed essential to prevent this. To this end, an increase of wages was deemed necessary.[9]

MILITARIZATION OF EAST-WEST CONFLICT

Communist attack against South Korea on 25 June 1950 basically changed the situation in Europe. As the sources now available indicate, Western assumption that this aggression had to be attributed to the USSR was basically correct. Kim Il-sung's decision had been approved by Stalin; his military action was supported by both arms deliveries from the USSR and Soviet pilots put at North Korean disposal. After some hesitation, the Kremlin leader had allowed himself to be persuaded that there was no risk of American intervention.[10] President Truman, however, sent troops to save South Korea. Stalin saw himself trapped. He suspected a premeditated fraud to stigmatize the socialist camp as aggressor and to create a general feeling of threat in the West to justify massive armament.[11]

This was a misperception based on the wrong interpretation of a statement by Secretary of State Acheson, who had failed to include Korea in the U.S. defense parameter. When Stalin had accepted the conclusion that the United States would acquiesce in the conquest of South Korea, he had not taken into account that the evidence provided by Kim Il-sung did not apply to the scenario of the war unleashed on 25 June 1950. When Secretary of State Dean Acheson had failed to include Korea in the U.S. defense perimeter, he had referred to the contingency of a global war, when it would have made no sense to commit scarce military forces to this theater. The Western countries, for their part, also misperceived the other side's intent. It was almost generally felt that attack against South Korea was an overture of a similar action against Western Europe. In fact, however, Stalin wanted to avoid war with the United States. As long as American troops would remain on the Continent, he was determined not to seek armed conflict.

This mutual failure to interpret the opponent's behavior correctly had far-reaching consequences. While North Korea was unexpectedly involved in confrontation with the United States, East-West conflict was generally militarized. The starting point was that the West Europeans felt acutely threatened by the supposed prospect of Soviet attack in the near future. They realized that the military forces available to the West did not allow for sustained defense. The fact that South Korea had been raided also put the deterrent effect of American power in question. The U.S. pledge under the North Atlantic Treaty not to leave the allies to their fate but to send forces to Europe could be put into practice only after the United States had created sufficient military capabilities during an extended period of rearmament as it had done in World War II. Hence Western Europe would be conquered and subjected to cruel Soviet occupation. Liberation by the United States would follow only much later and entail massive devastation through warfare. To avert this prospect, the organization of efficient forces to resist attack seemed indispensable. The West Europeans wanted an operational defense system which, in their view, required the Americans to take the biggest share. Washington responded that it was unable to shoulder such an immense burden. The allies had to exploit their own resources to the full extent. This required including soldiers from the Federal Republic. Only on this basis was the United States willing to contribute to the military effort.

Response to the Prospect of Western Rearmament

For the Kremlin, contemplated Western rearmament was a challenge. Countermeasures deemed necessary would create an economic burden and infringe on reconstruction. If the West Europeans were made to feel that they were not under Soviet military threat any longer, this would shift the concentration of forces on the Continent. Buildup of West German troops in a Western alliance framework was seen as particularly harmful.[12] To be sure, Stalin understood that there was no immediate military danger. For some years to come, the Western formations in Europe would continue to be inferior to the Soviet army. But the Western military and political bloc would be fortified; the Americans would reinforce their ties with their European allies and mobilize their greatly superior economic resources for armament; West German units would both strengthen the military capabilities of the North Atlantic alliance and terminate the chance that the *Bereitschaften* in the GDR might be employed one day as a force to support action for German unification. As a country that would make a substantial contribution to Western military power, the Federal Republic would be a weighty international actor capable of fostering both national unification on a Western basis and the revision of Eastern borders.

The first response by the Kremlin was political. Stalin wanted to make the Cominform a full-fledged center of communist policy coordination with a well-known party leader from Western Europe at its top. As the French party chairman Thorez was seriously ill, his Italian counterpart was the only candidate. But Togliatti wanted to stay in his home country and stubbornly refused to accept the proposal. The argument that the international communist movement needed a competent leader to be on Eastern territory when war was approaching failed to make him change his mind. In his view, the prospect that Comintern principles would be expressly introduced again was highly undesirable. In December 1950 and January 1951, Togliatti had heated discussions with Stalin but stuck to his position. Upon this, the Kremlin leader abandoned the Cominform scheme altogether.[13]

Rearmament in the West made Stalin also feel that there was a need for military measures. The Soviet Union and the aligned socialist countries were unprepared for a "big war" against well-armed adversaries in Europe. While such a war was not a prospect for the time being, the challenge would emerge within a few years. For this reason, the Eastern armies had to be increased and modernized; massive weapons production was required.[14] On 9 January 1951, Stalin spoke to the party leaders and the defense ministers of the dependent communist countries.

> In recent time, the opinion has emerged that the United States is an invincible power and that it is willing to start a third world war. But reality has shown that the United States is not only unwilling to start the third world war but that it is unable to cope with a small war such as the one in Korea. It is clear that the United States is unprepared and that they will need some years to get prepared. The United States has put itself into a situation of constraint and is involved in Asia for a number of years. This provides us and the revolutionary world movement with the most favorable condition that the United States is involved in Asia for two, three years. These two, three years must be skilfully exploited. The United States has atomic energy; we also have it; the United States has a big

navy but its navy can't take a decisive role in war; the United States has a modern air force but its air force is weak, weaker than ours.

Our task is to exploit the two, three years we have for building a modern and efficient army. We dispose of all conditions to build such an army, and we can do this. China has created a better army than ours, the army of the people's democracies. It is not normal that you have weak armies. This situation must be eliminated. In two, three years, you must create modern and efficient armies in the people's democratic countries which, at the end of the three-year period, should be fully prepared for struggle. This is the objective of our consultations. I draw your attention to [the fact] that his consultation is inofficial and strictly secret.

After Stalin had made clear what he was up to, the East European defense ministers reported on their military situation. All of them felt unprepared for war, displayed little willingness to increase armament, and stated that little had been done to coordinate efforts with the USSR. On this basis, Stalin concluded:

The comrades from the people's democratic countries must be given aid more quickly. One must transmit the necessary technical documentation to them more quickly. I have decided this matter, and I do not know why this decision is not implemented. . . . You must prepare yourselves well. For this, a plan of six years as with the Poles is not good. What plan is this which takes six years? Who will guarantee these six years to you? Two, three years is a good plan, a plan which will work. In the people's democratic countries, we must organize armies which in war, in a first case of need, include 2–2.5 million men. And all this [must be] planned carefully so that this fighting force is well-equipped with everything it will need. What do you say, Vasil'evskii [Soviet defense minister], are 2–2.5 million sufficient?

Vasil'evskii (supported by [Chief of General Staff] Shtemenko): No, the people's democratic countries can easily provide 4 million.

Stalin: If there will be 4 million, they will be equipped badly. Better 3 million in the first case of need, and these well-organized and well-equipped. The proposal by the Romanian comrades [to put up 3 million] is alright. We feel that the proposal by the Romanian comrades must be accepted and that we must entrust the body which will discuss the proposal, with the problem of the army. This commission, whatever we will call it, must guarantee a sufficient quantity of modern means of combat to the army so that, at the end of the three-year period, everything will be ready. . . . Not every country must do everything itself. The tasks must be distributed. Not everyone must produce tanks and canons. Limit yourselves to two, three countries which can produce them quickly and well. For this, we will need a coordinating committee consisting of competent people. We propose that also all the military will enter it. From us [the USSR], too, military men will go into it. I remind [you] once more: You need a fleet of jet fighters, at minimum one division for each country, with reliable and carefully selected pilots who will not flee with their aircraft across the border. We also need bombers for attack, at the beginning, one division at minimum for each country. This equipment with modern means must be guaranteed by the committee. We need such a committee. I propose that we form a commission at once to investigate the problem. The commission is to submit proposals within 2–3 days.

On 11 January, the commission chaired by Vasil'evskii envisioned a permanent coordination committee that would meet regularly to discuss problems of military equipment. The next day, Stalin, Molotov, Malenkov, Beria, and the commission met to ratify this agreement and to fix the military contributions by the people's democracies. Concluding the session, Stalin admonished the East European leaders:

> I draw your attention to [the fact] that the two, three years which lie before us, are a time span not to work but to arms ourselves and to arm ourselves well. Why is this necessary? It is necessary since the imperialists have their own logic: They use to attack unarmed or weakly armed countries to annihilate them; but they avoid the well-armed countries. Therefore, it is necessary that you arm yourselves well in order to be respected by the imperialists and to be left by them in peace.[15]

Stalin's instruction was directed to Poland, Czechoslovakia, Hungary, Romania, and Bulgaria. Both being geographically separated from the Soviet bloc and having but a tiny potential, Albania was left out. East Germany did not participate either. To justify the official claim that it was an acceptable nucleus of national unification, it continued to be officially ascribed an "antifascist-democratic" character and thus was not to be part of the socialist camp.

Struggle Against "West German Remilitarization"

The Federal Republic's prospective rearmament was not simply a challenge but also provided an opportunity for appeals to the other European countries, notably France, where Nazi aggression and occupation had not been forgotten. Soviet propaganda warned them not to allow for the reemergence of "German militarism" in the Federal Republic, which allegedly was threatened with repetition of their terrible experience.[16] This was not the only chance to exploit fears that past dreads might return. In the Federal Republic as well, there were apprehensions of being victimized by war. Given that the public was unaware that military units did exist already in the GDR, antimilitary sentiment was reinforced by the argument that the buildup of an army in West Germany was bound to entail similar measures in the East. Then "Germans" would have to "fight against Germans." The lesson derived from devastating war and postwar reeducation was that the recruitment of troops would entail another military disaster.[17]

To be sure, the Kremlin opposed any steps of Western armament; but the military effort by the West Europeans did not offer an expedient target of denunciation. For this reason, propaganda polemics were directed at "West German remilitarization" as the very threat to peace in Europe. Emphasis was also put on depicting the U.S. presence as a source of war. The "American imperialists" were portrayed as criminals who, in conjunction with the "reactionary forces" in the Federal Republic, wanted to involve the Europeans in an offensive war against the "camp of peace" in the East. The slogan "Ami go home" was widely disseminated. In the intra-German context, it was also argued that "remilitarization" of the country's Western part would deepen national partition and put an end to the chance of reunification. The SED appealed to the nation: "Fight against West Germany's remilitarization!" and: "Prevent restoration of German militarism!" To this end, "unity of action" was alleged to be required. It would have to include not only workers of any political orientation but also "the bourgeoisie's leading intellectual forces." The splitting activities by the "German and foreign warmongers" had to be stopped for the sake of restoring national unity.[18]

As previously, the campaign in West Germany was organized by KPD cadres under SED and, ultimately, Soviet control. The starting point was the creation of committees that included people from all parts of society to conceal the communist initiative. After this, a "referendum" was initiated. The West Germans were requested to put their signatures under a text that called for termination of "remilitarization" and conclusion of a peace treaty. The action was prohibited by the Ministry of the Interior in Bonn on 24 April 1951. Upon this, the Eastern side tried to initiate mass protest. The occupation powers and Adenauer's government were accused of a "terrorist campaign" against "patriots and fighters for peace." A "Committee for Protection of Democratic Rights in Western Germany" was founded. Also, thousands of allegedly spontaneous letters were sent from the GDR to individuals in the Federal Republic. All of them requested protest against imminent "remilitarization" and early conclusion of a peace treaty.[19]

"Bourgeois" audiences in the Federal Republic, such as former Nazis and professional soldiers, notably generals and SS leaders, were paid particular attention. The objective was to dissuade them from any support of West European defense. Eastern efforts to cultivate "bourgeois" opposition were greatly encouraged when, on 11 October 1950, Gustav Heinemann resigned as minister of the interior to protest against Chancellor Adenauer's policy of "remilitarization" and "cementing national partition." Given Heinemann's close links with the Protestant Church, the Kremlin and the East German regime expected that this would trigger a broad "antimilitarist" movement and split the West German "bourgeoisie." A popular front would result to replace the pro-Western government in Bonn. Willingness for an alliance with "progressive bourgeois forces" in the Federal Republic did not change the "class orientation" underlying Moscow's policy. As previously, the GDR was seen as the model to transform the prospective all-German state. Free elections continued to be unacceptable as a basis of unification. Heinemann and his associates did not accept this and refused cooperation. Soviet plans to set up a joint political front against "West German remilitarization" failed to materialize.[20]

Program of German Unification

At a suggestion from East Berlin,[21] the Kremlin convened the bloc foreign ministers in Prague on 20–21 October 1950 to define domestic modalities of German unification. The declaration that had been prepared by the USSR and was unanimously approved called for renouncing the plans of "West German remilitarization" and claimed that it offered an attractive chance of reunification to the Germans. On the basis of parity, representatives of either government were to form an "All-German Constituent Council" that had to agree on the system and regime of united Germany, set up a provisional government, and define the fundamentals of the prospective state structures. The decisions to result from the negotiations between the two states might not be discussed, let alone revised in subsequent quadripartite peace treaty talks.[22] This program of action basically reaffirmed the positions defined in 1948 and 1949 on how German unity might be achieved.[23]

The envisaged procedure had three major implications. The SED leadership would have a veto on any matter. Any West German attempt to reject socioeconomic and other domestic transformation that, in communist interpretation, was required by the Potsdam Agreement (expressly mentioned as the obliging basis), was bound to elicit the response that this was a *sine qua non* of agreement. Given that any political step of the GDR was thoroughly controlled by the USSR, whereas policy in the Federal Republic was essentially shaped by domestic forces, the Prague proposal also implied that, in the four-power context, the Western powers would be unilaterally excluded from decisions on the modalities of German unification. This disequilibrium not only provided for weakness on the Western side as Bonn was unable to match Moscow's political weight but also allowed for inclination to prevail among West Germans (who might not understand all resulting consequences) that unification required maximum concessions. In addition to this, the Federal Republic was likely to be deprived of support by the Western powers once it alienated them by entering negotiations against their will (as it was not permitted under the Occupation Statute of 1949).

To make the West Germans put pressure on their government to agree to the proposal, a propaganda campaign was launched.[24] The Prague Declaration was presented as a program to overcome partition. All political parties were called upon to fight Adenauer and the Western "splitters." These "warmongers" had to be deprived of their capacity to "remilitarize" the country. The concept that had been reaffirmed in Prague was explained in more detail by Grotewohl. In a letter that, on precise Soviet instructions, he addressed to Chancellor Adenauer on 30 November 1950 (and which was instantly published), he proposed that each of the two German governments nominate negotiators to decide on problems relating to creation of an All-German Constituent Council. Six representatives were envisaged for either side but numbers were declared not to be "fundamentally important." What really mattered was mutual "understanding," that is, decisions had to be taken unanimously. The all-German government to be set up by the council would, inter alia, "prepare conditions for holding free elections." Neither date nor procedure were indicated. Any commitment was thus avoided on holding elections prior to basic decisions on unification.[25]

Grotewohl's letter served as a basis for an intensified communist campaign in West Germany under the slogan: "Germans to one table!" The Western powers, notably the United States, were blamed for any conceivable infamy. "Ami go home!" was painted on the walls. Evidently, U.S. soldiers were to be given the feeling of not being welcome in the occupied country. Sharp polemics were directed also against the federal government, which was ascribed an intent to sabotage national unity. The internally stated objective was Adenauer's removal from office. To this end, a broad "alliance" of all potentially anti-Western groups was sought.[26] Particular attention was paid to extreme rightists in the Federal Republic.[27] Control of prospective united Germany was seen in Moscow as the key that would open the door to all of Europe.[28]

Failure of Cooperation with Adenauer's Domestic Opponents

The unification campaign failed to produce substantial results. The public generally felt that the Eastern refusal to allow for unification on the basis of free elections indicated a willingness for communist rather than democratic unification. To be sure, the leaders in both Moscow and East Berlin tried hard to conceal their underlying intents. As Grotewohl stated internally, they saw it as crucial to avoid any clarification of their German Constituent Council proposal before the Federal Republic would get involved in negotiations.[29] Unless the West Germans had irreversibly taken the road of seeking unification by agreement with the GDR, they were expected to reject the offer when they became aware of its implications. But people in the Federal Republic were skeptical even without clear insight into Eastern motivation. To be sure, quite a few among them suspected Adenauer of not being genuinely interested in national unity and opposed him for this reason, but hardly anyone was willing to talk with the SED and the USSR without their prior commitment to democratic self-determination. As was generally agreed, Soviet *diktat* and communist repression had be excluded prior to talks with the GDR. As a result, the Kremlin vainly hoped for support by Adenauer's critics. Notably, its expectation was utterly unrealistic that the SPD would accept "unity of action" with the communists and that parts of the "bourgeois camp" would oust the chancellor by unconstitutional action.

The attitude of Heinemann highlights the Soviet predicament. His disagreement with the "West German imperialistic bourgeoisie" under Adenauer and his orientation at the alliance with the United States was seen to conform to Soviet operational needs to the full extent.[30] But his underlying intent was completely different. The Kremlin's principal accusation against the chancellor was that he resisted implementation of the Potsdam Agreement as practiced in the GDR and rejected "unification of Germany on a democratic basis." This was attributed to his perception that this was a threat to "German imperialism," that is, to the capitalist system, which would entail loss of the "bourgeoisie's" economic and political positions.[31] These views were seen to shape Heinemann's attitude. To be sure, the Soviet side felt in Moscow that this point need not take precedence over exploiting a chance to promote policy on Germany by undermining Adenauer's position. But when Heinemann was confronted with a demand to accept joint action with the KPD to take the leading role, the attempt failed. To be sure, the GDR secret police *Stasi* managed to install an agent in his headquarters who monitored all his activities but was unable to control his policy.[32] Nonetheless, Heinemann was provided with occasional financial support through seemingly noncommunist channels. After all, he was useful as a challenge to Adenauer.[33]

In the Soviet view, political "allies" had to be under organizational and operational control.[34] The KPD willingly submitted but the Kremlin was interested in a broad front of opposition that not only implemented Soviet policy but had a noncommunist image. Joseph Wirth who, in the 1920s, had been prominent in the Catholic Zentrum party and, for a short while, had served as chancellor of the Reich, accepted the SED's conditions for cooperation. At the end of 1951, an organization was set up that he formally headed but it actually was controlled by cadres who received their instructions from East Berlin. To be sure, Wirth repeatedly made public statements not in accord with official policy, but his divergent pronouncements were often deemed useful as they were practically irrelevant but supported the official pretense that the organization was independent. Nonetheless, Wirth's SED connection transpired to the public. So even the small amount of personal authority and societal backing he had originally enjoyed was waning. Lack of trust in his integrity prevented political influence.[35]

Failure of the Paris Talks, March–June 1951

Ever since 1947, the Soviet leaders had pressed for negotiations for a German peace treaty but invariably insisted on restitution of full four-power control and satisfaction of all material and political demands. In 1950–1951, their plea for an alternative to "West German remilitarization" had some resonance in Western Europe. Particularly the French government felt that, given widespread attitudes in the country, this must not be ignored. Notably with a view on national elections in mid-1951, it sought diplomatic exchange with Moscow to discard the impression that it allowed for no arrangement but rearmament of the Federal Republic. Britain and the United States insisted on preparatory talks that would clarify whether the USSR was prepared to accept a balanced conference agenda with no inherent bias. Only on this basis, a chance for reasonable compromise might be expected.

Discussing the situation in Germany, the Soviet policy makers were concerned over Western plans to grant more independence to the Federal Republic. They did not want to reciprocate by making concessions to the SED regime's desire for more leeway.[36] Therefore, both improvement of West Germany's legal status and intensification of its integration into the West were seen as major challenges. The envisaged European Defense Community (EDC) and the Coal and Steel Community set up under the "Schuman Plan" were felt to frustrate hope for isolating West Germany. At the same time, Western advocacy of free elections as a basis of unification required an "expedient" response. Otherwise, this highly popular proposal would undermine the USSR's claim of being the champion of German unity. For these reasons, the Kremlin leadership rejected a suggestion by the Ministry of Foreign Affairs to reduce GDR dependence but decided that discussion on a peace treaty with Germany must be revived. An "Austrian solution," that is, creation of a united democratic state not aligned with the West, was seen to be out of the question.[37] The Ministry of Foreign Affairs suggested that peace treaty principles be worked out as a basis of propaganda.[38] Shortly afterward, the SED leaders asked for Soviet approval of their plan to direct a public appeal to West Germany to send a joint peace treaty petition to the four powers.[39] All this indicated little interest in serious negotiations.

During the preparatory talks for a prospective quadripartite conference that started on 5 March, the Western delegations were more flexible than had been anticipated in Moscow. It was felt that agreement on the agenda was not impossible. The Kremlin did not want this and instructed its delegation to insist that, at the prospective conference, the points of Soviet interest must be scheduled for decision before any Western desires would be discussed. The USSR would thus be able to press for fulfilment of its demands with no concessions in return. The leaders in Moscow knew, of course, that such a procedure provoked rejection.[40] Soviet unwillingness for compromise enabled the French government to tell its people that it had tried to open an alternative to West German rearmament but failed as a result of the other side's intransigence. Termination of the talks also allowed Britain and the United States to veil their preference for promoting progress of West European integration and to create an appearance that they had been prepared to reach agreement with the USSR on Germany.[41]

REORIENTATION OF POLICY ON GERMANY

In summer 1951, negotiations betweeen the Western powers and the Federal Republic on both a West German defense contribution and revision of the Occupation Statute resulted in consensus on the political framework. At this point, or possibly already before this,[42] Stalin decided that East Germany had to join Eastern preparations for war with the Western powers. In mid-1951, the Soviet General Staff worked out a document that "recommended" that not only the people's democracies but the GDR be included in the armament effort. Given the possibility that war would be "unleashed by the imperialistic forces of the West," all these countries were to put "investment in strategic development of their military forces" into the center of their economic plans.[43] The drafts worked out somewhat later by the Soviet foreign ministry on "fundaments of a peace treaty with Germany" (designed to justify East German creation of a full-fledged army as was expressly stated in internal communication)[44] postulated "national forces" consisting of ground, maritime, and aircraft units.[45] In November 1951, the USSR Council of Ministers (which was chaired by Stalin) ordered the Soviet ministry of armed forces to prepare for training of GDR military pilots.[46] Shortly afterward, military restructuring and armament industry buildup were initiated in the GDR.[47] When outlines for SED policy were defined in February 1952, "strengthening" of the domestic socialist order was added as a new postulate.[48]

These steps indicated a major change of policy. Until then, the "mission" assigned to the GDR had been to provide a basis for extending Soviet power and the socialist system to Germany as a whole. This presupposed that the GDR appeared as a country that had not been included in the "socialist camp" but was looking ahead to unite with the Western part of the nation. Secretly created, small-size military units designed for prospective civil war reflected this concept, while a mass army to support the USSR in war against the Western alliance amounted to joining the opposite side and thereby corroborating national partition. For the time being, it is true, Moscow continued to propagate German unification as an alternative to "remilitarization," but this position would have to be abandoned once the policy under preparation was implemented. This implied the task to make the German public feel that the Soviet Union wanted to abide by the goal of unity but was prevented from doing so by the West.

Initiation of a Public Proposal on German Unity

At the very time when the Kremlin looked forward to setting up GDR "national forces," it also took steps for offensively demanding German unity. Possibly in response to a hint by Soviet authorities, the SED leaders proposed to the Kremlin in August 1951 that Western advocacy of unification on the basis of free elections should be countered by a concrete peace treaty proposal. Referring to their suggestion, the responsible department of the foreign ministry in Moscow worked out a draft that, as the first step of the envisaged initiative, obliged the GDR government to drop its demand for numerical parity in talks with West Germany. This was a concession in appearance only. In reality, nothing would change since East German approval of any decision was postulated as before. The body designed to negotiate inter-German agreements would be renamed "All-German Consultation" and assigned, inter alia, the task to discuss free elections. But there was no indication about what criteria and procedures would qualify the elections to be free, and which role they would be allowed to play in the process of unification.[49] The draft was clearly intended to create an impression of willingness to accept free elections but to avoid any commitment. Everything would depend on what the SED regime would see fit. Employment of the term *free elections* was meaningless: GDR elections on the basis of one list of candidates were portrayed as "democratic" and "free,"[50] while voting in the Federal Republic was denounced as a mere fraud to conceal capitalist repression.[51]

Soviet Foreign Minister Vyshinskii recommended to the Politburo that the "struggle against remilitarization of West Germany" be reinforced and outlined a program of successive action to this end. The East Germans were to turn to the parliament in Bonn and suggest a conference of delegates from both states to discuss implementation of all-German elections for a national assembly, arguing that this would serve the "objective of creating a united, democratic, and peaceloving Germany." "Societal organizations" in East and West Germany would support the appeal and exploit it as a focus of an "active campaign under the slogan: "Germans to one table!" After the *Bundestag* would have rejected the appeal, the GDR government would ask the four powers for early conclusion of a peace treaty and withdrawal of the occupation troops. This would provide the USSR with an opportunity to present itself as the only country willing to meet German desires. After an appropriate time span, it would send a note to the Western governments with principles of a "democratic peace treaty with Germany" designed for immediate publication. Vyshinskii underlined that, unlike in previous proposals, the argument had to be focused on all-German elections, not inter-German negotiations, and on renunciation of the parity condition.[52] Another paper prepared by his subordinates for Stalin explained that the initiative would provide a "concrete platform of struggle for a united democratic Germany and against subjugation of West Germany by the Anglo-American imperialists."[53]

While Molotov advocated the proposal, Stalin hesitated to approve it for fear that the Western governments might accept negotiations. Only after he had been persuaded that they were certain to decline, he agreed.[54] The program of action was then modified. While the GDR government would start the initiative by reformulating the plan of inter-German negotiations as suggested, it would not send the envisaged appeal to the four powers when Bonn had already declined. Instead, it would wait for the Kremlin's signal that the time had come. Upon this, the USSR would pledge fulfilment of the alleged German desire and submit a proposal in due course.[55] The decision was officially taken on 8 September.[56] Three days later, the note of protest against "West German remilitarization" to Paris (which had equally been suggested by Vyshinskii) was approved.[57] As planned by the Kremlin, Grotewohl opened the new round of "German dialogue" by a government declaration on 15 September. On direct instructions from Moscow,[58] he announced that the GDR would be content to have fewer delegates than the Federal Republic in an all-German consultation. On the basis of free elections, a national assembly might be set up. He suggested that details should be discussed during prospective inter-German negotiations.[59] Explaining the implications to his cabinet colleagues, he underlined that any decision on unification would require mutual agreement.[60]

Controversy on Free All-German Elections

The Kremlin had realized at last that the West German public was willing to approve talks on unification only if it believed the GDR to be willing to allow for nationwide free elections. Adenauer was doubtful whether the SED regime was really prepared for this and sought to test this by defining fourteen criteria of implementation.[61] Grotewohl dodged by declaring that the chancellor's insistence on preceding fixation of details could not be admitted. Election procedures must not be "dictated." While "most" of the criteria were acceptable, decisions on them were not feasible before inter-German negotiations had started.[62] If the Federal Republic would have allowed for talks with no guarantee for the other side's willingness to acquiesce in genuinely free elections, it would have antagonized the Western powers with no Eastern promise of democratic unification. Despite sustained West German effort at clarification, the GDR refused to take a clear stand during subsequent months. As instructions from Moscow did not change, Grotewohl was unable to answer the key questions: What kind of procedure would be accepted to implement free elections? Would the deputies then elected be allowed to decide on the political bases of the prospective German state? Or would both constitutional order and government power be determined in advance in inter-German negotiations?[63]

When no response was forthcoming, the Federal Republic and the Western countries chose to test willingness to accept free all-German elections by proposing that a United Nations commission must supervise them.[64] The USSR and the GDR vehemently opposed assignment of any role to the UN, saying that the Germans were a civilized nation that must not be treated as a "colonial people." If supervision were required at all, it had to be entrusted to the Germans themselves. A commission with members from both states might do the job under a four-power roof.[65] This again implied a veto of the GDR, respectively the USSR, on the crucial issues. The Kremlin realized, however, that the Western demand of free elections was too popular to allow mere rejection. It therefore tried to regain the political initiative by submitting an allegedly positive proposal.

On 2 November 1951, the East German government made a commission draft an election law that might counter Adenauer's fourteen principles. Chaired by Ulbricht and in close contact with Soviet occupation authorities, this body prepared a text that was submitted to the Council of Ministers on 3 January 1952 and adopted by the People's Chamber six days later.[66] All parties, organizations, and associations recognized as "democratic" would be permitted political activity and participation in the elections for the "National Assembly." Voters had to be registered. Persons declared minor, deprived of civic rights by court of justice or by mere imprisonment, were not entitled to active and passive franchise. This was to apply even after elections had already been held and their results officially stated. An elected deputy might lose his seat at any time by renunciation, *a posteriori* loss of eligibility, annulment of his election, or *a posteriori* change of election results. Lists of candidates to stand for election had to be accepted with twenty signatures if the organization existed already. Otherwise, they would have to be signed by five hundred people. The election committees designed to exercise crucial influence, notably by counting the votes and reporting the results, were envisaged to be set up on grounds of the principle of "equal representation." The competences assigned to the central election committee did not allow for control of regional and local practices.[67]

These clauses were generally designed to allow for all kinds of intervention by those in power. Both the right to vote and eligibility could be easily denied. Power to determine medical judgment, to inflict sentences, and even simply to arrest people would automatically provide for convincing juridical argument to exclude opponents from active and passive participation in elections. Even when a position had been recognized as being righteously won, it might be taken away if its possessor failed to comply with the expectations of those in power. Besides deprivation of eligibility on the grounds already mentioned, compulsory renunciation of his mandate (a step which, significantly, might not be revoked once it had been enforced) and several variants of revising the election outcome were expressly envisioned. Another major point was inclusion of "societal organizations" set up to multiply communist representation. Their purpose was both to mislead noncommunist voters and to provide for communist dominance in election committees. Their participation in the elections throughout Germany would be assured by a low quorum of 20 signatures, while, in the GDR, a 500-signature-requirement was likely to deter groups outside the "antifascist" bloc from submitting lists since many people would have to expose themselves as opponents of the SED regime.

Absence of control by the central election committee was aimed at not allowing for an overall picture of irregular practices. This might favor communist manipulation not only in East Germany. Provided that the SED leaders managed to seize crucial power positions in all of Germany as had been presupposed by making unification conditional on "All-German Consultation," Ulbricht's draft would predictably be used as a basis to justify the elimination of any major opponents. To be sure, West German acceptance of such a scenario was very unlikely. The proposal appeared nonetheless useful: It contributed to preventing Bonn from seeking unification but, hopefully, made the public believe that the GDR wanted national unity.

Preparation of "Principles of a German Peace Treaty"

Public advocacy of free all-German elections on the basis of inter-German negotiations was only one part of the action program approved by Stalin in early September 1951. It had also been decided to send a Soviet note to the Western governments to enter negotiations on a peace treaty. To make this appear attractive, "principles" of the envisaged contents were to be attached. Diplomatic personnel prepared drafts and submitted them to Politburo members, notably foreign policy expert Molotov, who read them thoroughly and suggested detailed corrections. Quite a few successive drafts were written and sent back and forth several times to refine them in both substance and form. As it appears, Stalin did not see any of these papers. But Gromyko, Vyshinskii's deputy in charge of European affairs, kept him informed on the process and put questions before him whenever he deemed his comment or decision necessary. The expressly stated purpose was propaganda to mobilize the German "masses."[68]

In the early drafts, the official position on German unification was explained in much detail. As was alleged, the Yalta and Potsdam decisions had obliged the Germans to "eradicate the remnants of fascism and mili-tarism," to prohibit any activity by "fascist and militarist organizations," and to adopt "the democratic changes [already] enforced in East Germany." Organizations and individuals who sought "abolition of the democratic rights of the people, revival of German militarism and fascism, and cultiva-tion of revanchist ideas" must be prosecuted. The government would have "to reinforce the democratic transformations in industry, agriculture, and other branches of economy (transfer of war and nazi criminals' property to the German people, land reform and others) and to continue their enforce-ment." Economic disarmament required total annihilation of "cartels, trusts, syndicates, and other monopolistic associations in the realms of pro-duction, commerce, banking and other spheres of economy" and their transfer to state ownership. Liquidation of "all authorities created by for-eign powers to control the Ruhr [industries]" would put an end to partici-pation in the European Coal and Steel Community.[69]

Molotov and other supervisors felt that detailed presentation of demands was inexpedient. Soviet conditions for German unification should be stated in more general terms. As Gromyko explained to Stalin, detailed explana-tion of the Soviet position would deter potential sympathizers and invite exploitation by enemy propaganda. Any reference to "inexpedient" detail had to be avoided. Attention had to be focused on the "question of strug-gle for unity of Germany." Additional explanation should not be given.[70] In subsequent drafts, the Soviet attitude on delicate issues, notably on the sys-tem and regime to be introduced in united Germany, was circumscribed in a way that appeared to fulfill hope in the West but made the communist cadres understand that orientation at socialism was envisioned. For exam-ple, concretization of the postulated political order was replaced by the statement that united Germany would be a "democratic and peaceloving" state. The demand that it was envisaged to be "independent," respectively "sovereign," indicated that integration into the West was inadmissible in any form. Emphasis that both people's rights and any parties or organiza-tions that would be allowed freedom of activity would have to be "demo-cratic" was meant to indicate that Eastern rather than Western standards would provide the fundament. Organizations "opposed to democracy and to the cause of peace," that is, in sympathy with the West, would be banned. In the final stages of preparing the note, a previous reference to the need to eliminate big monopolist capitalism was dropped, being seen as too frank a statement.[71]

Only in one of his many messages to Stalin, Gromyko expressed concern that, contrary to expectation, the West might possibly accept the offer for negotiations. He felt that this was most undesirable and recommended precautions to prevent such a response.[72] Intention to elicit rejection can also be gathered from postulated treaty regulations. By being strikingly asymmetrical, envisaged clauses on borders, reparations, and debts were clearly designed to be unattractive to the Western powers. Inter alia, annexation of large East German provinces by the USSR and Poland would have to be finalized, but the French Saar protectorate was due for cancellation. Uncondititional fulfilment of any Soviet reparation demand was envisaged, whereas even repayment of Anglo-Saxon postwar food deliveries and Marshall Plan credits was excluded. Contemplated military arrangements were bound to result in a Soviet triumph over NATO. While national German rearmament and withdrawal of occupation troops would deprive the emerging West European defense system of both its American and West German backbones, the Soviet army would retain a presence in the close vicinity of Central Europe.

The Kremlin was interested in making the addressees of the prospective note, the three Western governments, reject negotiations for primarily two reasons. The West was certain to initiate diplomatic discussion on liquidation of the GDR in the public limelight. This would boost hope among the population to get rid of communist rule by democratic reunification and thus destabilize the SED regime. Any such challenge had to be avoided. At the same time, Soviet control of East Germany was absolutely required for nuclear armament. Production of atomic and fusion bombs depended on uranium mining in southern Saxony that had been started by the USSR and made a direct part of its economy in 1946. As this was the only uranium resource available, the Kremlin felt that it could not possibly allow for even minor uncertainty of control.[73]

From the very beginning, the authors of the peace treaty principles stipulated an obligation by Germany to renounce the option of entering "coalitions or military alliances" directed against any country whose forces had fought against it in World War II. This demand had been raised all the time but the clause on creating "national" land, sea, and air forces was a major departure from the previous position. As a result, denunciation of any German rearmament was no longer possible. After the note and the attached peace treaty principles had been published, it was therefore substituted by polemics against the prospective West German "mercenary army" alleged to offend against the national interest. To be sure, the size of the posited forces was to be limited to requirements of defense, but the initial plan to make this limit binding by defining it in concrete terms[74] was abandoned. Underlying this was a remarkable Soviet interest to make any German nationalists and military support GDR armament. In January 1952, a point was included in the peace treaty principles that former Nazis and Wehrmacht professionals must be accorded full civil and political rights for the purpose of "creation of a democratic and peaceful Germany."[75]

Publication of the Soviet Peace Treaty Proposal and Subsequent Disputes

When the Federal Republic and the Western powers had achieved agreement on the crucial issues in early 1952, Stalin decided that the time had come to propose peace treaty negotiations.[76] As had been planned before, the first step was to make the GDR government issue an appeal to the four powers to provide for early conclusion of a peace treaty. On the basis of Soviet instructions, East Berlin prepared a draft that was submitted to the Ministry of Foreign Affairs in Moscow. After major corrections had been inserted, the note was sent on 13 February.[77] As had been envisaged, the USSR replied affirmatively,[78] while the Western governments failed to respond. After a few weeks' delay designed to create the appearance that the proposal had been worked out in response to the East German request, Moscow directed a note to the three Western governments that declared that negotiations on a peace treaty with united Germany were necessary "in the nearest future." The principles that had been worked out in Moscow were attached to provide guidance. The note was transmitted by diplomatic channels and published on 10 March 1952.[79] The East Berlin leaders, who had been informed of its contents only the preceding evening,[80] instructed the communists in West Germany to start to mobilize and organize the "masses" in support of the Soviet bid for reunification by a massive propaganda campaign.[81]

In the "Principles for Conclusion of a Peace Treaty with Germany" attached to the note, it was taken for granted that unified German had to accept the peace treaty agreed upon among the four powers and then approved by all countries previously at war with Germany as an obliging *octroi*. Any indication was missing on how unification would be achieved and an all-national be created. Official comments from Moscow and East Berlin made clear that, in conformity with the decision taken by Stalin in September 1951, any progress toward unity must result from agreement in "All-German Consultations" between the two states.[82] As Soviet insiders have emphasized, the Kremlin's position in spring 1952 fully conformed to its attitude in previous years.[83] In winter 1951–1952, when Churchill had tried to elicit Soviet interest in unifying Germany as a democratic but neutral country, Moscow declined.[84] Major Western leaders (but not Adenauer) knew about this but the public was unaware. Hence many people felt that the USSR might be willing to accept democratic unification in exchange for a guarantee that the country would not join the Western alliance.[85]

Such hope was encouraged notably among West German democratic opponents of military integration. Heinemann and others felt that renunciation of armaments would buy democratic unification, while many people in the SPD including Schumacher saw a need to test the Soviet "offer" by negotiations. As adherents of this view had a strong voice even in the CDU/CSU, Adenauer faced a challenge from within his own party. He might have been toppled if his critics had been encouraged by some concrete prospect of democratic unity.[86] Among the leaders in Western capitals (including Bonn), there was much concern that the USSR might be willing to compromise on Germany. Encouraged by Adenauer's statement that peace treaty negotiations were undesirable, the three governments reaffirmed their position that unification required the creation of a German government on the basis of free elections under supervision by a UN commission. When Vyshinskii read their reply on 25 March, his face spontaneously expressed joy.[87] This was understandable given that Stalin had threatened to call him and other initiators of the note to account if, contrary to their prediction, the Soviet proposal for negotiations would be accepted.[88]

Underlying this was that Stalin was as much concerned about the possible diplomatic discussion on Germany as were his Western adversaries. This was demonstrated again when, a few weeks later, U.S. Ambassador George Kennan arrived in Moscow to seek agreement on Germany at his personal initiative. He was denied any chance of talking with Soviet officials. And, after months of total isolation, he chose to leave.[89] In accordance with the action program approved by Stalin in September 1951, the USSR stated on 9 April in its reply to the Western note of 25 March that free all-German elections were possible. Supervision by a joint commission under a four-power roof was also accepted.[90] Either statement simply reiterated previous positions. Willingness to allow for free elections (as had already been expressed by Grotewohl in September 1951 on the basis of Stalin's preceding decision) was based both on a specifically Soviet idea of what this meant in practical terms, and on the prerequisite of preceding all-encompassing agreement in the the postulated "All-German Consultations." Acceptance of supervision was linked to implementation essentially by the two German states, with but a minor role to be accorded to the four powers. Significantly, the "struggle for free all-German elections" was internally seen as an instrument for Adenauer's overthrow and promotion of "working class unity."[91]

In the West, these implications escaped attention. As a result, official policy was exposed to attack by domestic opponents. In the Federal Republic, pressure from both the social democrats and critics within the CDU/CSU was strong enough to make Adenauer feel that he was bound to allow for a test of Soviet intent. In Western countries, it was increasingly felt that there was a chance to prevent undesirable West German rearmament by a negotiated arrangement on free all-German elections. Leading politicians notably in Paris wanted the Western High Commissioners in Germany to meet with their Soviet counterpart to discuss modalities. Agreement would, hopefully, be reached before other unification problems were put on the table. Adenauer did not object. But before there had been time for making a try, the U.S. government put an end to the initiative.[92]

While many people in Western countries had indulged in the illusory hope for agreement on Germany, Soviet sympathizers were irritated by the 10 March 1952 proposal and hesitated to identify with it. Objections focused on the Kremlin's advocacy of German national forces. In many cases, even communist cadres were exasperated by Soviet attitudes on this issue. As a result of decreasing sympathy for Moscow's position, opposition in West Germany to participation in West European defense was weakened, if temporarily. Those who were concerned about a "revival of militarism" tended to feel that the creation of a national army with no international control regime was worse than integration in the projected (West) European Defense Community.[93] The Kremlin tried to overcome ill-feeling by arguing on the basis of Marxist-Leninist doctrine that military buildup in support of the "cause of peace" was no deviation from previous "anti-militaristic" policy. Only the recruitment of "mercenary units" in the West that served "imperialistic" designs was unacceptable. In contrast to this, the creation of national defense forces in the GDR fostered "strengthening of peace."[94]

ASSIGNMENT OF
A MILITARY AND SOCIALIST ROLE TO THE GDR

The policy that had culminated in the note of 10 March implied that East Germany had to be fully included in the socialist camp and must no longer be subjected to military and systemic restrictions. In the Kremlin's view, East German contributions to Soviet military strength were particularly urgent. In April 1952, the SED regime was made to initiate an intensified campaign for "defense of the homeland." This effort to make a reluctant population willing to accept militarization was accompanied by an equally intensified effort to recruit young men for military units, to create a premilitary training network, and to use major industrial capabilities for armament production. Previous restraint designed to allow for unification appeals to the West German public was abandoned.[95] The implications were far-reaching. Propaganda of German unity lost credibility when the GDR embarked on undisguised large-scale militarization and took increasingly less care to veil socialist transformation. While the East European party leaders had raised strong economic objections when, in January 1951, Stalin had imposed intensified armaments on their countries,[96] their SED colleagues, notably Ulbricht, were quite happy in spring 1952 to be allowed to take part in the Soviet program of heavy armament and accelerated socialism, feeling that this would rid them of previous restrictions. The new course, however, entailed highly negative economic, social, and political consequences. Dissatisfaction with the material hardships of life was reinforced by latent opposition to the regime that increased repression. This development made masses of people seek escape from socialism by leaving for West Germany.

Stalin's Instructions to the SED Leaders

As early as three days before Western rejection of negotiations, on 22 March, Ulbricht expressed satisfaction in a draft submitted to the Soviet leadership that the recent change of policy had ridded the GDR of previous regard for requirements of German unity. The Kremlin did not deny that priorities had shifted but stressed that unification propaganda must nonetheless continue.[97] But at the same time, separation from, and confrontation with, the Federal Republic was under preparation. This became clear when, on 25 March, the occupation authorities invited the SED leaders to see Stalin in Moscow and informed them on the topics to be discussed.[98]

At the first meeting on 1 April, Stalin mainly listened to their situation report and their ideas on how to topple Adenauer's government by exploitation of the slogan of free elections, to achieve "working class unity," to mobilize support by bourgeois "patriots," to organize resistance against a communist party ban, to wage a struggle for the conclusion of a peace treaty and against West German integration into the Western alliance, and to provide for military protection against "the threat from the West." The Kremlin leader agreed that the police, that is, the *Bereitschaften*, must not be equipped with old Wehrmacht weapons any longer but with modern light arms that East Germany would be authorized to produce. Upon this, the SED representatives raised the question of whether steps toward setting up a full-fledged army should be taken. Stalin replied that he wanted not steps but an army. This, however, created a major problem for propaganda. As people in the GDR had internalized pacifism, they had to be persuaded that military defense was required. Given that, at the same time, remilitarization in West Germany continued to be condemned, it was crucial to explain the fundamental difference between the two sides. Stalin emphasized that pacifism as such was bad and must not be permitted. For the time being, however, he did not want intensified propaganda for military defense. No noise must be made before the army was there.

In the course of further discussion, Stalin came back to the problem of military buildup by asking who was in charge of the "police." Ulbricht answered that formal responsibility was with the Ministry of the Interior, while actual control was exercised by a state secretary who in fact worked under the Ministry of State Security and the chairman of the Council of

Ministers. Stalin suggested setting up an embryonic military leadership closely linked to the Ministry of State Security, voiced interest in East German heavy, notably steel industry, and authorized tank production.[99]

Given that domestic problems had increased compared to 1951, Pieck emphasized on behalf of the SED the need for intensified repression. But such action was impeded by considerations resulting from the struggle for German unity. He advocated harsh measures against "enemy activities" by *kulaks* [big peasants], the churches, and others. Stalin's question whether *kolkhoses* [large state farms] had been set up, was answered in the negative. Pieck bemoaned the economic losses created by specialists' flight to the West but Stalin saw this as a political benefit [as the GDR was thereby relieved of "bourgeois elements"] and advised the East German leaders to substitute the old intelligentsia by a new one. Pieck also complained about a "difficult situation" in Berlin "as a result of the split of the city in two parts." The "reaction" had concentrated in the Western sectors. From there, the United States was seeking to undermine the GDR by "many reactionary newspapers" and "three powerful radio stations broadcasting to the GDR." Social democratic control of the West Berlin administration also provided for negative influence. Molotov felt that free movement across the sectoral border must be terminated by a system of permits, but Stalin only agreed to intensified control of the access routes.[100]

Six days later, Stalin had made up his mind on the details of future policy.

> Comrade Stalin believes that regardless of what proposals we make on the German issue, the Western powers will not agree with them and nonetheless will not leave West Germany. To think that compromise will be reached or that the Americans would accept the peace treaty project would be mistaken. The Americans need an army in West Germany, in order to keep Western Europe in their hands. They say that they have the army there against us. Actually, the mission of their army is to keep Europe. The Americans will pull Germany into the Atlantic pact. They will create West German troops. Adenauer is in the Americans' pocket. All the former fascists and generals as well. In fact, an independent state is being set up in West Germany. And you, too, must organize a state of your own. The demarcation line between West and East Germany must be considered a border—and not a mere border, but a dangerous border. We need to reinforce protection of this border. At the first line of its defense, the Germans will stand, but at the second line we will put Russian troops. All too freely, the agents of Western countries are moving around in the German Democratic Republic. They can take extreme measures and kill you or Comrade Chuikov. One has to take this into account. Therefore, a strong border protection is required. Then, continues Comrade Stalin, we want to revive the offices of [Soviet] military commandants [in the GDR]. This is another good measure against possible diversions. Our forces, too, must have secure protection. And also you will need it; you will then be stronger.

Stalin announced that the police-in-barracks, that is, the troops, would receive Russian weapons. All kinds of them including tanks and pieces of artillery would be provided.[101] He then drew attention to salaries and criticized the GDR for paying not much more to engineers and technicians than to unskilled workers.

> Technology has become so complex compared to the times of the Commune [in 1871 when Marx advocated equal salaries] that an engineer and even a qualified worker must learn much to master this technology. An engineer must have an opportunity to become more perfect, to read books, [and] to write—there can be no engineer without it. The same applies to the army. Marx and Engels believed that we needed a militia-army.[102] In our first years, we also thought that a militia-army was needed. And during the first years, we [too] have regarded only a militia-army to be necessary. Life has shown that this is wrong. Today, in order to defend the country, a modern army is required with many specialists. A militia-army is only good if war is decided by rifle. Today, one must get rid of this old militia-army. Today, the army is not a manufacture army but a machine army. Therefore, we need people in the army who know machines.

Seeking to make the GDR fully adopt the Soviet model, Stalin went on to explain that payment had to be highly differentiated for simple workers on the one hand and well-trained specialists on the other. After this, he raised the subject of collectivization in agriculture.

> He, Stalin, has understood [the SED leaders as saying] that the GDR has no collective farms at all, and the machine-rental stations serve only private peasant farms. Comrade Ulbricht confirms that and adds that we have even prohibited the organization of collective farms where the peasants wanted this, in order not to impair the movement for a united Germany. Comrade Stalin says that you complain about the *kulaks*. What kind of tactic is that—complaining? The *kulaks* should be encircled, and you should create collective farms around them. In our country, organization of collective farms was going along with expropriation of the kulaks. This way [of doing it] will not be expedient for you. Let the *kulaks* sit at home, don't touch them. But besides the *kulaks*, there are poor peasants in your villages that live right next to the *kulak*. They must be drawn into production cooperatives. How many poor peasant farms will form a productive cooperative—5, 10, or 15—does not matter. What matters, is that they will be organized. Currently, the poor peasants have no machines, they don't have enough seed and appropriate knowledge and experience to manage their farms. That is why their harvest is so poor. In such a situation, poor peasants will ruin themselves and will join the ranks of the unemployed. If you will organize small collective farms and help them how to manage their farms, then the peasants will start thinking what is better—to join collective farms or to live separately?

Stalin did not accept the argument that the peasants were invariably prejudiced against *kolkhoses* so that any effort to introduce them would create tension. The state farms must be portrayed to be simply production cooperatives and be made attractive by material privileges. For rallying the peasants behind the working class, *kolkhoses* were indispensable. This would lay the fundament for building socialism. Stalin was reminded that, in order to lend credibility to the campaign for national unity, the SED had not advocated socialism yet but denied any such intention and exercised considerable restraint with regard to socialist measures.

> Comrade Stalin says that this was correct. Comrade Ulbricht asks whether we should continue this previous strategy after the deep split of Germany? Comrade Stalin says that even now you should not shout about socialism. But production cooperatives are small pieces of socialism. Enterprises owned by the people also mean socialism. Comrade Ulbricht says that so far we have never indicated that people's enterprises are socialist. To some extent, we have disguised the social relations which have emerged in the GDR [by the pretense of a bourgeois democratic development]. Comrade Stalin says that this disguise helped you not to scare the middle classes of West Germany. But if it [this disguise] had not existed, you might have attracted the lower strata [of the population] more strongly. The workers will be glad to learn that you nationalize industry. Otherwise, they will say that you have the same government as the one in Bonn. One can say that the GDR has a people's, a nationalized industry, whereas in West Germany there are a few capitalist-millionaires who dominate industry. You have to maneuver here—on the one hand, you should not scare the middle class away but you also should not offend the workers in the West.

As Stalin emphasized, unification propaganda must not be abandoned. It was very important to educate the people in West Germany. "Now it [advocacy of unification] is a weapon in your hands, and you should always hold it in your hands. We should continue to make proposals regarding German unity also in order to expose the Americans."[103]

Implementation

Stalin's instructions on East German military buildup did not specify details but the SED triumvirate received partial information on this while still in Moscow. The prospective army was to be staffed by three hundred thousand men in thirty divisions; their leading cadres would be trained in the USSR; heavy weapons including submarines and fighter aircraft were envisioned. Also, a number of pre- and paramilitary organizations must be created.[104] After the SED leaders had returned home, they received additional instructions. GDR (but not East Berlin) borders to the Federal Republic and to West Berlin had to be closed with only few checkpoints to remain. A very tight control regime was designed to prevent unauthorized crossing. Massive increase of the border police (which, besides the military *Bereitschaften*, was another armed organization deployed in barracks) and large-scale evacuation of a five-kilometer control zone were envisaged.[105] As the Soviet Council of Ministers decided on 14 April, the measure was to be announced and implemented when the treaties between the Federal Republic and the Western powers were signed.[106] Recurrent SED requests to authorize closure of the sectoral border in Berlin were declined.[107] The Kremlin only permitted East German border guards "to put an end to uncontrolled access to East Berlin from the Western sectors" by occcasional luggage checks.[108]

To create the impression that GDR measures were taken in response to the Western challenge, Stalin had instructed the SED leaders not to "shout" about military buildup and socialist measures for the time being. His willingness to allow for their being initiated even before "remilitarization" would have started in the Federal Republic was based on the assumption that the treaties of the Federal Republic with the West would be ratified soon and that creation of West German troops was imminent. Then the time would come to explain openly what had been prepared in the GDR. But creation of the EDC was delayed. In spring and early summer 1952, the emerging situation in East Germany made it increasingly difficult to abstain from announcing the measures that were already being taken. Antimilitary feeling among the population made a massive campaign for "armed protection of the homeland" appear necessary. To be sure, existence of a military organization in the country was not admitted but when young men recruited allegedly for service in the police saw themselves put into a military environment, it proved impossible to respond to their protest by assuring them that the GDR rejected the creation of military forces. Another problem resulted when the peasants were vehemently hostile to collectivization and argued that, since the (alleged) cooperatives had been declared to result from their members' initiative, they were under no obligation to join. To justify the enforcement of collectivization, official orders were required.

Against this background, the SED leaders asked Stalin on 1 July 1952 for permission to proclaim "transition to construction of socialism and creation of the fundaments for socialism in agriculture." Domestic difficulties would only be overcome if they were allowed to press for socialism openly. In their portrayal, the "broad masses of the working class and the working population" in the Federal Republic would respond favorably, if "their" party was authorized to announce a people's democracy. In the GDR, "the initiative of the working class and the working population" would "considerably develop."[109] As the Western treaties had not been ratified, let alone implemented yet, the plea from East Berlin implied that the Kremlin was to abandon the tactical approach that any divisive measures must appear imposed by preceding Western action.

Stalin hesitated. Only when the SED pressed for an affirmative answer did he agree at last a few hours before the Second SED Party Conference opened on 9 July.[110] At its first session, Ulbricht announced "construction of the fundaments of socialism." In addition to the measures taken in previous years, collectivization of agriculture would be initiated. The assembly rubber-stamped the decision and postulated national forces.[111] The Kremlin had failed to authorize their proclamation. While a full-scale GDR army was in fact in the process of being set up by restructuring and enlarging the *Bereitschaften*, it was officially termed "People's Police in Barracks" (Kasernierte Volkspolizei, KVP). As previously envisaged, the formation of national forces would be announced only after the initiation of military buildup in the Federal Republic.

Stalin's Political Heritage

When Stalin died on 5 March 1953, his empire was in disarray. He had antagonized not only the countries of the West. Except for the East European satellites and the communist regimes in Beijing and Pyongyang dependent on Soviet support, the USSR was isolated. Turkey, which in the interwar period entertained very friendly relations with the leaders in Moscow, had joined its traditional enemy Greece in resisting Soviet pressure. In 1952, both countries had entered NATO. Threat by the Kremlin had made Yugoslavia, a radically anti-Western ally in the early postwar years, depend on U.S. backing and aid, and to conclude the Balkan Pact with Greece and Turkey. Traditionally neutral states—the Netherlands, Denmark, and Norway—had entered the North Atlantic Alliance and taken an active role in West European defense. Other countries maintained neutrality but were willing to side with NATO in the event of war. Finland, which had been made by Stalin to accept an alliance if war with Germany would break out, wanted to avoid obligations to the USSR as much as possible. Even relations with China were strained by Stalin's insistence that, for the purpose of engaging the Americans, its involvement in Korea must continue.

Ever since Stalin had asserted his power in Moscow, the Soviet Union had accorded priority to armament. This had been a major impediment to economic and social reconstruction after World War II. The problem was intensified when Stalin decided in 1950–1951 to increase the military effort even more. Propaganda justified emphasis on armament by pointing out that Western aggression was likely. This created a widespread feeling of insecurity among both the population and the elite. The policy makers in Moscow were concerned over the size of U.S. potential and Soviet technological inferiority. For example, they were unable to prevent American overflights deep into their country.[112] More acute still were domestic problems. The economy and society continued to suffer from wartime destruction.

The armament effort imposed on them proved beyond their capacity. Budgetary deficit had become abnormally high.[113] Crucial consumer goods were lacking; hunger and misery were ubiquitous. Only repressive machinery (which had put 4 million people into jail and forced labor camps and inflicted banishment on more than 2.5 million[114]) had prevented mass riots. When, after the dictator's death, the feeling of terror lessened, both in the USSR[115] and in the people's democracies[116] an explosive situation emerged.

In all the satellite countries, acute dissatisfaction resulted in strikes. Given that strikes were officially seen as absolutely unacceptable under socialism (which claimed to have put an end to exploitation and repression of the "working class"), this challenged not only totalitarian control but jeopardized the ideological fundament as well. The situation grew particularly tense in Hungary.[117] Early in May, Bulgarian policy, which promised relief but failed to fulfill expectations thus created, entailed strikes at the major industrial center Plovdiv, but the government managed to control the situation by skilfully negotiating with the workers.[118] At the end of the month, a currency measure in Czechoslovakia deprived people of their savings. This caused exasperation among the population. In the second-biggest Bohemian city, Plzeň, insurgents temporarily took over and were crushed only by security forces called in from outside.[119] There was unrest also in Poland[120] and Romania,[121] but in these two countries, maintenance of the communist regime was not endangered.

In East Germany, there was no open protest during spring. Below the surface, however, the situation was unstable. There was an enormous amount of discontent and opposition[122] but the pot was prevented from boiling over by the "open border" in Berlin. The tide of fugitives was growing to such an extent that the material and moral basis of the GDR was increasingly threatened. According to official Soviet counts, 57,230 people had left in the first half of 1952, their number had risen to 78,831 during the following six months, while in the first quarter of 1953—that is, in only half the time—84,034 East Germans turned their backs on their home country.[123] Even before Stalin had died (who had always exploited dependent countries and never granted aid to them), Ulbricht had asked the Kremlin for aid and argued that otherwise instability would result. The Soviet Control Commission, too, was deeply concerned and, in early 1953, made a "group of responsible functionaries from the SED Central Committee and the GDR government" investigate the situation. In mid-April, a report was tabled that concluded that current policies were untenable and must be revised.[124] As subsequent events would demonstrate, the leaders in both Moscow and East Berlin were unable to cope with the problems. The uprising of 17 June was the result.

NOTES

1. "Militarizm," *Bol'shaia Sovetskaia Èntsiklopediia, Vol. 13* (Moscow: Gosu-darstvennoe izdatel'stvo "Bol'shaia Sovetskaia Èntsiklopediia" 1952), pp. 481–82; "Imperializm," *Bol'shaia Sovetskaia Èntsiklopediia, Vol. 17* (1952), pp. 568–84.

2. Leonid Gibianskii, "The Last Conference of the Cominform," Giuliano Procacci (ed.), *The Cominform. Minutes of the Three Conferences 1947/1948/1949* (Milan: Feltrinelli Editore Milano 1994), p. 651; Grant M. Adibekov, *Das Kominform und Stalins Neuordnung Europas* (Frankfurt/Main: Peter Lang 2002), pp. 198–201.

3. Adibekov, *Das Kominform*, pp. 201–11. For the minutes of the third Cominform conference see Procacci, *The Cominform*, pp. 671–1003.

4. Michael Lemke, "Die infiltrierte Sammlung. Ziele, Methoden und Instrumente der SED in der Bundesrepublik 1949–1957," Tilman Mayer (ed.), *"Macht das Tor auf." Jakob-Kaiser-Studien* (Berlin: Berlin Verlag Arno Spitz GmbH 1996), pp. 176–77, 180.

5. See Lemke, "Die infiltrierte Sammlung," Mayer (ed.), *"Macht das Tor auf,"* pp. 173–83; S. Tiul'panov to V. Semënov, 29 July 1949, AVPRF, 0457a, 7, 39, 10, pp. 72–75; SED Politburo sessions (protocol excerpts), 19, 20, and 22 August 1949, Federal Ministry of the Interior (ed.), *Dokumente zur Deutschlandpolitik, Series II, Vol. 2/2* (Munich: Oldenbourg 1996), pp. 399–443; session of the SED Party Executive, 24 August 1949, *Dokumente zur Deutschlandpolitik, II, 2/2*, pp. 444–47; reports by W. Ulbricht, A. Ackermann, S. Tiul'panov, and F. Sperling, 19, 20, and 22 August 1949, *Dokumente zur Deutschlandpolitik, II, 2/2*, pp. 402–5, 409, 413, 417; joint sessions Western Commission and Politburo of the SED, 16, 21, 28, and 30 January, 6 February 1950, SAPMO-BArch, NY 4036 Vol. I/2 649, pp. 60–67, 68–70, 75–79, 80–85, 87–91; report by Fred Oelssner on visit in the USSR, 21 February 1950, SAPMO-BArch, IV 2/2/73, p. 2; SED Western Commission to the SED Politburo, 2 March 1950, SAPMO-BArch, NY 4036 Vol. I/2 649, pp. 184–85; protocol of SED Secretariat sessions on 17 March 1950, 21 March 1950, SAPMO, IV 2/2/77, pp. 17–26, 47–55; session of SED West Commission Secretariat, 12 June 1950, *Dokumente zur Deutschlandpolitik, Series II, Vol. 3/2* (1997), pp. 809–12; W. Pieck to V. Semënov, 11 July 1950, *Dokumente zur Deutschlandpolitik, II, 3/2*, pp. 867–68; SED Politburo report, 19 July 1950, SAPMO-BArch, IV 2/2/99, pp. 15–19; Michael Lemke, "Eine neue Konzeption? Die SED im Umgang mit der SPD 1956 bis 1960," Jürgen Kocka (ed.), *Historische DDR-Forschung* (Berlin: Akademie Verlag 1993), pp. 363–66. For operative detail see Heike Amos, *Die Westpolitik der SED 1948/49–1961. "Arbeit nach Westdeutschland" durch die Nationale Front, das Ministerium für Auswärtige Angelegenheiten und das Ministerium für Staatssicherheit* (Berlin: Akademie Verlag 1999), pp. 50–67.

6. For the integration concept's genesis and development see Dieter Krüger, *Sicherheit durch Integration? Die wirtschaftliche und politische Zusammenarbeit Westeuropas 1947 bis 1957/58* (Munich: Oldenbourg 2003).

7. Report on conversation I. V. Stalin–W. Pieck, W. Ulbricht, O. Grotewohl, 4 May 1950, *Istochnik*, 3/2003 (63), pp. 108–9.

8. Report on conversation I. V. Stalin–W. Pieck, W. Ulbricht, O. Grotewohl, 4 May 1950, *Istochnik*, 3/2003 (63), pp. 110–11.

9. Report on conversation I. V. Stalin–W. Pieck, W. Ulbricht, O. Grotewohl, 4 May 1950, *Istochnik*, 3/2003 (63), pp. 104–8.

10. Chen Jian, *The Sino-Soviet Alliance and China's Entry into the Korean War*, Cold War International History Project, Working Paper No. 1, Washington D.C., June 1992, pp. 18–21; Kathryn Weathersby: "The Soviet Role in the Early Phase of the Korean War," *Journal of American-East Asian Relations* 2, no. 4 (Winter 1993), pp. 425–58; Kathryn Weathersby (ed.), "Korea, 1949–50: To Attack, or Not to Attack? Stalin, Kim Il Sung, and the Prelude to War," *Cold War International History Project Bulletin*, 5 (Spring 1995) (Washington D.C.: Woodrow Wilson International Center for Scholars), pp, 1–9; Kathryn Weathersby (ed.), "New Russian Documents on the Korean War. Introduction and Translations," *Cold War International History Project Bulletin*, 6–7 (Winter 1995/1996) (Washington D.C.: Woodrow Wilson International Center for Scholars), pp. 30–40; Evgeni Bajanov, "Assessing the Politics of the Korean War, 1949–1951," *Cold War International History Project Bulletin*, 6–7 (Winter 1995/1996), pp. 54, 87–88; Hyun-su Jeon and Gyoo Kahng, "The Shtykov Diaries," *Cold War International History Project Bulletin*, 6–7 (Winter 1995/1996), pp. 69, 92–93; A. S. Orlov, "Sovetskaia aviatsiia v Koreiskoi voine 1950–1953 gg.," *Novaia i noveishaia istoriia*, 4/1998, pp. 121–46. Cf. Shen Zhihua, "Sino-North Korean Conflict and Its Resolution during the Korean War," *Cold War International History Project Bulletin*, 14–15 (Winter 2003/Spring 2004) (Washington D.C.: Woodrow Wilson International Center for Scholars), pp. 9–24. See also Soviet and Chinese documents in *Cold War International History Project Bulletin*, 6–7, pp. 4–20, 27–29 (translation from Russian), 148–69 (translation from Chinese); *Novaia i noveishaia istoriia*, 4–5/1994 (Russian original text to translation on pp. 27–29), pp. 132–40; Rolf Steininger, *Der vergessene Krieg. Korea 1950–1953* (Munich: Olzog 2006), pp. 31–36.

11. See Foreign Minister Vyshinskii's remark as quoted by Glenn D. Paige, "Comparative Case Analysis of Crisis Decisions—Korea and Cuba," C. F. Hermann (ed.), *International Crises* (New York: Free Press 1972), pp. 48–49.

12. N. I. Egorova, "Evropeiskaia bezopasnost' i 'ugroza' NATO v otsenkakh stalinskogo rukovodstva," A. O. Chubar'ian (ed.), *Stalinskoe desiatiletie kholodnoi voiny. Fakty i gipotezy* (Moscow: "Nauka" 1999), pp. 68–69.

13. Retrospective reports by Togliatti's partner Leonilde Jotti, and his party comrades Amendola, Secchia, and Natta (in German transl.), *Osteuropa*, 10/1970, pp. A 703–718; Adibekov, *Das Kominform*, 304–18.

14. Egorova, "Evropeiskaia bezopasnost'," Chubar'ian (ed.), *Stalinskoe desiatiletie*, p. 72; A. M. Filitov, "Stalinskaia diplomatiia i germanskii vopros: poslednii god," Chubar'ian (ed.), *Stalinskoe desiatiletie*, p. 85; Karel Kaplan, *Dans les archives du Comité Central. Trents ans de secrets du Bloc soviétique* (Paris: Albin Michel 1978), pp. 162–66 (report based on reminiscences by Czechoslovakian defense minister Čepička who participated in the conference); Alexandru Osça and Vasile Popa, "Stalin a decis. Lagrul socialist se înarmează," *Buletinul Arhivelor Militare Române*, 2–3/1998, pp. 71–72.

15. Report on sessions in Moscow 10–12 January 1951, 15 January 1951, written by E. Bodnăraş on the basis of notes taken during the sessions, signed by [Gh.] Gheorghiu-Dej, E. Bodnăraş, Alexandru Osça and Vasile Popa, "Stalin a decis. Lagrul socialist se înarmează," *Buletinul Arhivelor Militare Române*, 2–3/1998, pp. 72–76.

16. Egorova, "Evropeiskaia bezopasnost'," Chubar'ian (ed.), *Stalinskoe desiatiletie,* p. 68.

17. For Soviet perception of the 1950 situation see Egorova, "Evropeiskaia bezopasnost'," pp. 68–69.

18. SED working plan for September-October 1950, 7 September 1950, *Dokumente zur Deutschlandpolitik, II, 3/2,* pp. 971–72; SED Politburo decision, 3 October 1950, *Dokumente zur Deutschlandpolitik, II, 3/2,* pp. 1051–52; GDR National Front resolution, 14 November 1950, *Dokumente zur Deutschlandpolitik, II, 3/1,* p. 434.

19. Draft [by the West Commission] for the SED Politburo, 2 October 1950, SAPMO-BArch, NY 4036 Bd. I;2, pp. 186–90; SED Politburo session, 3 October 1950, SAPMO-BArch, IV 2/2/111, pp. 2–3; SED Politburo session, 17 October 1950, SAPMO-BArch, IV 2/2/114, pp. 9–10; SED Politburo session, 31 October 1950, SAPMO-BArch, IV 2/2/116, pp. 6–7; report to the SED West Commission, 8 January 1951, SAPMO-BArch, NY 4182 Vol. II 868, pp. 2–20; memorandum by F. Dahlem, H. Axen on meeting with G. Heinemann, H. Grüber, 10 January 1951, SAPMO-BArch, NY 4036 Bd. I/2 649, pp. 192–94; SED document on developments in the KPD, 13 March 1951, SAPMO-BArch, IV 2/2/138, pp. 493–96; KPD report to the SED Politburo, 16 April 1951, SAPMO-BArch, NY 4036 Vol. I/2 649, pp. 197–245; SED Politburo decision, 22 May 1951, SAPMO-BArch, IV 2/2/149, pp. 309–12; SED Politburo decision, 5 June 1951, SAPMO, IV/2/2/151, unpaginated; SED Politburo session, 26 June 1951, SAPMO-BArch, IV 2/2/154, pp. 1–2; SED Politburo paper, 28 August 1951, SAPMO-BArch, IV 2/2/163, unpaginated; SED Politburo session, 23 October 1951, SAPMO-BArch, IV 2/2/172, p. 2; SED Politburo session, 27 November 1951, SAPMO-BArch, 2/2/179, p. 2.

20. SED Politburo session, 30 December 1950, *Dokumente zur Deutschlandpolitik, II, 3/2,* pp. 1194–98; F. Dahlem to W. Pieck, O. Grotewohl, W. Ulbricht, 9 August 1951, SAPMO-BArch, DY 4036 Bd. I/36 649, pp. 252–54; Lemke, "Die infiltrierte Sammlung," Mayer (ed.), *"Macht das Tor auf,"* pp. 182–90.

21. Foreign Minister Dertinger's report on the Prague conference, 23 October 1950, SAPMO, NY 4090 Bd. I 459, pp. 2–18 (notably pp. 4–6); *Dokumente zur Deutschlandpolitik, II, 3/2,* pp. 1071–80.

22. Prague declaration of the Eastern foreign ministers, 21 October 1950, *Dokumente zur Deutschlandpolitik der Sowjetunion, Vol. I* ([East] Berlin: Rütten and Löning 1957), pp. 245–54, and *Dokumente zur Deutschlandpolitik, Series II, Vol 3/1: Published Documents 1 January–31 December 1950,* ed. [German] Federal Ministry of the Interior in conjunction with the Federal Archive (Munich: Oldenbourg 1997), pp. 382–84.

23. Declaration by the Eastern foreign ministers, 24 June 1948, *Vneshniaia politika Sovetskogo Soiuza. Dokumenty i materialy. 1948 god. Chast' pervaia: Ianvar'–iiun' 1948 goda* (Moscow: Izdatel'stvo politicheskoi literatury 1950), pp. 238–48; proposal by A. Ia. Vyshinskii at the Paris session of the Council of Foreign Ministers, 10 June 1949, *Dokumente zur Deutschlandpolitik der Sowjetunion, I,* p. 228.

24. Massenmobilisierung für die Prager Beschlüsse in Westdeutschland/Auswertung der Aktionseinheits-Konferenz, 31 October 1950, SAPMO-BArch, IV 2/2/116, unpaginated, and *Dokumente zur Deutschlandpolitik, II, 3/2,* pp. 1093–97.

25. O. Grotewohl to K. Adenauer, 30 November 1950, *Dokumente zur Deutschlandpolitik, II, 3/1,* pp. 452–53; Lemke, "Die infiltrierte Sammlung," Mayer (ed.), *"Macht das Tor auf,"* p. 183; Amos, *Die Westpolitik der SED,* pp. 67–76.

26. Michael Lemke, "Doppelte Alleinvertretung," *Zeitschrift für Geschichtswissenschaft*, 2/1992, p. 538. In particular, the communists tried to mobilize the West German youth: Michael Herms and Karla Popp (eds.), *Die Westarbeit der FDJ 1946–1989. Eine Dokumentation* (Berlin: Metropol Verlag 1997), pp. 83–86, 147–77.

27. Wolfgang Buschfort, "Aufbau des behördlichen Verfassungsschutzes in Nordrhein-Westfalen," Wolfgang Buschfort, Philipp-Christian Wachs, Falco Werkentin, *Vorträge zur deutsch-deutschen Nachkriegsgeschichte* (Berlin: Der Landesbeauftragte für die Unterlagen des Staatssicherheitsdienstes der ehemaligen DDR 2001), pp. 21–23.

28. Stein Bjørnstad, *Soviet German Policy and the Stalin Note of 10 March 1952* (Hovedoppgrave, University of Oslo, Department of History, fall 1996), p. 90.

29. Statement by O. Grotewohl at GDR government session, 29 January 1951, BArchB, C 20 I/3-42, pp. 195–218.

30. M. G. Pushkin, Ėkonomicheskii i politicheskii obzor polozheniia Germanii v 1951 godu, 15 March 1952, AVPRF, 082, 40, 254, 6, pp. 124–25.

31. M. G. Pushkin, Ėkonomicheskii i politicheskii obzor polozheniia Germanii v 1951 godu, 15 March 1952, AVPRF, 082, 40, 254, 6, pp. 125–28.

32. Lemke, "Die infiltrierte Sammlung," Mayer (ed.), *"Macht das Tor auf,"* pp. 183–202; Amos, *Die Westpolitik der SED*, pp. 99–114.

33. Lemke, "Die infiltrierte Sammlung," Mayer (ed.), *"Macht das Tor auf,"* pp. 193–95; Amos, *Die Westpolitik der SED*, pp 77–114; Wolfgang Stock, "Geld aus dem Osten," *Frankfurter Allgemeine Zeitung*, 21 March 1994; Hans Bodensteiner, "Wahlkampfgeld vor 40 Jahren" (letter to the editor), *Frankfurter Allgemeine Zeitung*, 6 April 1994; Helmut Lenders, "Nicht mit dem Bund der Deutschen" (letter to the editor), *Frankfurter Allgemeine Zeitung*, 6 April 1994. The money was channeled to Heinemann through intermediaries to make him not suspect the source.

34. M. G. Pushkin, Ėkonomicheskii i politicheskii obzor polozheniia Germanii v 1951 godu, 15 March 1952, AVPRF, 082, 40, 254, 6, pp. 128–29.

35. F. Dahlem to W. Ulbricht, 30 December 1951, SAPMO-BArch, NY 4182 Vol. II 870, pp. 17–24; F. Dahlem to W. Ulbricht, 31 December 1951, SAPMO-BArch, NY 4182 Vol. II 870, pp. 27–28; F. Dahlem to W. Pieck, O. Grotewohl, W. Ulbricht, 20 March 1952, SAPMO-BArch, NY 4182 Vol. II 870, pp. 97–98; J. Wirth to G. Dertinger, 31 March 1952, PAAA-MfAA, A 14852 (Akte Ministerbüro), pp. 56–57; Filitov, "Stalinskaia diplomatiia i germanskii vopros," Chubar'ian (ed.), *Stalinskoe desiatiletie*, pp. 87–88; Lemke, "Die infiltrierte Sammlung," Mayer (ed.), *"Macht das Tor auf,"* pp. 197–203; Amos, *Die Westpolitik der SED*, pp. 99–106; Ulrich Schlie, "Diener vieler Herren," *Frankfurter Allgemeine Zeitung*, 8 February 1997; Robert Becker, "Im Bunde mit der Gesamtdeutschen Volkspartei" (letter to the editor), *Frankfurter Allgemeine Zeitung*, 14 February 1997.

36. As late as in fall 1951, an East German request to be allowed to issue entrance visas was turned down (report on conversation A. I. Vyshinskii–R. Appelt, 28 September 1951, AVPRF, 082, 38, 221, 3, pp. 82–86). Only in March 1954 was the GDR accorded some measure of independent action.

37. M. G. Gribanov to A. A. Gromyko, 9 July 1951, AVPRF, 082, 38, 239, 108, pp. 126–34 (German transl.: Jürgen Zarusky (ed.), *Die Stalin-Note vom 10. März 1952. Neue Quellen und Analysen* [Munich: Oldenbourg 2002], pp. 66–70); M. G. Gribanov to A. A. Gromyko, 3 August 1951, AVPRF, 082, 38, 230, 47, p. 12 (German transl.), Zarusky (ed.), *Die Stalin-Note*, p. 71; Egorova, "Evropeiskaia bezopasnost',"

Chubar'ian (ed.), *Stalinskoe desiatiletie,* pp. 67–70, 72–75; Filitov, "Sovetskii Soiuz i germanskii vopros," Chubar'ian (ed.), *Stalin i kholodnaia voina* (Moscow: Institut vseobshchei istorii RAN 1997), pp. 319–20, 323, 327–28.

38. M. G. Gribanov to A. A. Gromyko, 24 February 1951, AVPRF, 082, 38, 230, 47, p. 1 (German transl.: Zarusky, *Die Stalin-Note,* p. 63).

39. S. M. Kudriavtsev to V. A. Zorin, 6 March 1951, AVPRF, 082, 38, 230, 47, p. 2 (German transl.: Zarusky, *Die Stalin-Note,* pp. 64–65).

40. S. M. Kudriavtsev to V. A. Zorin, 6 March 1951, AVPRF, 082, 38, 230, 47, p. 2 (German transl.: Zarusky, *Die Stalin-Note,* pp. 64–65); Egorova, "Evropeiskaia bezopasnost'," Chubar'ian (ed.), *Stalinskoe desiatiletie,* pp. 70–71.

41. Hanns Jürgen Küsters, *Der Integrationsfriede. Viermächte-Verhandlungen über die Friedensregelung mit Deutschland 1945–1990* (Munich: Oldenbourg 2000), pp. 538–44.

42. Stalin's decision in April 1951 to set up a nucleus of an East German military "sea police" (USSR Council of Ministers decision No. 1708-665ss, 25 April 1951, signed by I. Stalin and countersigned by M. Pomaznev, AVPRF, 0458, 264ss, 314, 0036, pp. 24–38) may have been intended to create a navy rather than a maritime "police" force for civil war landing operations in West Germany. As it appears, Soviet preparations for an air force (which certainly was designed for employment in a "big," not civil war) started as early as at the end of 1950 (Rüdiger Wenzke, "Auf dem Weg zur Kaderarmee," Bruno Thoss [ed.], *Volksarmee schaffen—ohne Geschrei! Studien zu den Anfängen einer "verdeckten Aufrüstung" in der SBZ/DDR 1947–1952* [Munich: Oldenbourg 1994], p. 250).

43. Tadeusz Pióro, *Armia ze skazą. W Wojsku Polskim 1945–1968. Wspomnienia i refleksje* (Warsaw: Czytelnik 1994), p. 163.

44. S. Den'gin to V. S. Semënov, 18 March 1952, AVPRF, 0457a, 13, 66, 5, p. 71. See also Major V. I. Kuskov, *Sozdanie i razvitie Natsional'noi Narodnoi Armii GDR (1956–1974 gg.). Avtoreferat dissertacii na soiskanie uchënoi stepeni kandidata istoricheskikh nauk, spetsial'nost' No. 07.00.07yh Voennaia istoriia* (Moscow: Institut voennoi istorii Ministerstva oborony SSSR 1976), pp. 9–11.

45. See drafts of 7 September 1951 through 25 February 1952: Zarusky (ed.), *Die Stalin-Note,* pp. 80–106, 110–12.

46. USSR Council of Ministers decision No. 4594-2025ss, 15 November 1951, as referred to by Army General Maladin to Airforce Colonel General P. F. Zhigarev, Colonel General V. I. Beloskokov, 21 November 1951, AVPRF, 0458, 264ss, 314, 0036, pp. 40–41.

47. Torsten Diedrich, "Das Jahr 1952—Schlüsseljahr der Aufrüstung in der DDR," Falco Werkentin (ed.), *Der Aufbau der "Grundlage des Sozialismus in der DDR 1952/53* (Berlin: Landesbeauftragter für die Unterlagen des Staatssssicherheitsdienstes der ehemaligen DDR 2002), pp. 41–48. Cf. Gerhard Wettig, "Neue Erkenntnisse aus sowjetischen Geheimdokumenten über den militärischen Aufbau in der SBZ/DDR 1947–1952," *Militärgeschichtliche Mitteilungen,* 53, no. 2 (1994), pp. 406–7.

48. Stenographic protocol of the 8th SED Central Committee plenum, 21–23 February 1952, SAPMO-BArch, DY 30/IV 2/1/101, pp. 1–162; protocol of SED Politburo session, 18 March 1952, SAPMO-BArch, DY 30/IV 2/2/202, pp. 1–3; protocol of SED Politburo session, 20 March 1952, SAPMO-BArch, DY 30/IV 2/2/203,

pp. 1–4. Soviet archival documents equally indicate that the policy change had been under preparation for a long time: A. O. Chubar'ian, "Novaia istoriia 'kholodnoi voiny,'" *Novaia i noveishaia istoriia*, 6/1997, p. 19.

49. M. G. Gribanov to A. A. Gromyko, 15 August 1951, AVPRF, 082, 38, 230, 47, pp. 14–16 (German transl.: Zarusky, *Die Stalin-Note*, pp. 72–73).

50. GDR government declaration of 15 November 1951, Otto Grotewohl, *Im Kampf um die einige Deutsche Demokratische Republik*, Vol. II ([East] Berlin: Dietz 1959), pp. 251–53.

51. Statement by S. I. Tiul'panov at SED Politburo session, 19 August 1949, *Dokumente zur Deutschlandpolitik*, II, 2/2 (1996), p. 242; resolution of the SED Party Executive, 24 August 1949, *Dokumente zur Deutschlandpolitik*, II, 2/2 (1996), p. 444; assessment of both the Western demand for free elections and the GDR election procedure by W. Pieck in his notes for a conversation with Stalin on 4 May 1950, Rolf Badstübner and Wilfried Loth (eds.), *Wilhelm Pieck—Aufzeichnungen zur Deutschlandpolitik 1945–1953* (Berlin: Akademie Verlag 1994), pp. 346–47. See also Michael Lemke, "Die DDR und die deutsche Frage 1949–1955," Wilfried Loth (ed.), *Die deutsche Frage in der Nachkriegszeit* (Berlin: Akademie Verlag 1994), p. 145.

52. A. Ia. Vyshinskii to V. M. Molotov for I. V. Stalin, 26 August 1951, AVPRF, 07, 24, 388, 33, pp. 127–31 (German transl.: Zarusky, *Die Stalin-Note*, pp. 74–75).

53. V. S. Semënov, M. G. Gribanov, M. G. Pushkin to A. Ia. Vyshinskii for I. V. Stalin, 28 August 1951, AVPRF, 082, 38, 222, 13, pp. 1–6 (German transl.: Zarusky, *Die Stalin-Note*, pp. 76–79). On the basis of its contents, this letter gives the impression that it must have preceded Vyshinskii's proposal while its date, if correct, excludes this possibility.

54. Wladimir S. Semjonow, *Von Stalin bis Gorbatschow. Ein halbes Jahrhundert in diplomatischer Mission 1939–1991* (Berlin: Nicolai 1995), p. 392 (postscript by Iu. A. Kvitsinskii on what Semënov as an official present told his friends many years later).

55. See for reference to this in the following documents: A. A. Gromyko to I. V. Stalin, undated [21 January 1952 at latest], AVPRF, 07, 25, 13, 144, pp. 26–29 (German transl.: Zarusky, *Die Stalin-Note*, pp. 107–9); A. A. Gromyko to I. V. Stalin, undated [21 January 1952 at latest], AVPRF, 07, 25, 13, 144, pp. 30–37; A. A. Gromyko to I. V. Stalin, 28 January 1952, AVPRF, 07, 25, 13, 144, pp. 41–51.

56. See agenda of Politburo session, 8 September 1951, Federal Archival Service, RGASPI (ed.), *Politbiuro TsK RKP(b). Povestki dnia zasedanii 1919–1952. Katalog. Vol. III: 1940–1952* (Moscow: ROSSPÉN 2001), p. 818. For reference to the decision see M. G. Gribanov, M. G. Pushkin, M. E. Koptelov to I. V. Stalin, undated [between 16 and 20 January 1952], AVPRF, 07, 25, 13, 144, p. 38 (German transl.: Zarusky, *Die Stalin-Note*, p. 105).

57. See agenda of Politburo session, 11 September 1951, Federal Archival Service, RGASPI (ed.), *Politbiuro*, p. 818.

58. Bjørnstad, *Soviet German Policy*, p. 103. To allow no doubt on Soviet attitude, SCC head V. I. Chuikov gave an interview by which he identified with Grotewohl's policy declaration: *Dokumente zur Deutschlandpolitik der Sowjetunion*, I, pp. 278–79.

59. Grotewohl, *Im Kampf*, pp. 444–64. The People's Chamber duly took a corresponding resolution: *Neues Deutschland*, 16 September 1951.

60. Grotewohl at the GDR government session, 14 September 1951, BArchB, C 20 I/3-67, pp. 177–212.

61. Federal Ministry for All-German Affairs, ed., *Die Bemühungen der Bundesregierung um Wiederherstellung der Einheit Deutschlands durch gesamtdeutsche Wahlen. Dokumente und Akten, Vol. I: October 1949–October 1953* (Bonn: Deutscher Bundes-Verlag 1958) (4th ed.), pp. 40–43.

62. GDR government declaration of 10 October 1951, Grotewohl, *Im Kampf,* pp. 509–27.

63. See, for example, his GDR government declaration, 15 November 1951, Grotewohl, *Im Kampf,* pp. 253–71.

64. For relevant documents see *Die Bemühungen der Bundesregierung,* pp. 51–55, 59.

65. GDR President Pieck to Federal President Heuss, 2 November 1951, *Die Bemühungen der Bundesregierung,* pp. 56–57; statement by Soviet Foreign Minister Vyshinskii at U.N. plenary session, 13 November 1951, *Dokumente zur Deutschlandpolitik der Sowjetunion, I,* pp. 280–87.

66. Protocol of GDR government session, 2 November 1951, BArchB, DC 20 I/3-76, pp. 6–7; protocol of GDR government session (with attachments), 3 January 1952, BArchB, DC I/3-88, pp. 1–27; Filitov, "Sovetskii Soiuz," Chubar'ian (ed.), *Stalin i kholodnaia voina,* pp. 330–31. As publication in the SCC daily paper *Tägliche Rundschau* indicates, the text had been prepared in cooperation with the Soviet side.

67. Draft of all-German electoral law, *Tägliche Rundschau,* 10 January 1952.

68. See, inter alia, A. Gromyko to I. V. Stalin, undated [20 January 1952 at latest], AVPRF, 07, 25, 13, 144, pp. 25–37; M. G. Gribanov to V. I. Chuikov, V. S. Semënov, undated [January 1952], AVPRF, 082, 40, 255, 11, pp. 10–11; A. Gromyko to I. V. Stalin, 23 January 1952, AVPRF, 082, 40, 255, 144, p. 14; A. Gromyko to I. V. Stalin, 28 January 1952, AVPRF, 07, 25, 13, 144, pp. 41–51; proekt pis'ma pol'skomu pravitel'stvu, undated [February 1952], AVPRF, 082, 40, 255, 11, pp. 23–24.

69. Plan by M. G. Gribanov to guide drafting peace treaty principles, undated [July–August 1951 with a handwritten addition of 7 September 1951], AVPRF, 082, 38, 230, 47, pp. 22–34 (German transl.: Zarusky, *Die Stalin-Note,* pp. 80–87). Similarly: draft of peace treaty, undated [after 8 September 1951], AVPRF, 082, 40, 255, 11, pp. 31–46 (German transl.: Zarusky, *Die Stalin-Note,* pp. 88–100); M. G. Gribanov to A. E. Bogomolov, AVPRF, 082, 38, 250, 122, pp. 21–34.

70. A. A. Gromyko to I. V. Stalin, undated [20 January 1952 at latest], AVPRF, 07, 25, 13, 144, pp. 25–37. To be sure, Gromyko's argument (which was approved by Stalin) referred to a suggestion that a complete peace treaty proposal should be publicized but is equally valid for any more detailed clarification of the Soviet position.

71. Draft of peace treaty principles, 25 February 1952, AVPRF, 07, 25, 13, 144, pp. 99–102 (German transl.: Zarusky, *Die Stalin-Note,* pp. 110–12); Soviet note to the Western governments (with attachment "Principles of a Peace Treaty with Germany"), 10 March 1952, *Pravda,* 11 March 1952.

72. A. A. Gromyko to I. V. Stalin, undated [21 January 1952 at latest], AVPRF, 07, 25, 13, 144, pp. 30–37.

73. Winfried Halder, *"Modell für Deutschland." Wirtschaftspolitik in Sachsen 1945–1948* (Paderborn: Schöningh 2001), pp. 446–50; Winfried Halder, "Was die Russen wirklich wollten. Zur Bedeutung des Uranbergbaus in der SBZ/DDR

1945–1954," Elke Mehnert (ed.), . . .*'s kommt alles vom Bergwerk her. Materialien zum 7. Deutsch-tschechischen Begegnungsseminar Gute Nachbarn—Schlechte Nachbarn* (Frankfurt/Main: Peter Lang 2005), pp. 63–89. As the only firm in the GDR, the mines continued to be Soviet-owned until 1990 when Germany was reunified.

74. Plan by M. G. Gribanov to guide drafting peace treaty principles, undated [July–August 1951? with a handwritten addition of 7 September 1951], AVPRF, 082, 38, 230, 47, pp. 27–28 (German transl.: Zarusky, *Die Stalin-Note*, pp. 83–84).

75. In the final version of 10 March 1952 this conditionality was not expressed that clearly. But that this was the underlying meaning can be seen from an early draft which expressly promised such rights to "all former nazis who had broken with fascist ideology and joined the democratic forces of the German people in reconstructing peaceful, democratic Germany": draft of peace treaty principles by M. G. Gribanov, M. G. Pushkin, 4/10 January 1952, AVPRF, 07, 25, 13, 144, pp. 3–4 (German transl.: Zarusky, *Die Stalin-Note*, p. 102). The interpretation also conforms to Stalin's remarks to the SED leaders on 31 January 1947, creation of the National-Democratic Party in 1948, and outspoken Soviet interest in 1952 to win sympathizers and adherents among former military and Nazi people (including SS circles) in West Germany (Filitov, "Sovetskii Soiuz," Chubar'ian (ed.), *Stalin i kholodnaia voina*, pp. 324–25, 347; A. M. Filitov, *Germanskii vopros: ot raskola do ob-edineniiu* [Moscow: "Mezhdunarodnye otnosheniia" 1993], p. 139).

76. Postanovlenie TsK VKP(b): O meropiiatiiakh po uskoreniiu zakliucheniia mirnogo dogovora s Germaniei i sozdaniiu edinogo, demokraticheskogo miroliubivogo germanskogo gosudarstva, 8 February 1952, AVPRF, 07, 25, 13, 144, p. 125 (German transl.: Zarusky, *Die Stalin-Note*, p. 113).

77. A. Ia. Vyshinskii to V. I. Chuikov, V. S. Semënov, undated [8 February 1952], AVPRF, 07, 25, 13, 144, pp. 126–28 (German transl.: Zarusky, *Die Stalin-Note*, 113–15); Filitov, "Sovetskii Soiuz," pp. 335–36. For the resultant text see *Dokumente zur Aussenpolitik der Regierung der Deutschen Demokratischen Republik, Vol. 1* ([East] Berlin: Rütten and Löning 1954), pp. 73–76.

78. Note of the USSR to the GDR, 21 February 1952, *Dokumente zur Deutschlandpolitik der Sowjetunion, I*, p. 288.

79. Text: *Izvestiia*, 11 March 1952.

80. Pieck's notes on conversation, 9 March 1952, 10:30 P.M., Badstübner and Loth (eds.), *Wilhelm Pieck*, p. 381.

81. Laure Castin-Chaparro, *Puissance de l'URSS, misères de l'Allemagne. Staline et la question allemande, 1941–1955* (Paris: Publications de la Sorbonne 2002), pp. 339–42.

82. Transcript of SED Central Committee plenary session, 21–23 February 1952, SAPMO-BArch, DY 30/IV 2/1/101, pp. 5–6; protocol of SED Politburo session, 11 March 1952, SAPMO-BArch, IV 2/2/200, pp. 1–3; statement by O. Grotewohl in the People's Chamber, 14 March 1952, Grotewohl, *Im Kampf*, pp. 79, 88; A. Ia. Vyshinskii in a conversation with U.S. Chargé d'Affaires Cumming, 25 March 1952, *Associated Press from Moscow*, 27 March 1952; *Radio Moscow broadcast in Russian*, 25 March 1952, 9.25 GMT; speech by W. Ulbricht, 3 May 1952, Walter Ulbricht, *Zur Geschichte der deutschen Arbeiterbewegung, Vol. IV* ([East] Berlin: Dietz 1964), p. 336; V. S. Semënov to V. M. Molotov [in retrospection], 2 May 1953, AVPRF, 082, 41 271, 18, pp. 52–55.

83. I. Turaginov to M. Gribanov, 18 April 1953, AVPRF, 082, 41, 271, 18, pp. 3–28; V. S. Semënov to V. M. Molotov, 2 May 1953, AVPRF, 082, 41, 271, 18, pp. 52–55; Semjonow, *Von Stalin bis Gorbatschow,* p. 266 (reference to Manifest on the German Question adopted by the Third SED Party Congress, *Dokumente der Sozialistischen Einheitspartei Deutschlands, Vol. 3* ([East] Berlin: Dietz 1952), pp. 184–88).

84. Klaus Larres, "Integrating Europe or Ending the Cold War? Churchill Postwar Foreign Policy," *Journal of European Integration History,* 1/1996, pp. 35–36.

85. Political controversy on whether Stalin was willing to accept democratic unification, if the West would renounce military integration of the Federal Republic, has subsequently been transformed into a debate among historians. This has been answered affirmatively by Michael Lemke, *Einheit oder Sozialismus? Die Deutschlandpolitik der SED 1949–1961* (Cologne: Böhlau 2001), pp. 207–19; Rolf Steininger, *Eine Chance zur Wiedervereinigung? Darstellung und Dokumentation auf der Grundlage unveröffentlichter britischer und amerikanischer Akten. Archiv für Sozialgeschichte, Beiheft 12* (Bonn: Dietz Nachf 1985); Wilfried Loth, "Das Ende einer Legende. Hermann Graml und die Stalin-Note. Eine Entgegnung," *Vierteljahrshefte für Zeitgeschichte,* 4/2002, pp. 653–64. The opposite view has been taken by Hermann Graml, "Nationalstaat oder westdeutscher Teilstaat?" *Vierteljahrshefte für Zeitgeschichte,* 25 (1977), pp. 821–64; Hermann Graml, "Die Legende von der verpassten Gelegenheit," *Vierteljahrshefte für Zeitgeschichte,* 31 (1983), pp. 307–41; Peter März, *Die Bundesrepublik zwischen Westintegration und Stalin-Noten. Zur deutschlandpolitischen Diskussion 1952 in der Bundesrepublik vor dem Hintergrund der westlichen und sowjetischen Deutschlandpolitik* (Frankfurt/Main: Peter Lang 1982), pp. 127–70; Ruud van Dijk, *The 1952 Stalin Note Debate: Myth or Missed Opportunity for German Unification?* Working Paper No. 14, Cold War International History Project (Washington D.C.: Woodrow Wilson Center, May 1996); Iu. F. Rodovich, "O 'note Stalina' ot 10 marta 1952g. po germanskomu voprosu," *Novaia i noveishaia istoriia,* 5/2002, pp. 63–79; A. M. Filitov, "Nota 10 marta 1952 goda: prodolzhaiushchaia diskussiia," B. M. Tupolev (ed.), *Rossiia i Germaniia/Russland und Deutschland, Vol. 3* (Moscow: "Nauka" 2004), pp. 311–30 [with some minor modifications]. For presentation of both views see Zarusky (ed.), *Die Stalin-Note.* Analyzing the problem in a larger con-text in 1996–1997, Bernd Bonwetsch (who has written the respective part of the article) felt that there was not sufficient evidence yet to arrive at a final judgment: Bernd Bonwetsch and Aleksej Filitov, "Die sowjetische Politik und die SED-Diktatur. Handlungs- und Verantwortungsspielräume der KPD/SED/DDR 1945–1963," Deutscher Bundestag (ed.), *Materialien der Enquete-Kommission "Überwindung der Folgen der SED—Diktatur im Prozess der deutschen Einheit," Vol. VIII/1: Das geteilte Deutschland im geteilten Europa* (Baden-Baden: Nomos 1999), pp. 869–72.

86. Graml, "Die Legende von der verpassten Gelegenheit," pp. 307–41.

87. Report by Chargé d'Affaires Cumming to the State Department cited by Graml, "Die Legende von der verpassten Gelegenheit," p. 329.

88. Semjonow, *Von Stalin bis Gorbatschow,* p. 392.

89. George F. Kennan, *Memoirs 1950–1963* (London: Hutchinson 1963), pp. 107, 112–67. For Kennan's attitude see also Hans-Peter Schwarz, *Adenauer, Vol. I: Der Aufstieg 1876–1952* (Stuttgart: Deutsche Verlags-Anstalt 1986, 2nd ed.), p. 923.

90. Note of the USSR to the Western governments, 9 April 1952, *Pravda*, 10 April 1952.

91. On the basis of preceding information by Semënov, Pieck included this statement in his report to Stalin who tacitly agreed, see conversations I. V. Stalin–W. Pieck, W. Ulbricht, O. Grotewohl, 1 and 7 April 1952, *Istochnik*, 3/2003 (63), pp. 115–28.

92. Schwarz, *Adenauer, I*, pp. 916–24.

93. Nikolaus Meyer-Landrut, *Frankreich und die deutsche Einheit. Die Haltung der französischen Regierung und Öffentlichkeit zu den Stalin-Noten 1952* (Munich: Oldenbourg 1988), pp. 74–106.

94. This argument was reflected in a draft by M. G. Gribanov, M. G. Pushkin (German transl.), 15 September 1951, Zarusky, *Die Stalin-Note*, pp. 97–100.

95. Wettig, "Neue Erkenntnisse," pp. 408–12; Torsten Diedrich, "Das Jahr 1952," pp. 33–52; Falco Werkentin (ed.), "Die 2. Parteikonferenz der SED im Juli 1952," Werkentin, *Der Aufbau*, pp. 53–70; Jens Schöne, "'Wir sind dafür, dass über diese Fragen keine Berichterstattung erfolgt.' Die Kollektivierung der Landwirtschaft in der DDR 1952/53," Werkentin (ed.), *Der Aufbau*, pp. 71–94.

96. "'Liudiam svoistvenno oshibat'sia'. Iz vospominanii M. Rakoshi," *Istoricheskii arkhiv*, 3/1998, pp. 11–12; interview with Edward Ochab by Teresa Torańska, *Oni. Stalin's Polish Puppets* (London: Collins Harvill 1987), p. 46; Pióro, *Armia ze skazą*, pp. 161–63.

97. Bjørnstad, *Soviet German Policy*, pp. 121–22.

98. Plan for conversation in Moscow, undated, Badstübner and Loth (eds.), *Wilhelm Pieck*, pp. 383–85.

99. Conversation I. V. Stalin–W. Pieck, W. Ulbricht, O. Grotewohl, 1 April 1952, *Istochnik*, 3/2003 (63), pp. 115–16, 119–21.

100. Conversation I. V. Stalin–W. Pieck, W. Ulbricht, O. Grotewohl, 1 April 1952, *Istochnik*, 3/2003 (63), pp. 116–18, 120–21.

101. Conversation I. V. Stalin–W. Pieck, W. Ulbricht, O. Grotewohl, 7 April 1952, *Istochnik*, 3/2003 (63), p. 122.

102. It should be noted that this term is ambivalent: On the one hand, it refers to the idea of a militia as outlined by Marx and Engels, but on the other, *militsiia* means in Russian "police" and thus refers to the military units that already existed in the GDR. These were no militia but troops-in-barracks alleged to be mere police units. During the conversations of both 1 and 7 April, it was explicitly stated that this organization was meant when transformation into a full-scale army was talked about.

103. Conversation I. V. Stalin–W. Pieck, W. Ulbricht, O. Grotewohl, 7 April 1952, *Istochnik*, 3/2003 (63), pp. 122–25. The need to continue unification propaganda had already been stressed before, cf. transcript of the 8th SED CC plenum, 21–23 February 1952, SAPMO-BArch, DY 30/IV 2/1/101, pp. 1–162; protocol of the SED Politburo session, 18 March 1952, SAPMO-BArch, IV 2/2/202, pp. 1–3; protocol of the SED Politburo session, 20 March 1952, SAPMO-BArch, IV 2/2/203, pp. 1–4. The 21–23 February plenum had been convened on Soviet initiative: Haritonow, *Ideologie*, p. 161.

104. Notes taken by W. Pieck in Badstübner and Loth (eds.), *Wilhelm Pieck,* p. 306. The editors have put them into the context of the conversation on 1 April 1952—an assumption falsified by the fact that they clearly refer to subjects of discussion on 7 April.

105. Pieck's notes on conversations with I. V. Chuikov, 14 and 18 April 1952, Badstübner and Loth (eds.), *Wilhelm Pieck,* pp. 400–402.

106. Pieck's notes on conversation with V. I. Chuikov, 18 April 1952, Badstübner and Loth (eds.), *Wilhelm Pieck,* p. 402; Stefan Creuzberger, "Abschirmungspolitik gegenüber dem westlichen Deutschland im Jahre 1952," Gerhard Wettig (ed.), *Die sowjetische Deutschland-Politik in der Ära Adenauer* (Bonn: Bouvier 1997), pp. 22–33; Silke Schumann, *Parteierziehung in der Geheimpolizei. Zur Rolle der SED im MfS der fünfziger Jahre* (Berlin: Ch. Links 1997), pp. 25–26; Torsten Diedrich, "Die Grenzpolizei der SBZ/DDR (1946–1961)," Diedrich, Ehlert, and Wenzke (eds.), *Im Dienste der Partei,* pp. 208–10; *Die Sperrmassnahmen der DDR vom Mai 1952. Faksimilierter Nachdruck des Weissbuches von 1953* (Bonn: Federal Ministry of Intra-German Relations 1987).

107. Chubar'ian, "Novaia istoriia," p. 19; M. G. Gribanov, Spravka ob ustanovlenii okhrany na sektornoi granitse v Berline, 4 December 1952, AVPRF, 082, 40, 98, 266, p. 15; A. Ia. Vyshinskii und V. S. Semënov to I. V. Stalin, 20 December 1952, AVPRF, 082, 40, 98, 266, pp. 18–22; V. M. Molotov, G. M. Pushkin to the Presidium of the Ministers Council of the USSR, 18 March 1953, Christian F. Ostermann (ed.), *The Post-Stalin Succession Struggle and the 17 June 1953 Uprising in East Germany. The Hidden History. Declassified Documents from US, Russian, and other European Archives* (Washington D.C.: Cold War International History Project 1996) (mimeographed), document No. 4 [AVPRF, 06, 12, 18, 283, pp. 1–2].

108. CPSU CC resolution, 2 January 1953, Ostermann, *Post-Stalin Succession,* p. 43.

109. Wilfriede Otto, "Eine edle Idee im Notstand. Zur Zweiten Parteikonferenz der SED im Juli 1952 (mit zwei Dokumenten)," *Jahrbuch für Forschungen zur Geschichte der Arbeiterbewegung,* 2/2002, pp. 4–5, 10–11.

110. Transcript of session of the SED Politburo, 8 July 1952, *Jahrbuch für Forschungen zur Geschichte der Arbeiterbewegung,* 2/2002, pp. 13–17.

111. For principal documents see Ulbricht, *Zur Geschichte der deutschen Arbeiterbewegung, IV,* pp. 371–499, and *Dokumente der Sozialistischen Einheitspartei Deutschlands, IV,* pp. 70–78.

112. R. Cargill Hall, "The Truth About Overflights. Military Reconnaissance Missions Over Russia Before the U-2," *Quarterly Journal of Military History* 9, no. 3 (Spring 1997), pp. 27–32.

113. Iu. N. Zhukov, *Tainy Kremlia. Stalin, Molotov, Beriia, Malenkov* (Moscow: "Terra" 2000), p. 606.

114. Dmitrii Volkogonov, *Sem' vozhdei, Vol. I* (Moscow: "Novosti" 1995), p. 357.

115. V. P. Naumov, "K istorii sekretnogo doklada N.S. Khrushchëva na XX s-ezde KPSS," *Novaia i noveishaia istoriia,* 4/1996, p. 153.

116. Jan Foitzik, "Ostmitteleuropa zwischen 1953 und 1956," Jan Foitzik (ed.), *Entstalinisierungskrise in Ostmitteleuropa 1953–1956. Vom 17. Juni bis zum ungarischen Volksaufstand. Politische, militärische, soziale und nationale Dimensionen* (Paderborn: Schöningh 2001), pp. 21–34.

117. János M. Rainer, "Ungarn 1953–1956: Die Krise und die Versuche ihrer Bewältigung," András B. Hegedüs and Manfred Wilke (eds.), *Satelliten nach Stalins Tod. Der "Neue Kurs," 17. Juni in der DDR, Ungarische Revolution 1956* (Berlin: Akademie Verlag 2000), pp. 137–42; János M. Rainer, "Der 'Neue Kurs' in Ungarn 1953," Christoph Klessmann and Bernd Stöver (eds.), *1953—Krisenjahr des Kalten Krieges in Europa* (Cologne: Böhlau Verlag 1999), pp. 71–77; György T. Varga, "Zur Vorgeschichte der ungarischen Revolution von 1956," Foitzik, *Entstalinsierungskrise,* pp. 55–56. For relevant documents see *Vostochnaia Evropa v dokumentakh rossiiskikh arkhivov 1944–1953 gg. Sbornik dokumentov,* ed. by Rossiiskaia Akademiia Nauk, Institut slavianovedeniia i balkanistiki, Rossiiski Tsentr khraneniia i izucheniia dokumentov po noveishei istorii, and Gosudarstvennyi arkhiv Rossiiskoi Federatsii, *Vol. II: 1949–1953* (Moscow and Novosibirsk: Sibirskii khronograf 2002), pp. 935–38; *Sovetskii faktor v Vostochnoi Evrope 1944–1953 gg. Dokumenty, Vol. II: 1949–1953,* ed. by Rossiiskaia politicheskaia éntsiklopediia, Institut slavianovedeniia RAN, Gosudarstvennyi arkhiv Rossiiskoi Federatsii, and Rossiiskii gosudarstvennyi akhiv sotsial'no-politicheskoi istorii (Moscow: ROSSPÈN 2002), pp. 786–92.

118. Mark Kramer, "The Early Post-Stalin Succession Struggle and Upheavals in East Central Europe (Part 1)," *Journal of Cold War Studies* 1, no. 1 (Winter 1999), pp. 15–17; *Sovetskii faktor,* pp. 756–58.

119. Kramer, "The Early Post-Stalin Succession Struggle," pp. 17–33; Jiří Pernes, "Die politische und wirtschaftliche Krise in der Tschechoslowakei 1953 und Versuche ihrer Überwindung," Klessmann and Stöver (eds.), *1953—Krisenjahr des Kalten Krieges in Europa,* pp. 93–103; *Vostochnaia Evropa, II,* pp. 918–26; Karl-Heinz Gräfe, "Die Krise des sowjetischen Imperiums und der Neue Kurs in Osteuropa," Klaus Kinner (ed.), *Menetekel 17. Juni 1953. Reader der Konferenzen anlässlich des 50. Jahrestages des 17. Juni 1953* (Leipzig: Rosa-Luxemburg-Stiftung Sachsen 2003), pp. 115–17; *Sovetskii faktor, II,* pp. 758–62, 764–67, 768–72.

120. *Sovetskii faktor, II,* pp. 775–79; *Vostochnaia Evropa, II,* pp. 943–45.

121. *Vostochnaia Evropa, II,* pp. 939–43; *Sovetskii faktor, II,* pp. 779–86.

122. Rolf Stöckigt, "Ein forcierter stalinistischer Kurs führte 1953 in die Krise," *Berliner Zeitung,* 8 March 1990.

123. Paper submitted by Beria to the CPSU Central Committee Presidium on 6 May 1953, Sergej Kondraschow, "Über Ereignisse des Jahres 1953 und deren Bewertung von Aufklärungsdiensten einiger Länder," Heiner Timmermann (ed.), *Juni 1953 in Deutschland. Der Aufstand im Fadenkreuz von Kaltem Krieg, Katastrophe und Katharsis* (Münster: LIT-Verlag 2003), p. 26.

124. Heinz Lippmann, "Der 17. Juni im Zentralkomitee der SED," *Aus Politik und Zeitgeschichte. Beilage zur Wochenzeitung "Das Parlament,"* 13 June 1956, p. 374. Lippmann was vice-chairman of the communist youth organization and a member of the group.

6

Stalin's Role
in Cold War Interaction

STALIN AS SOVIET POLICY MAKER

Stalin controlled everything. In all his career as head of the communist party in the USSR, he had never failed to have his designs executed even at times when conditions had been unfavorable. In foreign policy, he decided both major and minor details. To the extent that documents are available, they indicate that, when Soviet envoys served on major missions abroad, he even felt a need for intensified day-to-day control.[1] As Norman Naimark has observed, Stalin, his views, and his ability to implement them were the central factor of decision making. He "had the intention, the means, and the ability to control the overall design, as well as the thrusts and parries of Soviet foreign policy." While he allowed "bold subordinates" to write down ideas of their own outside bureaucratic strictures, the course of action subsequently taken depended exclusively on him. Once he had "made up his mind and closed down alternatives, he just as quickly removed his patronage from various underlings and abandoned them to meaningless jobs." The people around him "were just errand boys."[2] Stalin encouraged and incited rivalries and infighting among his subordinates but did not allow this to be connected to political issues, and he used to create and maintain submissiveness by humiliating his aides.[3] John Lewis Gaddis has rightly pointed out that Soviet policy "reflected the priorities and the practices of a single individual—a latter-day tsar, in every sense of the word. Just as it would have been impossible to separate the Soviet Union's internal structure from the man who ran it, so too the Soviet sphere of influence in Eastern Europe took on the characteristics of Stalin himself."[4]

241

Stalin paid major attention to exercising maximum influence on the domestic affairs of other countries. As conditions for this were best in occupied countries, his effort was devoted particularly to them. He got most
strongly involved where and when he faced potential or actual resistance by
the Anglo-Saxon powers, notably the United States. As a result, policy on
Germany was accorded the highest priority from 1945 onward.[5] Occupation officers were generally forbidden to discuss "big policy."[6] Both they
and the native communist leaders were assigned the role of administrators
who simply executed orders.[7] They would act only on detailed instructions
from Moscow and seek to avoid any appearance of acting on their own.[8]

Stalin saw "class struggle" as the essence of politics not only in domestic
affairs but in the international context as well. In spite of his need to maintain cooperative relations, he perceived his major wartime allies and occupation partners in Germany—the "capitalistic" powers the United States
and Britain—as antagonists on the basis of systemic principle. In the countries conquered by the Red Army, he sought to impose both the socialist system and Soviet power. In his view, the two aspects were invariably interconnected.[9] As a result, his demand for "friendly governments" in the
neighborhood around the USSR, for Soviet security against possible future
aggression, implied socialist transformation of the countries in question. To
be sure, Stalin was aware that the "correlation of forces" did not always allow for the pursuit of systemic objectives. He therefore did not insist on enforcement of systemic postulates in marginal countries (Finland in 1940,
1944, and 1948 and Austria in 1945) if too big an effort would have been
required or major advantages elsewhere were put at risk. Stalin saw socialist transformation as nonenforcable in regions outside the Red Army's
reach. Nonetheless, for some while he tried to make the West allow him
seizure of, participation in, or control of major sea exits (notably the Turkish Straits) and the industrial heartland of West Germany (the Ruhr District), and even made a short-lived attempt to acquire maritime bases in the
Eastern Mediterranean, which clearly belonged to the Anglo-Saxon sphere
of power. All these initiatives failed and provided for the increase of anti-
Soviet feeling in the outside world.

In contrast to Lenin, Stalin did not believe that revolutionary action by
political forces outside his country was useful. Socialism had to spread from
the USSR to other countries by a process of military expansion.[10] Wherever
conquest by the Red Army had created favorable conditions, Stalin imposed
Soviet control and socialist transformation. He saw attainment of but one
of these objectives as insufficient. Dominant influence simply on foreign
and military affairs of a foreign country would not guarantee good political
behavior. Equally, a socialist regime with no control by the USSR was inherently unreliable. This is why Stalin refused to ascribe legitimacy to Béla
Kun's communist revolution in Hungary after World War I. Significantly,

one of the very first tasks the German "action groups" had to fulfill when they arrived from Moscow in the Soviet zone was to combat indigenous communists who had initiated socialist transformation on their own. From the very start, Stalin was uneasy about the independent position acquired by the communist leaders of Yugoslavia at the end of World War II. To be sure, he willy-nilly acquiesced in their orientation at immediate radical domestic transformation and their far-reaching expansionist ambitions (the risks of which he was unwilling to share) but he always felt that, in spite of their enthusiastic profession of allegiance, they could not be trusted. Suspicion that Tito was willing to defect resulted in a self-fulfilling prophesy when Stalin provoked refusal by insisting on unconditional submission.

SETTING THE STAGE FOR THE COLD WAR

The takeover by the communists in Russia added systemic antagonism to traditional international conflict. This was already an essential precondition for the Cold War which, however, did not break out yet. Except for the early years when East Central Europe and Germany were in turmoil as a result of World War I, the USSR was too weak to challenge outside countries by revolutionary subversion or military attack. As Stalin realized when he announced "socialism in one country," the Soviet regime was unable to abide by the ideological principle to expose capitalism ("imperialism" in its current form) to major challenges for the time being. This allowed the restoration of traditional interstate patterns for one and a half decades.

To be sure, the leaders not only of the USSR but other countries as well continued to be aware of the Soviet threat, notably in Eastern Europe, which would be incapable of warding off Soviet invasion by forces of their own. Their fear of being victimized by "revolution" imposed on them by the Red Army according to Stalin's concept was demonstrated when, in the late 1930s, the British and French sought Soviet military assistance against Hitler's expansion, and the Kremlin leader made any support dependent on freedom of action in Eastern Europe. When, as a result of their refusal to accept entrance of the Red Army, the Anglo-French attempts failed, Stalin sided with Hitler and thus was enabled to take the road of territorial and systemic expansion. Less than two years later, however, the USSR was raided by Hitler's troops. Stalin's calculation proved wrong that internecine struggle among the other powers would allow him to stay out of military conflict until the situation would allow him to export "revolution," that is, to impose Soviet control and the socialist system, by superior armed strength.

From the moment that, by the pact with Hitler in 1939, Stalin had broken out of containment and embarked on expansion, systemic antagonism had become a crucial issue of international relations. Nonetheless, Britain and the United States largely chose to ignore this when, as a result of the German raid in 1941, they found themselves in an alliance with the USSR. Feeling that the requirements of warfare to defeat Hitler had to take precedence, the Anglo-Saxon powers sought to strengthen Soviet military capabilities as much as possible, needlessly allowed advance by the Red Army into important regions, and did little to prevent the Soviet side from imposing its control and system on Eastern Europe. Stalin contributed to their neglect by an approach designed to make Soviet intervention in domestic affairs of conquered countries appear as resulting from indigenous will, and to conceal that it was directed at imposing the socialist system to ensure both permanent Soviet control and communist rule. This kind of domestic change in conquered countries, which also implied a generally anti-Western orientation, was crucial in undermining cooperative relations with the Anglo-Saxon powers and creating the conditions for the Cold War to break out some years later.

It has occasionally been argued that there was no premeditated concept of transforming the domestic structures of foreign countries.[11] According to another opinion, Stalin pursued "military and political interests" in Poland, Finland, and Romania "which overlapped, not coincidentally, with traditional Russian tsarist foreign policy aims," but he displayed "enormous variation and flexibility" when he defined short- and medium-term goals in Hungary, Czechoslovakia, Austria and Germany, France, and Italy.[12] Surprisingly, Finland (which was spared sovietization) is put here into one category with Poland and Romania (where the socialist system was imposed against particularly strong resistance), whereas Hungary, Czechoslovakia (which were also sovietized), and Germany (where the Soviet-occupied part was subjected to socialist transformation) are seen to have been treated in essentially the same way as Austria, France, and Italy (which were allowed to take the road of Western democracy). Soviet policy on these countries differed basically in dependence on the extent to which they were controlled by the Red Army. Except for Austria, which was seen in the Kremlin as a marginal country, sovietization took place wherever Stalin was able to enforce it.

It can be argued that the sequence of measures and the modalities of enforcement differed from country to country. This, however, was inevitable as Stalin was confronted with most different situations. He could not possibly stick to an inflexible timetable of prefixed action to cope with unforeseen challenges. At various places and moments, he had to face quantitatively and qualitatively different resistance and different reaction by the Anglo-Saxon leaders (with whom he wanted to avoid rupture). Stalin had to adapt his responses to the needs of the given moment and place. As he saw it, the respective "correlation of forces" had to be taken into account. For this reason, suggestions that identical successive action must serve as the criterion for making a judgment on whether a common concept was underlying policy in occupied countries[13] do not fit the purpose. What really matters is whether Stalin was oriented at the achievement of similar objectives relying on the same methods.

Therefore, inference on whether a general concept was underlying the enforcement of socialist transformation in Soviet-occupied countries must be based on evidence to allow for judgment on whether there was a common strategy which, to be sure, was bound to be tactically varied according to circumstances. The existence of such a strategy must indeed be taken for granted, given that direction and goal were always the same, bloc politics invariably applied (except for Czechoslovakia where Stalin ordered a putsch when his hope for attainment of socialism by other methods was disappointed), and measures were taken such as, notably, expropriation of industry, banking, and land, compulsory inclusion of the social democrats in the communist party, and liquidation, at least satellization when special conditions were seen to require this, of the "bourgeois" bloc parties. In addition to this, there is direct evidence that, in occupied countries, Stalin acted on the basis of such principles to enforce transformation. It should also be noted that socialism and communist rule were not introduced in response to confrontation with the West. The fundaments had been laid a long time before the Cold War broke out.[14]

INCREASE OF TENSION RESULTING IN COLD WAR

Only during the last months of World War II, when both accomplished facts in Eastern Europe and conditions for decisive Soviet influence on Germany had already been created, did the Anglo-Saxon governments begin to realize that their Soviet wartime ally both took an antagonistic attitude on grounds of principle and sought maximum extension of its power and system. In 1944–1945 when Stalin and Molotov refused to satisfy moderate Anglo-Saxon demands on Poland, notably on substantial political participation by members of the exile government and creation of democratic patterns, doubts on the political fundament of cooperation began to spread in Washington and notably London. Nonetheless, the Anglo-Saxon leaders continued to accept assertions that Soviet policy in occupied countries was basically determined by a strongly felt need for Soviet security against the dreaded threat of another German attack. However, they saw this as no longer credible when, in response to a U.S. proposal on long-time German disarmament, the Kremlin argued in 1946 that protection against the defeated country was possible only by its systemic transformation.

The final rupture, however, was triggered by another issue. Ever since Germany had been subjected to the occupation regime by the four powers, the

USSR failed to take the vital interest of the two Anglo-Saxon countries into account to put an end to a situation in which their taxpayers had to pay for sizeable food deliveries to prevent mass starvation in the defeated country. The practical consequence, that the Germans must be permitted industrial production for export to allow them to pay for their imports, was vehemently rejected by the Kremlin. It is surprising that Stalin, who stepped up Soviet zone industrial production in 1946 to satisfy Soviet reparation demands, saw no need to accept any similar arrangement to provide for self-support of the population in the British and American zones. Given that the United States had indicated willingness to withdraw from Europe (which made him feel that, as after World War I, it would choose isolationism), he saw no need to concede anything. Accordingly, he felt that there was no power left to oppose the USSR.

Stalin had miscalculated. As a result of successive frustrations by Soviet attitudes and a growing feeling of Soviet threat to democracy, the leaders in Washington agreed with the British at last that the United States must commit itself to defending "freedom" against the communist threat. After a last-ditch attempt for compromise with the USSR had failed in spring 1947, they shortly afterward announced the Marshall Plan, which was designed to stabilize the democratic countries by initiation of economic recovery. Inclusion of West Germany deprived Stalin of his veto power on the Western zones. This implied that the Kremlin leader was no longer in a position to prevent implementation of any undesirable policy in Germany and, on this basis, to insist on an agreement that would allow for extension of Soviet zone "democratization" to the country as a whole—a demand that he justified by alleged Western obligations under the Potsdam Agreement of summer 1945. The preceding extreme unilateralism in Stalin's part of Germany ever since 1945 did not prevent him from vehemently protesting against the Marshall Plan as an intolerable unilateralist Western policy that provoked the USSR and made further cooperation impossible. Stalin made the USSR, the satellite countries, and the communist parties in the West take a course of absolute hostility. This resulted in the open outbreak of the Cold War.

STALIN'S INITIATION OF STRUGGLE FOR A SOCIALIST GERMANY

The disputed country was Germany, which the Soviet leaders had always seen as the door to all of Europe. Even before his rupture with the West, Stalin had tried to make its population support his policy against his occupation partners. When the Marshall Plan and ensuing plans to set up a West German state frustrated his hope that they would eventually accept, or at minimum acquiesce in, the achievement of his objectives, Stalin wanted the

Germans to undermine the Western powers in their zones by rallying behind the Soviet program for reunification and by joining communist-controlled organizations. The attempt failed, however, since most people were suspicious of Eastern designs. Another approach was required. The 1948–1949 blockade of Berlin was directed at forcing the Western powers to choose between termination of their presence in the city or abandonment of their plans to create a West German state. In either event, they would have to accept political defeat. To be sure, the loss of West Berlin (which Stalin expected to be their preferred choice) would not be crucial by objective criteria. But decisive change would result on the basis of subjective factors. The Germans would realize that, given the Western powers' inability to defend their position in Berlin, they would not rely on them any longer but seek alignment with the USSR as the winning side.

To everyone's surprise, an airlift allowed the supply of 2.4 million people in the Western sectors who strongly identified with the West. As a result, Stalin failed to dislocate the enemy from Berlin and, diametrically opposed to what he had sought, he had increased West German attachment to the West. He concluded that the Soviet zone, which already had central institutions, must constitute itself as a state as soon as West Germany had been created. This was not intended as a signal that partition would be accepted. Instead, the Kremlin leader intended the "German Democratic Republic" (GDR), set up on the basis of detailed instructions from Moscow, to be both the political home of all "patriots" in either part of the divided country and the nucleus of the prospective united Germany. The GDR was assigned an "all-German mission." To make commitment to the cause of reunification with alleged disregard for communist goals appear credible, Stalin instructed the SED leaders to pretend that they continued to pursue a "bourgeois-democratic" course of policy and remained outside the socialist camp. In fact, however, sovietization had been promoted since fall 1947 at an accelerated pace. The "all-German mission" was put into practice by intensified campaigns for reunification on the basis of negotiations between the two states (which would implicitly allow for exercise of veto power by the Kremlin), and creation of military units labelled as a police organization but designed for employment in civil war.

Failure of the Berlin Blockade also confronted Stalin throughout the "free world" with a rising tide of anti-Soviet feeling and resolve to meet the Soviet challenge. The North Atlantic alliance founded on 4 April 1949 included not only the two Anglo-Saxon powers and France (which until then had stayed aside) but traditionally neutral countries as well and provided for express U.S. commitment to protection of the European members—the very thing Stalin had wanted to prevent. The preceding "great debate" in the United States had taken place under the strong influence of the perception that the Soviet action against the position in Berlin indicated a threat that had to be warded off.

Stalin responded by initiating a peace campaign in the West focused on the dangers alleged to result from American possession of the atomic bomb. This propaganda continued to the full extent and was even stepped up when the USSR broke the U.S. monopoly by exploding an atomic device in summer 1949 and subsequently engaged in nuclear armament.

Until 1950, coexistence of the North Atlantic pact and Soviet bilateral alliances (which had been concluded in previous years) did not entail major preparations for the contingency of war. To be sure, the Soviet forces had been reduced much less than the Western armies and, as a result, were overwhelmingly superior in the European theater, but Stalin had failed to orient his troops at attack (which, according to Leninist military doctrine, was the only acceptable method of waging war). He wanted to avoid war which might involve the United States. As the USSR had suffered large-scale destruction in World War II and had not yet overcome the resultant exhaustion, he felt that restoration of the economic fundament had to precede massive armament. One exception to this was an effort to create strong nuclear forces. Stalin felt that the best chance to develop and expand power was to preserve peace for a long period of time. There was no need to enhance military buildup since the enemy was unable to attack. On the Western side, the military tended to be concerned that, due to lacking forces, effective defense was unfeasible, but the political leaders were satisfied by U.S. political commitment to the allies' security as a (hopefully) reliable deterrent of Soviet attack.

STALIN'S STRUGGLE FOR GERMANY AGAINST THE BACKGROUND OF ARMAMENT IN THE WEST AND EAST

Negligence for the war contingency by both the West and the USSR ceased when, on 25 June 1950, communist North Korea invaded the southern part of the country. Underlying this raid was a mutual misperception of policy. In the West, Stalin, who supported the aggression by providing indispensable military support, was wrongly seen as having initiated it. To be sure, he had given his approval when the plan had been submitted to him but had done so only after having been persuaded by Kim Il-sung that the United States would not intervene but allow for military success within a very few months. Accordingly, operations would be a minor affair of short duration and would not entail military conflict with the Americans. When this expectation was disproved by President Truman's immediate decision to send troops to Korea and save the noncommunist South, Stalin suspected Washington of having deliberately given wrong signals in early 1950 to provoke attack and then exploit it for propaganda purposes, to make public opinion in the West support the preparation of war against the USSR.

Stalin concluded this when the invasion of South Korea spurred Western determination to create a system of effective defense against Soviet attack. From his point of view, the underlying perception was absolutely incomprehensible. He had not initiated aggression against South Korea and was even less willing to take similiar action against Western Europe, as he was suspected by the West of intending. He could not imagine that Western Europe might indeed feel directly threatened. After all, there was a most crucial difference between Korea and the European theater: While U.S. troops had left the Korean peninsula, they continued to be present in Europe. For this reason, initiation of war was a priori excluded there but not in Korea (where, additionally, the USSR was not directly involved). This invited the conclusion that West European feelings of threat had been artificially created by American propaganda intended to generate what in fact resulted: West European demands for military protection.

Stalin saw achievement of his goals put in jeopardy by Western reaction. The United States, which had sent almost any available troops to Korea, took the road of armament which, due to its greatly superior economic resources, was bound to create an enormous military challenge. Even more importantly, the West Europeans were not willing any longer to accept their security to be based simply on political commitment by the United States. The prospect appeared intolerable that, if war were to break out, the Americans would evacuate and leave the continent to the Soviet invaders. To be sure, it was generally taken for granted that, as in World War II, they would mobilize their superior resources in order to rearm, return to Europe, liberate allied territory, and defeat the USSR. This, however, implied the dire prospect of having both to endure extreme hardships of Soviet occupation and communist repression and to suffer massive destruction by the military struggle that would follow. To prevent this, the Western European governments sought to create sizeable forces and asked for U.S. combat units to be deployed on their continent. (By then, all American military personnel in Germany were employed in administration and envisaged to be evacuated in the event of war.) The leaders in Washington agreed but demanded that the allies on their part must exploit all available resources and, notably, accept a military contribution by West Germany.

In Stalin's perception, implementation of these plans would result in the consolidation of West European independence from the USSR, the prevention of German unification along Soviet lines, and the creation of Western offensive military power. He responded by initiating massive Soviet and East European armament and an intensified political campaign against "West German remilitarization." While, in Western Europe, he focused public attention on alleged revival of aggressive "militarism" as the very threat to international security, Eastern propaganda in the Federal Republic aimed at both demonstrating the negative implications for reunification and persuading people that an "army of mercenaries" was on the agenda which must be prevented. Young men were exhorted to protest against military service. These appeals had major resonance but Stalin felt that the North Atlantic pact nations, which set up military organization as a basis of common defense in early 1951, would succeed in including West German units. As a result, Western forces would be greatly strengthened. Stalin also foresaw frustration of his plan to extend the GDR to all of Germany: Any hope that the United States would withdraw at a later date was waning, and West German soldiers tied to NATO would not allow for GDR "police" forces to wage and win war against the Federal Republic of Germany.

In view of the changed situation, Stalin felt that regard for the need to make East Germany appear credible as a champion of reunification must no longer take precedence over the requirement to include it more fully in the political and military framework of the socialist camp. When, in mid-1951, he made up his mind on this, it necessarily implied that the units thus far designed for employment in intra-German civil war had to be restructured and enlarged as an army that might support Soviet forces in prospective military conflict with the West. However, denunciation of "West German remilitarization" and advocacy of a "united Germany on a democratic basis" was to continue. On the recommendation of the foreign policy establishment, Stalin decided in September to have a proposal for agreement on a peace treaty with united Germany prepared as a propaganda ploy to justify planned armament and sovietization of the GDR as an inescapable result of the Western failure to accept a reasonable solution of the unification problem. To create an appearance of strong Soviet interest in immediate unification, a "program of action" was initiated to provide for successive steps that would culminate in a note to the Western governments.

Stalin acted on the assumption that the inclusion of the Federal Republic in Western military preparations must be expected very soon. But negotiations in the West lasted longer than anticipated. So the time to send and publicize the note came only in March 1952. In subsequent propaganda, the Eastern side ascribed the preconceived measures in the GDR on separation, sovietization, and militarization to Western "splitting policy" and pretended that the USSR continued to be the only champion of German unity. After the Western treaties with the Federal Republic had been concluded at the end of May, endless delays in the ratification process followed. In spite of this, Stalin always felt that the creation of forces in the Federal Republic was imminent and that, for the time being, the Kremlin had lost on Germany. At the same time, he failed to understand that Western integration policy provided for a new pattern of relations among the countries concerned. He therefore took consolation from the expectation that, as a result of developing "interimperialistic contradictions," Western victory would entail defeat later. When Chou En-lai asked him whether the prospective West German army might eventually turn its weapons against the United States, he answered in the affirmative. Stalin even declared in public that West Germany would not permanently accept the subordinate role assigned to it by the West. To expect anything else would be tantamount to "believing in miracles."[15]

PERCEPTIONS UNDERLYING STALIN'S FOREIGN POLICY

Stalin's attitude toward political actors in the outside world was shaped by the ideological premise of an antagonistic relationship. The imperative of "class struggle" against capitalism did not allow for any exception. To be sure, there might be compelling reasons for cooperation in a given situation such as the need to face a common challenge, to seek mutual benefit, or to elicit material support, but Stalin invariably acted on the assumption that this was but a temporary requirement and must not prevent simultaneous action to oppose the other side and inflict failure on it. Any goodwill by the "class enemy" had to be exploited against him. It was crucially important to differentiate antagonists by the role assigned to them momentarily: Foreign powers declared to belong to the "imperialistic" variant of capitalism, and politicians, respectively parties, labelled "reactionaries," were the main enemy in the current struggle, while the other "forces of capitalism" were left aside for the time being. To the extent that they were willing to serve the Soviet cause in one way or another, they were credited with a "progressive," respectively "democratic," orientation until Stalin felt that priority must be given to fighting them. The ultimate goal was to defeat capitalism and to put the USSR's power and system in its stead worldwide. When this would be achieved was not defined, but seeking progress to this end appeared necessary all the time. Stalin's premise that political actors outside his control were bound to be enemies was a self-fulfilling prophesy; it was his attitude that, sooner or later, made them turn against him.

As can be seen from these explanations, Stalin's view was that adherence to either the socialist or capitalistic system was the determining factor in world politics. As a result, the domestic order of other countries was a crucial factor in international relations which, besides traditional interaction among states, had a very important "societal" dimension. It was logical, therefore, that Stalin saw systemic transformation as a task of high priority in countries occupied by the Red Army. To achieve this end, he felt that the "working class's" attitude was decisive on the level of domestic politics. He ascribed the fact that, before Soviet troops had entered the respective country, the capitalistic system had been able to maintain itself to noncommunist influence on the workers (as notably in Germany) or to the absence of a sufficiently strong "working class" (in predominantly agrarian Eastern Europe). To overcome these barriers, Stalin ordered the destruction of "bourgeois" social power by the expropriation of industry, banks, and land, and the enforcement of communist control of the "working class" by the elimination of both "bourgeois" influence and the social democratic competitor for "working class" representation. To this end, he envisaged "unification of the two workers' parties" under communist leadership. Also, the role of the "working class" had to be enhanced by control of the "means of production" and industrialization of agrarian regions.

Stalin took it for granted that, on the basis of "class interest," the workers could not but rally behind the communist party, which was guided by the prescripts of Marxist-Leninist doctrine. If the workers failed to conform to this expectation, this had to be attributed to their own lack of insight into their true needs. An effort was then required to make the workers understand how they must perceive their own situation and interest. The premise that the communist cadres must direct their effort primarily at seeking "working class" support was not allowed to be put into question by deviating experience. When, for example, there was a much greater chance to make West German "bourgeois" circles accept the Soviet position on unification than workers under social democratic influence, the official line continued to emphasize the need for appealing to the latter. In Stalin's view, the idea that everything ultimately depended on the "working class" was immutable. The "law of historical development" on which it was based equally implied that the socialist system was superior to capitalism by innate necessity and that it would ultimately prevail in all countries. This perspective did not allow for a passive atttitude but required maximum effort. It provided, however, for an expectation that, in spite of any setback, the USSR would be victorious in the end.

On the basis of the confidence thus created, Stalin—in striking contrast to Hitler—felt no need to take avoidable risk and to hurry success when it could not be achieved by normal effort. In particular, he did not want war unless victory appeared certain with little sacrifice. This feeling intensified when the USSR suffered extraordinary annihilation and devastation by German invasion and was then seeking to overcome resultant exhaustion. The Kremlin leader saw maintenance of peace rather than another military conflict as providing for the best possible development of Soviet prosperity and power. To be sure, he always abided by the ideological position that war was indispensable for the final triumph of socialism. But he felt that armed struggle must not be waged prematurely, nor under inappropriate conditions at that. During all his lifetime, Stalin had expected the prediction to come true that "contradictions" inherent in the "system of imperialism" (the current variant of capitalism) were bound to involve the major foreign powers in internecine conflict that would totally exhaust them and trigger revolution by their "working class." It was only then that the USSR would intervene and enforce socialism on a worldwide scale. While this ideological tenet expressed political intent, it contrasted with the fact that, when Stalin died, the expansion of Soviet power and the socialist system had been stopped and tension within the Soviet empire was approaching crisis.

NOTES

1. Cf. Vladimir Pechatnov (ed.), "'Soiuzniki nazhimaiut na tebia dlia togo, chtoby u tebia slomit' voliu . . .' (Perepiska Stalina s Molotovym i drugimi chlenami Politbiuro po vneshnepoliticheskim voprosam v sentiabr'—dekabr' 1945g.)," *Istochnik*, 2/1999, p. 70; Grant M. Adibekov, *Das Kominform und Stalins Neuordnung Europas* (Frankfurt/Main: Peter Lang 2002), pp. 73–86.

2. Norman M. Naimark, "Stalin and Europe in the Postwar Period, 1945–53: Issues and Problems," *Journal of Modern European History* 2, no. 1 (2004), pp. 28–29.

3. Cf. O. V. Khlevniuk, *Politbiuro. Mekhanizm politcheskoi vlasti v 1930-e gody* (Moscow: ROSSPÈN 1996); A. A. Danilov and A. V. Pyzhikov, *Rozhdenie sverkhderzhavy. SSSR v pervy poslevoennye gody* (Moscow: ROSSPÈN 2001); "Vvedenie," O. V. Khlevniuk, I. Gorlitskii, L. P. Kosheleva, A. I. Miniuk, M. Iu. Prozumen'shchikov, L. A. Rogova, S. V. Somonova (eds.), *Politbiuro CK VKP(b) i Sovet Ministrov SSSR 1945–1953* (Moscow: ROSSPÈN 2002).

4. John Lewis Gaddis, *We Now Know. Rethinking Cold War History* (Oxford: Clarendon Press 1998), pp. 51–52.

5. N. G. Pavlenko, *Razmyshleniia o sud'be polkovodtsa* (Moscow: Znanie 1989), pp. 48–49; R. C. Raack, "Stalin Plans His Post-War Germany," *Journal of Contemporary History*, 28 (1993), pp. 64–65; "Vvedenie," *SSSR i germanskii vopros 1941–1949. Dokumenty iz Arkhiva vneshnei politiki Rossiskogo Federatsii*, ed. by Historico-Archival Department of the Russian Ministry of Foreign Affairs and the Potsdam Center for Contemporary Historical Research, Vol. II: *9 maia 1945 g.–3 oktiabria 1946 g.* (Moscow: "Mezhdunarodnye otnosheniia" 2000), pp. 14, 15–16, 620; Nina Petrov, "Zur Geschichte der sowjetischen Repressionsorgane (NKVD/MVD) in der SBZ 1945/46," Andreas Hilger, Mike Schmeitzner, and Ute Schmidt (eds.), *Diktaturdurchsetzung. Instrumente und Methoden der kommunistischen Machtsicherung in der SBZ 1945–1955* (Dresden: Hannah-Arendt-Institut für Totalitarismusforschung 2001), p. 32; Alexandr Haritonow, *Ideologie als Institution und soziale Praxis. Die Adaption des höheren sowjetischen Parteischulungssystems in der SBZ/DDR (1945–1956)* (Berlin: Akademie Verlag 2004), pp. 72–73, 79.

6. Wladimir S. Semjonow, *Von Stalin bis Gorbatschow. Ein halbes Jahrhundert in diplomatischer Mission 1939–1991* (Berlin: Nicolai 1995), p.157.

7. Jan Foitzik, *Sowjetische Militäradministration in Deutschland (SMAD) 1945–1949. Struktur und Funktion* (Berlin: Akademie Verlag 1999), pp. 136–37, 221–27, 242–43, 246, 259–70; Gerhard Wettig, "Autonomy and Dependence. The East German Regime's Relationship with the USSR, 1945–1949," Laurence McFalls and Lothar Probst (eds.), *After the GDR. New Perspectives on the Old GDR and the Young Länder* (Amsterdam and Atlanta, GA: Rodopi 2001), pp. 49–75.

8. Bernd Bonwetsch and Gennadij Bordjugov (eds.), "Die SED und die guten Er-fahrungen der Sowjetunion," *Deutsche Studien*, 121 (1994), p. 97. In the early occu-pation period when there was still much disorder and many lines of command had not been established yet, some military authorities enjoyed more leeway.

9. This point has been emphasized by Gaddis, *We Now Know*, p. 13, and Naimark, "Stalin and Europe," pp. 29–36. For the opposing view that the USSR pur-sued a policy of national security similar to those of Western countries see Vojtech Mastny, "Soviet Plans for Postwar Europe," Antonio Varsori and Elena Calandri (eds.), *The Failure of Peace in Europe, 1943–1948* (Houndmills and New York: Pal-grave 2002), pp. 64–65; Michael MccGwire, "National Security and Soviet Foreign Policy," Melvyn P. Leffler and David S. Painter (eds.), *Origins of the Cold War. An In-ternational History* (London and New York: Routledge 1995) (2nd ed.), pp. 53–76.

10. This view has been taken also by Gaddis, *We Now Know*, pp. 13–14.

11. Hannes Adomeit, *Imperial Overstretch: Germany in Soviet Policy from Stalin to Gorbachev* (Baden-Baden: Nomos 1998).

12. Naimark, "Stalin and Europe," p. 31.

13. Naimark, "Stalin and Europe," pp. 29–36. That there was "no timetable," has also been emphasized by Gaddis, *We Now Know*, p. 31.

14. Cf. Leonid Gibianskij, "Osteuropa: Sicherheitszone der UdSSR, sowjetisiertes Protektorat oder Sozialismus 'ohne Diktatur des Proletariats'?" *Forum für osteu-ropäische Ideen- und Zeitgeschichte*, 8, no. 2 (2004), pp. 120, 130–31.

15. "Stenogrammy peregovorov I.V. Stalina s Chzhou Ėn'laem v avguste-sentiabre 1952g.," *Novaia i noveishaia istoriia*, 2/1997, p. 84.

16. Stalin made this prediction in spring 1952 and included it in his report to the XIXth CPSU Party Congress: *Pravda*, 3 October 1952.

Bibliography

UNPUBLISHED ARCHIVAL SOURCES

Archive of the Russian Ministry of Foreign Affairs (Arkhiv vneshnei politiki Rossiiskoi Federatsii, AVPRF)

f. 06, op. 9, p. 43, d. 632, 639
f. 06, op. 9, p. 44, d. 660
f. 06, op. 11, p. 12, d. 174
f. 06, op. 12, p. 18, d. 283
f. 06, op. 35, p. 39, d. 13
f. 06, op. 35, p. 171, d. 75
f. 07, op. 22a, p. 10, d. 138
f. 07, op. 25, p. 13, d. 144
f. 082, op. 10, p. 36, d. 488
f. 082, op. 31, p. 187, d. 40
f. 082, op. 34, p. 154, d. 79, 187
f. 082, op. 34, p. 71, d. 19, 20
f. 082, op. 36, p. 183, d. 12
f. 082, op. 38, p. 221, d. 3
f. 082, op. 38, p. 222, d.13
f. 082, op. 38, p. 231, d. 47
f. 082, op. 38, p. 239, d. 108
f. 082, op. 40, p. 254, d. 6
f. 082, op. 40, p. 255, d. 11
f. 082, op. 40, p. 266, d. 98
f. 082, op. 41, p. 271, d. 18
f. 0457a, op. 4, p. 19, d. 48
f. 0457a, op. 5, p. 28, d. 8

f. 0457a, op. 7, p. 33, d. 27
f. 0458, op. 266ss, p. 314, d. 0036
f. 0457a, op. 7, p. 39, 10–13
f. 0742, op. 4, p, 34, d. 60
f. Archivno-operativnaia biblioteka, op. 11zh, p. 71, d. 19, 20

Russian State Archive of Social and Political History (Rossiiskii gosudarstvennyi arkhiv sotsial'noi i politicheskoi istorii, RGASPI)

f. 17, op. 128, d. 149, 158, 324, 331, 568, 569, 1091, 1097, 1098, 1166
f. 17, op. 137, d. 92

State Archive of the Russian Federation (Gosudarstvennyi arkhiv Rossiiskoi Federatsii, GARF)

f. 7319, op. 19, d. 1
f. 9401, op. 2, d. 138

Foundation Archive Parties and Mass Organizations of the GDR within the German Federal Archive (Stiftung Archiv Parteien und Massenorganisationen der DDR im Bundesarchiv, SAPMO-BArch)

DY 30/3538
DY 30/IV 2/1/22, 73
DY 30/IV 2/2/73, 99, 116, 127, 138, 149, 151, 154, 163, 172, 179
DY 30/IV 2/2.1/120, 137, 147, 148, 149, 150, 151, 152, 153, 154
NY 4036 Bd. I,2 649
NY 4090 Bd. I,36 459, 649
NY 4109/5
NY 4182 Bd. II 870, Bd. III 1194

German Federal Archive Berlin (Bundesarchiv Berlin, BArchB)

C 20 I/3–42, 67
MdI 7/1, 42, 45, 421

[Archive of] The Federal Commissioner of the Materials of the State Security Service of the Former GDR (Bundesbeauftragte für die Unterlagen des Staatssicherheitsdienstes der ehemaligen DDR, BStU)

SdM No. 1405

Political Archive of the [German] Foreign Office, Files of the Ministry of Foreign Affairs of the Former GDR (Politisches Archiv des Auswärtigen Amtes, Bestände des Ministeriums für Auswärtige Angelegenheiten der ehemaligen DDR (PAAA-MfAA)

A 14852

PUBLICATIONS OF ARCHIVAL AND OTHER PRIVATE SOURCES

Anderson, K. M., and Chubar'ian, A. O., eds. *Komintern i vtoraia mirovaia voina*, Vols. *1–2*. Moscow: Institut vseobshchei istorii RAN / RTsKhIDNI 1994, 1998.

Badstübner, Rolf, and Loth, Wilfried, eds. *Wilhelm Pieck—Aufzeichnungen zur Deutschlandpolitik 1945–1953*. Berlin: Akademie Verlag 1994.

Barth, Bernd-Rainer, and Schweizer, Werner, eds. *Der Fall Noel Field. Schlüsselfigur der Schauprozesse in Osteuropa*, 2 vols. Berlin: BasisDruck 2007.

Bayerlein, Bernhard H., Babichenko, Leonid G., Firsov, Friedrich I., and Vatlin, Aleksandr Ju., eds. *Deutscher Oktober 1923. Ein Revolutionsplan und sein Scheitern.* Berlin: Aufbau-Verlag 2003.

Bayerlein, Berhard H., Narinski, Mikhail, Studer, Brigitte, and Wolikow, Serge, eds. *Moscou, Paris, Berlin (1939–1941). Télégrammes chiffrés du Komintern*. Paris: Tallandier 2003.

Bezymenski, Lev, ed. "Die Rede Stalins am 5. Mai 1941," *Osteuropa*, 3/1992, pp. 242–64.

Bonvech, Bernd, ed. "'Skostit' polovinu summy reparatisii . . . my mozhem.' Vstrechi Stalina s rukovodstvom" SEPG [April 1952], *Istochnik*, 3/2003 (63), pp. 100–127.

Bonwetsch, Bernd, and Bordjugov, Gennadij [Bordiugov, Gennadii], eds. "Die SED und die guten Erfahrungen der Sowjetunion. Pieck und Grotewohl informieren sich in Moskau," *Deutsche Studien*, 121 (1994), pp. 95–107.

Bonvech [Bonwetsch], Bernd, Bordiugov, Gennadii, and Neimark [Naimark], Norman, eds. *SVAG. Upravlenie propagandy (informatsii) i S. I. Tiul'panov. 1945–1949*. Moscow: "Rossiia molodaia" 1994. Enlarged German edition, Bonwetsch, Bernd, Bordjugov, Gennadij [Bordiugov, Gennadii], and Naimark, Norman M., eds. *Sowjetische Politik in der SBZ 1945–1949. Dokumente zur Tätigkeit der Propagandaverwaltung (Informationsverwaltung) der SMAD unter Sergej Tjul'panov*. Bonn: Dietz Nachf. 1998.

Die Sowjetunion auf internationalen Konferenzen während des grossen Vaterländischen Krieges 1941 bis 1945, published by the Ministry of Foreign Affairs of the USSR, Vol. VI: *Die Potsdamer (Berliner) Konferenz der höchsten Repräsentanten der drei alliierten Mächte—UdSSR, USA und Grossbritannien (17 July–2 August 1945). Dokumentensammlung*. Moscow: Progress; [East] Berlin: Staatsverlag der DDR 1986.

Dimitroff, Georgi. *Tagebücher 1933–1943*, ed. Bernhard H. Bayerlein. Berlin: Aufbau-Verlag 2000.

Documents on Germany 1944–1985, Department of State Publication 9446. Washington D.C.: Government Printing Office 1985.

"Dokumente und Materialien. Sicherheits—und militärpolitische Konzepte der SED in der SBZ von 1948. Eine Dokumentation," *Beiträge zur Geschichte der Arbeiterbewegung*, 4 (1992), pp. 58–71.

Erler, Peter, Laude, Horst, and Wilke, Manfred, eds. *"Nach Hitler kommen wir." Dokumente zur Programmatik der Moskauer KPD-Führung 1944/45 für Nachkriegsdeutschland*. Berlin: Akademie Verlag 1994.

Federal Archival Service, RGASPI, ed. *Politbiuro TsK RKP(b). Povestki dnia zasedanii 1919–1952. Katalog. Vol. III: 1940–1952*. Moscow: ROSSPÉN 2001.

Federal Ministry of the Interior, ed. *Dokumente zur Deutschlandpolitik: Die Konferenz von Potsdam, Series II, Vols. 1/1–3.* Kriftel: Metzner 1992.

———, ed. *Dokumente zur Deutschlandpolitik: Unveröffentlichte Dokumente, Series II, Vols. 2/1–3/2.* Munich: Oldenbourg 1996–1997.

Firsov, F. I., ed. "Arkhivy Komintern i vneshniaia politika SSSR v 1939–1941 gg.," *Novaia i noveishaia istoriia,* 6/1992, pp. 12–35.

Foreign Relations of the United States [FRUS]. Diplomatic Papers. 1943, Vol. I: General, Department of State Publication 7585; *The Conferences of Cairo and Tehran 1943,* Department of State Publication 7187; *The Conferences at Malta and Yalta 1945,* Department of State Publication 6199; *The Conference of Berlin (The Potsdam Conference) 1945,* Department of State Publication 7163; *1947, Vol. II: Council of Foreign Ministers, Germany and Austria,* Department of State Publication 8530; *1948, Vol II: Germany and Austria,* Department of State Publication 8660; *1949, Vol II: Germany and Austria,* Department of State Publication 8752. Washington D.C.: Government Printing Office 1963, 1961, 1955, 1960, 1972, 1973.

Friedrich, Thomas, ed. "Antworten der SED-Führung auf Fragen Stalins 1948," *Beiträge zur Geschichte der Arbeiterbewegung,* 3/1991, pp. 364–73.

Germany 1947–1949. The Story in Documents. Department of State Publication 3556. Washington D.C.: Government Printing Office 1950.

Goroshkova, G. N. *Dvizhenie nemetskogo narodnogo kongressa za edinstvo i mirnyi dogovor.* Moscow: Izdatel'stvo Institut mezhdunarodnykh otnoshenii 1959.

Gruner, Gert, and Wilke, Manfred, eds. *Sozialdemokraten im Kampf um die Freiheit. Die Auseinandersetzungen zwischen SPD und KPD in Berlin 1945/46. Stenografische Niederschrift der Sechziger-Konferenz am 21./22. Dezember 1945.* Munich: Piper 1981.

Herms, Michael, and Popp, Karla, eds. *Die Westarbeit der FDJ 1946–1989. Eine Dokumentation.* Berlin: Metropol Verlag 1997.

"I. V. Stalin o 'Kratkom kurse istorii VKP(b)," *Istoricheskii arkhiv,* 5/1994, pp. 4–31.

Karner, Stefan, Stelzl-Marx, Barbara, and Tschubarjan, Alexander, eds. *Die Rote Armee in Österreich. Sowjetische Besatzung 1945–1955, Krasnaia Armiia v Avstrii. Sovetskaia okkupatsiia 1945–1955. Vol. II: Dokumente / Dokumenty (bilingual edition).* Vienna: Oldenbourg 2005.

Keiderling, Gerhard, ed. *"Gruppe Ulbricht" in Berlin April bis Juni 1945. Von den Vorbereitungen im Sommer 1944 bis zur Wiedergründung der KPD im Juni 1945. Eine Dokumentation.* Berlin: Berlin Verlag 1993.

"'Lozhnye ustanovki v dele vospitaniia i propagandy.' Doklad nachal'nika Glavnogo politicheskogo upravleniia RKKA L.Z. Mekhlisa o voennoi ideologii. 1940 g.," *Istoricheskii arkhiv,* 5–6/1997, pp. 82–99.

Mar'ina, V. V. "Dnevnik G. Dimitrova," *Voprosy istorii,* 7/2000, pp. 32–55.

Mastny, Vojtech, ed. "The Beneš-Stalin-Molotov-Conversations in December 1943" [minutes taken by J. Smutný], *Jahrbücher für Geschichte Osteuropas,* NF 20 (1972), pp. 367–402.

Narinskii, M. M., ed. "I. V. Stalin i Moris Torez. Zapis' besedy v Kremle. 1947 g.," *Istoricheskii arkhiv,* 1/1996, pp. 4–26.

"'Nasha liniia takaia . . . 'Dokumenty o vstreche I. V. Stalina s rukovoditeliami SEPG. Ianvar'—fevral' 1947 g.," *Istoricheskii arkhiv,* 4/1994, pp. 22–44.

"Obsuzhdenie v SSSR amerikanskogo predlozheniia o zakliuchenii dogovora o ra-zoruzhenii i demilitarizatsii Germanii (1945–1947 gg.)," *Mezhdunarodnaia zhizn'*, 8/1996, pp. 69–76.

Orlik, Igor', ed. "'V Rumynii teplee, chem eto nuzno dlia strany.' Priëm Stalinym rumynskoi pravitel'stvennoi delegatsii" [on 3 February 1947], *Istochnik*, 2/2002, pp. 92–99.

Osça, Alexandru, and Popa, Vasile. "Stalin a decis. Lagrul socialist se înarmează" [Romanian document on Stalin's talks with communist party heads and the defense ministers of the East European countries, 9–12 January 1951], *Buletinul Arhivelor Militare Române*, 2–3/1998, pp. 71–76. German translation (with introduction): Wettig, Gerhard, "Stalins Aufrüstungsbeschluss. Die Moskauer Beratungen mit den Parteichefs und Verteidigungsministern der Volksdemokratien vom 9. bis 12. Januar 1951," *Vierteljahrshefte für Zeitgeschichte*, 4/2005, pp. 635–49.

"'Oshibki imeiutsia i u menia, i u moikh sotrudnikov.' Zapis' besedy I. V. Stalina i Sharlia de Gollia," *Vestnik*, 5/1996, pp. 105–7.

Paczkowski, Andrzej, ed. "The Polish Contribution to the Victory of the 'Prague Coup' in February 1948," *Cold War International History Project Bulletin*, 11 (Winter 1998), pp. 141–48.

Pechatnov, Vladimir O., ed. *The Big Three after World War II. New documents on Soviet Thinking about Post War Relations with the United States and Great Britain.* Working Paper No. 13, Cold War International History Project. Washington D.C.: Woodrow Wilson International Center for Scholars 1995.

——, ed. "Kak Stalin pisal F. Ruzvel'tu (po novym dokumentam)," *Istochnik*, 6/1999, pp. 82–87.

——, ed. "'Na ètom voprose my slomaem antisovetskoe uporstvo . . .' (Iz perepiski Stalina s Molotovym po vneshnepoliticheskim delam v 1946 godu)," *Istochnik*, 3/1999, pp. 92–104.

——, "Ne mif: rech' Stalina 19 avgusta 1939 goda," *Novaia i noveishaia istoriia*, 8/2005, pp. 3–20.

——, ed. "'Soiuzniki nazhimaiut na tebia dlia togo, chtoby u tebia slomit' voliu . . .' (Perepiska Stalina s Molotovym i drugimi chlenami Politbiuro po vneshnepoliticheskim voprosam v sentiabr'–dekabr' 1945 g.)," *Istochnik*, 2/1999, pp. 70–85.

Petrov, Nikita V., Lavinskaia, Olga V., and Nachotovich, Dina N., eds. *SVAG i nemetskie organy samoupravleniia 1945–1949. Sbornik dokumentov.* Moscow: ROSSPÈN 2006.

"Posetiteli kremlevskogo kabineta I. V. Stalina. Zhurnaly (tetradi) zapisi lic priniatykh pervym gensekom. 1924–1953 gg. Alfavitnyi ukazatel'," *Istoricheskii arkhiv*, 4/1998, pp. 3–191.

Procaccio, Giuliani, ed. *The Cominform. Minutes of the Three Conferences 1947/1948/1949* (bilingual Russian and English edition of documents with introductory parts). Milan: Feltrinelli Editore 1994.

Protokolle der erweiterten Sitzung des Sekretariats des Zentralkomitees der KPD Juli 1945 bis Februar 1946. Dokumente zur Geschichte der kommunistischenBewegung in Deutschland. Reihe 1945/1946. Munich: K. G. Saur 1994.

[Rákosi, Mátyás.] "'Liudiam svoistvenno oshibat'sia'. Iz vospominanii M. Rakoshi," *Istoricheskii arkhiv*, 3/1998, pp. 3–63; 5–6/1997, pp. 153–212.

Reale, Eugenio. *Avec Jacques Duclos au banc des accusés.* Paris: Hachette 1958.

Rupieper, Hermann-Josef, ed. *Die Zwangsvereinigung von KPD und SPD. Einige ausgewählte SMAD Dokumente, 16. Januar–7. Juni 1946.* Halle/Saale: Gesellschaft für Demokratie- und Zeitgeschichte, University of Halle 1997.

Scherstjanoi, Elke, and Semmelmann, Rolf, eds. "Die Gespräche Stalins mit der SED-Führung im Dezember 1948 und im April 1952," *Zeitschrift für Geschichtswissenschaft,* 2/2004, pp. 138–66; 3/2004, pp. 238–69.

Semënova, Elena, and Chavkin, Boris, eds. "Aus den persönlichen Tagebüchern des sowjetischen Diplomaten V. S. Semenov," *Forum für osteuropäische Ideen- und Zeitgeschichte,* 2/2004, p. 252, 36–38.

Sovetskaia voennaia administratsiia v Germanii 1945–1949. Politika SVAG v oblasti kul'tury, nauki i obrazovaniia: Tseli, metody, rezul'taty. Sbornik dokumentov pod obshchei redaktsiei Kh. Mëllera [H. Möller] i A. O. Chubar'iana [Dokumenty SVAG]. Moscow: ROSSPÈN 2006.

Sovetskii faktor v Vostochnoi Evrope 1944–1953. Dokumenty, ed. by Rossiiskaia politicheskaia èntsiklopediia, Institut slavianovedenija RAN, Gosudarstvennyi arkhiv Rossiiskoi Federatsii, and Rossiiskii gosudarstvennyi akhiv sotsial'no-politicheskoi istorii, Vols. I–II. Moscow: ROSSPÈN 1999, 2002.

Sovetskii Soiuz na mezhdunarodnykh konferentsiiakh perioda Velikoi otechestvennoi voiny 1941–1945 gg. Sbornik dokumentov. Vol. I: Moskovskaia konferentsiia ministrov inostrannykh del SSSR., SShA i Velikobritanii, 19–30 oktiabria 1943 g.; Vol. II: Tegeranskaia konferentsiia trëkh soiuznykh derzhav—SSSR, SShA i Velikobritanii (28 noiabria–1 dekabria 1943 g.); Vol. IV: Krymskaia konferentsiia rukovoditelei trekh soiuznykh derzhav—SSSR, SShA i Velikobritanii (4–11 fevralia 1945 g.). Moscow: Izdatel'stvo politicheskoi literatury 1978, 1978, 1984.

Sovetsko-amerikanskie otnosheniia. Rossiia XX vek. Dokumenty pod obshchei redaktsiei Akademika A. N. Iakovleva, Vols. 1939–1945 and 1945–1948. Moscow: Izdatel'stvo "Materik" 2004.

"Stalin's Plan to Assassinate Tito," *Cold War International History Project Bulletin,* 10 (March 1998). Washington D.C.: Woodrow Wilson International Center for Scholars, p. 137.

"Stenogrammy peregovorov I. V. Stalina s Chzhou Èn'laem v avguste-sentiabre 1952 g.," *Novaia i noveishaia istoriia,* 2/1997, pp. 69–86.

Suckut, Siegfried, ed. *Blockpolitik in der SBZ/DDR. 1945–1949. Die Sitzungsprotokolle des zentralen Einheitsfrontausschusses.* Cologne: Wissenschaft und Politik 1986.

Volokitina, T. V., Murashko, G. P., and Noskova, A. P., eds. *Tri vizita A.Ia. Vyshinskogo v Bukharest 1944–1946. Dokumenty rossiiskikh arkhivov.* Moscow: ROSSPÈN 1998.

Vostochnaia Evropa v dokumentakh rossiiskikh arkhivov 1944–1953 gg., ed. Rossiiskaia Akademiia Nauk, Institut slvavianovedeniia i balkanistiki, Rossiiski Tsentr khraneniia i izucheniia dokumentov po noveishei istorii, Gosudarstvennyi arkhiv Rossiiskoi Federatsii, Vols. I–II. Moscow and Novosibirsk: "Sibirskii khronograf" 1997, 2002.

Weathersby, Kathryn, ed. "Korea, 1949–50: To Attack, or Not to Attack? Stalin, Kim Il Sung, and the Prelude to War," *Cold War International History Project Bulletin,* 5 (Spring 1995). Washington D.C.: Woodrow Wilson International Center for Scholars, pp. 1–9.

———, ed. "New Russian Documents on the Korean War. Introduction and Translations," *Cold War International History Project Bulletin*, 6–7 (Winter 1995/1996). Washington D.C.: Woodrow Wilson International Center for Scholars, pp. 30–40.

Werblan, Andrzej, ed. "The Conversation between Władysław Gomułka and Jozef Stalin on 14 November 1945," *Cold War International History Project Bulletin*, 11 (Winter 1998), pp. 134–40.

"'Zaniat'sia podgotovkoi budushchego mira,'" *Vestnik Arkhiva Prezidenta Rossiiskoi Federatsii* (supplement to *Istochnik*), 4/1995, pp. 114–58.

PUBLISHED SOURCES

Acheson, Dean. *Strengthening the Forces of Freedom. Selected Speeches February 1949–April 1950*, Department of State Publication 5852. Washington D.C.: Government Printing Office 1950.

Ackermann, Anton. "Gibt es einen besonderen deutschen Weg zum Sozialismus?" *Einheit. Organ zur Vorbereitung der Vereinigung der Arbeiterparteien*, 9 February 1946, pp. 22–32.

Bol'shaia Sovetskaia Èntsiklopediia, Vols. 13, 17, 27. Moscow: Gosudarstvennoe nauchnoe izdatel'stvo 1952, 1954.

Deutsche Gesellschaft für Auswärtige Politik / Senate of [West] Berlin, eds. *Dokumente zur Berlin-Frage 1944–1963*. Munich: Oldenbourg 1963; shorter version in English: *Documents on Berlin, 1943–1963*. Munich: Oldenbourg 1963.

Deutsches Armeemuseum, ed. *Ich schwöre. Eine Bilddokumentation*. [East] Berlin: Ministry of National Defense 1969.

Die Sperrmassnahmen der DDR vom Mai 1952. Faksimilierter Nachdruck des Weissbuches von 1953. Bonn: Federal Ministry of Intra-German Relations 1987.

Dokumente der Sozialistischen Einheitspartei Deutschlands, Vols. I–IV. [East] Berlin: Dietz 1951–1953.

Dokumente zur Aussenpolitik der Regierung der Deutschen Demokratischen Republik, Vol. 1. [East] Berlin: Rütten and Löning 1954; Vol. 2. [East] Berlin: Staatsverlag der DDR 1956.

Dokumente zur Deutschlandpolitik der Sowjetunion, Vol. 1. [East] Berlin: Rütten and Löning 1957.

Federal Ministry for All-German Affairs [of West Germany], ed. *Die Bemühungen der Bundesregierung um Wiederherstellung der Einheit Deutschlands durch gesamtdeutsche Wahlen. Dokumente und Akten, Vol. I: October 1949–October 1953*. Bonn: Deutscher Bundes-Verlag 1958 (4th ed.).

Grieder, Peter. *The East German Leadership, 1946–1973*. New York: Manchester University Press 1999.

Grotewohl, Otto. *Im Kampf um die einige Deutsche Demokratische Republik. Reden und Aufsätze, Vols. I–III*. [East] Berlin: Dietz 1959.

Karlsch, Rainer. *Uran für Moskau. Die Wismut—Eine populäre Geschichte*. Berlin: Ch. Links 2007.

Karner, Stefan, Reiter, Erich, and Schöpfer, Gerald, eds. *Kalter Krieg. Beiträge zur Ost-West-Konfrontation 1945 bis 1990*. Graz: Leykam 2002.

Molotov, V. M. Address at the CPSU celebration of the October Revolution anniversary, 6 November 1948, *Bol'shevik*, 21/1948, pp. 12–13.

———. *Fragen der Aussenpolitik. Reden und Erklärungen April 1945–Juni 1948*. Moscow: Verlag für fremdsprachliche Literatur 1949.

Oelssner, Fred. Unser Kampf gegen den Militarismus, *Neues Deutschland*, 18 February 1946.

Ruggenthaler, Peter. *Stalins großer Bluff. Die Geschichte der Stalin-Note*. Munich: Oldenbourg 2007.

Spilker, Dirk. *The East German Leadership and the Division of Germany. Patriotism and Propaganda 1945–1953*. Oxford and New York: Oxford University Press 2006.

Stalin, I. V. Report to the XIXth CPSU Party Congress, 2 October 1952, *Pravda*, 3 October 1952.

———. *Sochineniia, Vol. 13*. Moscow: Politizdat 1951.

———. Speech in his Moscow electoral district, 9 February 1946, *Pravda*, 10 February 1946.

———. "SSSR v avangarde bor'by za prochnyi mir" (editorial), *Bol'shevik*, 23/1948, pp. 2–5.

Ulbricht, Walter. "Der deutsche Plan," *Neues Deutschland*, 2 September 1947.

———. *Zur Geschichte der deutschen Arbeiterbewegung, Aus Reden und Aufsätzen, Vols. III–IV*. [East] Berlin: Dietz 1961, 1964.

———. *Zur Geschichte der neuesten Zeit, Vol. III*. [East] Berlin: Dietz 1959.

Vneshniaia politika Sovetskogo Soiuza. Dokumenty i materialy. 1946 god; 1948 god: Chast' pervaia: Ianvar'–iiun' 1948 goda. Moscow: Gosudarstvennoe izdatel'stvo politicheskoi literatury 1950, 1952.

Vneshniaia politika Sovetskogo Soiuza. 1949 god. Moscow: Gosudarstvennoe izdatel'stvo politiceskoi literatury 1953.

"Vorschlag der DDR für gesamtdeutsche freie Wahlen," *Tägliche Rundschau*, 10 January 1952.

Wettig, Gerhard. "Der 17. Juni 1953 in sowjetischer Sicht," *Militärgeschichtliche Zeitschrift*, 1/2007, pp. 145–57.

———. "Die Vereinbarungen der Siegermächte über Berlin und die Deutschlandpolitik der UdSSR 1943–1945, " *Kie Vier Mächte in Berlin: Beiträge zur Politik der Alliierten in der besetzten Stadt*, ed. Michael Bienert, Uwe Schaper, and Andrea Theissen. Berlin: Landesarchiv Berlin 2007, pp. 17–29.

MEMOIRS AND REMINISCENCES

Aleksandrov-Agentov, A. M. *Ot Kollontai do Gorbacheva. Vospominaniia diplomata, sovetnika A. A. Gromyko, pomoshchnika L. I. Brezhneva, Iu. V. Andropova, K. U. Chernenko i M. S. Gorbacheva*. Moscow: "Mezhdunarodnye otnosheniia" 1994.

Becker, Robert. "Im Bunde mit der Gesamtdeutschen Volkspartei" (letter to the editor), *Frankfurter Allgemeine Zeitung*, 14 February 1997.

Bereschkow, Valentin M. *Ich war Stalins Dolmetscher. Hinter den Kulissen der politischen Weltbühne*. Munich: Universitas 1991.

Bodensteiner, Hans. "Wahlkampfgeld vor 40 Jahren" (letter to the editor), *Frankfurter Allgemeine Zeitung*, 6 April 1994.

Bouvier, Beatrix W., and Schulz, Horst-Peter, eds. *" . . . die SPD hat aufgehört zu existieren" Sozialdemokraten unter sowjetischer Besatzung*. Bonn: Dietz Nachf 1991.

Catroux, Georges. *J'ai vu tomber le rideau de fer a Moscou 1945–1948*. Paris: Hachette 1952.

Djilas, Milovan. *Conversations with Stalin*. New York: Harcourt 1962.

———. *Jahre der Macht. Kräftespiel hinter dem Eisernen Vorhang. Memoiren 1945–1966*. Munich: Molden-Seewald 1983.

Gniffke, Erich W. *Jahre mit Ulbricht*. Cologne: Wissenschaft und Politik 1966.

Gromyko, A. A. *Pamiatnoe, Vol. 1*. Moscow: Izd. pol. lit. 1991 (2nd ed.).

Howley, Frank. *Berlin Command*. New York: Putnam 1950.

Kariagin, V. V. *Diplomaticheskaia zhizn' za kulisami i na stsene*. Moscow: "Mezhdunarodnye otnosheniia" 1994.

Kennan, George F. *Memoirs 1950–1963*. London: Hutchinson 1963.

Khrushchëv, N. S. *Vospominaniia. Vremia, liudi, vlast', Vol. I*. Moscow: "Moskovskie novosti" 1999.

Koval', K. I. *Poslednii svidetel'. "Germanskaia karta" v kholodnoi voine*. Moscow: ROSSPÈN 1997.

———. "Rabota v Germanii po zadaniiu GKO," *Novaia i noveishaia istoriia*, 2/1995, pp. 101–14.

———. "Zapiski upolnomochennogo GKO na territorii Germanii," *Novaia i noveishaia istoriia*, 3/1994, pp. 124–47.

Lenders, Helmut. "Nicht mit dem Bund der Deutschen" (letter to the editor), *Frankfurter Allgemeine Zeitung*, 6 April 1994.

Leonhard, Wolfgang. *Die Revolution entlässt ihre Kinder*. Cologne: Kiepenheuer and Witsch 1955.

Novikov, N. V. *Vospominaniia diplomata. Zapiski 1938–1947*. Moscow: Izd. pol. lit. 1989.

Ratchford, B. U., and Ross, M. W. D. *Berlin Reparations Assignment*. Chapel Hill: University of North Carolina Press 1947.

Schollwer, Wolfgang. *Potsdamer Tagebuch 1948–1950. Liberale Politik unter sowjetischer Besatzung, Vols. 1–2*. Munich: Oldenbourg 1988.

Semiriaga, M. M. *Kak my upravliali Germaniei*. Moscow: ROSSPÈN 1995.

———. *Russkie v Berline v 1945 gody, Mezhdunarodnaia zhizn'*, 9/1994, pp. 115–23.

Semjonow, Wladimir S. *Von Stalin bis Gorbatschow. Ein halbes Jahrhundert in diplomatischer Mission 1939–1991*. Berlin: Nicolai 1995.

Smith, Walter Bedell. *My Three Years in Moscow*. Philadelphia and New York: Lippincot 1950.

Sto sorok besed s Molotovym. Iz dnevnika F. Chueva. Moscow: Terra 1991.

Tuominen, Arvo. *Stalins Schatten über Finnland. Erinnerungen des ehemaligen Führers der finnischen Kommunisten*. Freiburg/Breisgau: Herderbücherei 1986.

"Wollte Stalin Togliatti kaltstellen?" *Osteuropa*, 10/1970, pp. A 703–718.

ACADEMIC AND OTHER WORKS

Adibekov, G. M. *Kominform i poslevoennaia Evropa, 1947–1956 gg.* Moscow: Rossiia molodaia 1994. German version: *Das Kominform und Stalins Neuordnung Europas,* ed. Bernhard H. Bayerlein and Jürgen Mothes. Frankfurt/Main: Peter Lang 2002.

———. "Ot ispolkoma Kominterna do otdela mezhdunarodnoi informatsii," *Bulgarian Historical Review,* 25 (2–3/1997), pp. 156–79.

Adomeit, Hannes. *Die Sowjetmacht in internationalen Krisen und Konflikten.* Baden-Baden: Nomos 1983.

———. *Imperial Overstretch. Germany in Soviet Policy from Stalin to Gorbachev.* Baden-Baden: Nomos 1998.

Amos, Heike. *Die Westpolitik der SED 1948/49–1961. "Arbeit nach Westdeutschland" durch die Nationale Front, das Ministerium für Auswärtige Angelegenheiten und das Ministerium für Staatssicherheit.* Berlin: Akademie Verlag 1999.

Bajanov, Evgeni. "Assessing the Politics of the Korean War, 1949–1951," *Cold War International History Project Bulletin,* 6–7 (Winter 1995/1996). Washington D.C.: Woodrow Wilson International Center for Scholars, pp. 54, 87–88.

Banac, Ivo. *With Stalin Against Tito. Cominformist Splits in Yugoslav Communism.* Ithaca, NY, and London: Cornell University Press 1988.

Batiuk, V., and Evstaf'ev, D. *Pervye zamoroski. Sovetsko-amerikanskie otnosheniia v 1945–1950 gg.* Moscow: Rossiiskii nauchnyi fond 1995.

Bauer, Theresia. *Blockpartei und Agrarrevolution von oben. Die Demokratische Bauernpartei Deutschlands 1948–1963.* Munich: Oldenbourg 2003.

Bauernkaemper, Arnd, ed. *"Junkerland in Bauernhand"? Durchführung, Auswirkungen und Stellenwert der Bodenreform in der Sowjetischen Besatzungszone, Beiheft 20 zu den Historischen Mitteilungen der Ranke-Gesellschaft.* Stuttgart: Steiner Verlag 1996.

Baus, Ralf Thomas. *Die Christlich-Demokratische Union Deutschlands in der sowjetisch besetzten Zone 1945 bis 1948. Gründung-Programm-Politik.* Dusseldorf: Droste 2001.

Bayerlein, Bernhard H. *"Der Verräter, Stalin, bist Du!" Vom Ende der linken Solidarität 1939–1941. Mit einem Vorwort von Wolfgang Leonhard.* Berlin: Aufbau-Verlag 2006.

Behring, Rainer, and Schmeitzner, Mike, eds. *Diktaturdurchsetzung in Sachsen. Studien zur Genese der kommunistischen Herrschaft 1945–1952.* Cologne: Böhlau 2003.

Békés, Csaba. "Soviet Plans to Establish the Kominform in Early 1946: New Evidence from Hungarian Archives," *Cold War International History Project Bulletin,* 10 (March 1998). Washington D.C.: Woodrow Wilson International Center for Scholars, pp. 135–36.

Berghe, Yvan Vanden. *Der Kalte Krieg 1917–1991.* Leipzig: Leipziger Universitätsverlag 2002.

Beyer-Thoma, Hermann. *Kommunisten und Sozialdemokraten in Finnland 1944–1948.* Wiesbaden: Harrassowitz 1990.

Bezymenski, Lev. "Chto zhe skazal Stalin 5 maia 1941 goda?" *Novoe vremia,* 19/1991, pp. 36–40.

———. *Stalin und Hitler. Das Pokerspiel der Diktatoren.* Berlin: Aufbau Verlag 2002.

Bienert, Michael, Schaper, Uwe, and Theissen, Andrea, eds. *Die Vier Mächte in Berlin. Beiträge zur Politik der Alliierten in der besetzten Stadt.* Berlin: Landesarchiv Berlin 2007.

Bjørnstad, Stein. *Soviet German Policy and the Stalin Note of 10 March 1952.* Hovedoppgrave, University of Oslo, Department of History, fall 1996 (mimeographed study).

Bode, Bernard. *Liberal-Demokraten und "deutsche Frage." Zum Wandel einer Partei in der Sowjetischen Besatzungszone und in der DDR zwischen 1945 und 1961.* Frankfurt/Main: Peter Lang 1997.

Bonwetsch, Bernd. "Vom Hitler-Stalin-Pakt zum 'Unternehmen Barbarossa,'" *Osteuropa*, 6/1991, pp. 562–79.

Bonwetsch, Bernd, and Bordjugov, Gennadij. "Stalin und die SBZ. Ein Besuch der SED-Führung in Moskau vom 30. Januar–7. Februar 1947, *Vierteljahrshefte für Zeitgeschichte*, 2/1994, pp. 279–303.

Buchstab, Günter, ed. *Verfolgt und entrechtet. Die Ausschaltung ChristlicherDemokraten unter sowjetischer Besetzung und SED-Herrschaft 1945–1961. Eine biographische Dokumentation.* Dusseldorf: Droste 1997.

Bukharkin, I. V., and Gibianskii, L. Ia. "II. [k konfliktu s Tito:] Pervye shagi konflikta," *Rabochii klass i sovremennyi mir*, 5/1990, pp. 152–63.

Bullock, Alan. *Hitler und Stalin—Parallele Leben. Überarbeitete Neuausgabe.* Berlin: Siedler 1999.

Buschfort, Wolfgang, Wachs, Philipp-Christian, and Werkentin, Falco. *Vorträge zur deutsch-deutschen Nachkriegsgeschichte.* Berlin: Der Landesbeauftragte für die Unterlagen des Staatssicherheitsdienstes der ehemaligen DDR 2001.

Castin-Chaparro, Laure. *Puissance de l'URSS, misères de l'Allemagne. Staline et la question allemande, 1941–1955.* Paris: Publications de la Sorbonne 2002.

Chubar'ian, A. O. "Novaia istoriia 'kholodnoi voiny,'" *Novaia i noveishaia istoriia*, 6/1997, p. 19.

———, ed. *Stalin i kholodnaia voina. Fakty i gipotezy.* Moscow: Institut vseobshchei istorii RAN 1997.

———. *Stalinskoe desiatiletie kholodnoi voiny. Fakty i gipotezy.* Moscow: "Nauka" 1999.

Ciesielski, Stanisław, ed. *Umsiedlung der Polen aus den ehemaligen polnischen Ostgebieten nach Polen in den Jahren 1944–1947.* Marburg: Herder Institut 2006.

Ciesla, Burghard, Lemke, Michael, and Lindenberger, Thomas, eds. *Sterben für Berlin? Die Berliner Krisen 1948 : 1958.* Berlin: Metropol 2000.

Courteois, Stéphane. "Thorez, Stalin und Frankreichs Befreiung im Lichte von Moskauer Archiven," *Jahrbuch für Historische Kommunismusforschung*, 1998, pp. 77–85.

Coutouvidis, John, and Reynolds, Jaime. *Poland 1939–1947.* Leicester: Leicester University Press 1986.

Creuzberger, Stefan. *Die sowjetische Besatzungsmacht und das politische System der SBZ.* Weimar: Böhlau 1996.

———. "Klassenkampf in Sachsen," *Historisch-Politische Mitteilungen*, II (1995), pp. 119–30.

Creuzberger, Stefan, and Görtemaker, Manfred, eds. *Gleichschaltung unter Stalin? Die Entwicklung der Parteien im östlichen Europa 1944–1949.* Paderborn: Schöningh 2002.

Crockett, Richard. *The Fifty Years War. The United States and the Soviet Union, 1941–1991.* London and New York: Routledge 1995.

Danilov, A. A., and Pyzhikov, A. V. *Rozhdenie sverkhderzhavy. SSSR v pervy poslevoennye gody.* Moscow: ROSSPÈN 2001.

Davies, Norman. *Aufstand der Verlorenen. Der Kampf um Warschau 1944.* Munich: Droemer 2004.

Deutscher Bundestag, ed. *Materialien der Enquete-Kommission "Aufarbeitung von Geschichte und Folgen der SED—Diktatur in Deutschland im Prozess der deutschen Einheit" (13. Wahlperiode des Deutschen Bundestages), Vol. VIII/1–3.* Baden-Baden: Nomos; Frankfurt/Main: Suhrkamp 1999.

Diedrich, Torsten, Ehlert, Hans, and Wenzke, Rüdiger, eds. *Im Dienste der Partei. Handbuch der bewaffneten Organe der DDR.* Berlin: Ch. Links 1998.

Diedrich, Torsten, and Wenzke, Rüdiger. *Die getarnte Armee. Geschichte der Kasernierten Volkspolizei der DDR 1952 bis 1956.* Berlin: Ch. Links 2001.

Dijk, Ruud van. *The 1952 Stalin Note Debate: Myth or Missed Opportunity for German Unification?* Working Paper No. 14, Cold War International History Project. Washington D.C.: Woodrow Wilson Center, May 1996.

Dilks, D. "Cherchill' i operatsiia 'Nemyslimoe', 1945 g.," *Novaia i noveishaia istoriia,* 3/2002, pp. 126–42.

Dockrill, Michael L. *The Cold War, 1945–1963.* Basingstoke: Macmillan 1988.

Dockrill, Saki, Frank, Robert, Soutou, Georges-Henri, and Varsori, Antonio, eds. *L'Europe de l'Est et de l'Ouest dans la Guerre froide 1948–1953.* Paris: Presse de l'Université de Paris Sorbonne 2002.

Duda, Gerhard. *Jenö Varga und die Geschichte des Instituts für Weltwirtschaft und Weltpolitik in Moskau 1921–1970.* Berlin: Akademie Verlag 1994.

Dülffer, Jost. *Europa im Ost-West-Konflikt 1945–1991.* Munich: Oldenbourg 2004.

Ehlert, Hans, and Wagner, Armin, eds. *Genosse General! Die Militärelite der DDR in biographischen Skizzen.* Berlin: Ch. Links 2003.

Erler, Peter. "'Moskau-Kader' der KPD in der SBZ," Wilke, Manfred, ed., *Anatomie der Parteizentrale. Die KPD/SED auf dem Weg zur Macht.* Berlin: Akademie Verlag 1998, pp. 229–91.

Ermer, Matthias. *Von der Reichsmark zur Deutschen Mark der Deutschen Notenbank. Zum Binnenwährungsumtausch in der Sowjetischen Besastzungszone Deutschlands (Juni/Juli 1948).* Stuttgart: Franz Steiner 2000.

Farquharson, John. "The Essential Division. Britain and the Partition of Germany, 1945–49," *German History,* 3/1991, pp. 23–45.

Filippovykh, D. N. *Sovetskaia voennaia administratsiia v Germanii: Voenno-politicheskii aspekt deiatel'nosti (1945–1949 gg.).* Moscow: Voennyi universitet (mimeographed) 1995.

Filitov, A. M. *Germanskii vopros: ot raskola k ob-edineniiu.* Moscow: "Mezhdunarodnye otnosheniia" 1993.

———. "Nota 10 marta 1952 goda: prodolzhaiushchaia diskussiia," Tupolev, B. M., ed., *Rossiia i Germaniia/Russland und Deutschland, Vol. 3.* Moscow: "Nauka" 2004, pp. 311–30.

Fischer, Alexander. *Sowjetische Deutschlandpolitik 1941–1945.* Stuttgart: Deutsche Verlagsanstalt 1975.

———, ed. *Studien zur Geschichte der SBZ/DDR*. Berlin: Duncker and Humblot 1993.

Fleischhauer, Ingeborg. *Der Pakt. Hitler, Stalin und die Initiative der deutschen Diplomatie 1938–1939*. Frankfurt/Main: Ullstein 1990.

Florath, Bernd, Mitter, Armin, and Wolle, Stefan, eds. *Die Ohnmacht der Allmächtigen*. Berlin: Ch. Links 1992.

Foitzik, Jan, ed. *Entstalinisierungskrise in Ostmitteleuropa 1953–1956. Vom 17. Juni bis zum ungarischen Volksaufstand. Politische, militärische, soziale und nationale Dimensionen*. Paderborn: Schöningh 2001.

———. *Sowjetische Militäradministration in Deutschland (SMAD): 1945–1949. Struktur und Funktion*. Berlin: Akademie Verlag 1999.

Frieser, Karl-Heinz. *Krieg hinter Stacheldraht. Die deutschen Kriegsgefangenen in der Sowjetunion und das Nationalkomitee "Freies Deutschland."* Mainz: v. Hase and Koehler 1981.

Gaddis, John Lewis. "The Emerging Post-Revisionist Synthesis on the Origins of the Cold War," *Diplomatic History* 7, no. 3 (Summer 1983), pp. 171–200.

———. *We Now Know. Rethinking Cold War History*. Oxford: Clarendon Press 1998.

Garelow, M. A. [pseudonym for M. A. Gareev]. "Woher droht Gefahr?" *Einheit*, 6/1989, pp. 573–89.

Gibianskii, L. Ia. "I. [k konfliktu s Tito:] U nachala konflikta: Balkanskii uzel," *Rabochii klass i sovremennyi mir*, 2/1990, pp. 171–85.

———. "III. [k konfliktu s Tito:] Vyzov v Moskvu," *Politicheskie issledovaniia*, 1/1991, pp. 195–207.

Gibianskij,[Gibianskii] Leonid. "Osteuropa: Sicherheitszone der UdSSR, sowjetisiertes Protektorat oder Sozialismus 'ohne Diktatur des Proletariats'?" *Forum für osteuropäische Ideen- und Zeitgeschichte*, 8, no. 2 (2004), pp. 113–37.

Gieseke, Jens. *Mielke-Konzern. Die Geschichte der Stasi 1945–1990*. Stuttgart: Deutsche Verlags-Anstalt 2001.

Gobarev, Victor. "Soviet Military Plans and Actions during the First Berlin Crisis, 1948–49," *The Journal of Slavic Military Studies* 10, no. 3 (September 1997), pp. 1–24.

Gori, Francesca, and Pons, Silvio, eds. *The Soviet Union and Europe in the Cold War, 1943–53*. Basingstoke: Macmillan; New York: St. Martin's Press 1996.

Gorodetsky, Gabriel. *The Grand Delusion*. New Haven, CT: Yale University Press 1999.

———, ed. *Soviet Foreign Policy 1917–1991. A Retrospective*. London: Frank Cass 1994.

Graml, Hermann. "Die Legende von der verpassten Gelegenheit," *Vierteljahrshefte für Zeitgeschichte*, 31 (1983), pp. 307–41.

———. "Nationalstaat oder westdeutscher Teilstaat?" *Vierteljahrshefte für Zeitgeschichte*, 25 (1977), pp. 821–64.

Halder, Winfried. "*Modell für Deutschland.*" *Wirtschaftspolitik in Sachsen 1945–1948*. Paderborn: Schöningh 2001.

———. "Was die Russen wirklich wollten. Zur Bedeutung des Uranbergbaus in der SBZ/DDR 1945–1954," Mehnert, Elke, ed., *. . . 's kommt alles vom Bergwerk her. Materialien zum 7. Deutsch-tschechischen Begegnungsseminar Gute Nachbarn—Schlechte Nachbarn*. Frankfurt/Main: Peter Lang 2005, pp. 63–89.

Hall, R. Cargill. "The Truth About Overflights. Military Reconnaissance Missions Over Russia Before the U-2," *Quarterly Journal of Military History* 9, no. 3 (Spring 1997), pp. 27–32.

Haritonow, Alexandr. *Ideologie als Instiution und soziale Praxis. Die Adaption des höheren sowjetischen Parteischulungssystems in der SBZ/DDR (1945–1956)*. Berlin: Akademie Verlag 2004.

———. *Sowjetische Hochschulpolitik in Sachsen 1945–1949*. Cologne: Böhlau 1995.

Hasanli, Jamil. *At the Dawn of the Cold War: The Soviet-American Crisis Over Iranian Azerbaijan, 1941–1946*. Boulder, CO: Rowman & Littlefield 2006.

Haslam, Jonathan. *The Soviet Union and the Struggle for Collective Security in Europe 1933–1939*. London and Basingstoke: Macmillan 1984.

Hegedüs, András B., and Wilke, Manfred, eds. *Satelliten nach Stalins Tod. Der "Neue Kurs," 17. Juni in der DDR, Ungarische Revolution 1956*. Berlin: Akademie Verlag 2000.

Hermann, C. F., ed. *International Crises*. New York: Free Press 1972.

Heuser, Beatrice. *Western "Containment" Policies in the Cold War. The Yugoslav Case, 1948–1953*. London and New York: Routledge 1989.

Hilger, Andreas, Schmeitzner, Mike, and Schmidt, Ute, eds. *Diktaturdurchsetzung. Instrumente und Methoden der kommunistischen Machtsicherung in der SBZ/DDR 1945–1955, Berichte und Studien Nr. 35*. Dresden: Hannah-Arendt-Institut für Totalitarismusforschung 2001.

Hilger, Andreas, Schmeitzner, Mike, and Vollnhals, Clemens, eds. *Sowjetisierung oder Neutralität? Optionen sowjetischer Besatzungspolitik in Deutschland und Österreich 1945–1955*. Göttingen: Vandenhoeck & Ruprecht 2006.

Hoffmann, Dierk, and Wentker, Hermann, eds. *Das letzte Jahr der SBZ. Politische Weichenstellungen und Kontinuitäten im Prozess der Gründung der DDR*. Munich: Oldenbourg 2000.

Holtsmark, Sven G. *A Soviet Grab for the High North and Northern Norway 1920–1953*. Oslo: Institutt for Forvarsstudier 1993.

Jarausch, Konrad, and Siegrist, Hannes, eds. *Amerikanisierung und Sowjetisierung in Deutschland 1945–1970*. Frankfurt/Main: Campus Verlag 1997.

Jensen, Bent. "Sowjetische Okkupation neuen Typs. Die lange Befreiung der dänischen Insel Bornholm 1944 bis 1946," *Osteuropa*, 4/1999, pp. 397–416.

Jeon, Hyun-su, and Kahng, Gyoo. "The Shtykov Diaries," *Cold War International History Project Bulletin*, 6–7 (Winter 1995/1996) (Washington D.C.: Woodrow Wilson International Center for Scholars), pp. 69, 92–93.

Jian, Chen. *The Sino-Soviet Alliance and China's Entry into the Korean War*, Cold War International History Project, Working Paper No. 1, Washington D.C., June 1992, pp. 18–21.

Kaff, Brigitte, ed. *"Gefährliche politische Gegner." Widerstand und Verfolgung in der scwjetischen Zone/DDR*. Düsseldorf: Droste 1995.

Kaplan, Karel. *Dans les archives du Comité Central. Trents ans de secrets du Bloc soviétique*, Paris: Albin Michel 1978.

Karbovskii, A. S. "Ust'e Odera v sovetskoi vneshnei politike 1945–1956 gg.," *Baltiiskii region v istorii Rossii i Evropy*, ed. Baltiiskii mezhdunarodnyi institut obshchevestvennykh nauk, Kaliningrad: Izdatel'stvo Rossiiskoi gosudarstvennogo universiteta im. I. Kanta 2005, pp. 109–14.

Karner, Stefan, and Stelzl-Marx, Barbara, eds. *Die Rote Armee in Österreich. Sowjetische Besatzung 1945–1955. Vol. I: Beiträge*. Vienna: Oldenbourg 2005.

Keesings Archiv der Gegenwart, Vol. *XV (1945).* Frauenfeld: Huber and Co., undated [1946].

Kennedy-Pipe, Caroline. *Soviet Strategies in Europe, 1943 to 1956.* Manchester and New York: Manchester University Press 1995.

Kersten, Krystyna. *The Establishment of Communist Rule in Poland, 1943–1948.* Berkeley: University of California Press 1991.

Khlevniuk, O. V. *Politbiuro. Mekhanizm politcheskoi vlasti v 1930-e gody.* Moscow: ROSSPÈN 1996.

Khlevniuk, O. V., Gorlitskii, I., Kosheleva, L. P., Miniuk, A. I., Prozumen'shchikov, M. Iu., Rogova, L. A., and Somonova, S. V., eds. *Politbiuro CK VKP(b) i Sovet Ministrov SSSR 1945–1953.* Moscow: ROSSPÈN 2002.

Kinner, Klaus, ed. *Menetekel 17. Juni 1953. Reader der Konferenzen anlässlich des 50. Jahrestages des 17. Juni 1953.* Leipzig: Rosa-Luxemburg-Stiftung Sachsen 2003.

Kleinmann, Hans-Otto. *Die Geschichte der CDU 1945–1982.* Stuttgart: Deutsche Verlags-Anstalt 1993.

Klessmann, Christoph, and Stöver, Bernd, eds. *1953—Krisenjahr des Kalten Krieges in Europa.* Cologne: Böhlau Verlag 1999.

Kley, Stefan. *Hitler, Ribbentrop und die Entfesselung des Zweiten Weltkrieges.* Paderborn: Schöningh 1996.

Kocka, Jürgen, ed. *Historische DDR-Forschung. Aufsätze und Studien.* Berlin: Akademie Verlag 1993.

Kondraschow, Sergej. "Über Ereignisse des Jahres 1953 und deren Bewertung von Aufklärungsdiensten einiger Länder," Timmermann, Heiner, ed., *Juni 1953 in Deutschland. Der Aufstand im Fadenkreuz von Kaltem Krieg, Katastrophe und Katharsis.* Münster: LIT-Verlag 2003, pp. 26–43.

König, Helmut. "Der Konflikt zwischen Stalin und Togliatti um die Jahreswende 1950/51," *Osteuropa,* 10/1970, pp. 699–706.

Kramer, Mark. "The Early Post-Stalin Succession Struggle and Upheavals in East Central Europe (Part 1)," *Journal of Cold War Studies* 1, no. 1 (Winter 1999), pp. 3–55.

Kostka, Bernd von. "Die Berliner Luftbrücke 1948/49. Krisenmanagement am Beginn des Kalten Krieges, " *Die Vier Mächte in Berlin: Beiträge zur Politik der Alliierten in der besetzten Stadt,* ed. Michael Bienert, Uwe Schaper and Andrea Theissen. Berlin: Landesarchiv Berlin 2007, pp. 81–92.

Krüger, Dieter. *Sicherheit durch Integration? Die wirtschaftliche und politische Zusammenarbeit Westeuropas 1947 bis 1957/58.* Munich: Oldenbourg 2003.

Krüger, Dieter, and Wagner, Armin, eds. *Konspiration als Beruf. Deutsche Geheimdienstchefs im Kalten Krieg.* Berlin: Ch. Links 2003.

Kuskov, Major V. I. *Sozdanie i razvitie Natsional'noi Narodnoi Armii GDR (1956–1974 gg.). Avtoreferat dissertatsii na soiskanie uchënoi stepeni kandidata istoricheskikh nauk, spetsial'nost' Nr. 07.00.07 Voennaia istoriia.* Moscow: Institut voennoi istorii Ministerstva oborony SSSR 1976.

Küsters, Hanns Jürgen. *Der Integrationsfriede. Viermächte-Verhandlungen über die Friedensregelung mit Deutschland 1945–1990.* Munich: Oldenbourg 2000.

Kynin, G. P. "Die Antihitlerkoalition und die Nachkriegsordnung in Deutschland. Die Haltung der UdSSR nach Dokumenten des Archivs für Aussenpolitik

Russlands," *Berliner Jahrbuch für osteuropäische Geschichte,* 2/1995, pp. 187–99.

————. "Germanskii vopros vo vzaimootnosheniiakh SSSR, SShA i Velikobritanii," *Novaia i noveishaia istoriia,* 4/1995, pp. 105–32.

Larres, Klaus. "Integrating Europe or Ending the Cold War? Churchill Postwar Foreign Policy," *Journal of European Integration History,* 1/1996, pp. 15–49.

Laufer, Jochen. "Die UdSSR und die deutsche Währungsfrage 1944–1948," *Vierteljahrshefte für Zeitgeschichte,* 3/1998, pp. 455–85.

————. "Die UdSSR und die Ursprünge der Berliner Blockade," *Deutschland Archiv,* 4/1998, pp. 564–77.

————. "Die UdSSR und die Zoneneinteilung Deutschlands (1943/44)," *Zeitschrift für Geschichtswissenschaft,* 4/1995, pp. 309–31.

————. "Verfassungsgebung in der SBZ 1946–1949," *Aus Politik und Zeitgeschichte. Beilage zur Wochenzeitung "Das Parlament,"* B 32–33/98, 31 July 1998, pp. 30–33.

Lebedeva, N., and Narinskii, M. "Rospusk Kominterna v 1943 godu," *Mezhdunarodnaia zhizn',* 5/1994, pp. 81–88.

Leffler, Melvyn P., and Painter, David S., eds. *Origins of the Cold War. An International History.* London and New York: Routledge 1995 (2nd ed.).

Lel'chuk, V. S., and Pivovar, E. I. *SSSR i kholodnaia voina.* Moscow: Mosgorarkhiv 1995.

Lemke, Michael. "Die infiltrierte Sammlung. Ziele, Methoden und Instrumente der SED in der Bundesrepublik 1949–1957," Mayer, Tilman, ed., *"Macht das Tor auf." Jakob-Kaiser-Studien.* Berlin: Berlin Verlag Arno Spitz GmbH 1996, pp. 171–234.

————. "Doppelte Alleinvertretung," *Zeitschrift für Geschichtswissenschaft,* 2/1992, pp. 531–43.

————. *Einheit oder Sozialismus? Die Deutschlandpolitik der SED 1949–1961.* Cologne: Böhlau 2001.

Lindner, Bernd. "Trennung, Sehnsucht und Distanz. Deutsch-deutsche Verwandtschaftsverhältnisse im Spiegel der Zeitgeschichte," *Deutschland Archiv,* 6/2004, pp. 991–1000.

Lipinsky, Jan. *Das Geheime Zusatzprotokoll zum deutsch-sowjetischen Nichtangriffsvertrag vom 23. August 1939 und seine Entstehungs- und Rezeptionsgeschichte von 1939 bis 1999.* Frankfurt/Main: Peter Lang 2005.

Lippmann, Heinz. "Der 17. Juni im Zentralkomitee der SED," *Aus Politik und Zeitgeschichte. Beilage zur Wochenzeitung "Das Parlament,"* 13 June 1956, p. 374.

Loth, Wilfried. "Das Ende einer Legende. Hermann Graml und die Stalin-Note. Eine Entgegnung," *Vierteljahrshefte für Zeitgeschichte,* 4/2002, pp. 653–64.

————, ed. *Die deutsche Frage in der Nachkriegszeit.* Berlin: Akademie Verlag 1994.

————. *Stalins ungeliebtes Kind. Warum Moskau die DDR nicht wollte.* Berlin: Rowohlt 1994. English edition: *Stalin's Unwanted Child: The Soviet Union, the German Question, and the Founding of the GDR.* Basingstoke: Macmillan 1997.

Löwe, Heinz-Dietrich. *Stalin. Der entfesselte Revolutionär, Vols. 1–2.* Göttingen: Musterschmidt 2002.

Lundestad, Geir. "How (Not) to Study the Origins of the Cold War," Westad, Odd Arne, ed., *Reviewing the Cold War. Approaches, Interpretations, Theory.* London: Frank Cass 2000.

Maetzke, Heinrich. *Der Union Jack in Berlin. Das britische Foreign Office, die SBZ und die Formulierung britischer Deutschlandpolitik 1945/47.* Konstanz: Universitätsverlag 1996.

Mählert, Ulrich. *Die Freie Deutsche Jugend 1945–1949. Von den "antifaschistischen Jugendausschüssen" zur SED-Massenorganisation: Die Erfassung der Jugend in der Sowjetischen Besatzungszone.* Paderborn: Schöningh 1995.

Mählert, Ulrich, and Weber, Hermann, eds. *Terror. Stalinistische Parteisäuberungen 1936–1953.* Paderborn: Schöningh 1998.

Mai, Gunther. *Der Alliierte Kontrollrat in Deutschland 1945–1948. Alliierte Einheit— deutsche Teilung?* Munich: Oldenbourg 1995.

Major, Patrick. *The Death of the KPD. Communism and Anti-Communism in West Germany, 1945–1956.* Oxford: Clarendon Press 1997.

Malycha, Andreas. *Partei von Stalins Gnaden? Die Entwicklung der SED zur Partei neuen Typs in den Jahren 1946 bis 1950.* Berlin: Dietz 1996.

Mar'ina, V. V. "Sovetskii Soiuz i Chekhoslovakiia. 1945 god," *Novaia i noveishaia istoriia,* 3/2005, pp. 38–64.

———. *Zakarpatskaia Ukraina (podkarpatskaia Rus') v politike Benesha i Stalina, 1939–1945 gg.* Moscow: "Novyi khonograf" 2003.

Mark, Eduard. *Revolution by Degrees: Stalin's National-Front Strategy for Europe, 1941–1947.* Working Paper No. 31, Cold War International History Project. Washington D.C.: Woodrow Wilson International Center for Scholars 2001.

März, Peter. *Die Bundesrepublik zwischen Westintegration und Stalin-Noten. Zur deutschlandpolitischen Diskussion 1952 in der Bundesrepublik vor dem Hintergrund der westlichen und sowjetischen Deutschlandpolitik.* Frankfurt/Main: Peter Lang 1982.

Mastny, Vojtech. *Russia's Road to the Cold War. Diplomacy, Warfare, and the Politics of Communism, 1941–1945.* New York: Columbia University Press 1979.

Mehringer, Hartmut, ed. *Von der SBZ zur DDR. Sondernummer Schriftenreihe der Vierteljahreshefte für Zeitgeschichte.* Munich: Oldenbourg 1995.

Melis, Damian van. *"Republikflucht." Flucht und Abwanderung aus der SBZ/DDR 1945 bis 1961. Schriftenreihe der Vierteljahreshefte für Zeitgeschichte.* Munich: Oldenbourg 2006.

Meyer-Landrut, Nikolaus. *Frankreich und die deutsche Einheit. Die Haltung der französischen Regierung und Öffentlichkeit zu den Stalin-Noten 1952.* Munich: Oldenbourg 1988.

Miagkov, M. Iu. "SSSR, SShA i problema Pribaltiki v 1941–1945 godakh," *Novaia i noveishaia istoriia,* 1/2005, pp. 50–59.

Mitteilungen der Gemeinsamen Kommission fuer die Erforschung der juengeren Geschichte der deutsch-russischen Beziehungen / Soobshcheniia Sovmestnoi komissii po izucheniiu noveishei istorii rossiisko-germanskikh otnoshenii (bilingual German-Russian publication), prepared by Eberhard Kuhrt, Vol. 1, Berlin: Federal Ministry of the Interior 2003; Vol. 2, Munich: Oldenbourg 2005.

Morré, Jörg. *Hinter den Kulissen des Nationalkomitees. Das Institut 99 in Moskau und die Deutschlandpolitik der UdSSR 1943–1946.* Munich: Oldenbourg 2001.

Müller, Werner. "Noch einmal: Stalin und die Demokratie in Nachkriegsdeutschland," *Jahrbuch für Historische Kommunisforschung,* 1998, pp. 203–16.

Muraschko, Galina P., Noskowa, Albina F., and Wolokitina, Tatjana W. "Das Zentralkomitee der WKP(B) und das Ende der 'nationalen Wege zum Sozialismus,'" *Jahrbuch für Historische Kommunismusforschung,* 1994, pp. 9–37.

Naimark, Norman M. "Die sowjetische Militäradministration in Deutschland und die Frage des Stalinismus. Veränderte Sichtweise auf der Grundlage neuer Quellen aus russischen Archiven," *Zeitschrift für Geschichtswissenschaft*, 4/1995, pp. 293–307.

——. *Fires of Hatred. Ehtnic Cleansing in Twentieth Century Europe.* Cambridge, MA: Harvard University Press 2001.

——. *The Russians in Germany. A History of the Soviet Zone of Occupation, 1945–1949.* Cambridge, MA: Harvard University Press 1997.

——. "Stalin and Europe in the Postwar Period, 1945–53: Issues and Problems," *Journal of Modern European History* 2, no. 1 (2004), pp. 28–58.

Naimark, Norman, and Leonid Gibianskii, eds. *The Establishment of Communist Regimes in Eastern Europe, 1944–1949.* Boulder, CO: Westview 1997.

Narinskii, M. M. "Berlinskii krizis 1948–1949 gg. Novye dokumenty iz rossiiskikh arkhivov," *Novaia i noveishaia istoriia*, 3/1995, pp. 16–29.

——, ed. *Kholodnaia voina. Novye podkhody, novye dokumenty.* Moscow: Institut vseobshchei istorii RAN 1995.

Naumov, V. P. "K istorii sekretnogo doklada N.S. Khrushchëva na XX s-ezde KPSS," *Novaia i noveishaia istoriia*, 4/1996, pp. 147–68.

Nekrich, Aleksandr M. "The Two Nazi-Soviet Pacts and their Consequences," Pike, David Wingate, ed., *The Opening of the Second World War.* New York: Peter Lang 1991, pp. 44–98.

Nezhinskii, L. N., and Chelyshev, I. A. "O doktrinal'nykh osnovakh sovetskoi vneshnei politiki v gody 'kholodnoi voiny,'" *Otechestvennaia istoriia*, 1/1995, pp. 3–27.

Nordling, Carl O. *Defence or Imperialism? An Aspect of Stalin's Military and Foreign Policy 1933–1941.* Uppsala: Uppsala universitet Reprocentralen HSC 1984.

Noskova, A. F. "Moskovskie sovetniki v stranakh Vostochnoi Evropy (1945–1953 gg.)," *Voprosy istorii*, 1/1998, pp. 104–13.

——, ed. *Moskva i vostochnaia Evropa. Stanovlenie politicheskikh rezhimov sovetskogo tipa. 1949–1953. Ocherki istorii.* Moscow: ROSSPÈN 2002.

Orlov, A. S. "Sovetskaia aviatsiia v Koreiskoi voine 1950–1953 gg.," *Novaia i noveishaia istoriia*, 4/1998, pp. 121–46.

Ostermann, Christian F., ed. *The Post-Stalin Succession Struggle and the 17 June 1953 Uprising in East Germany. The Hidden History. Declassified Documents from US, Russian, and other European Archives.* Washington D.C.: Cold War International History Project 1996 (mimeographed).

——. *Uprising in East Germany 1953. The Cold War, the German Question, and the First Major Upheaval Behind the Iron Curtain.* Budapest and New York: Central European University Press 2001.

O'Sullivan, Donal. *Stalins "Cordon Sanitaire." Die sowjetische Osteuropapolitik und die Reaktionen des Westens 1939–1949.* Paderborn: Schöningh 2003.

Otto, Wilfriede. "Eine edle Idee im Notstand. Zur Zweiten Parteikonferenz der SED im Juli 1952 (mit zwei Dokumenten)," *Jahrbuch für Forschungen zur Geschichte der Arbeiterbewegung*, 2/2002, pp. 4–34.

——. *Erich Mielke—Biographie.* Berlin: Dietz 2000.

Pavlenko, N. G. *Razmyshleniia o sud'be polkovodtsa.* Moscow: Znanie 1989.

Pietrow-Ennker, Bianka, ed. *Präventivkrieg? Der deutsche Angriff auf die Sowjetunion.* Frankfurt/Main: Fischer Taschenbuch Verlag 2000.

———. *Stalinismus, Sicherheit, Offensive. Das "Dritte Reich" in der Konzeption der sowjetischen Aussenpolitik 1933–1941*. Melsungen: Schwartz 1983.

———. "Stalin-Regime und Aussenpolitik in den dreissiger Jahren," *Jahrbücher für Geschichte Osteuropas*, NF 33 (1985), pp. 495–507.

Pike, David Wingate, ed. *The Opening of the Second World War*. New York: Peter Lang 1991.

Pikhoia, R. G. *Sovetskii Soiuz. Istoriia vlasti*. Moscow: Izd. RAGS 1998.

Pióro, Tadeusz. *Armia ze skazą. W Wojsku Polskim 1945–1968. Wspomnienia i refleksje*. Warsaw: Czytelnik 1994.

Polonsky, Antony, and Drukier, Bolesław, eds. *The Beginnings of Communist Rule in Poland*. London and Boston: Routledge and Kegan Paul 1980.

Pons, Silvio. "Stalin, Togliatti, and the Origins of the Cold War in Europe," *Journal of Cold War Studies* 3, no. 2 (Spring 2001), pp. 3–18.

Popplewell, Richard J. "The KGB and the Control of the Soviet Bloc: The Case of East Germany," *Intelligence and National Security* 13, no. 1 (Spring 1998), pp. 254–85.

Raack, R. C. "Stalin Plans His Post-War Germany," *Journal of Contemporary History* 28 (1993), pp. 53–73.

Read, Anthony, and Fisher, David. *The Deadly Embrace. Hitler, Stalin, and the Nazi-Soviet Pact 1939–1941*. London: Michael Joseph 1988.

Rentola, Kimmo. "1948: Which Way Finland?" *Jahrbuch für Historische Kommunismusforschung*, 1998, pp. 99–124.

Richter, Michael. *Die Ost-CDU 1948–1952. Zwischen Widerstand und Gleichschaltung*. Dusseldorf: Droste 1991.

Richter, Michael, and Rissmann, Martin, eds. *Die Ost-CDU. Beiträge zur Entstehung und Entwicklung*. Weimar: Böhlau 1995.

Riklin, Alois. *Das Berlinproblem. Historisch-politische und völkerrechtliche Darstellung des Viermächtestatus*. Cologne: Verlag Wissenschaft und Politik 1964.

Roberts, Geoffrey. "Moscow and the Marshall Plan: Politics, Ideology, and the Cold War, 1947," *Europe-Asia Studies* 46, no. 8 (1994), pp. 1371–86.

———. *The Soviet Union and the Origins of the Second World War. Russo-German Relations and the Road to War, 1933–1941*. London and Basingstoke: Macmillan 1995.

Robrieux, Philippe. *Histoire intérieure du parti communiste, Vol. II: 1945–1972*. Paris: Fayard 1981.

Rodovich, Iu. F. *Germanskaia problema v 1945–1955 gg. i pozitsiia SSSR. Kontseptsiia i istoricheskaia praktika*. Tula: Kontsern 1997.

———. "O 'note Stalina' ot 10 marta 1952 g. po germanskomu voprosu," *Novaia i noveishaia istoriia*, 5/2002, pp. 63–79.

Roman, Eric. *Hungary and the Victor Powers, 1945–1950*. Basingstoke: Macmillan 1996.

Rucker, Laurent. *Moscow's Surprise. The Soviet-Israeli Alliance of 1947–1949*. Cold War International History Project, Working Paper No. 46. Washington D.C.: Woodrow Wilson International Center for Scholars, July 2005.

Sakharov, A. S. *Rossiia: Narod, Praviteli, Tsivilizatsii*. Moscow: Institut Rossiskoi istorii RAN 2004.

Sattler, Friederike. "Die Gründung der DDR begann in Prag," *Zeitschrift des Forschungsverbunds SED-Staat*, 6/1998, pp. 96–116.

Schenk, Fritz. "Mit Geheimbefehl Nr. 01 wurden 1945 die Tresore ausgeplündert," *Frankfurter Allgemeine Zeitung*, 2 June 1998.

Scherstjanoi, Elke, ed. *"Provisorium auf längstens ein Jahr . . . ."* Berlin: Akademie Verlag 1993.

Schlaga, Rüdiger. *Die kommunisten in der Friedensbewegung—erfolglos? Die Politik des Weltfriedensrates im Verhältnis zur Aussenpolitik der Sowjetunion und zu unabhängigen Friedensbewegungen im Westen (1950–1979).* Münster: LIT-Verlag 1991.

Schlie, Ulrich. "Diener vieler Herren," *Frankfurter Allgemeine Zeitung*, 8 February 1997.

Schmidt, Gustav, ed. *Ost-West-Beziehungen. Konfrontation and Détente 1945–1989,* Vol. 3. Bochum: Universitätsverlag Dr. N. Brockmeyer 1995.

Schroeder, Klaus, ed. *Geschichte und Transformation des SED-Staates. Beiträge und Analysen.* Berlin: Akademie Verlag 1994.

Schumann, Silke. *Parteierziehung in der Geheimpolizei. Zur Rolle der SED im MfS der fünfziger Jahre.* Berlin: Ch. Links 1997.

Schwarz, Hans-Peter. *Adenauer, Vol. I: Der Aufstieg 1876–1952; Vol. 2: Der Staatsmann 1952–1967.* Stuttgart: Deutsche Verlags-Anstalt 1986 (2nd ed. 1991).

———. *Vom Reich zur Bundesrepublik. Deutschland im Widerstreit der aussenpolitischen Konzeptionen in den Jahren der Besatzungsherrschaft 1945–1949.* Neuwied: H. Luchterhandt 1966.

Semiriaga, M. I. "Sovetskii Soiuz i predvoennyi politicheskii krizis," *Voprosy istorii,* 9/1990, pp. 49–64.

Sevostianov, G. N., ed. *Fevral' 1948. Moskva i Praga. Vzgliad cherez polveka. Materialy vtorogo zasedaniia komissii istorikov i arkhivistov Rossii i Chekhii, Moskva, 26–30 aprelia 1997 g.* Moscow: Institut slvavianovedeniia i balkanistiki RAN 1998.

Sharp, Tony. *The Wartime Alliance and the Zonal Division of Germany.* Oxford: Clarendon Press 1975.

Smirnova, N. D. "Gretsiia v politike SShA i SSSR, 1945–1947 gg. Novye arkhivnye dokumenty," *Novaia i noveishaia istoriia,* 5/1997, pp. 21–34.

Smith, Jean Edward. *The Defense of Berlin.* Baltimore: Johns Hopkins University Press 1963.

Smyser, W. R. *From Yalta to Berlin. The Cold War Struggle Over Germany.* Houndmills and London: Macmillan 1999.

Sokolov, V. V. "Narkomindel Viacheslav Molotov," *Mezhdunarodnaia zhizn',* 5/1991, pp. 99–112.

———. "Neizvestnyi Chicherin," *Novaia i noveishaia istoriia,* 2/1994, pp. 3–18.

Sommer, Ulf. *Die Liberal-Demokratische Partei Deutschlands. Eine Blockpartei unter der Führung der SED.* Münster: Agenda Verlag 1996.

Sovetskaia vneshniaia politika v gody "kholodnoi voiny" (1945–1985). Novoe prochtenie, ed. Insitut rossiskoi istorii RAN. Moscow: "Mezhdunarodnye otnosheniia" 1995.

SSSR i germanskii vopros 1941–1949. Dokumenty iz Arkhiva vneshnei politiki Rossiskogo Federatsii, ed. Historico-Archival Department of the Russian Ministry of Foreign Affairs and the Potsdam Center for Contemporary Historical Research, *Vol. I: 1941–1945.* Moscow: "Mezhdunarodnye ostnosheniia" 1996.

SSSR i germanskii vopros 1941–1949. Dokumenty iz Arkhiva vneshnei politiki Rossiskogo Federatsii, ed. by Historico-Archival Department of the Russian Ministry of Foreign Affairs and the Potsdam Center for Contemporary Historical Research, *Vol. II: 9 maia 1945 g.–3 oktiabria 1946 g.* Moscow: "Mezhdunarodnye otnosheniia" 2000.

SSSR i germanskii vopros 1941–1949. Dokumenty iz Arkhiva vneshnei politiki Rossiiskoi Federatsii, ed. by Istoriko-Dokumental'nyi Departament MID Rossii / Zentrum für Zeithistorische Forschung Potsdam, *Vol. III: 6 oktiabria 1946 g.–15 iiunia 1948 g.* Moscow: "Mezhdunarodnye otnosheniia" 2003.

Stavrakis, Peter J. *Moscow and Greek Communism, 1944–1949.* Ithaca, NY, and London: Cornell University Press 1989.

Steininger, Rolf. *Der Kalte Krieg.* Frankfurt/Main: Fischer Kompakt 2003.

———. *Der vergessene Krieg. Korea 1950–1953.* Munich: Olzog 2006.

———. *Eine Chance zur Wiedervereinigung? Darstellung und Dokumentation auf der Grundlage unveröffentlichter britischer und amerikanischer Akten. Archiv für Sozialgeschichte, Beiheft 12.* Bonn: Dietz Nachf 1985.

Stock, Wolfgang. "Geld aus dem Osten," *Frankfurter Allgemeine Zeitung,* 21 March 1994.

Stöckigt, Rolf. "Ein forcierter stalinistischer Kurs führte 1953 in die Krise," *Berliner Zeitung,* 8 March 1990.

Stourzh, Gerald. *Um Einheit und Freiheit. Staatsvertrag, Neutralität und das Ende der Ost-West-Besetzung Österreichs 1945–1955.* Vienna: Böhlau 1998.

Stöver, Bernd. *Der Kalte Krieg.* Munich: C. H. Beck 2003.

Strelis, Uldis Pauls. "Deportation als Vernichtungsmethode," *Terroropfer unter zwei Diktaturen in den baltischen Ländern / Divu diktaturu terora upuri Baltijas valstis.* Riga: Tapals 2005.

Suckut, Siegfried. "Die Entscheidung zur Gründung der DDR," *Vierteljahrshefte für Zeitgeschichte,* 1/1991, pp. 125–75.

———. "'Wenn die Nation erhalten bleibt, werden alle administrativen Spaltungsmassnahmen eines Tages zergehen und zerfallen.' Zur Vorgeschichte der DDR-Gründung," *Die Deutschlandfrage von Jalta und Potsdam bis zur staatlichen Teilung Deutschlands 1949, Studien zur Deutschlandfrage Vol. 12.* Berlin: Duncker and Humblot 1993, pp. 117–85.

———. "Zur Vorgeschichte der DDR-." *Vierteljahrshefte für Zeitgeschichte,* 1/1991, pp. 157–58.

Suckut, Siegfried, and Süss, Walter, eds. *Staatspartei und Staatssicherheit. Zum Verhältnis von SED und MfS.* Berlin: Ch. Links 1997.

Swain, Geoffrey. "Stalin's Vision of the Postwar World," *Diplomacy and Statecraft 7,* no. 1 (March 1996), pp. 73–96.

Tantzscher, Monika. "Vorläufer des Staatssicherheitsdienstes," *Jahrbuch für Historische Kommunismusforschung,* 1998, pp. 125–56.

Tessmer, Carsten. "Gleichgeschaltet? Deutschlandpolitische Anstrengungen der Liberal-Demokraten," *Deutschland Archiv,* 1/1991, pp. 137–40.

Ther, Philipp, and Siljak, Ana, eds. *Redrawing Nations: Ethnic Cleansing in East-Central Europe, 1944–1948.* Boulder, CO: Rowman & Littlefield 2001.

Thoss, Bruno, ed. *Volksarmee schaffen—ohne Geschrei! Studien zu den Anfängen einer "verdeckten Aufrüstung" in der SBZ/DDR 1947–1952.* Munich: Oldenbourg 1994.

Tillotson, H. M. *Finland at Peace and War 1918–1993.* Norwich: Michael Russell 1993.

Timmermann, Heiner, ed. *Die DDR—Analysen eines aufgegebenen Staates*. Berlin: Duncker and Humblot 2001.

Torańska, Teresa, Oni. *Stalin's Polish Puppets*. London: Collins Harvill 1987.

Torkunov, A. V. *Zagadochnaia voina. Koreiskii konflikt 1950–1953 godov*. Moscow: ROSSPÈN 2000.

Trachtenberg, Marc. *A Constructed Peace. The Making of the European Settlement 1945–1963*. Princeton, NJ: Princeton University Press 1999.

Upton, Anthony F. *Finland in Crisis, 1940–1941*. London: Faber and Faber 1964.

Varsori, Antonio. "Reflections on the Origins of the Cold War," Westad, Odd Arne, ed., *Reviewing the Cold War. Approaches, Interpretations, Theory*. London: Frank Cass 2000.

Varsori, Antonio, and Calandri, Elena, eds. *The Failure of Peace in Europe, 1943–48*. Houndmills and New York: Palgrave 2002.

Volkogonov, Dmitrii. *Sem' vozhdei, Vol. I*. Moscow: "Novosti" 1995.

Volkov, V. K. *Uzlovye problemy noveishei istorii Tsentral'noi i Iugo-Vostochnoi Evropy*. Moscow: Izdatel'stvo "INDRIK" 2000.

Volokitina, T. V., Murashko, G. P., and Noskova, A. F. *Narodnaia demokratiia: Mif ili real'nost'?* Moscow: "Nauka" 1993.

Vorholt, Udo, and Zaib, Volker. "Die Deutschlandpolitik der SED in den Jahren 1947/48," *Deutschland Archiv*, 12/1995, pp. 1279–91.

Wall, Irwin M. *French Communism in the Era of Stalin. The Quest for Unity and Integration, 1945–1962*. Westport, CT, and London: Greenwood 1983.

Weathersby, Kathryn. "The Soviet Role in the Early Phase of the Korean War," *Journal of American-East Asian Relations* 2, no. 4 (Winter 1993), pp. 425–58.

Wenzel, Otto. *Die gescheiterte deutsche Oktoberrevolution*. Münster: LIT-Verlag 2003.

Werkentin, Falco, ed. *Der Aufbau der "Grundlage des Sozialismus" in der DDR 1952/53*. Berlin: Der Landesbeauftragte für die Unterlagen des Staatssssicherheitsdienstes der ehemaligen DDR 2002.

Westad, Odd Arne, Holtsmark, Sven, and Neumann, Iver B., eds. *The Soviet Union in Eastern Europe 1945–89*. New York: St. Martin's Press 1994.

Wettig, Gerhard. "All-German Unity and East German Separation in Soviet Policy, 1947–1949," *Jahrbuch für Historische Kommunismusforschung*, 1994, pp. 122–39.

———. "Autonomy and Dependence. The East German Regime's Relationship with the USSR, 1945–1949," McFalls, Laurence, and Probst, Lothar, eds., *After the GDR. New Perspectives on the Old GDR and the Young Länder*. Amsterdam and Atlanta, GA: Rodopi 2001, pp. 49–75.

———. *Bereitschaft zu Einheit in Freiheit? Die sowjetische Deutschland-Politik 1945–1955*. Munich: Olzog 1999.

———. "Das Bemühen der sowjetischen Führung und der SED um Sozialdemokraten und bürgerliche Oppositionskreise in Westdeutschland 1946–1953," Hübsch, Reinhard, ed. *"Hört die Signale!" Die Deutschlandpolitik von KPD/SED und SPD 1945–1970*. Berlin: Akademie Verlag 2002, pp. 139–66.

———. *Das Vier-Mächte-Abkommen in der Bewährungsprobe. Berlin im Spannungsfeld von Ost und West*. [West] Berlin: Berlin Verlag 1982 (2nd ed.).

———. "Der Konflikt der Ost-CDU mit der Besatzungsmacht 1945–1948 im Spiegel sowjetischer Akten," *Historisch-Politische Mitteilungen*, 6 (1999), pp. 109–37.

———. "Die Deutschland-Note vom 10. März 1952 nach sowjetischen Akten," *Die Deutschlandfrage von der staatlichen Teilung Deutschlands bis zum Tode Stalins, Studien zur Deutschlandfrage 13.* Berlin: Duncker and Humblot 1994, pp. 281–96.

———. "Die Frage der deutschen Einheit im Kalten Krieg. Konzepte und Bemühungen," *Deutschland Archiv*, 5/2003, pp. 820–43.

———. "Die Interessen der Mächte angesichts der Stalin-Note vom 10. März 1952. Stand der Ost-West-Konfrontation in Deutschland 1952," *Deutschland Archiv*, 2/2002, pp. 231–36.

———. "Die Lage in der Deutschland-, Europa- und Sicherheitspolitik bei den West-verträgen von 1952," Timmermann, Heiner, ed., *Deutschlandvertrag und Pariser Verträge. Im Dreieck von Kaltem Krieg, deutscher Frage und europäischer Sicherheit.* Münster: LIT-Verlag 2003, pp. 58–74.

———. "Die sowjetische Besatzungsmacht und der politische Handlungsspielraum in der SBZ," Pfeil, Ulrich, ed., *Die DDR und der Westen. Transnationale Beziehungen 1949–1989.* Berlin: Ch. Links 2001, pp. 39–62; French version: "L'occupant soviétique et la marge de manoeuvre polititique en zone d'occupation soviétique 1945–1949," Pfeil, Ulrich, ed., *La RDA et l'Occident (1949–1990). Préface d'André Fontaine.* Asnières: Etudes de l'Institut Allemand 2000, pp. 59–80.

———, ed. *Die Sowjetische Deutschland-Politik in der Ära Adenauer.* Bonn: Bouvier 1997.

———. "Entwicklungen zur Nationalen Volksarmee und zum Warschauer Pakt," *Deutschland Archiv*, 2/2005, pp. 280–89.

———. "Neue Erkenntnisse aus sowjetischen Geheimdokumenten über den militärischen Aufbau in der SBZ/DDR 1947–1952," *Militärgeschichtliche Mitteilungen*, 53, no. 2 (1994), pp. 399–419.

———. *Politik im Rampenlicht. Aktionsweisen moderner Aussenpolitik.* Frankfurt/Main: Fischer Bücherei 1967.

———. "Sowjetische Machtapparate als integraler Bestandteil des SED-Regimes. Anfänge organisatorischer Durchdringung 1945 bis 1954," *Osteuropa*, 10/2000, pp. 1149–63.

———. "Stalin and German Reunification: Archival Evidence on Soviet Foreign Policy in Spring 1952," *The Historical Journal* (Cambridge), 37, 2/1994, pp. 411–19.

———. "Vorgeschichte und Gründung des Warschauer Paktes," *Militärgeschichtliche Zeitschrift*, 64, no. 1 (2005), pp. 151–76.

———. "Wer kontrolliert die Währung? Neue Aufschlüsse über die sowjetische Politik während der Berliner Blockade 1948," *Deutschland Archiv*, 1/2001, pp. 117–22.

Wetzlaugk, Udo. *Berlin und die deutsche Frage.* Cologne: Wissenschft und Politik 1985.

Wilke, Manfred, ed. *Die Anatomie der Parteizentrale. Die KPD/SED auf dem Weg zur Macht.* Berlin: Akademie Verlag 1998.

———. *Die SBZ-CDU 1945–1947. Zwischen Kriegsende und Kaltem Krieg.* Munich: Herbert Utz Verlag Wissenschaft 1998.

Wohlfahrt, William Curt. *The Elusive Balance. Power and Perceptions during the Cold War.* Ithaca, NY: Cornell University Press 1993.

Yergin, Daniel. *Shattered Peace. The Origins of the Cold War and the National Security State.* Boston: Houghton Mifflin 1978.

Young, John Wilson. *Coldwar Europe 1945–1991.* London: Arnold 1996.

Zarusky, Jürgen, ed. *Die Stalin-Note vom 10. März 1952. Neue Quellen und Analysen. Mit Beiträgen von Wilfried Loth, Hermann Graml und Gerhard Wettig. Schriftenreihe der Vierteljahrshefte für Zeitgeschichte 84.* Munich: Oldenbourg 2002.

———. *Stalin und die Deutschen. Neue Beiträge zur Forschung.* Munich: Oldenbourg 2006.

Zhelitski, Bela. "Postwar Hungary, 1944–1946," Naimark, Norman, and Gibianskii, Leonid, eds., *The Establishment of Communist Regimes in Eastern Europe 1944–1949.* Boulder, CO: Westview 1997, pp. 76–91.

Zhihua, Shen. "Sino-North Korean Conflict and Its Resolution during the Korean War," *Cold War International History Project Bulletin,* 14–15 (Winter 2003/Spring 2004), pp. 9–24. Washington D.C.: Woodrow Wilson International Center for Scholars.

Zhukov, Iu. N. *Tainy Kremlia. Stalin, Molotov, Beriia, Malenkov.* Moscow: "Terra" 2000.

Zinner, Paul E. *Communist Strategy and Tactics in Czechoslovakia, 1918–48.* New York and London: Praeger 1963.

Zschaler, Frank. "Die vergessene Währungsreform. Vorgeschichte, Durchführung und Ergebnisse der Geldumstellung in der SBZ 1948," *Vierteljahrshefte für Zeitgeschichte,* 2/1997, pp. 191–223.

Zubok, Vladislav, and Pleshakov, Contantine. *Inside the Kremlin's Cold War. From Stalin to Khrushchev.* Cambridge, MA: Harvard University Press 1996.

Index

About the Author

Gerhard Wettig was born in 1934 in Gelnhausen (West Germany). He received his Ph.D. in modern history from the University of Göttingen and was, until his retirement, director of foreign policy and international security studies at the Federal Institute of East European and International Studies, Cologne. He is currently external research associate of the Institute of Contemporary History, Munich/Berlin. He has published a large number of books and articles (in collective volumes and academic journals) in Germany, Britain, the United States, Russia, and France, notably on the history of the Cold War in Germany and Europe with particular attention to Soviet policy. His most recent book publication is *Khrushchev's Berlin Crisis of 1958–1963* (in German, with a translation into Russian to follow in 2007). He is currently working on a research project on Soviet policy toward the West from 1953 to 1958.